Praise for

GETTING STARTED ON SOCIAL ANALYSIS IN CANADA, Fourth Edition

This new edition of successfully brings together in one handy package topical issues of serious concern to activists and newcomers to social movement activities. It contains the necessary analytical tools for understanding our world so we can change it. Teachers and facilitators whose passion is involving others in a political project for social justice and change will find this an invaluable resource.

> — Maureen MacDonald, MLA, Nova Scotia,
> The Maritime School of Social Work, Dalhousie University, Halifax

Getting Started hooks the reader in, chapter after chapter, using engaging examples from daily life that most Canadians can easily connect with. This new edition is an excellent resource for ordinary citizens wanting tools to analyze the world around them. It is also an excellent text for introducing students to important social issues in Canada. At the same time, it helps them develop their critical analysis skills.

> — Vicki L. Nygaard,
> Sociology, University of Victoria

Excellent, just what we have been waiting for . . . With updated facts and figures, this fourth edition builds on the successful social analysis approach of the earlier editions. The expanded resource list, now including websites, is an excellent help. *Getting Started* is the best introduction to contemporary social issues and to working for social justice in Canada available today.

> — Bob McKeon,
> Theology and Social Ethics, Newman Theological College,
> University of Alberta, Edmonton

Finally, an introduction to sociology textbook that will challenge my students to think critically, but taking it a step further and challenging them to take action to realize a more just and equitable society. Addresses key social issues and problems in clear language, topics of concern that students and other Canadians face today. Excellent resources and discussion questions.

> — E. Wilma van der Veen,
> Sociology and Criminology, St. Mary's University, Halifax

It's clear and to the point. The section on supermarkets just blew my students' minds. They had no idea about how few companies were involved in the food system. That raised some WONDERFUL discussion. We could take political economy theory and communications theory using that issue and play with it a lot.

> — Margaret Malone,
> School of Nursing, Ryerson University, Toronto

Getting Started
on Social Analysis in Canada

Fourth Edition

Jamie Swift

Jacqueline Davies

Robert G. Clarke

Michael Czerny S.J.

Between the Lines
Toronto

Getting Started on Social Analysis in Canada, Fourth Edition

First published in Canada in 2003 by
Between the Lines
720 Bathurst Street, Suite #404
Toronto, Ontario M5S 2R4
1-800-718-7201
www.btlbooks.com

National Library of Canada Cataloguing in Publication

      Getting started on social analysis in Canada / Jamie Swift ... [et al.] ;
illustrations by Philip Street. – 4th ed.

Third ed. published as Getting started on social analysis in Canada / Michael Czerny,
Jamie Swift, Robert G. Clarke ; illustrations by Carlos Freire.
Includes bibliographical references and index.
ISBN 1-896357-77-6

     1. Canada–Social conditions–1971-. 2. Social problems–Canada. I. Swift, Jamie, 1951-

HN103.5.C98 2003   361.1'0971   C2003-901253-0

Cover and text design by Margie Adam, ArtWork
Printed in Canada

Between the Lines gratefully acknowledges assistance for its publishing activities from the Canada Council for the Arts, the Ontario Arts Council, and the Government of Canada through the Book Publishing Industry Development Program.

Canada

To

Doris Marshall
(1911–2003)

dian marino
(1941–1993)

Jim McSheffrey S.J.
(1945–1999)

and

Morgan Bickenbach-Davies

Contents

Preface to the Fourth Edition

Getting Started on Social Analysis in Canada is a textbook that helps readers unpack social issues. It is also a book with a long history.

It stands apart from textbook projects that are developed by transnational publishing enterprises after exhaustive market analysis. The book was conceived in the early 1980s at Toronto's Jesuit Centre for Social Faith and Justice, a small activist organization in a gritty working-class neighbourhood dotted with aging factories and newly gentrified houses. Lead contamination was an urgent local issue, and the popular struggles to rid Central America of military dictatorships animated a small staff eager to put liberation theology into practice.

The Jesuits and those they hired to help them often carried out educational retreats and workshops with community and church groups, religious orders, and teachers. They were repeatedly asked about ways of analyzing – "reading" – Canadian society, ways of understanding the problems that confront Canadians. There was an apparent need for social analysis that was clear, Canadian, and practical. The people at the Jesuit Centre decided to produce a book that would help to fill this need.

The resulting text turned out to be remarkably successful. Getting Started proved popular with groups and individual activists steeped in that part of the Christian tradition that emphasizes justice and participation.

As it happened, the book also proved as popular with college and university instructors as it did with faith- and community-based groups. Some twenty years later, this fourth edition brings a new generation of readers up to date with an array of information – data, events, prominent discussions, observable trends. It frames its argument in ways that reflect changes in analytical approaches, integrating more thoroughly issues of gender and race, challenging readers to imagine the experience of excluded people as the norm. It maintains the social justice perspective that has always provided a strong line of continuity and made the earlier editions so useful.

As in previous editions, Getting Started IV divides its explorations of key social issues into three major parts; and each of them concludes with a reflective chapter that draws attention both to the tools available to social analysts and to the skills developed as they make their way through the book. The chapter "Welcome to Social Analysis" considers the economy and the culture of coffee as a means of introducing the questioning awareness of society that runs throughout. The following "basic needs" section, "Issues in the Everyday," includes chapters on health, housing, food, and the world of work.

A second reflective chapter, "Social Analysis Again," shifts the focus from our immediate experience as individuals to the larger world of surrounding people and communities. Under the heading "The World Around Us," the next set of issue chapters addresses the natural environment, new technology, and globalization.

The transition chapter "Media and Ideology" then explores how the mass media represent, shape, and often distort our understanding of the issues that require social analysis. Looking at how this happens – and especially at the role played by popular stereotypes and commonly held prejudices – this chapter also reveals how some groups of people are more misrepresented or under-represented in the media than others.

The following set of issue chapters, "People and Perspectives," takes yet another tack. The chapters consider the ways in which "Issues in the Everyday" are experienced by three groups of people whose concerns are often ignored or shunted to one side: old people, Aboriginal peoples, and women. Heeding how these groups see things not only tells us about their lives but also presents us with different ways of looking at the world. These perspectives in turn suggest responses to social problems that might not otherwise have come to the surface.

The concluding chapter, "We Have Just Begun," examines the connection between social analysis and social action – in a world in which the deluge of information and the enormity of problems can overwhelm individual citizens. The content and consequences of analysis can include victories, not just setbacks. *Getting Started IV* examines impediments, priorities, and political power, and then steps beyond social analysis.

Against this background it appears that, contrary to the sharp dictum of former British prime minister Margaret Thatcher ("There Is No Alternative"), social analysis can help the reader transcend an approach that emphasizes individual solutions. With a nod to C. Wright Mills in its examination of the polarized job market, *Getting Started IV* explains that – unlike private troubles – issues are public matters.

This edition of *Getting Started* was revised by Jackie Davies of Queen's University, Jamie Swift, one of the book's original authors, and Robert Clarke, who was also responsible for the revisions that produced the third edition. Michael Czerny S.J. now works as the co-ordinator of the African Jesuit AIDS Network, based in Nairobi. He was unable to assist this time around, but much of his original work is still here as a tangible, and important element. He remains an encouraging friend of this publication.

Several other people provided valuable help along the way. Freelance writer Ann Silversides did the bulk of the writing and research for chapter two, "In Sickness and in Health." Greg Michalenko and students in the Department of Environment and Resource Studies at the University of Waterloo sent along information on websites. Monica Rahman and Bob Darwish provided research assistance for a number of the chapters, and Bonita Lawrence offered helpful comments and suggestions. Thanks go as well to Zöe Druick for her astute suggestions in the early stage of this project.

We also want to thank Margie Adam, ArtWork, for her skill and solidarity; David Nazar S.J. for his enthusiastic interest; and Jean-Marc Laporte S.J., Provincial, Jesuits of Upper Canada, for his moral and practical encouragement. Paul Eprile of Between the Lines guided this project through from start to finish. We thank him and all the other staff at BTL for their constant support.

A Note from Jack Costello S.J.

With this fourth edition, the authors of *Getting Started* have followed an approach to social analysis that draws less directly on Christian and Jesuit sources. It seems fair to flag this shift, especially for readers who are aware of recent developments in the Jesuit approach to social issues and may have anticipated finding signs of them in these pages.

Although no longer actively involved in the production of *Getting Started*, the Canadian Jesuits maintain their encouragement and financial support for this new edition. *Getting Started IV* continues to examine the elements required for a genuinely social understanding of our individual lives and public actions in society. Its proposals clearly serve its goal: to enhance the formation of participatory and responsible communities, locally and globally.

The Jesuit Centre for Social Faith and Justice continues to work with hope and enthusiasm for this same goal. We walk with the authors of *Getting Started* as companions on the way.

Chapter One

Welcome to Social Analysis

"Let's have another cup of coffee."

A friendly way to carry on a conversation . . . and a good way to begin social analysis. Most of us probably don't think twice about having a cup of coffee (unless it's to heed the warnings about too much caffeine). But if we stop to think about it, a coffee can quickly get some questions going.

- "Yes, I'd like a cup." The coffee beans may come from one of those small Central American countries that drift in and out of the news. Do you know what the local producers get paid for their work? What happens as the coffee beans make their way to us?

- "How much do I owe you for that?" Now and then we hear about a slump in coffee prices, like the one in 2001, when producer prices reached a thirty-year low.[1] It seems coffee prices have been in a continuing downward spiral (which is not reflected at the cash register of trendy cafés). What does news like this have to do with Canada?

- "Let me fill the kettle." With tap water? Is the water filtered? Is it safe? Given the tainted water scandals of Walkerton, Ontario, and North Battleford, Saskatchewan – and doubts in many other communities across the country – you might prefer to use bottled water. But does this option carry a cost to the environment as well as at the check-out counter?

- "I'll put on a pot." If the coffee is filtered, check the paper filter. Did its material originate with a logging company embroiled in a land dispute like the one that has frustrated Alberta's Lubicon Cree for decades? Is the filter "whiter than white"? According to one study, "The principal agent of paper's dazzling whiteness – chlorine – is guilty of creating some of the most toxic pollutants ever discharged into our environment."[2]

- "A coffee to go." The drink could come in a cheap, disposable styrofoam cup fashioned from petroleum (there may be a shortage or a glut). The styrofoam might have been manufactured using chemicals that contribute to the depletion of the ozone layer. You'll probably get a plastic stir-stick. When you throw these things away, where do they go?

- "A spoonful of instant." The makings of that coffee may have come from a dozen different countries, but where was it processed? What is the nationality of the company that processed and markets the instant? What else does it sell? Who controls the "coffee market"? Does it make any difference?

- "Do you take sugar?" Sugar (which is apparently not all that good for us) is produced in about 120 countries around the world, including Canada. But 85 per cent of the sugar consumed in Canada is imported, much of it from Third World countries. The aid agency Oxfam has linked the agricultural policies of the European Union – which subsidizes sugar production, leading to low prices – with the plight of farmers in poorer countries who rely on sugar for their livelihoods.[3]

- "Would you like cream?" Dairy farms have gone the way of other small farms in Canada – they either grow larger or they have trouble surviving, and disappear. What impact does the trend towards agribusiness have on the quality

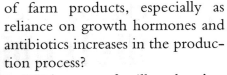

of farm products, especially as reliance on growth hormones and antibiotics increases in the production process?

- "We're out of milk – here's a whitener." What's on the list of ingredients? Is the whitener an edible oil product? Do you have any idea what the ingredients do to your health?

- "Good to the last drop." A cup of coffee does not just happen. Many people are involved in getting it ready, from planting the seedling and maintaining the clean water supply, through all the stages of processing, to serving the coffee and washing the cup: owner, planter, picker, shipper, buyer, insurer, processor, packer, advertiser, seller, shopper, consumer, dishwasher. How are all these people – and jobs – related to each other, to their communities, and to the natural environment? Which leads to our final question:

- Is there any fair trade coffee around here? Fairly traded foods ensure that producers are paid a decent price for their work. Fair trade links producers more closely with consumers, reducing the need for middle people and guaranteeing a minimum price to the workers. You can look for a fair trade label on produce, coffee, tea, paper products, and clothing.

A Questioning Awareness

Social analysis begins with *questions* like these. As they surface, they start us thinking about a particular issue, like Third World exports, or our health, or a whole cluster of issues like the coffee cycle. Similar questions can prompt us to think about Canadian society. This is what social analysis means – acquiring the habit of questioning the world around us and looking for patterns that raise new questions. There are many different approaches to social analysis, and many theories. One book is too short to discuss them all. But here is a preliminary definition that will serve people using this book.

Social analysis, as we are using the term, means *raising questions* about society and *seeking answers*. Its purpose is not only to *develop a critical awareness of the world* but also *to lead towards social justice.*

The process of social analysis also gives rise to further questions about what is going on and who is benefiting and who is getting hurt. This leads to further research. The process brings out the links or connections between different social issues. It helps us find out what is really going on beneath the surface of society, or beyond the appearances. It encourages group discussion.

Social analysis helps people become *critical*. Critical does not mean being negative, or condemning the society we live in, or showing a lack of gratitude for the good things it has to offer. Critical means becoming conscious, aware, questioning. It means developing a discerning attitude, a habit of trying to get to the bottom of things.

All the questions that arise from this process cannot be answered right away. Some open up topics that require *research*. This means taking time to pursue the questions as far as we possibly can. For example, after a discussion of the coffee cycle, we might want to look for additional information about the health hazards of caffeine, sugar, or whitener; the system that ensures the purity of the water we drink; the workings of the international coffee and sugar markets and the possibilities of fair trade; or the situation of coffee-producing peoples and their needs. It is also important to question the information we gather – to make sure it is accurate and thorough.

Critical questions lead to an awareness of previously unsuspected *connections* between issues. For example, thinking about where a cup of coffee comes from and how its ingredients get to us can quickly lead to questions about the international balance of trade, the structure of the food industry, the science, economics, and politics of maintaining a clean water supply, and the effects of caffeine and sugar on health.

Or take another example: a comparative analysis of a particular industry in Canada and a Third World country might soon uncover a common tendency to export relatively unprocessed raw materials. Social analysis tries to trace the links connecting issues, in order to understand how society works and fails to work.

Why raise questions, become critical, do research, and trace connections? Social analysis is not motivated merely by intellectual or scientific curiosity. The purpose is to seek the truth of a situation – whether it is the coffee cycle or unemployment in Canada – in order to lay bare any injustice that characterizes the situation. Social analysis is oriented towards *social justice* – towards taking some action, towards promoting change where this is judged necessary. It hopes to contribute effectively to the quest for greater social justice.

Social analysis is preferably done *in a group*, where one comment can spark new thoughts and people's opinions can get refined by coming up against other points of view. As the members of a group gain a picture of an issue, they move from analysis of a problem that has been identified, through a discussion of possible action, to making decisions, distributing tasks, contacting other groups, and taking action.

Doing social analysis does not mean agreeing with everything in *Getting Started,* but it does require a commitment to honest questioning. It is irresponsible to take an opposing viewpoint simply for the fun of it, or to protect a prejudice that you know is there but you don't want to admit to. But simply agreeing with everything in this book would be equally irresponsible. If you disagree with an approach taken in *Getting Started*, an emphasis given, a line of argument used, or a conclusion, take that disagreement as an opportunity to develop an alternative analysis that raises questions, traces connections, takes a critical stance, and proposes an alternative solution.

Some people say, "I have other things to do." Or, "I can't be bothered about dealing with that. Let other people – politicians, experts – figure it out." But the alternative to social analysis is to accept the surface meanings; to think what we are told to think; to consume, not only goods and services, but also the slogans, meanings, and values of society that go along with them. If we leave all the interpretation and direction of society in the hands of a few people, we may not like the results.

One day, seeing that things have gone too far, we might object, "I wasn't consulted!" By then it may be too late.

Towards Social Justice

Social analysis leads to action on behalf of justice. Such action may entail looking up more information, organizing a group to take action about an issue, making a small gesture of protest, or contributing to a national campaign that is tackling an important issue. Whatever the action, it will in turn raise new questions and once again involve people more deeply in the process of social analysis.

It doesn't take long for social analysis to begin uncovering the deep inequities and structural problems that characterize Canadian society. These matters can be stated starkly, even simply. But practical solutions are rarely black or white, and usually they are quite messy. They need to be hammered out in an often difficult process of compromise. In most cases, *Getting Started* poses the questions rather than proposes solutions.

> The choice of public justice is more than individual. It is a communal decision to favour all instead of some. And it is a political decision. It calls for engagement, for debate, for respectfully listening to each other. And for considering the consequences of policies not only for the majority, but also on the vulnerable and marginalized.
>
> — Louise Slobodian,
> Public Justice Resource Centre and Citizens for Public Justice,
> "From a Justice Perspective," 2001.

Social analysis opens up the need for political analysis, which is in turn basic to the task of developing the organizations of civil society and finding workable solutions. But political analysis is outside the range of this book, which limits itself to raising social questions without proposing political answers; it is an introduction to social analysis. (The conclusion, chapter fourteen, has more on the political consequences of social analysis.)

Without making specific proposals, *Getting Started* nevertheless does take a stand. It analyzes issues from the perspective of the many Canadians who feel relatively helpless in the face of the social issues that shape their lives. It deliberately opts for their interests. It favours those whose viewpoint is usually not heard and whose dignity is most often neglected and violated.

Some of *Getting Started*'s suggestions may in effect challenge the status quo, for social analysis as we define it here is not detached from the social reality under study. It is unabashedly involved in and committed to greater justice in Canada.

Everyone Is Welcome

The task of analyzing the social situations in Canada belongs to all of us, no matter what group, religious community, school, union, or political party we belong to. Among others, Canadian churches have been especially insistent in calling for social analysis.

In 1983 the Catholic bishops of Canada described the steps leading to and flowing from social analysis:

a) being present with and listening to the experiences of the poor, the marginalized, the oppressed in our society (e.g., the unemployed, the working poor, the welfare poor, exploited workers, native peoples, the elderly, people with disabilities, small producers, racial and cultural minorities, etc.);

b) developing a critical analysis of the economic, political and social structures that cause human suffering;

c) making judgments in light of Gospel principles and social teachings of the Church concerning social values and priorities;

d) stimulating creative thought and action regarding alternative visions and models for social and economic development; and,

e) acting in solidarity with popular groups in their struggles to transform economic, political and social structures that cause social and economic injustices.[4]

I believe passionately, people do care. They hurt, they suffer when their job is cut, when their plant closes, when families struggle in poverty, when asthma in children rises because of global warming and pollution, when people beg on the streets, when farmers get sunk by multinationals and when violence and discrimination increase.

People do care.

Our job as activists is to make the links and connections better between what is happening on a daily basis, and how it is connected to our union, social movement or group.

— Libby Davies,
Member of Parliament, East Vancouver, May 2002.

The values and methods of social analysis have a continuing relevance. They are echoed, for example, in the efforts of students, writers, labour unionists, members of church groups, and other people from all walks of life to address questions of social justice within the framework of globalization. Among the actions taken and analysis provided at the People's Summit in Quebec City in April 2001, the Canadian Council of Churches affirmed:

We believe that the new millennium can see human societies move towards equality and justice. We are not doomed to recycle old wrongs! Our peoples need policies that restore right relationships, preserve responsible communities, shrink economic inequalities, and allow space for all of creation to flourish in its diversity.[5]

Social analysis can also motivate self-examination, and churches are not exempt from this responsibility as they examine their own participation in situations of injustice. Social analysts themselves do not escape scrutiny under the light shed by critical questioning. In their social analysis they need to look both inward, at themselves, and outward, at the rest of the world.

Social analysis is also not limited to students,

or churchgoers, or members of particular organizations, or experts in any one field. In the end, all of us are responsible for analyzing the situation in Canada. Social teaching makes a special claim on all people of good will who want to contribute in a positive way to the human development of their sisters and brothers.

Getting Started is written for all people who:

■ feel paralyzed and baffled by the workings of Canadian society;

■ are concerned about a particular social issue and want to begin thinking about it;

■ are already working on an issue and want to see how it relates to other issues;

■ have done some social analysis and want to further develop their skills in critical thinking, questioning, and reflecting;

■ want to teach social analysis to others, lead group discussions, or encourage a community response; and,

■ share the desire to make Canada a better, more just country to live in – part of a more just global community.

How to Use This Book

Getting Started is divided into three main parts, and each part contains three or four chapters of analysis. A chapter of reflection brings each part to a close and prepares the way for the next set of chapters. The parts of the book are arranged as follows.

Issues in the Everyday — People often run up against immediate problems in their everyday lives, problems that seem overwhelming. The analysis in this part discusses how to connect a basic, everyday (and seemingly individual) problem to a larger social issue that helps to explain its root causes.

Reflection — Learning how to use the tools of social analysis is like learning to understand a language and its grammar.

The World Around Us — Examining the issues in our everyday lives is a good start, but it is not enough. Placing these issues in larger contexts stimulates analyses from broader perspectives, and encourages us to look for larger patterns and structures to explain what we see. Asking critical questions from these perspectives also makes us ask about the broader impact of the actions we take in our daily lives. It encourages us also to think about how our lives are influenced by events that are changing the shape of our world at personal everyday and global levels — events in the natural environment, in the rapidly shifting domain of technology, and in the realm of global economics.

Reflection — When we analyze issues at the everyday and global levels it becomes apparent that the media are entangled in all these phenomena. The reflection introduces a prevailing set of assumptions – or a dominant ideology – that is geared to justify what is happening.

People and Perspectives — So far the analysis has dealt with the issues and structures of Canadian society in general. But there are many particular groups of people who suffer injustices of a different and distinct kind. This part of the book explores the experiences, troubles, and contributions of old people, Aboriginal peoples, and women. This not only tells us about their lives but also offers new perspectives on mainstream conditions and approaches. Social analysis reveals connections between the issues faced by specific groups and the ways in which Canadian society is structured in general.

Reflection — The last chapter looks at what social analysis can mean in concrete action. It also reveals that the content and consequences of analysis can include victories, not just setbacks. It looks at impediments to analysis, at the issue of priorities and political power, and at steps beyond social analysis.

Many readers will want to work their way through the chapters in the order presented. Others may prefer to go directly to a chapter treating an issue of greatest concern or interest to them. In any case, readers should work through at least one or two of the appropriate issue chapters before delving into the reflection chapters (six, ten, and fourteen).

Most chapters end with a question section aimed at helping readers begin discussion and at encouraging further reading or research.

In each chapter we also suggest resources to follow up the analysis: books and other print materials, videos, websites, and groups to contact for further information and orientation. A warning to readers, though: all of us need to use discretion and critical judgement in using web material. The Library and Documentation website of the United Nations Framework Convention on Climate Change (UNFCCC) lists criteria that can be used in evaluating websites <unfccc.int/resource/library/criteria>.

At the back of the book, the Notes identify sources of quotations within the text and give details on other sources used in writing this book.

Because *Getting Started* provides only a representative sample of Canadian issues, the treatment of each one is necessarily very introductory. Furthermore, many possible topics are not treated. For instance: the specific problems of young people, lesbians and gays, refugees, or people with disabilities; agriculture, fisheries, forestry, and manufacturing; regional disparities, constitu-

tional questions, or the many issues raised by Quebec nationalism; the role of schools, colleges, and universities; militarism and national security; the list could go on.

In planning the chapters on old people and Aboriginal peoples, the authors of *Getting Started* faced a particular difficulty. We do not belong to either group. Although this is undoubtedly a handicap, we believe it is both possible and necessary for social analysis to listen to and engage with the experience of other groups and to find a way to make their concerns our own.

We debated whether issues related to old people, Aboriginal peoples, and women should be treated in separate chapters or integrated into the other chapters. In fact we do both. The advantages of a chapter dedicated, in a frankly introductory way, to some of each group's issues seem to outweigh the risk of tokenism (that is, giving the impression that a separate chapter takes care of all of their problems).

One further note on content: when it comes to the very important issues of abortion and reproductive rights, Canadians disagree strongly. Even among the Christian churches of Canada, there is profound disagreement. Similarly, the authors of *Getting Started* are not able to agree on a common approach to these issues. They have therefore been deliberately omitted.

Resources

• Beginning to do social analysis in a workshop, classroom, or group discussion is really no harder than arranging a kettle of water, coffee mug, styrofoam cup, plastic stir-stick, creamer or whitener, bowl of sugar, and jar of instant coffee on a low table. Everyone can be invited to mention the ideas or questions that these items suggest – similar to the comments that opened this chapter – and a record of points can be kept on paper or a blackboard. In no time there will be plenty of suggestions for discussion, further research, liaison with other groups, and proposals for action.

• After a group sees how quickly it can generate questions for social analysis, another session might consider why anyone would deliberately remain unaware. What is it in people that blocks their analysis of social reality? Why are people reluctant to take part in social analysis? Are they just too busy or preoccupied with other things, or is it something else? Can specific fears be identified, and how might each one be allayed?

• The following Social Paralysis Quiz has been used successfully in classes and workshops. Each member of the group should get a copy of the quiz and be asked to rate the statements as they apply personally.

Social Paralysis Quiz

5	4	3	2	1
strongly agree	agree	don't know	disagree	strongly disagree

☐ Canadian society is too complicated for me to understand.

☐ In Canada there's a premium on authority and obedience: the prudent thing, whenever there's social tension, is to stay out of it.

☐ Things are always getting worse and I feel the news is too awful to take in.

☐ If the experts cannot agree among themselves on any social problem, much less the solution, I haven't a chance.

☐ Faced with issues too big and complicated for me, I feel overwhelmed – it's better not to start.

☐ Because decisions about social issues are very personal, I feel alone and isolated in facing the social world.

☐ There are too many facts to absorb, and it's like I'm drowning in a deluge of information.

☐ I have no control over the important decisions that shape life in Canada.

☐ Economics is a science so mysterious that even economists can't understand how the Canadian economy works.

☐ We will never reach a perfectly just society, because human greed and the lust for power will always reassert themselves, so why bother?

☐ I want to live a well-ordered life – I keep my world quite small.

☐ Social analysis might work in a Third World country, where the inequities are obvious, but it's nearly impossible to analyze a free society like Canada, with its complex issues.

☐ People used to understand the world from the viewpoint of the community they lived in all their lives, but now things are moving too fast for us to understand.

☐ There are tendencies towards evil built into human nature, and until individual hearts are changed there's no point in tampering with social structures.

☐ Political decisions are too weighty for most citizens to grasp.

☐ **Total score**

This quiz tests people's disposition towards social analysis. The higher you score, the more you have to struggle against social complacency or paralysis – the tendency to leave social concerns to experts, professionals, or activists. A lower score suggests that people believe they can understand their society and hope to have some impact on it.

In a group, everyone's scores could be averaged to see if they tend towards a belief that they have the power to change society for the better, or towards paralysis and disbelief. There could be a discussion of the items that group members tended to score on the pessimistic side.

Chapter Two

In Sickness and in Health

"I feel sick!" someone says.

"So, what's the problem? Where does it hurt?"

"I've got a sore throat. My head aches. I can't sleep."

Now what?

Most of us respond to a sick feeling by trying to get rid of it as quickly as possible. We calm the cough, kill the pain, take a pill. That's how aches and pains are usually handled. Nowadays we are bombarded daily with ads and commercials and advice about health products that will get us back on our feet and off to school or work in no time at all. The new ads stress ever more strongly the power of products that can suppress the problems.

But sometimes that initial help doesn't work, and we begin to see the cough and pain in a different light. Instead of nagging irritants, they become persistent symptoms, which tell us that something is wrong inside and needs to be put right. They are the starting point for a more thorough investigation. Usually with outside help we try to trace our way back to the probable causes of the symptoms – their roots – and figure out

which of those causes is the most likely. Eventually, if all goes well, the investigation leads to an appropriate cure. This activity of identifying what's wrong is called *diagnosis*.

The advantage of diagnosis – compared with the immediate elimination of any sick feeling – is that it seeks out the root causes and works towards a cure. It doesn't merely treat the effects or symptoms, like a cold remedy does, for instance. Diagnosis analyzes symptoms in the context of the whole body, and many factors come into play. Diagnosis is a combination of science and art, experience and intuition, dialogue and consultation.

Social analysis works in a similar way. In looking at society we run into problems that are urgent and painful, and often we find they don't yield to immediate solutions. Often the solutions that we or others come up with only cover up the problems – they are called "Band-aid solutions." The task of social analysis is to work back from the symptoms of those problems to the root causes. This means that we can find and adopt an effective, long-lasting solution, even if it is more demanding and harder to achieve than a quick cure.

All of us have some experience of physical symptoms and how diagnosis works. These experiences help to get social analysis started. As the old proverb says, "An ounce of prevention is worth a pound of cure." Certainly, both prevention and cure are needed, and this chapter looks at both. The first part, "An Ounce of Prevention," examines what we know about health, some of the causes of illness, and steps that can be taken to improve health. The second part, "A Pound of Cure," takes a look at the health-care (or, as some say, "illness-care") system in Canada – its history, its strengths and weaknesses, and the threats to its well-being.

"An Ounce of Prevention"

How healthy we are as a society is inextricably linked to the kind of society we have. The causes of illness and disease are not merely biological, and the "cures" are not necessarily medical. They are also social. In the countries of the Third World, for example, poverty can mean inadequate nutrition, poor housing, and a lack of clean water. These factors in turn give rise to widespread malnutrition, rampant infectious disease, and high rates of infant mortality. In short, poverty breeds disease – as surely as germs do.

That same link holds fast not only in poor nations, but also in wealthier ones such as Canada, the United States, and Britain. Studies show that poorer people in Canada are more vulnerable to health problems. People in lower socio-economic groups experience worse health and die sooner than people in middle-income groups; but people with middle incomes in turn have worse health and die sooner than people in higher income groups. Health is significantly determined by economic class. And economic class is also often determined by other factors: some groups are more likely to be poor in Canada – for instance, Aboriginal people, single women with one or more children, and people of colour – and therefore more likely to have poor health. Gender is also a key factor. Indeed, as one Canadian research organization states: "Issues related to gender, language, and cultural background have a profound impact on people's roles, how they view and use health care services, and how they respond to different programs and approaches to care."[1]

A Definition of Health

Health is a state of complete physical, mental and social well-being and not merely the absence of disease or infirmity.

— Preamble to the Constitution of the World Health Organization, as adopted by the International Health Conference, New York, June 19-22, 1946.

Illness and the Determinants of Health

The idea of determinants of health forms a link between *individual* health problems and the social and physical *environments* we live in. The determinants of health are the conditions that have an impact on health – from genetics to lifestyle (such as smoking or drinking or eating certain kinds of foods) to economic status. These conditions include early childhood experience; hierarchical positions at work; workplace hazards; family and friendship supports; employment status; and environmental factors.

Analysts conclude that socio-economic status is the single most important determinant of health. If you are the two-year-old child of a semi-employed single mother who smokes and lives near a paint factory, your chances of enjoying a healthy life are not the same as those of a child who lives in more favourable circumstances – no matter how many visits to a doctor you can make. Children born to poor parents are more likely than those from more affluent families to have low birth weights, experience difficulty in school, eat less wholesomely, and drop out of school. All of these factors put their health at risk. As income rises, parents are able to furnish better diet, shelter, and hygiene for their offspring, and fewer children die in the early years of life. The wealthiest Canadians can expect to live four years longer than the poorest Canadians.[2]

One of the most glaring disparities shows up in the health of Canada's Aboriginal peoples, who have average incomes far below those of most Canadians. Compared to the Canadian average, more than twice as many First Nations children die in their first year of life. The life expectancy of Aboriginal people in Canada is shorter than for the population as a whole – by about seven years for men and five years for women. The burden of illness is also far greater. For Manitoba First Nations people, the chances of having diabetes is more than four times the Canadian average, and the chance of undergoing amputation as a result of diabetes is sixteen times higher. Hospitalization rates for Manitoba First Nations people are double the rate of other Manitobans.[3] Aboriginal

people who live in the North often don't have adequate access to health care (see also chapter twelve).

The 1997 report of the National Forum on Health put it this way:

> Being healthy requires clean, safe environments, adequate income, meaningful roles in society, and good housing, nutrition, education, and social support in our communities. In fact, actions on these broad determinants of health through public policies have led to most of the improvement in health status of Canadians over the last century."[4]

One sure way to improve the health of Canadians is to reduce poverty and to support conditions that foster health. Urban air pollution is a growing health concern, especially given that more than half of all Canadians live in just four urban centres. Long-term exposure to tiny particles in the air (by-products of fossil-fuel combustion) increases the risk of death from lung cancer and heart disease. Statistics Canada reports that air pollution is linked to the premature deaths of up to sixteen thousand Canadians a year, and in Ontario alone smog is estimated to cost taxpayers more than $1 billion a year from increased hospital visits and admissions and lost work days. Yet fuel efficiency standards for vehicles have not improved since 1980, and air pollution is getting worse.[5]

A society's overall life expectancy is a reasonable index of health status. Countries with the longest life expectancy rates are not the wealthiest countries, but rather those with the smallest spread of incomes and the smallest proportion of the population living in relative poverty.[6] Hence life expectancy in the United States is significantly below that of Canada, and the infant mortality rate south of the border is 40 per cent higher than here. The United States is a wealthier, but far more unequal, society.[7]

"Choice" and Blaming the Victim

Cancer and heart disease are major killers in Canada, and at first glance both of the diseases and the preventive measures necessary can be all too easily linked to individual choice and personal lifestyle. For example, smoking habits contribute to both the major killers. (Although much attention is paid to smoking and cancer, cigarettes kill more people by causing heart disease than by causing lung cancer.) By the late 1980s, tobacco use was *quite simply the single greatest cause of disease and disability in Canada.*[8] Health advocates argued that cutting down on smoking would reduce the number of people who suffer from both diseases – and thereby save on health dollars. To some extent the "smoking message" got through. The percentage of smokers dropped to a historic low of 23 per cent in 2001. (In 1965 the number of smokers was as high as 50 per cent.)[9]

But the reduction of smoking, though important, is an individual solution to a larger problem. In Canada – and around the world – smoking is more prevalent among poorer people than among wealthier people. In North America that is at least partly because people with lower incomes have fewer alternatives that they can turn to for coping with their problems. "When you have income that is very minimal, you can't plan, you can't look ahead . . . you don't know if you're gonna still be in the same place two months from now," one low-income person said.[10] As a result, U.S. public health researcher Nancy Milo says, many poor people "turn to what is at hand – alcohol, cigarettes, food – all economically accessible in an affluent society if substituted for other things. And they turn most to the least costly (cigarettes) or most available (excess calories)."[11]

That doesn't mean we should abandon efforts aimed at lowering smoking rates. But in a complex society, choice is not all that simple a matter. *Blaming the victim* (or "poor-bashing") is an easy but insufficient analysis. Freedom of choice falters before the massive avalanche of advertising and marketing techniques let loose on Canadian society by the multibillion-dollar food, alcohol, and tobacco industries. Meanwhile, too many health promotion activities "are passive and biased to middle and upper social class cultures." That was the conclusion of a Manitoba study that found that low-income citizens were not only more often hospitalized for illness but also suffered disproportionately from some illnesses.[12]

Public Health Measures

One means of promoting safer living and working conditions is through public health measures. In Canada, many diseases like typhoid and cholera – often spread by contaminated water and food – have been dramatically reduced or even eliminated thanks to the generally higher level of prosperity. Public health organizations are responsible for monitoring water supply and food-handling, implementing prevention programs for sexually transmitted diseases such as AIDS and syphilis, and overseeing the safe disposal of garbage and sewage. Public health measures are the most effective way of preventing many diseases.

Yet a very small proportion of our health-care dollars goes into the public health sector – just over 1 per cent. In recent years the underpinnings of public health – things like air and water quality, food monitoring, road safety, and work safety inspections – have been under threat.[13] When the public health sector is cut back, the results can be catastrophic. In Ontario in the 1990s the Conservative provincial government made deep cuts to the Ministry of the Environment and jeopardized, among other things, water testing. One result? In the town of Walkerton in 2000, seven people died and 2,300 became ill – some suffering lifelong health consequences – because their water supply was contaminated. This was a completely preventable catastrophe, a problem that belonged in the nineteenth century rather than the late twentieth.[14] The Walkerton experience showed that public health cannot be taken for granted.

Ill health is not a random event – often, it is all too easy to predict. For instance, cutbacks to social services and housing programs in the 1990s led to a dramatic increase in the number of homeless people in Canada's inner cities (see chapter three). This situation had a number of immediate health consequences, among them an increase in the incidence of tuberculosis, an infectious disease that easily spreads when people are crowded into emergency shelters. Before the cuts to social programs, tuberculosis had been virtually eliminated.

Government policy in many different areas has a direct impact on the health of Canadians. The health(illness)-care system, which treats individuals, gets an enormous amount of attention. But many other policy areas – education, housing, recreation, social assistance, public health – have a much more significant, if less immediately obvious, impact on health.

Still, when we become sick, have an accident, or contract a disease, we look to the health-care professionals and the health-care system for help.

"A Pound of Cure"

From the beginning of time communities have recognized certain men and women as possessing the skill and power to heal. These healers could be herbalists, midwives, shamans, priests, or physicians. There were women physicians in ancient Rome, and, originally, women witches were healers with practical knowledge and skill – though in more recent times we have had the stereotype of the wild-eyed "witch doctor" mumbling bizarre incantations. Traditionally women in the home provided most of the health care the family needed, and religious women established and ran hospitals.[15] In the nineteenth century, European-style "modern" medicine became concentrated in the hands of mostly male physicians, who worked vigorously to keep women out of their ranks. Women were relegated to the job of nursing – which they had to fight long and hard to professionalize. For people in need, there remained a wide range of medical options: from home remedies and folk cures to Thomsonians, Homeopaths, Eclectics, and Aboriginal healers, among others. Yet, then and now, all of them – from herbalists to neurosurgeons to nurses – have this in common: they are commissioned by the community to tend to the sick.

Modern medicine transformed medical practice into a professional business characterized by more private relationships. It centralized healthcare services and promoted increased specialization and the use of complex, expensive technology. By the 1990s the health-care system had become "the largest cluster of economic activity in all modern states."[16] The medical establishment now frowns on the activities of competitors whom it sees as "less professional" – acupuncturists, chiropractors, midwives, naturopaths, and homeopaths, for instance – especially those not based on the "Western" scientific tradition.

In the days before medicare – which really weren't so long ago – the prevailing arrangement in Canada was "pay-as-you-go." Each patient paid for medical services either personally or through an insurance policy sold by a private firm. That system led to a number of typical experiences.

- Children of poorer families rarely saw a doctor or nurse.
- Severe illness often forced elderly people to sell off their homes or other assets to raise cash to pay medical bills.
- Those who could not afford to pay avoided the doctor altogether, humbly asked for free care or credit, or went to the emergency department and the public ward. Patients sometimes felt like beggars, and doctors decided who deserved "charity medicine."
- The inability to predict medical expenses and the pressure to budget for expensive health insurance were common sources of anxiety.
- Those most in need of medical attention – the poor, especially the borderline poor who did not qualify for welfare – were least likely to get it.

Good access to medical care also depended on where you lived. In 1959 Newfoundland, for instance, had one doctor for every 2,190 residents, compared to the Canadian average of one per 938. In Atlantic Canada access to prepaid medical coverage was 50 per cent less than for the country as a whole, and in the rural areas of the Prairie provinces, coverage was much lower than in the cities.[17]

It's worth remembering what the "facts of life" used to be under an arrangement that still characterizes health care in the United States, where about forty-three million citizens have no health insurance of any kind, and at least as many have such inadequate coverage that a major illness would lead to personal bankruptcy.

Under Canada's medicare program, the situation is markedly different. Medicare is Canada's publicly funded health insurance system, designed to give all members of society reasonable access to medical attention. Compared with the hardships and inequities of the out-of-pocket arrangement, medicare seems fair and effective to most Canadians.

Justice Emmett Hall is one of the founders of medicare in Canada. After conducting a comprehensive review of the system in 1980, Justice Hall assured Canadians, "I found no one – not any Government or individual, not the Medical Profession nor any organization – not in favour of Medicare."[18]

Yet medicare has always had its enemies. When it was introduced in 1965, and passed the following year, the federal Medical Care Insurance program was opposed by the medical profession, the insurance industry, chambers of commerce, and several provincial governments. In 1982 Dr. Marc Baltzan, president of the Canadian Medical Association (CMA), stated baldly, "There are at least three distinct disadvantages to Canadian medicare: it is a threat to civil liberty, it is a threat to health and it is economically inefficient."[19] But *Limits to Medicine*, Ivan Illich's classic critique of modern health-care systems, begins with just the opposite assessment: "The medical establishment has become a threat to health. The disabling impact of professional control over medicine has reached the proportions of an epidemic."[20] Other critics say that despite the benefits of medicare, the Canadian health-care system is based on an overly institutionalized, top-down delivery model, with hospitals and doctors at the apex and patients at the

bottom. To be more effective, some say, the system should be broader, more holistic, and more focused on the needs of patients.

A Health Charter for Canadians

Medicare was first proposed by the Liberal Party as early as 1919. The Co-operative Commonwealth Federation (CCF) and all the major labour unions pushed for it during the 1930s and 1940s. In 1962, when the CCF government in Saskatchewan moved towards a system of publicly funded health insurance, doctors warned of chaos in medicine and launched a strike to protest the government's action. After a bitter struggle, Saskatchewan residents became the first in the country to be covered by medicare. But the government backed down from its original plan to put many doctors on salary, agreeing instead on a system, called fee-for-service, based on payment for each consultation or procedure.

Prepaid insurance for medical care and hospital treatment, as a right for all Canadians, was established by the federal Medical Care Act of 1966 and reaffirmed in the Canada Health Act of 1984. Although the health field comes under provincial jurisdiction, the federal government has exercised influence by paying a share of the costs of medicare in any province whose program meets five criteria:

- *Universality* – everyone must be covered. Insured health services must be available to all residents, without discrimination.
- *Accessibility* – people must have reasonable access to services, without prohibitive extra charges.
- *Comprehensiveness* – a full range of health services must be available and covered by the program.
- *Portability* – Canadians must be able to carry their medical insurance from province to province, to be covered anywhere in the country.
- *Public administration* – plans must be run on a non-profit basis by a public agency of the provincial government (which limits the role of the public insurance industry).

Medicare is sometimes loosely referred to as

"free," although it is neither free nor a government handout. The public pays for it through taxes; in Alberta and British Columbia individual citizens who want to be covered also pay annual premiums, like those of a conventional insurance plan.

Under medicare, doctors are independent professionals/entrepreneurs who receive payments for their services from a government health-insurance agency. The fee schedule is set by each province after negotiation with the provincial medical association. Fee-for-service allows doctors to control their incomes. Those who practice "revolving door" medicine, ushering patients in and out of the office at brief intervals, can earn considerably more than those who take more time with individual patients.

The Changing Face of Medicare

Medicare has gone a long way towards "curing" the major financial difficulties that used to prevent the sick from getting medical attention.

In the first year after the introduction of Quebec's medicare plan, poor families in Montreal increased their visits to the doctor by 18.2 per cent. Among low-income, pregnant women, the rate of prenatal consultations more than doubled with the advent of medicare. But once these previously underserved groups were attended to, the statistics levelled off, indicating that medicare did not lead to overuse on the part of the poor. Research in Alberta, Saskatchewan, Ontario, and Canada as a whole suggests that health insurance has improved access to medical care by the poor. Average medical services per family still tend to increase with family income, but research shows different patterns of use.[21] A Manitoba study found that dollars spent on physician visits tend to increase with education and income, while the number of short hospital stays goes up as both income and education levels decline. "The better off you are the less likely you are to be hospitalized," the report concludes (reminding us again of the determinants of health).[22]

Health-care expenditures grew rapidly in the 1950s and 1960s, helped by government subsidies for hospitals and hospital insurance. But in the 1970s, under medicare, the total cost of health care (public and private) remained constant, hovering between 7.5 and 8 per cent of the Gross Domestic Product (GDP). The 1980s saw a new surge in health-care expenditures, with costs steadily increasing from $22.7 billion in 1980 to $61.8 billion, or 9.5 per cent of GDP, in 1990[23] and then 10.2 per cent in 1992. Developments in medicine, sophisticated surgical procedures, organ replacements, the rising cost of prescription drugs, and reliance on expensive equipment represent some of the heaviest financial burdens on the health-care system.

In the 1990s, federal and provincial governments, worried about ballooning deficits, began to reduce health-care spending. Between 1992 and 1997 the expenditures dropped in absolute terms for the first time in the history of medicare. Spending on hospitals and doctors was reduced — and as a result health-care spending as a percentage of GDP dropped down to 9.2 per cent in 1997. In all, $30 billion was taken out of the health-care system during the 1990s.[24] The cuts put significant strains on the system, resulting in large-scale layoffs of nurses and other hospital employees. These moves sometimes put patient safety in serious jeopardy. In Ontario Premier Mike Harris did nothing to help morale when thousands of Ontario nurses faced job loss as a result of the recommendations of a hospital restructuring commission. Asked what advice he had for those about to lose their jobs, Harris compared the hospitals to Hula Hoop factories. When Hula Hoops went out of fashion, factory workers had to find other employment. Nurses could do the same, he suggested.[25]

The cuts proved to be too crude and too deep, and a few years later governments began to restore health-care spending. In 2001 spending went up by 4.3 per cent over the year before.[26] But a critical shortage of nurses in Ontario and elsewhere in the country remained.

In the United States medical expenditures

In short, the U.S. experience has shown that private markets and commercial competition have made things worse, not better, for our health care system. That could have been predicted, because health care is clearly a public concern and a personal right of all citizens. By its very nature, it is fundamentally different from most other goods and services distributed in commercial markets. Markets simply are not designed to deal effectively with the delivery of medical care – which is a social function that needs to be addressed in the public sector.

— Dr. Arnold Relman,
Harvard Medical School, addressing the Standing Senate Committee on Social Affairs, Science and Technology, Feb. 21, 2002.

followed a steady upward trend, but the costs were consistently and substantially higher than those in Canada. By 1993 U.S. health-care costs had reached 14 per cent of GDP,[27] and that level of spending stayed constant through the rest of the decade.

Although Canada's health-system spending is second only to that of the United States, it is roughly in line with spending in Germany and only slightly higher than spending in other industrialized nations, such as France and the Netherlands. Given that we are a relatively rich country, our overall spending on health care appears to be affordable.

However, the federal share of public health-care spending dropped to less than 30 per cent during the 1990s from about 40 per cent in the 1970s. Federal money to the provinces now comes through the 1995 Canada Health and Social Transfer (CHST), giving the provinces leeway to spend federal dollars where they want. One of the key recommendations of the 2002 Romanow report on the future of health care was that the CHST be scrapped in favour of a dedicated health fund that would allow greater accountability for health-care expenditures. Indeed, the Royal Commission suggested that "accountability" be added as a sixth principle of the Canada Health Act.[28]

The falling federal contribution to health care

raised concerns about the federal government's ability to enforce the Canadian Health Act. Provinces have already tolerated measures that reduce the accessibility, comprehensiveness, or universality of ensured services – measures such as extra charges, reduced services, and the use of premiums. These measures are regressive because the burden falls most heavily on those least able to bear it. Alberta, for example, has allowed private for-profit cataract clinics to operate in the province. While a rationale was to provide better access, a study by the Consumers Association of Canada found that waiting lists and costs for surgery were highest, and waiting lists longest, in regions of Alberta dominated by private clinics.[29]

Meanwhile, during the public spending cuts of the 1990s, Alberta's cuts to the hospital sector were twice the national average. In 2000 Alberta introduced a law to make it easier for private clinics and hospitals to operate.[30] A couple of years later Ontario introduced legislation that would allow for private MRI (magnetic resonance imaging) and CT (computed tomography) clinics in the province. Such clinics already existed in Alberta, Quebec, and British Columbia, and the result there was queue-jumping – patients willing to pay cash got far faster access to scans.[31]

Such queue-jumping is in direct contravention of the Canada Health Act. But the federal government has not defended the Act. In 1999 the auditor general reported, "The federal government has never imposed discretionary financial penalties on provinces for non-compliance with the five criteria of the Canada Health Act."

While total health-care spending between 1992 and 1997 dropped as a percentage of GDP, and public spending dropped, private spending on health care increased. Spending on drugs, dentistry, and the private part of institutional care rose by 16.4 per cent. As well, provincial governments eliminated some medical procedures from public medicare coverage, leaving patients to pay on their own for some treatments. The net result was that private spending on health care – out of pocket spending, or through private insurance – increased to 30 per cent of total spending in 1997, up from 26 per cent just five years earlier.[32]

Medicare under Fire

As a result of all these changes, medicare has come under more fire from those who believe in expanding the private delivery of health services. People who derive their income from the system are vocal if they believe that their interests are being jeopardized or harmed. This is especially true of the most powerful groups. Organized medicine (comprising the federal and provincial doctors' associations), hospital associations, and the pharmaceutical industry usually have strong links to key government officials and use their connections to lobby hard when they feel their interests are threatened. (It is always useful to ask "in whose interests?" when such groups take stands on medicare – for example, when they promote for-profit medicine.)

As well, the financing and operation of the health-care system provide a natural target of political debate and attack. After all, the system is funded with tax dollars and represents the single largest item in provincial budgets (close to one-third of each province's total expenditures go to health, up from 27 per cent in 1975). When things go demonstrably wrong – when patients are harmed or die unnecessarily, when there are long waiting lists for medical procedures, when money is obviously wasted – the incidents are debated openly in the press and in provincial legislatures, with the health minister often in the hot seat. This kind of focused, public scrutiny does not happen in countries with a largely private system of health care, such as the United States.

During U.S. president Bill Clinton's failed attempt at health-care reform in the early 1990s, Canada's system came under serious attack by U.S. private health insurers fighting against reform in their country. These private companies were anxious to discredit a public system of medicare (which would eliminate the need for private insurers) and made every effort to portray it as inefficient, unfair, and just plain chaotic, wildly exaggerating actual problems. Today U.S. private, for-profit health-care firms continue to search aggressively for opportunities to expand into Canada.

Medicare does, of course, have its very real difficulties, including hospital bed shortages, long waits for some procedures, clogged emergency wards, inadequate home-care services, a shortage of doctors in some areas, and expensive drugs. Provincial and federal inquiries and commissions on medicare have become regular events. The Commission on the Future of Health Care, chaired by Roy Romanow, a former Saskatchewan premier, delivered its report in November 2002, making forty-seven recommendations covering ten critical areas. In addition to raising the issue of accountability, it called for an increase in federal health-care funding to the provinces, the expansion of fully financed home care for certain groups, drug payments for people who spend more than $1,500 a year on prescriptions, and the introduction of a Canadian Health Covenant, which would explain the rights and responsibilities of everyone in the system.[33]

Canadians have legitimate concerns about the state of our health-care system. But once again we need to look behind the symptoms, identify the causes, and consider alternatives that could remedy at least some of the (seemingly never-ending) growing pains of the Canadian health system.

In Search of the Proper Prescription

People with a vested interest in dismantling medicare – since such a move would lead to their financial benefit – consistently argue that the legitimate concerns constitute a "crisis" or often a "crisis in funding." Many of these critics go on to argue that the solution is more private health care.

The hallmark of medicare in Canada is now public payment for privately delivered hospital and medical care. Tommy Douglas, the Saskatchewan premier who was the driving force behind medicare, aimed to remove "the financial barrier between those who need care and those who provide for it." And medicare went a long way towards doing that. But Premier Douglas envisioned a second stage for medicare: one that would implement a new type of delivery system that would include community-based care, preventive medicine, and different ways of paying doctors. That new system has not yet become a reality.

Since medicare was established, patterns of illness in Canada have changed. Acute problems, such as injuries, tuberculosis, and diphtheria, used to be the main health issues. Today, chronic illnesses – heart disease, diabetes, asthma – have become a much greater burden. These illnesses can be better managed with a more co-ordinated system of care.[34]

Because medicare guarantees payment only for health care provided in hospital or by doctors, many other health professionals are underutilized. A great deal of the routine work done by family physicians, such as immunizations and checkups, could be handled by nurses and nurse practitioners working in a team with family doctors. Such an arrangement would leave family doctors free to deal with more serious and complex health issues, and would help address concerns about the shortage of family doctors. Canadians have indicated that they would happy to receive care from a team of health-care professionals including nurses, doctors, and pharmacists.[35] But the system offers no financial incentive for this kind of arrangement, and it is rare. Nurse practitioners are employed successfully, but usually only in areas where there are doctor shortages or in multidisciplinary health-care clinics where doctors have agreed to be paid by salary. The Romanow Report called for $2.5 billion in new federal spending to stimulate "primary health care," stating: "No other initiative holds as much potential for improving health and sustaining our health care system."[36] The money would go to supporting teams of professionals, not just doctors; treatment combined with disease prevention and health promotion; integration of prevention and promotion targeting tobacco and obesity; and a national immunization strategy.[37]

The Canada Health Act does not cover home care, and funding of such care is left primarily to provinces. As a result, there is a threefold variation in home-care entitlement from province to province and no national standards for care. Yet the pressure on hospitals, together with the trend to shortened hospital stays and more out-patient treatment, means that more and more people are forced to rely on home care as they convalesce.[38] In several provinces, private for-profit firms have moved into the home-care field, and when provinces like Ontario insist on competitive bidding to provide care, the result is a home-care workforce largely made up of badly paid, non-union, often part-time workers. Even nurses who work in home care are typically paid less than their hospital counterparts. Because of the inadequacies of home care, many patients are not getting the care they need at home, and an often overwhelming burden is placed on family members, mostly women, who serve as informal, unpaid caregivers. Family members are "fearful of being overwhelmed," according to the National Forum on Health, which recommended that home care become an integral part of publicly funded health services, with national standards.[39]

Prescription drugs make up a large and growing proportion of health-care costs in Canada. In 1980, they accounted for 8.4 per cent of total health-care spending; by 1996 that proportion had climbed to 12.3 per cent. Five years later, spending on drugs had, at 15 per cent of total health spending, surpassed spending on doctors' services (which amounted to 14 per cent of health-care costs). At the same time, more than three million Canadians – mainly the poor and those with low incomes – lack any drug insurance.[40] This group of people is increasingly hard hit with shorter hospital stays and more out-patient care. In many provinces, drug costs are only covered while patients are in hospital – when they leave the hospital they have to pay for their own drugs. As with home care, there is a threefold variation in the way provinces cover prescription drugs for citizens. Some provinces, like British Columbia, provide prescription drugs to all citizens, subject to some restrictions. Provinces like Ontario provide coverage only for the elderly, the disabled, and those on social assistance.

In 1997 the ruling federal Liberal Party endorsed a national pharmacare program as a "long-term national objective" and pledged to ensure that all Canadians have access to medically necessary drugs within the health-care system. Such coverage is taken for granted in many other countries with public health-care systems. But the powerful pharmaceutical industry staunchly opposes a national plan. The drug companies are concerned that such a program would give governments such buying power that they could drive down the price of drugs.

Proposals for anything like an extensive pharmacare program are usually attacked because they would be expensive. But according to Dr. Joel Lexchin, "There is compelling evidence that a national drug plan would actually reduce overall costs, not increase them." He argues that overall drugs costs to Canadians would fall by 10 per cent – or $650 million less a year – "because drug prices would inevitably drop (by about 15%) under a public plan, and so would administrative costs."[41] (See also chapter nine, pp.120-21.)

Doing Things Differently

Those who stand to gain from for-profit medical care promote the addition of a private tier as the solution to what ails Canada's health-care system. But any expansion of private for-profit medicine in Canada would weaken and, eventually, destroy the universal public system that Canadians are so proud of. Quite simply, the first priority of for-profit corporations is shareholders and top-echelon employees, not citizens; and care offered by such corporations is by no means better. One study found that the mortality rate at for-profit hospitals in the United States was 2 per cent higher than at U.S. non-profit hospitals. The study suggested that hospital deaths would increase by as many as 2,200 a year in Canada if U.S.-style for-profit hospitals were introduced into our health-care system.[42]

If private care is not the answer, health care in

Canada can still be significantly improved by changes in the delivery system. Wait lists for surgery and other procedures often become a flashpoint for dissatisfaction with medicare. While waiting lists are inevitable in any health-care system, there should be agreed-upon criteria for placement on the list, and both the lists and criteria should be regularly monitored. This is, of course, particularly important in cases involving life-threatening conditions. Because of concerns about the wait for heart surgery patients in the late 1980s, Ontario created a cardiac care network in 1990. The network, which includes regional cardiac care co-ordinators who work with health professionals and patients, tracks patient conditions and wait lists across the province. After the network was implemented, Ontario saw a 33 per cent increase in operations and a drop in the surgery mortality rate – the province now has one of the best cardiac surgery outcomes in the world.[43] A decade after starting the cardiac network, Ontario began work on a network for patients waiting for joint replacement.

A co-ordinated, multidisciplinary approach to the delivery of primary health care would address troubling issues such as overcrowded hospitals and emergency wards and shortages of family doctors. In Victoria, B.C., for example, a multidisciplinary team – available fifteen hours a day – assesses elderly patients in emergency wards and immediately organizes the services required for them to convalesce at home. In Edmonton, day health centres for the frail elderly focus on health promotion by offering help with nutrition and exercise and by providing social contact. Teams of health professionals, including dentists and foot-care specialists, also regularly monitor the health of the participants. The program has led to a significant decrease in hospital and nursing home costs.[44]

In 2000, Canada's health-care ministers agreed to pursue an "integrated services" model of primary health care, and the federal government contributed $200 million a year for four years to help spur reform.[45] The goal is in some

If we were building a health care system today from scratch, it would be structured much differently from the one we now have and might be less expensive. The system would rely less on hospitals and doctors and would provide a broader range of community-based services, delivered by multidisciplinary teams with a much stronger emphasis on prevention. We would also have much better information linking interventions and health outcomes. However, because we are not starting with a blank slate, we must be careful about the pace of change so that both the public and the health care providers maintain their confidence in the system – a difficult balancing act.

— National Forum on Health,
Canada Health Action: Building on the Legacy, 1997.

ways a restatement of Tommy Douglas's original vision of a second stage of medicare, a new type of delivery system – one that focuses on maintaining health and employs alternative mechanisms (besides fee-for-service) for paying health professionals.

Already, most provinces have decentralized health care to regional authorities. These authorities receive a lump sum of funding from the provincial government to organize and pay for a wide range of services at the local level. A regionalized system offers the possibility of more co-ordinated care for patients, compared to a system in which various parts (hospitals, home care, long-term care) operate in isolation from – and often in competition with – each other.

Organizations for Health

One way of bringing together the curative and preventive dimensions of health care is through a communal and structural approach that places a greater emphasis on health promotion – an emphasis that is not as likely to occur in the private fee-for-service practice of medicine or in hospital treatment. Community Health Centres (CHCs), or in Quebec the CLSCs (Centres local de services communautaires), are examples of this. The CHC/CLSC (we use them interchangeably here) is an organization designed to

implement or follow the criteria of the Canadian health charter – that is, to offer health care that is accessible, comprehensive, and universal – and to address "social diseases" like cancer.

CHCs, though definitely part of the medicare system, differ from both private practice and larger hospitals. They are often located in a refurbished storefront or public building and seem more open and welcoming than a typical doctor's office, far less impersonal and intimidating than a big hospital. The friendly atmosphere, informal dress, and simplified procedures can help to reduce some of the anxieties usually associated with seeking medical aid.

CLSCs offer a wide range of curative, preventive, and social services, including prenatal and postnatal care, nutrition, mutual help groups, and testing for environmental hazards. Instead of responding only to patients who are sick, the CLSCs try to address the social causes of sicknesses and educate people to take care of their health. CLSCs also set up their own telephone network – where Quebeckers can call and get medical advice from a nurse – long before such telephone referral systems (often run by private companies) were introduced in other provinces.

The staff of a CHC is a multidisciplinary team of physicians and health-care and social-service workers. This takes the focus off the doctor and makes room for other contributors to the health of individuals and the community.

Usually the staff is paid salaries, which removes individual financial transactions from the doctor-patient relationship and frees the staff to provide a more comprehensive range of services. The people who use the centre and are thus directly affected by its quality of health care select a community board of directors. The board is responsible for planning, setting priorities, and preparing budgets. In effect, the whole health team is accountable to its patients.

There are over two hundred such health centres across Canada. Because of their philosophy, staffing, funding arrangements, and community control:

■ CHCs are more accessible to the poor, elderly,

disadvantaged, and people of colour, who have difficulty gaining access to private doctors and often need more comprehensive care. Accessibility is also increased for people who cannot afford the premiums in Alberta and British Columbia.

- CLSCs are able to link illnesses to the patient's family, housing (see chapter three), environment (see chapter seven), and economic and social problems. By taking these determinants into account, they provide more comprehensive care than hospitals or private practice can offer.

- Besides helping patients treat their sickness, CHCs can actively promote health, develop ways of preventing disease, and tackle environmental or social problems in the neighbourhood. They can organize activities in which people can learn what is threatening their health and figure out what to do about it.

- CLSCs allow people from the community and health workers to be partners, making decisions together.

The CHC/CLSC is an innovative structure. It goes beyond the merely curative to make holistic, communal, preventive and positive, participatory and empowering health care possible. It is a structure within which people – professionals, volunteers, the ill, the poor, from different ethnic backgrounds – can co-operate on these important ideals.

There are 140 CLSCs in Quebec, where they are fully integrated in the health-care system and widely used by all parts of the the population. There are fifty-six CHCs in Ontario and less than ten elsewhere in the country. Ontario also has ten Aboriginal Health Access Centres, which are similar to CHCs, but funded by the federal government.

As the Association of Ontario Health Centres puts it, "CHCs suffer from a lack of recognition."[46] But their approach is based on more than just addressing the symptoms of the health system's malaise. Rather, the community-based approach emphasizes participation and is rooted in a diagnosis of the causes of health-care problems, both individual and social.

> Canada is a diverse country, and that diversity should be reflected in our health care system. The care we deliver should match the needs of different groups of Canadians, from men and women, to new Canadians, to visible minorities, people with disabilities and others . . .
>
> Equity means that citizens get the care they need, without consideration of their social status or other personal characteristics such as age, gender, ethnicity or place of residence . . .
>
> [Canada should] improve access and quality for minority language communities and meet the differing health care needs of men and women, visible minorities, people with disabilities and new Canadians.
>
> — Canadian Institutes of Health Research (CIHR), Institute of Gender and Health, Recommendations to the Romanow Commission, 2002.

Getting Better

Social analysis, like diagnosis, begins with symptoms or problems on the surface and works its way back to whatever is causing them. Like diagnosis, social analysis is a combination of science and art, experience and intuition, dialogue and consultation.

After finding out they have an illness, few people say, "It's too difficult to get rid of, I'll live with it." At first health care may seem as simple as one patient's relationship with one doctor. But health care soon proves to be a broader system that affects everyone. And people working in groups can have some effect on that system. Social analysis can be a tool used in improving health. It leads us to consider what is causing problems in the workings of our health system, to discover the sometimes hidden causes of ill health or a particular disease – and to find out, as well, what makes us feel healthy, feel "well." Doing something about these causes is obviously essential to the effort of preventing disease and promoting health – even if doing so may challenge things as they are.

How do we improve the health of Canadians? How do we improve the health-care system? To begin with, the health of Canadians is a reflection of the larger inequalities in Canadian society. Tackling those inequalities through social and economic policy initiatives would go a long way towards improving the health of individuals and the population as whole. After all, people in societies with the narrowest gap between the rich and the poor enjoy better overall health. People who volunteer and work to improve social justice are also working to improve health.

Medicare as an institution is also a reflection of the larger inequalities in Canadian society. A complex society may seem to require a complex medical system with high technology, well-established institutions, and efficient business practices. But Canadian communities also need centres of healing in the more traditional sense. The knowledge and resources exist: to learn how to avoid getting sick in the first place, to attack disease in a more systematic way, to develop more effective structures like the CHCs/CLSCs, and to promote health positively by encouraging preventive medicine and public health.

Questions

❑ What stories have you heard – or can you find – about being sick before the days of medicare? Are similar experiences occurring nowadays? Is medicare "in crisis"?

❑ Do a survey of your community's health needs and resources. Does everyone in your community have equal access to health care? What forms of extra-billing or extra charges do people encounter? Your provincial Health Coalition is part of a national movement to preserve the original principles of medicare; for further information, contact the Canadian Health Coalition, 2841 Riverside Drive, Ottawa, Ont. K1V 8X7, ph. 613-521-3400, e-mail <info@healthcoalition.ca>.

❑ What constitutes a healthy lifestyle? Is yours healthy? What helps people develop such a lifestyle? What are the economic and political barriers? Is there a CHC/CLSC in the neighbourhood? If so, is it community-controlled? If not, to explore setting up such a centre, contact your provincial association of CHCs/CLSCs (address available from Canadian Health Coalition, above).

❑ Is environmental pollution in your community causing illnesses, including cancer? What measures have been taken to clean up the pollution and prevent the illness? Are there problems with occupational health and safety? For further information, contact the Canadian Centre for Occupational Health and Safety, 250 Main Street East, Hamilton, Ont. L8N 1H6, ph. 416-523-2981, e-mail <clientservices@ccohs.ca>.

❑ Audit your personal health-care expenses. How do you pay for health care? What goods and services are paid in part by the government, or by private or employer insurance, and what are paid out of pocket? Consider everything from dentist bills to prescription and over the counter drugs to fitness club memberships.

❑ Healthy ways of living are sometimes discussed as though all that is needed is willpower and the ability to make the right choices. What kinds of changes (such as quitting smoking, having less stressful work, or less stressful family commitments) would support your own desires to live a healthier lifestyle?

Resources

• Pat Armstrong and Hugh Armstrong. *Wasting Away: The Undermining of Canadian Health Care.* 2nd ed. Toronto: Oxford University Press, 2003. The authors examine and assess the development of the Canadian health-care system, breaking the analysis down into accessible units: who provides (the institutions and the people); who pays (funding sources); and who decides (public, private, and patients).

• Colleen Fuller. *Caring for Profit: How Corporations Are Taking over Canada's Health Care System.* Vancouver: New Star Books, 1998. Fuller traces alliances between private insurers and the medical profession and provides a "who's who" of the key people and corporations making money in Canada's health-care sector.

• Joel Lexchin. *The Real Pushers.* Vancouver: New Star Books, 1984. A critical report on the drug industry in Canada.

• Michael Rachlis, Robert G. Evans, Patrick Lewis, and Morris L. Barer. *Revitalizing Medicare: Shared Problems, Public Solutions.* A study prepared for the Tommy Douglas Research Institute, Vancouver, January 2001. A cogent analysis of factors such as hospital admissions, waits for care, and the cost of medications, combined with suggestions for innovation. The authors argue that "the crisis of medicare" is more rhetoric than reality.

• Terrence Sullivan and Patricia Baranek. *First Do No Harm: Making Sense of Canadian Health Reform.* Toronto: Malcolm Lester, 2002. A primer that provides a broad-based understanding of the issues surrounding Canada's health-care reform debate.

• Kevin Taft and Gillian Steward. *Clear Answers: The Economics and Politics of For-Profit Medicine.* Edmonton: Duval House Publishing, University of Alberta Press, and Parkland Institute, 2000. A rebuttal of the argument that privately run health care is less expensive and more efficient than public health care.

• *Drug Deals: The Brave New World of Prescription Drugs.* Canada, 2001. Directed by Erna Buffie and Elise Swerhone. NFB and Merit Motion Pictures. Video. 50 min. Examines the degree to which universities, hospitals, doctors, researchers, and health protection agencies all find themselves increasingly influenced by the power and money behind the pharmaceutical industry.

• *Healing Spirit.* Canada, 1992. Directed by Hubert Schuurman. National Film Board of Canada (NFB), Montreal. Video. 57 min. Connecting spiritual healing and medical technology, this film shows women and men suffering from ailments as diverse as depression and AIDS, and physicians practising both conventional and holistic medicine.

• *How Can We Love You?* 2002. Produced and directed by Laura Sky. Sky Works Charitable Foundation. Toronto. Video. 60 min. and 71 min. versions. This documentary film, which focuses on women with metastatic breast cancer, was designed to inform and inspire women with breast cancer, their families and caregivers, the health-care community, and anyone dealing with a life-threatening illness.

Websites:

The website for the Canadian Centre for Policy Alternatives contains a wealth of current research information on health and other social issues, as well as providing links to other organizations and material.

See also the sites for the Canadian Health Coalition, an organization that includes unions, seniors, churches, women, students, and health professionals; the Canadian Institute for Health Information, an independent, pan-Canadian, not-for-profit organization; and (for federally funded research information) the Canadian Institutes of Health Research (CIHR).

Another good source of information is the site of the Tommy Douglas Research Institute, an independent non-profit Canadian economic and social research and educational body named after the acknowledged father of medicare in Canada.

Chapter Three

No Place Like Home

Home: The word gives most people a feeling of belonging and security. Home is, usually, the place where we grew up, a place to live out our everyday lives. Home can be a special place to arrange and furnish; it can be an expression of the personalities of the people who live there. It is made not just of bricks and mortar, wood and nails, but also of human relationships. It is a place of security and a source of comfort – or at least it should be.

According to the Universal Declaration of Human Rights, everyone has the right to an adequate standard of living, and this right includes housing: a minimum amount of decent, affordable shelter. Housing is a material need; a home is a spiritual and cultural necessity. Having a home and being adequately housed are basic to human well-being, as basic as being adequately clothed and fed.

To look at the Real Estate or Homes sections of Canadian newspapers, though, you might think that housing was little more than another of the wide array of consumer goods available to those with the wealth to invest in them. In these sections, almost wholly made up of advertisements, "luxurious enclaves of prestigious town homes" vie with "elegant" or "graceful" houses in new suburbs. Discerning buyers can choose between a "country style charmer," a "spacious south side beauty," or a "pretty condo." This is hardly the language of human rights and necessities of life. It is the language of the housing industry, an industry that is in the business of marketing a commodity.

Although the real estate sections display no shortage of properties, there is lots of talk these days about a housing crisis. In 1998 the mayors of Canada's largest cities declared homelessness a national disaster. They added that homelessness is only the most visible symptom of a larger crisis, the acute and growing shortage of affordable housing in Canada. In 2001, for instance, more than 13 million people — 40 per cent of the population — were living in the 4.8 million renter households in the country. According to one report, they faced "a crisis of rising rents, stagnant or falling incomes, and a dwindling supply of affordable units." Almost one in five households is on the brink of homelessness.[1] Cities large and small across the country are opening up "warming rooms" in church basements and community centres just to get people in from the winter cold.

How we address these problems depends in part on what kind of problems we think they are. What we think about them — how we analyze problems — depends in part on the framework that we use to describe them. First we need to think about, to identify, all the "players" in this field. People concerned about human needs and rights will frame the problems of housing in one way. People involved in the business — real estate firms, investors, and developers — will tend to frame their accounts of the opportunities and risks represented by housing in another way. In thinking about housing, we need to examine both of these frameworks, and then the relationship between them. We also need to consider how government has responded to the relationship, overlap, and sometimes conflict between these two sets of needs.

A focus on the human right to adequate housing for all Canadians, which was the basis of [Canadian] housing policy from the mid-1960s to the mid-1980s, is essential for the promotion of sustainable urban development, human development and social cohesion. As Article 22 of the Universal Declaration of Human Rights asserts, everyone is entitled to "the economic, social and cultural rights indispensable for his dignity and the free development of his personality." Human poverty is a denial of basic human rights. Human development, the process of enlarging people's choices, requires respect for and leads to the further realization of all human rights — economic, social, cultural, civil and political. Individual and community well-being are intertwined, and human development requires strong social cohesion and equitable distribution of the benefits of progress to avoid tension between the two.

— J. David Hulchanski,
"Housing and a Sustainable Social Fabric,"
September 2002.

In Search of a Home of One's Own

In Canada, home ownership has long been the dominant mode of housing, and most Canadians are well housed compared to people in many other countries. Most people in Canada strive to own a home. Often, as a kind of long-term investment, home ownership helps people to maintain, and build, a certain standard of living.[2]

Today the country's housing stock consists of over ten million units, and of that total, roughly 62 per cent is owner-occupied. About 30 per cent is private market rental. Only about 7 per cent is social housing — a term used to describe all forms of publicly assisted housing: public, non-profit, and co-op.[3] In Canada it seems there is "a pervasive cultural and institutional bias against renting, as there is in the United States."[4] And in recent years there has been little government support for social housing.

But during the housing crisis of the early 1980s a magazine article told readers bluntly, "If you don't own the roof over your head today, you probably never will."[5] Increasing real estate prices combined with the collapsing incomes of those who do not already own homes make that claim even truer today. By the late 1990s, carrying a mortgage (plus taxes and other costs) on an average starter home in Toronto, for example, took a minimum household income of almost $65,000 – which put it out of the reach of over 65 per cent of the city's families.[6]

Affordability is not only a big-city problem, or one restricted to depressed areas. Doug Faulkner, mayor of the new city of Fort McMurray, Alberta, the "oil capital of Canada," has a blunt assessment of the situation. "Greed," he says, "has taken over in many of these rapid-growing areas of our country, where the developers are more interested in the markup on the homes than they are in providing shelter for people."[7]

Most Canadians live in urban areas, and almost one-third of them live in the three largest cities in the country: Toronto, Montreal, and Vancouver. For too many Canadians, finding a suitable and affordable place to live is a continuing struggle. Dan Devaney, a Vancouver resident, reveals some of the barriers that he came up against in his quest for housing:

> Before living in a housing co-op I was renting a one-bedroom unit in an apartment complex. As a single parent in a wheelchair living on a fixed income, my housing choices were very limited. Rental housing that I could afford and that could accommodate my wheelchair was extremely hard to find. In addition to the actual physical barriers such as stairs, the rent for a two-bedroom unit for my daughter and I would be at least $850 per month in Vancouver. Finding any apartment in Vancouver is a challenge as vacancy rates are routinely at one per cent and there are similar shortages in all cities across Canada.[8]

As a tenant, Dan Devaney is a member of the group faced with one of the largest housing obstacles: affordability. The Canadian government defines affordable housing as costing less than 30 per cent of total household income. Among homeowners, affordability is a problem for 20 per cent of women, compared with 12 per cent of men. Among tenants, affordability is a problem for 46 per cent of women and 27 per cent of men.[9]

The housing affordability gap reflects a growing income gap between tenants and homeowners. A few decades ago, in the 1960s, the income gap between homeowners and renters was about 20 per cent. That was when a great deal of private rental housing was built. Since then the gap between the median income of homeowners and renters has grown considerably. In 1984, homeowners had almost double the income of renters (192 per cent), and by 1999 the gap had increased to more than double (208 per cent). From 1984 to 1999 the wealth of homeowners increased from being twenty-nine times to seventy times that of renters. As University of Toronto housing policy professor David Hulchanski puts it, "Poverty and housing tenure are now much more closely connected."[10]

Barriers to Housing

Household income growth has not kept up with real estate prices. Indeed, it has been stagnant. Between 1989 and 1998, total real household income increased by only 2.7 per cent, while single people and single-parent families saw their real incomes decline. For people on moderate to low incomes, renting is often the only alternative, but rents have also been driven up and vacancy rates are at very low levels. Ten of Canada's fifteen major metropolitan areas saw private apartment rents increase by at least 20 per cent between 1989 and 1999. Some areas saw increases of up to 42 per cent. Meanwhile, by 2001, nine of Canada's twenty-six metropolitan areas had rental vacancy rates at or below 1 per cent, well below the 3 per cent level that is considered necessary to make the market function competitively. The rental rate for the country as a whole was 1.1 per cent.[11] This means that rental prices went up, and up, and up. By 1996, 46 per cent of Canadian tenants were spending more than 30 per cent of their income on rent – with 21.6 per cent devoting half or more of their income to rent. The majority of these households are made up of Aboriginal people, seniors, and families with children.[12]

Factors contributing to the increase in rents include the elimination of rent controls and new laws favouring landlords. Ontario's ironically named Tenant Protection Act, for instance,

makes it easier for landlords to evict tenants who get behind on their rent. Previously only a judge could order a person evicted. The threat of eviction puts many people in a precarious housing situation. It moves them into the "at risk" category used by social analysts studying homelessness. One study found that in Toronto "in any year 25,000 people have some episode of literal homelessness, while 85,000 are at risk of that condition if one additional life crisis occurred."[13]

Other factors combine with economics to

Percentage of Tenant Income Spent on Rent, 1991 and 1996, Canada and the Provinces and Territories

| | Paying 30% or more of income on rent | | | | Paying 50% or more of income on rent | | | |
| | 1991 | | 1996 | | 1991 | | 1996 | |
	no.	%	no.	%	no.	%	no.	%
Canada	1273175	34.8	1670770	43.2	583710	16	833555	22
Nfld.	12555	33.9	18285	43.3	6215	17	9430	22
P.E.I.	4200	36.3	5605	42.2	1835	16	2325	18
N.S.	34330	36.8	47030	47.3	16620	18	23310	24
N.B.	23770	36.7	29360	42.1	10290	16	13575	20
Que.	404035	35.1	518705	42.6	194220	17	273825	23
Ont.	432915	33.3	615985	44.5	194920	15	300645	22
Man.	46250	35.8	52445	40.6	20165	16	23485	18
Sask.	32675	32.5	38820	36.7	14950	15	18980	18
Alta.	106210	33.3	115275	37.7	46570	15	51240	17
B.C.	174075	39.7	226665	46.9	77115	18	115525	24
Yukon	745	19.2	1125	28.1	255	6.6	560	14
N.W.T.	1365	12.5	1465	12.8	540	4.9	650	5.7

Source: Federation of Canadian Municipalities, "National Housing Policy Options Paper: A Call For Action," Ottawa, June 1999, p.14; reproduced in Jack Layton, *Homelessness: The Making and Unmaking of a Crisis*, 2000, p.210.

create even greater barriers to suitable housing. Like racial discrimination, or discrimination on the basis of sexual orientation, discrimination against a prospective tenant receiving social assistance is illegal. Yet it occurs routinely. A study of 61,000 Toronto apartments found that 92 per cent of the buildings put up explicit barriers to welfare recipients. Of the twenty-seven different corporations managing these buildings, six admitted openly that they did not rent to people on welfare. Another nineteen said that they had income requirements that effectively blocked welfare recipients from moving in.[14] Poor tenants, including the working poor and those living on old age or disability pensions, are also effectively discriminated against by the requirement to pay the first and last months' rent in order to secure lodging. New immigrants can find themselves in even more dire straits. They have trouble arranging for housing because they lack a Canadian rental history or credit rating. Some landlords demand six months' rent in advance before they will let them have an apartment.[15]

Amina Ahmed, a housing help worker, says she routinely encounters racism in her work on behalf of people of colour who are looking for a place to live. Talking to a *Globe and Mail* reporter, she pointed out a nicely finished apartment with a "clipped green lawn and neatly tended flower beds." The management "throws up a no vacancy-sign whenever they see her coming," she says. "It's a nice building, but you wouldn't be able to get any of my clients in there. I've been there with many people and miraculously, the vacancies disappear every time."[16]

When they do find accommodation, people of colour or new immigrants often find themselves having to cope with substandard housing. This kind of racism has a dual effect: the direct negative effect on the quality of life of those forced to live in slum-like conditions, and the indirect effect of the stigma attached to the people who must live there. But, oddly, the drop in quality does not translate into a drop in rents. Low-income visible minority immigrants not only end up paying comparably higher rents for poor quality housing, but also, as one researcher puts it, get stereotyped by the slum conditions they are forced to endure.[17]

As social vulnerability increases, so too does vulnerability to substandard housing. Zarina Sherazee, a wife abuse counsellor with South Asian Family Support Services, reports that the single mothers she deals with are living in "cockroach-infested, mice-infested ghettos because the landlords know they are petrified and have nowhere else to go."[18] Tenants trapped by social conditions also become trapped, sometimes literally, in dangerous and dilapidated buildings that landlords know they can get away with neglecting. That happened, for example, to disabled and elderly tenants in a Scarborough high rise when their elevator remained broken for a month.

Aboriginal people all too often endure living conditions many times worse than those of the average Canadian, while paying rents only slightly below the norm. A study comparing Canadian and Aboriginal housing found that Aboriginal dwellings are twice as likely to be in need of repair, ninety times as likely to lack piped water, five times as likely to lack bathroom facilities, ten times as likely to lack flush toilets, and three times as likely to need central heating. But Aboriginal tenants on average pay only $51 per month less rent than non-Aboriginal tenants.[19]

In many countries social housing is a decent alternative for those who can't afford market rents. But Canada does not have the social housing necessary to meet current needs, never mind future needs. In Ontario some 275,000 households depend on social housing, with one-third of that total made up of people with disabilities and 40 per cent made up of the elderly. The remaining 28 per cent are mostly single-parent households. An Ontario family of four that qualifies for affordable housing can be on a waiting list for as long as eighteen years. Between 1997 and 1999 the waiting list for Edmonton's largest family-subsidized housing provider rose from zero to 865.[20] In Calgary the social housing waiting list grew between 1993 and 1998 by 64 per cent. The Calgary researchers also found that 80 per cent of women with disabilities lived on less than $5,000 per year.

Homelessness

One of the most obvious results of housing trends in Canada has been the phenomenon of homelessness. At least 250,000 people now experience homelessness during the course of a year. In hostels in seven Canadian cities, the number of homeless people using beds during a year doubled from 1987 to 1999.[21]

The "national disaster" that is homelessness is often met with stereotypes that blame the victims, presenting people who live in crisis as being responsible for their own misery or somehow simply beyond help. Is living "in the rough" really a lifestyle choice, as Ontario Premier Mike Harris once suggested? What about the other bad choices and personality flaws that bring people to the streets? According to Hulchanski, only a minority of the homeless fit the stereotypical profile of a substance-abusing or mentally ill street person.

> If any of us are houseless for a week, let's say – that means we're not eating right, we're not sleeping right – all kinds of bad personality traits each of us has will definitely come out. And when we bump into somebody on the street, what are we going to say? Here's a mentally ill person. And that's why there's this mistaken belief out there that the homeless are mentally ill people. The minority have some mental illness, but the majority don't. But boy, they don't look and act like the average Canadian. And neither would any one of us if we did not have a permanent base, our house and home, for even a period of a week.[22]

Although living with or recovering from addictions does involve choices, it makes little sense to speak of choosing addiction and even less to suppose that mental illness is a lifestyle preference. People with special needs require housing and other forms of community support too, yet they are among the most vulnerable to displacement. Integrating people with psychiatric disabilities into the community instead of keeping them in

institutions is a worthy goal, long favoured by patient advocates. But in recent years that goal has been embraced by governments concerned with cutting costs. Without community supports and affordable housing, the approach is a recipe for homelessness.

Worry and stress gnaw at everyone who falls into any of the various categories of "homelessness." Growing numbers of Canadians, young and old, face such stress. About 20 per cent of Toronto shelter users are children, about half in total are families. The struggle to keep lives together is constant. It means working or looking for work as well as accommodation: the majority of the people in Calgary's two largest shelter systems go to work every day. They have jobs, but what they make is not enough to pay for even the cheapest places.[23]

Up to a quarter of the homeless people in some Canadian cities are Aboriginal, and about 15 per cent of Toronto's hostel users are immigrants and refugees. The fastest-growing group among the homeless is now families, because some landlords refuse to rent apartments to families with children, single mothers, or to people on social assistance.[24]

Homelessness: Defining a Problem

Social analysts have defined homelessness in a variety of ways.
   They refer

. . . to **basic** shelter
   rooflessness (sleeping outdoors)
   houselessness (living in shelters, institutions, or short-term accommodation)
   insecure housing (squatters or people in refugee camps)
   inadequate or inferior housing (lacking basic facilities)

. . . to the **(in)security** of shelter
   absolute homelessness or shelterlessness: living in the street with no physical shelter of your own
   (includes emergency shelter users)
   relative homelessness: living in spaces that don't meet basic health and safety standards (for example,
   protection from the elements; access to safe water and sanitation; security of tenure and personal
   safety; affordability; accessibility to employment, education, health care; provision of minimum space
   to avoid overcrowding)

. . . to the **duration** of the problem
   chronic: living in emergency shelters or on the streets for years at a time
   episodic: circulating between emergency shelters and temporary places to live
   situational: loss of housing due to a significant life event such as a fire or domestic violence
   seasonal: finding housing during inclement weather only
   transitory: living in emergency shelter for only a month or two, then leaving for good.

Homelessness is a crisis across the country, even in places where people are not sleeping on the streets. Sam Synard, deputy mayor of Marystown, Newfoundland, has watched young people leaving town to go looking for jobs in other parts of Canada. The homeless people on the streets of big cities, he said – "They're our children, our people, they're from our communities." This means that homelessness is his community's problem – "even if we have no homeless people sleeping on our streets. Our homeless people are sleeping on other cities' streets."[25]

Men, women, and children are living and dying on the streets, in shelters, and in dangerously substandard firetraps. Unhoused and inadequately housed people die of violence; they die from the cold; and they die in fires. In one eighteen-month period, Toronto social service workers recorded a rate of one death a week related to homelessness. Fire-related deaths in substandard housing have risen to alarming levels.

In 1998 the mayor of Winnipeg reported that twenty-six people had died in slum-housing fires in the two previous years.[26]

The results of homelessness are not always that dramatic. Instead, the effects show up in basic health conditions. Research at the Inner City Health Research Unit at St. Michael's Hospital, Toronto, confirms that homeless people face high risks of premature death and suffer from a wide range of health problems, such as seizures, chronic obstructive pulmonary disease, musculoskeletal disorders, tuberculosis, and skin and foot ailments.[27]

All the talk about the problems facing people who have been dehoused rarely recognizes that they are exiles in their own land. According to Hulchanski, dehousing in Canada has produced "a diaspora of the excluded."

Homelessness is not *only* a housing problem, but it is *always* a housing problem. The central observation about the diverse group of

Canadians known as "the homeless" is that they are people who once had housing but are now unhoused. Canada's housing system once had room for virtually everyone; now it does not.[28]

> *Women living in poverty, visible minority women, Aboriginal women, especially single mothers, immigrant women, disabled women, young women, older women:*
>
> All of these groups of women share common characteristics of marginalization from policy making and from political power. Their housing crises are experienced in isolation from one another, in the context of a society in which women are made to feel ashamed if they cannot pay their rent or properly provide for their children. The challenge of understanding and properly conceptualizing women's homelessness is to counteract the marginalization of these women's experiences, not only within government policy making and program administration, but also within advocacy movements addressing poverty, homelessness or human rights.
>
> — Centre for Equality Rights in Accommodation (CERA), *Women and Housing in Canada: Barriers to Equality,* March 2002.

Development and Investment: Market Approaches to Housing

The production of housing is an indispensable step in the creation of homes, and the housing industry is in the business of producing housing. So you might think that whatever is good for the housing industry is good for those who need a home.

Construction is one of Canada's most cyclical industries, subject to massive swings in demand. This feature of the industry has a significant effect on construction workers, on investors who finance new projects, and ultimately on Canadians in needs of adequate housing. Because of the work's project-specific nature, unemployment in the construction industry is considerably

higher than in other sectors of the economy. Even in boom times, workers spend a significant amount of time between jobs. The strong seasonal and cyclical fluctuations of the industry lead to peaks and troughs in employment. To keep skilled workers, the industry generally provides higher wages than other sectors do.

The construction market can be subdivided into three subsectors: residential; institutional, commercial, and industrial; and engineering (roads, sewers, airports, pipelines, and all that is often collectively referred to as *infrastructure*). In recent years each of these subsectors has become riskier for and generally less attractive to potential investors.

A number of factors have depressed the market for new construction. The market for institutional, commercial, and industrial real estate has been flattened by government spending cuts, excess building capacity constructed during the 1980s, and slow growth in Canada's domestic economy. Some of the industry's spokespeople have expressed concerns that the construction market may be entering a "post-industrial" phase, with much of the infrastructure and buildings required by the Canadian economy already having been built. The market for engineering construction has also been hurt by government spending cuts. The residential market has been hit by declines in disposable income and job insecurity, and all markets were hurt by increases in interest rates.

As a result the industry has been looking increasingly to foreign markets for growth — to the United States, Third World countries, and Eastern Europe, among others. In 1995 Canada surpassed the United States as the world's largest supplier of prefabricated buildings to Japan. The federal government has supported, and encouraged, the industry players to move into new global markets.[29]

On the domestic scene, the picture is less rosy. Since the mid-1990s, housing starts have been well below projected demographic requirements, with little new rental housing being built. Rental dwelling starts averaged 7,200 units annually over the 1995-98 period — compared to

38,000 rental starts annually from 1986 to 1990. At the same time, demolition and conversion to condominiums have eaten away at the affordable rental stock.

For investors, it seems, rental housing is simply not an attractive proposition in most parts of Canada. Developers of new rental housing complain that they face the same regulations and municipal levies, fees, and charges experienced by developers of ownership housing – but have less to gain in return. They also face a less favourable federal and provincial tax environment than the one in place during the high-volume rental production period of the 1970s. Rather than building new rental accommodation, they find it makes more sense, from their point of view, to convert existing rental properties into condominiums that can be sold immediately on the marketplace.[30]

The supply and demand theory of the market insists that low supply results from low demand. Yet the demand for housing, especially for affordable rental housing, is high. The Canada Mortgage and Housing Corporation estimated in 2000 that Canada would need 45,000 new rental units each year for the next ten years just to keep up with current demand; at least half of those units would have to be affordable units. In 2001, concerned about this gap between housing needs and the available possibilities for meeting them, the Federation of Canadian Municipalities set targets for the next decade, calling for 20,000 new or acquired affordable units per year and 10,000 rehabilitated affordable units per year. The Federation suggested that for the next ten years, 40,000 households per year should receive enough income rental assistance to make their units affordable.[31]

Making sense of this discrepancy – between the supply that should be in place given the high demand for housing, and the reality of inadequate supply – depends on differentiating between housing as a commodity (something to be invested in with a view to the profit it can generate for shareholders) and housing as a human right (housing as a means of meeting a fundamental need). The development industry has little incentive to invest in affordable accommodation when market conditions make that investment a low-profit prospect.

Avoiding that path does not threaten the development industry, which has other options. But it does represent a big problem for people who need affordable housing.

Government Housing Policy – Under (De)construction

The federal government's response to the housing needs of Canadians reflects its more general vision: market forces and global trade are the keys to solving economic problems. Based on this view, solutions to social problems rest on economic pursuits. This approach may explain why Canada is the only Western nation without a housing policy. Indeed, the federal government has dismantled housing programs and devolved responsibility for housing onto levels of government that have less capacity to adequately meet the need for affordable housing.

Devolution is the opposite of evolution. It is also called "downloading." Since the mid-1980s Ottawa has devolved responsibility for housing to the provincial level. From there it has moved down to municipalities. This process has continued at an accelerating pace ever since then. The result is a patchwork of initiatives.[32] The federal level of government has the most effective levers in dealing with a problem like housing. Next

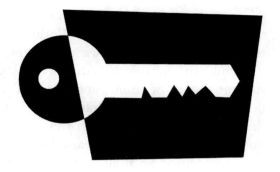

come the provinces. Then come municipalities, with little power to raise the tax money needed to build houses. Then come individual citizens and the groups they organize to help the homeless and push for decent housing for all. Citizens and cities have been leaders in raising awareness that money is the key to the problem.

Working with community groups across the country, the Federation of Canadian Municipalities proposed a detailed National Affordable Housing Strategy in 2000.[33] It included measures to attract new investment and to boost income supports. The Federation recognizes that housing is not the single responsibility of any one level of government. Yet the resources of municipalities are limited and increasingly strained by other downloaded responsibilities. In fact, only federal and provincial governments have the tax base needed to tackle the housing crisis.[34] Citizens groups, for their part, mounted a national campaign – complete with a little logo showing a "1%" figure being sheltered by a roof. The idea was to convince Canadians that the amount of money needed for affordable housing, though small, would ensure that no one was homeless.

Homeowners get indirect assistance through various tax breaks. While helping Canadians fulfil their dreams of owning their own homes is certainly laudable, a just approach to housing support would surely place equal emphasis on the needs of people who have no option but to rent. Whereas it was once possible for people with quite modest incomes to purchase a house, that is not true today, with the big income gap between owners and tenants.[35]

Social Housing: Participation and Justice

Aboriginal people, single parents, and people with disabilities – among the worst-housed groups in Canada – are also amongst those who most clearly recognize that we must treat housing as a human right rather than as a commodity. When combined with sufficient financial backing, this perspective has generated innovative approaches to housing.

To begin, it makes sense that the community takes collective responsibility for *physical* infrastructure – roads, sewers, and water purification, for example. These are the elements that make it possible for people to live in a community. People who drive often take for granted that the community provides roads, and keeps them in good repair. For others, it is more important that roads and sidewalks have wheelchair-accessible ramps, and that a building has a visual fire alarm system rather than just a siren, and that elevators have raised or Braille floor numbering. If a society places a high value on justice and equality, these elements of social infrastructure are a necessity, not a charitable extra. Disability rights activists, for instance, argue that if a society is committed to participation for all, all citizens have a right to the kind of infrastructure they need to participate equally in society.

Housing is a fundamental part of this infrastructure for social participation. If you have to deal with unsuitable and unsafe housing every day, or live with chronic housing insecurity when there is no suitable affordable housing, you will have little time or energy left to participate in the life of your community. So that community is robbed of the contributions you might have made.

Members of the "universal design movement" point out that it is much more efficient and inexpensive to take a barrier-free approach at the planning and building stage than to go back later and fix problems. Universal, barrier-free design means thinking ahead about the needs of all sorts of people – people using wheelchairs, scooters, walkers, white canes; people pushing

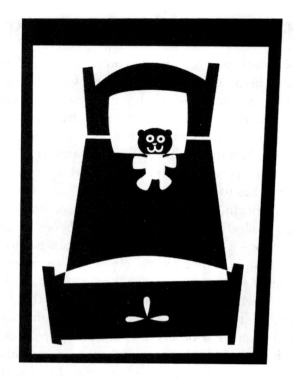

baby carriages; the blind and the hearing impaired; the elderly and the able-bodied. It costs only one-half of one per cent to make a new housing project accessible, but prices rise sharply when the work is done after the fact.[36] Activists argue that the longer the government postpones enacting legislation that would enforce equality of access to housing, jobs, and education, the longer money will be wasted on buildings that not only handicap a significant segment of the population now but will have to be retrofitted at high cost sometime later on.

Good social infrastructure is about more than just bricks and mortar, buildings and streets. It is also about how the various elements are designed and how different designs support community connections. In the years after the Second World War, the suburban environment consisted of pods of single-family homes, little or no public space, and streets designed primarily for vehicles. According to urban planner Elizabeth Plater-Zyberk, this design minimized possibilities for interaction with neighbours, isolating individual nuclear families in their own private space. This effect carries a toll for both family and community.

The fact that we've put so much emphasis on the nuclear family following World War II, the individual house for just the parents and the children, means that the psychological support system of family, aunts, uncles, even beloved neighbours, the ability to walk down the street to the coffee shop or even the bar, not being able to do that means that the family is so focused on itself that I think it certainly deserves looking at whether a lot of the broken households and family stress doesn't result from that inward focus which we've been forced into, in a sense, by our physical environment.[37]

Residents of North Winnipeg's Gilbert Park Housing Project testify to the importance of the support they draw on from their neighbours. To outsiders the buildings may seem unattractive, with their lack of trees and flowers. The residents are poor, and many are single parents. But they say they feel safe there. Their children are safe and everyone is close by. The community has a good transit system, a clinic, day cares, and stores. Gilbert Park also has its own tenants' council. Darlene Levasseur is enthusiastic about the council's positive impact:

> It's gotten better. Most of the time when they had this Gilbert Park Tenants Association, it got a lot better. They have a boys and girls club for the kids and everything, and then they have a food bingo, and they have a food bank. Block Parties: since they have this, it seems like there is more people coming out and more things happening.[38]

The goals of supporting a sustainable community were built right into the design and planning process of the Quebec village of Ouje-Bougoumou. Cree/Métis architect Douglas Cardinal followed traditional forms when he designed the village's housing, school, offices, community centre, nurses' residence, elders' residence, and clinic. He began by consulting elders and other community members, working to better understand the specific needs of this Cree community. The smaller buildings were organized in a circular pattern, which helped to emphasize a large gathering space. The village is heated by a community-owned system that burns waste wood from a nearby sawmill, a renewable energy source. The construction process also emphasized community needs, selecting procedures that would employ a maximum of local labour and cost-effective design. The planners made an inventory of the skills of band members, and the building techniques drew on those skills.

The village has been a resounding success, providing a new lease on life for a community that had suffered decades of forced relocations when previous village sites were destroyed to make way for the region's mining industry (see chapter 12). In 1995 the Ouje-Bougoumou Cree were presented with a United Nations award for being one of fifty exemplary communities chosen from around the world. They received international recognition again through their participation in the World's Fair, Expo 2000. Selected as a community that "represents a very tangible expression of the theme of the world's fair which is the balancing of humankind, nature and technology," they demonstrate an approach to housing that harmonizes the needs and builds on the strengths of community members as both workers and residents.[39]

Housing co-ops, a form of social housing, represent another solution to the housing shortage. The 2,100 non-profit housing co-ops in Canada – in every province and territory – are democratically owned and home to about a quarter of a million people. They provide decent, secure homes for Canadians on poverty-level incomes, yet without the social stigma of most social housing projects. More than five thousand co-op dwellings are home to at least one person with a physical disability.[40] Yet since the federal government dropped its funding for affordable housing in 1993, they have received little public support.

> While it is possible to convince ourselves that adequate, affordable housing alone will solve many problems, we know from experience that it is a base, not the whole structure of social and economic success. Immigration, demographic changes and social trends in our communities are pushing us to respond to needs which combine housing and specific services beyond housing. A housing policy that promotes a higher quality of life must go hand-in-hand with complementary policies in such sectors as health, social services, training and education, and employment.
>
> — Denise LeBlond,
> Canadian Housing and Renewal Association, 1993.

Building a Secure Home

If we think of a community as an organic whole, we can see housing at its heart. A place – a series of buildings and streets – becomes a community in the same way that a house becomes a home. It happens when the people who live there take an active hand in designing and decorating their surroundings. The key here, as in so much social analysis, is an understanding of just how important this sort of participation is. Communities like Ouje-Bougoumou thrive when they rely on their members to get things done – in the same way that houses are no longer commodities when people plant their own gardens or paint the back fence. Similarly, a housing co-op run – and perhaps even designed – by the people who live there is more than bricks and mortar. Like any neighbourhood it works best and feels most home-like when people share everything from cups of sugar to organizational skills.

Canada's capacity to construct a secure home for all its citizens, a home built on stable foundations, depends on establishing fundamental, shared priorities. Treating shelter as a commodity puts decent housing beyond the reach of a significant number of Canadians. It renders millions more insecure and vulnerable to anonymous-sounding "free-market forces." At the same time many others – especially the aged, single women supporting families, and people of colour – end

up paying large portions of their already inadequate incomes for shelter.

"Good, affordable, sustainable housing, in a society that makes room for all incomes, all ages, and all cultures is possible," the president of Canada Mortgage and Housing Corporation said over a decade ago.[41] But control has increasingly been concentrated in the hands of players who show little interest in affordable housing. How can those with the most power over what gets built be persuaded to realign their priorities or voluntarily reduce the cost of accommodation?

Ordinary people have a real, lasting interest in decent, reasonably priced houses or apartment buildings on a human scale in stable, friendly neighbourhoods. As individuals, people do not have much leverage when it comes to housing. But once organized, citizens can influence the supply and distribution of housing on the local level. They can continue to pressure the government to channel resources away from private developers and into non-profit housing and other consumer-centred solutions. Such policies would move us closer to an effective respect for everyone's right to adequate, decent shelter . . . so that everyone can rightfully feel *at home* in Canada.

Questions

❑ What is the vacancy rate in your municipality?

❑ Has the level of homelessness in your community been assessed recently? If so, what is it?

❑ Does your community provide emergency shelter for people facing homelessness? If so, do these shelters have adequate and secure funding? What are the shelters like? Are they comfortable and safe places to be?

❑ Does your community go beyond providing emergency shelter to provide support for long-term housing solutions?

❑ In every community, finding good solutions to housing problems requires paying attention to local conditions and the specific needs of community members. Make a list of social, cultural, economic, climactic, and environmental conditions in your community that a planner should take into consideration.

❑ Most of us count on one or another level of government to use tax dollars to ensure that essential services are available – water, roads, garbage removal, and sewer systems, for example. Should a particular level of government be responsible for ensuring that enough affordable housing is available so that no one is homeless?

❑ Does your municipality have a plan or strategy to encourage the construction of affordable housing units?

❑ Homeless people are rarely seen in suburbs — where there are rarely services for people facing a housing crisis. We tend to think, therefore, of homelessness as an inner-city problem. Should rural and suburban municipalities and residents share responsibility for solving the problem of homelessness in Canada?

❑ According to the Universal Declaration of Human Rights, everyone has the right to an adequate standard of living, and this right includes housing: a minimum amount of decent, affordable shelter. Discuss whether or not Canada is in violation of this UN Declaration.

❏ Most of us do not want simply to live in a housing "unit" – we want to have a home. When we think about homes, we think about how important needs are met in the neighbourhood as well as in the building we live in. For you and other members of your community, what sorts of things would make the difference between making a home and constructing a housing unit?

Resources

• Maureen Callaghan, Leilani Farha, and Bruce Porter. *Women and Housing in Canada: Barriers to Equality*. Toronto: Centre for Equality Rights in Accommodation, 2002. This national research report assesses federal programs and how well they assist low-income women meet their housing needs.

• Canada Mortgage and Housing Corporation (CMHC). *Housing for Persons with Disabilities*. Ottawa, 1996. Designed to help architects, builders, and homeowners who are planning residential accommodations for people with varying disabilities.

• Jack Layton. *Homelessness: The Making and Unmaking of a Crisis*. Toronto: Penguin Canada and McGill Institute, 2000. The book defines and documents the state of homelessness in Canada, offering solutions as well as an analysis of causes.

• Brendan O'Flaherty. *Making Room: The Economics of Homelessness*. Cambridge, Mass.: Harvard University Press, 1996. This economic analysis of homelessness evaluates responses to the problem in Toronto and five other big cities in the United States and Europe.

• John Sewell. *Houses and Homes: Housing for Canadians*. Toronto: James Lorimer and Company, 1994. An in-depth look at housing issues in Canada, including building good homes, designing good neighbourhoods, public and social housing, rent controls, and homelessness.

• *Sharing Successes in Native Housing: CMHC Housing Awards*. Canada, 1996. Produced by the Canada Mortgage and Housing Corporation.

Video. 20 min. Highlights 1994 prizewinning projects, the people and communities behind them, and the economic, environmental, and social challenges they faced together.

• *Building Futures: Rebuilding Our Lives*. Canada, 1996. Moving Images Productions. Video. 30 min. Profiles the development of Sandi Merriman House, a shelter for homeless women in Victoria, B.C., built by the women who would eventually use the service. Along with activist Jannit Rabinovitch, the women worked with three levels of government, their local neighbourhood, and business and trades people on a reconstruction project that changed more than a building.

• *Double or Nothing: The Rise and Fall of Robert Campeau*. Canada, 1992. Directed by Paul Cowan. NFB. 16mm and video. 92 min. A Study of the Canadian business magnate who once controlled one of the largest development companies in Canada.

• *Flemingdon Park: The Global Village*. Canada, 2002. Directed by Andrew Faiz. NFB. Video. 48 min. The story of a planned urban community, built in 1961 as a trendy Toronto home for artists and young professionals. Sold soon after as subsidized housing, it became home to refugees and new immigrants. Contains personal stories revealing the spirit and strength of this community.

• *Inherit the Earth*. Canada, 1995. Filmwest Associates. Video. 26 min. The story of the struggle of the Ouje-Bougoumou Cree to win band recognition, the land for a reserve, and the home they built on it. Interviews include Chief Abel Bossum and renowned Canadian architect Douglas Cardinal.

Websites:
The Canada Housing and Mortgage Corporation (CHMC) maintains a website with links to its extensive research and financing projects. It also contains useful information on the history of housing issues in Canada as well as current trends.

Following the 1989 fire that killed ten residents of the Rupert Hotel in Toronto, concerned tenants, landlords, community workers, and housing groups formed the Rupert Coalition to look for solutions to the housing crisis. The Rupert Coalition's website has lots of information about community organizing as well as fact sheets and links to activist and service-providing organizations.

The Centre for Equality Rights in Accommodation (CERA) is a Canadian non-profit human rights organization that promotes human rights in housing. Its website provides research reports and information about issues, programs, and international and Canadian law and policy, as well as links to related organizations.

Chapter Four
Lost in the Supermarket

The economy mystifies many Canadians. Data flood in on us every day: the inflation rate, the rise and fall of the Canadian dollar, the Dow Jones Industrial Average, Statistics Canada's "leading economic indicators." Neo-liberals, monetarists, and supply-siders lock horns in battle with Keynesians over terms like fiscal policy, money supply, structural adjustment, and recession and depression.

Statistics Canada produces monthly figures on the state of the economy, while university economists, business executives, union officials, and government policy-makers appear on TV to chew over the latest "indicators." Our leaders urge us in turn to save, spend, invest, compete, and lower our expectations.

Many Canadians may feel a bit like children overhearing the grown-ups arguing in the next room. While we know that the outcome of the argument affects us, we are not sure what the fight is really about.

Far removed from the realm of complicated financial statistics is economics in its more basic sense. The word "economy" comes from a Greek word that referred to household management or to a person who had this particular skill. This understanding of economics is still appropriate. People get paid for their work and spend those dollars on their personal and household needs and desires. Turning work into money and exchanging money for what people want: these are two major transactions that the economic system is supposed to make happen – at least from the perspective of the money economy, a system that tracks the flow of dollars and cents and defines productivity in terms of that flow.

In the money economy, "growth" is a measure of increases in national income, employment, or consumption. It may or may not contribute to environmental or human well-being. The costly cleanups of environmental disasters – like the oil spills that occurred after the supertanker *Exxon Valdez* ran aground off Alaska in 1989 or the *Prestige* sank off Spain in 2002 – stimulate the economy as crews scramble to contain the damage. A car accident creates work for doctors and nurses, body shops, and insurance adjusters.

Today's economic measures may include happenings that are downright destructive while excluding activities that are socially useful. Think of all the labour – unpaid and often unrecognized – that goes into keeping house and home together, caring for children and ailing relatives, contributing to the life of the community. Such work, often carried out by women, does not figure in conventional economic calculations.

The money economy and the activity of sustaining a household are not unrelated. They connect through the processes that make participation in the money economy possible. Children are raised and adults are nurtured, fed, clothed, housed, and generally cared for in ways that enable them to participate as workers in the (paid and unpaid) economy. As paid workers they can, in turn, participate in the money economy as consumers.

The money economy has another effect, related to the heavy time pressure that it puts on the household. When people's wages are lower and job insecurity higher, they have to put more time into performing paid work just to participate in the market economy at all. This limits the time available to look after themselves, their families, or their communities. But, of course, those homes and the people in them still need looking after. This creates a market for new commodities of convenience: like fast foods, unknown just a couple of generations ago.

There is a tendency to equate what is real with what is easily measurable, and activity in the money economy is easily measured in dollars and cents. It is easy, then, to see why all economic activity is reduced to money earned by our labour and money spent in the market. This view of reality not only leaves out a good deal of activity essential to sustaining human well-being, but also obscures well-being as a fundamental objective. Problems can arise when the standards set by the circulation of money replace the goals of human well-being. In this chapter we examine this approach to the market and ask what might be missing from social analyses that restrict themselves to this perspective.

Welcome to the Market

Markets are almost as old as human societies. Whether at points along First Nations trade routes, at a North African *souk*, or at a European fair, people have always gathered to barter, buy, and sell. The market has long been a place for people to trade news and gossip amidst the bustle of exchange and the strong smells of spices, fish, and fresh produce.

Most Canadians today arrive at a supermarket not to talk or trade, but to buy. One thing that strikes a shopper is the almost overwhelming quantity and variety of goods arrayed on shelves and stacked in wide aisles. There are staples like milk, skimmed to a precise degree of butterfat. There are bread packages marked with a certain percentage of whole wheat, or a non-wheat alternative. There are eggs accurately graded for size from factory layers or free-range hens raised on all-natural feed. There is every conceivable cut of meat packaged and (for the busy consumer) precooked and preportioned and ready for the microwave. For the really busy shopper – a growing market segment, according to industry analysts – there are packages that put the whole lot together in a box. More and more corporations, from Kraft to the International Menu Solutions Inc., are engaged in the business of selling not food, but "meal solutions" ready to be placed on the family table.[1]

On our supermarket shelves the products of the world jostle Canadian produce for attention: Mexican strawberries, Honduran bananas, Moroccan oranges, Indian tea, and coffee from a dozen tropical nations. Fresh, canned, and frozen edibles are supplemented by several aisles of non-food items, from toiletries to motor oil and housepaints. And the food on our tables is travelling increasingly long distances to get there. For the average American meal the distance is more than 1,500 miles.[2] Canada imports food and agricultural products from half the countries in the world, and more and more every year. Total shipments into Canada increased by 40 per cent in the relatively short period between 1995 and 1999.[3] Our accelerating import growth in food and agricultural products reflects a more general trend in globalization (see chapter nine).

At the supermarket nothing is out of place or out of season – if you can pay the price. That price includes not just the sticker price but also the hidden nutritional costs, the costs to the environment, and the costs to farmers at home and abroad.

According to many business and political leaders, the market system is the best, most efficient way of producing goods, providing services, and distributing those goods and services throughout the population. Influential economic theorists Milton and Rose Friedman even compare the activity of the marketplace with the workings of democracy. Although they see majority rule as a desirable if imperfect system, the Friedmans are satisfied that the market system represents a kind of perfect freedom: "When you vote daily in the supermarket, you get precisely what you voted for and so does everyone else."[4]

This, they say, is the key value of the market

A Trip to the Supermarket: Hidden Costs

To those folks who think they have "bargains" in their supermarket trolleys, or say, "Organic vegetables are so expensive," we should perhaps suggest that they whip out their calculators and figure out the true cost of those supermarket tomatoes or bananas or biscuits. Instruct them to factor in the cost of fossil fuels for farm machinery, transportation, refrigeration, etc.

Remind them to include the environmental and health costs related to pollution, global warming, soil quality and waste disposal, charged back to them as taxpayers. Let them work out what those imported products (not just avocados, but milk and potatoes!) have cost in terms of the loss of local sector employment in our own countries or exploited labour in someone else's. Have them figure out the true cost, to them, of government subsidies to agribusiness or the loss of fertile land to highways and parking lots.

— Marian Van Eyk McCain,
"True Bargains," *Resurgence*, March/April 2001.

---

system: when people get their wages they want to be able to spend them on the goods they need and desire; and the market system is the most efficient way of making those goods available as quickly and cheaply as possible. Everyone gets as much of what they want as it is possible for them to get, and so everyone's needs and desires are satisfied as well as they could be, given that the supply of goods is not limitless.

But is this system really the fairest and most efficient way of ensuring that everyone gets what they need and want? How much does voting with your dollars influence the choices you have? And what impact do other people's votes have on your choices and mine? Perhaps both supermarket and economy are more complicated, and less democratic, than the Friedmans and other advocates of the "free market" seem to think.

Who Does the Shopping?

Many Canadians, facing difficult economic times, have become acutely price conscious in their shopping. As long ago as 1982 the trade publication of the Canadian grocery business reported that 80 per cent of consumers viewed price as the most important factor in choosing where to shop. Because of lower prices, nearly half of the people surveyed had recently switched to a supermarket they liked less.[5] That was well before Big Box outlets such as Costco and Home Depot arrived in Canada. Over twenty years later many shoppers still remain acutely conscious of their limited food budgets.

The most commonly used measure of poverty in Canada is the low-income cut-off, or LICO, an official poverty line developed by Statistics Canada. It is set at the point where households spend 20 per cent more of their income than average on food, clothing, and shelter, adjusted for family and community size.[6] For example, for a large city, in 1997, the poverty lines were set at $17,409 for an individual and $32,759 for a family of four. On this measure the poverty rate in Canada was 17.5 per cent – which means one Canadian in six lives below the low-income cut-off.

Those who have the thinnest slice of the national economic pie must struggle to scrape by. Canada continues to show widespread poverty in spite of the abundance on supermarket shelves. Most people who are short of money pay the rent first, then buy food with what is left over. And more and more in the past two decades the poor and unemployed have had to turn to food banks as a last resort. Canada's food banks – the new symbol of hunger in the country – have multiplied since the first one was opened in Edmonton in 1981. By 1988 there were 126 food banks in Canada. By 1992 the number had more than doubled, to 292. In the following ten years the number doubled once again, until today there are at least 615 food banks, with an additional 2,213 agencies helping hungry people across the country.

The poverty that contributes to this phenomenon is not restricted to big cities. Some 267 food banks with thirty-eight agencies operate in communities of less than 10,000. And more are opening all the time: seventy-seven new food banks opened in Canada between 1995 and 2000 alone, and this during a period of economic growth. By 2002 the number of people using food banks had doubled in the past decade, with about 750,000 people – equivalent to the population of Ottawa – using food banks every month. According to the Canadian Association of Food Banks (CAFB), the fastest growing groups relying on food banks include not just women, seniors, and people with disabilities but also people with low-wage jobs.[7]

Food bank use alone does not accurately measure the degree of hunger or extreme food insecurity in the country. For one thing, food banks only provide a limited amount of food in a necessarily limited amount of time. For another,

---

Canadian Poverty Facts

As of 1997 the overall rate of poverty in Canada was 17.5 per cent.

Most at risk are women, the disabled, the elderly, the young, and those targeted by racism.

- The average income of *low-income families with children* is $8,942 – $10,057 below low-income lines.
- One in five Canadian *children* lives in poverty.
- Almost half of all *Aboriginal persons* receive less than $10,000.
- 40.9 per cent of *non-elderly unattached women* live in poverty.
- 42.7 per cent of *people with disabilities of working age* have incomes below $10,000.
- 45 per cent of *unattached seniors* live below the low-income cut-off.
- 60.7 per cent of *unattached youth* live below the low-income cut-off.

Sources: National Anti-Poverty Organization; The Aboriginal People's Survey; Statistics Canada, "Women in Canada."

as CAFB points out: "Only an estimated one in five food-insecure Canadians use food banks, soup kitchens, or other charitable programs. The majority are deterred by both the lack of a food bank in their vicinity and by the social stigma that is unfortunately associated with food bank use."[8]

Despite these daunting problems, bank economists and government ministers regularly report that Canada's "economic fundamentals" are strong, that the country is "firing on all cylinders."[9] Their optimism about the economy, based on the established indicators, such as growth in the Gross National Product, takes no account of the situations of the worst-off members of the community. What are the real "fundamentals" of society? What factors should be taken into account?

Among eighteen industrialized nations, Canada has the second-highest number of poor children. While Canada continues to be highly ranked on the United Nations Human Development Index, its standing continues to fall on the United Nation's human poverty index. In the year 2000, Canada fell from ninth to eleventh place among seventeen countries.[10] In general, Canadians express concern about the plight of children condemned to live in poverty, but withhold their sympathy from the adults with whom they live. U.S. economist Sylvia Ann Hewlett explains:

Now, you actually cannot really help children without also helping parents. And you see, I feel very profoundly that parents aren't any less good than they were in the past. They still desperately love their children. But increasingly as societies, we fail to produce the conditions that allow parents to come through for their kids. And again let me give you some examples: parents are at work 22 hours more a week than they were ten years ago. Work is increasingly eating them alive. And it's true of parents across the board, but it's particularly true of poor parents because no longer does one job or even two jobs keep a family above the poverty line.[11]

Those who have the thinnest slice of the economic pie must struggle to scrape by. Canada continues to show widespread poverty in spite of the abundance on supermarket shelves. The vast scale of disenfranchisement shows up in a comparison of income distributed among different segments of society. Social analysis can, for instance, divide the country's twelve million family units into five numerically equal groups called quintiles and then rank their aggregate wealth — the total economic pie — from the poorest fifth to the richest fifth. The people in the bottom quintile — the poorest 20 per cent of Canadians — owe more than they own. They hold minus .2 per cent of the country's personal wealth. Their aggregate wealth is *minus* $4.5 billion. The richest 20 per cent have an aggregate wealth of some 1.7 trillion, or 70.4 per cent — *well over two-thirds of the personal wealth in the country*. If the country's wealth is divided into two pieces, the results are even more startling: the top 50 per cent of Canadians hold 94.4 per cent of the country's wealth; the bottom half hold 5.6 per cent.[12]

Obviously, there are a certain number of shoppers who can take advantage of specials of exotic imports, fine cuts of meat, and conveniently prepackaged "meal solutions." A great many other Canadians, who feel pressure on both their time and their purses, scan the weekly specials on baloney and regular ground beef at nofrills, no-name outlets. In doing so, they often pay additional nutritional costs. The marketing strategies of food industry leaders reflect these differences. "Disposable income is less of a factor these days," said one representative of the food industry. "So, for a larger percentage of customers, if you can save them time, they will reward you with their business."[13]

Going back to the Friedmans' analogy between democracy and the market, if spending money at the supermarket is like voting in an election, the voting is rigged: some have many votes to cast and many more are lucky to have even one. "Economic votes" are not evenly distributed throughout the population.

The Wealth Pie

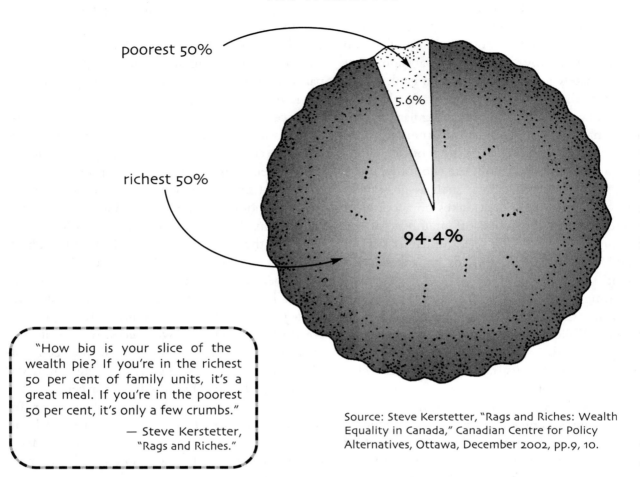

poorest 50%

5.6%

richest 50%

94.4%

> "How big is your slice of the wealth pie? If you're in the richest 50 per cent of family units, it's a great meal. If you're in the poorest 50 per cent, it's only a few crumbs."
>
> — Steve Kerstetter,
> "Rags and Riches."

Source: Steve Kerstetter, "Rags and Riches: Wealth Equality in Canada," Canadian Centre for Policy Alternatives, Ottawa, December 2002, pp.9, 10.

Big Is Beautiful

In a visit to the supermarket it is worth considering sheer size. The traditional supermarkets that revolutionized grocery shopping in the 1950s — and put many a neighbourhood grocery out of business — are virtually obsolete. Retailers like Safeway, Loblaws, and Loeb have abandoned the relatively small spaces they once had — of, say, between five thousand and thirty thousand square feet — and opened up much larger stores, usually in huge shopping malls with acres of "easy parking."

Now the neighbourhood branch of the big chain is being replaced by "superstores" and Big Box superwarehouses of a hundred thousand square feet. In the late 1980s, the U.S.-based Costco introduced new warehouse-style outlets of 120,000 square feet, selling everything from tea to tires. Since then, these "category killers" have all but broken down the traditional distinctions between food, hardware, furniture, and electronics outlets, while contributing to the decay of downtown areas. In 2001 Wal-Mart, the world's biggest corporation, decided to bring its giant Sam's Club discount outlets to Canada.

According to the economy of scale, bigger is better — or at least cheaper. The increased efficiency of running one huge store instead of several smaller ones should be reflected in lower prices. The same reasoning governs many economic decisions made by business and supported by government. But the size of the stores, and of the corporations that own them and control much of the economy, raises many a question for social analysis.

Survival of the Biggest

Large chain stores control a remarkable amount of the retail food market in Canada. The top six supermarket companies sell 86 per cent of all the groceries bought in Canada, compared to just 37 per cent for the top six supermarket companies in the United States. Canadian retailers are also watching, rather nervously, as Wal-Mart opens stores, and they are leery about the introduction of "Supercenters" to this country.[14] Wal-Mart Supercenters are 200,000-square-foot stores that combine typical Wal-Mart discount operations with supermarkets, extending Wal-Mart's immense buying power to the food industry. In 2000, Wal-Mart became the United States' largest grocer.

Burt Flickinger III, a U.S. retail consultant, explains Wal-Mart's success: "Wal-Mart is clearly investing in selling significantly below cost. It weeds out weaker food retailers, weaker discounters and weaker drug retailers."[15] "Strength" here is a measure of size, and not necessarily of the quality of the goods or services, or the desirability of the impact of the business on labour or environmental conditions. But size is an important predictor of success in the money economy, and by that measure Wal-Mart is formidable. In 1999 it ranked twenty-fifth among the world's top economies, which placed it above the nations of Poland, Norway, and Saudi Arabia.

Not only does Wal-Mart's strength enable it to undercut other retailers, and at least temporarily offer goods to consumers at lower prices, but its dominance as an employer has also had the effect of lowering the wages of workers at other retail outlets, as well as of workers who produce goods sold at below bargain-basement prices. The corporation – notorious for union-busting and employing part-time workers to avoid paying benefits – consolidates its power by putting the competition out of business. As labour markets become more dependent on giant corporations, local and national governments become more willing to lower corporate taxes and reduce regulations established to safeguard against traffic densities and other environmental effects of massive retail developments. In the process many of the costs of cheap retail goods sold at the megamarket remain hidden.

Again following the Friedman metaphor, "free market" democracy applied to the grocery business is like an election in which less well-financed candidates are squeezed out of the running.

An example of small enterprises squeezed out by bigger ones is health-food stores. They sprang up in the 1970s in response to consumer concern about chemical additives in the increasingly processed food offered by supermarkets. Since then many supermarkets have borrowed the health-food store idea of displaying bulk products and allowing shoppers to scoop the amount of food they want from the bins. A few bins contain so-called natural foods, while others hold everything from instant soup mixes to cheese puffs.

Some twenty years ago the trade magazine *Canadian Grocer* predicted that the big chains were "threatening to do to mom 'n' pop health food stores what they did to mom 'n' pop grocery stores – drive them out of business."[16] By 1993 it was reporting that Loblaws had taken a "vanguard position" in introducing a private label called "Too Good to Be True" and expanding that label tenfold in two years. "They've been cherry-picking what sells in health food stores," a health-food broker observed.[17]

Although "healthy food" is becoming an increasingly important part of their business, certain features of the chains' approach to health food are fundamentally at odds with the understanding of health and food that inspired the original movement. "Organic food isn't just a trend," Longo representative Dawn Defino says. "It's here to stay. We have to treat it with the same respect as we do the big brands like Coke and Hostess."[18]

The biggest companies keep on growing because joint purchasing, advertising, and sheer size give them an edge over smaller, independent operations. Supermarket chains are not the only big players in the grocery business. Corporate takeovers at the production end mean that ownership of the brands stocked on grocery shelves is concentrated in relatively few hands. Shoppers might be surprised by what causes are supported by their weekly "votes" at the check-out counter. For example, when they fill their carts with Miracle Whip, Kraft dinner, Kool-Aid, Post Raisin Bran, Maxwell House coffee, or a packet of Jell-O, even non-smokers are buying products from tobacco giant Philip Morris.

While there is some competition among the big players, whether at the production or the retail end of the grocery business, the market is dominated by a large and powerful few. Consumers may have a vote, but they have little control over whom or what to vote for.

Keeping up the Demand

"Consolidation, diversification and trade relations": these conditions, says an *Annual Report of the Grocery Industry*, are "enabling all segments of the industry to serve the consumer while preserving and, hopefully, growing the bottom line."[19] The key, indeed, is "growing the bottom line." But how is it done? In a word: demand. To ensure economic growth, the system must stimulate consumer demand, which, in turn, is stimulated by several factors, including the availability of credit, aggressive advertising, and, perhaps surprisingly, military spending.

The demand for consumer goods is likely to be an on-again off-again proposition when it depends on people saving up for what they need. One way to make sure it remains relatively steady is to extend consumer credit. Today virtually every retailer from the smallest hardware store to the largest Big Box outlet displays a cluster of familiar stickers indicating which credit cards they accept. More and more of the big chains offer their own credit cards, and an expanding range of other financial services to boot. At Loblaws, for instance, along with President's Choice Cookies and President's Choice Toilet Paper you will find President's Choice Financial Mastercard, provided by President's Choice Bank. Along with

fresh produce, you will find Loblaws' trade-marked Fresh Financial Thinking, which includes no-fee bank accounts with overdrafts available and grocery points offered as a bonus.

Advertising helps to direct the dollars that consumer credit makes available. It helps transform wants into needs, and helps us to feel good about buying things we might be better off without. "Part of a nutritionally balanced breakfast" is a common refrain in commercials advertising sugar-laden breakfast cereal. The truth of this claim is entirely dependent on what else you eat for breakfast.

In the early 1970s, federal government researchers found that cereals like Apple Jacks, Sugar Pops, and Count Chocula contained up to 54 per cent sugar by weight. A better choice for breakfast might be a Sara Lee Chocolate Cake (36 per cent sugar). When the government asked cereal manufacturers to voluntarily indicate on the labels the amount of sugar in their products, the reply was an emphatic "no". Instead, the companies that control Canada's breakfast-food market spend tens of millions of dollars a year on advertisements that offer virtually no useful information – with young children as the principal targets. By 2002 health campaigners had succeeded in pushing Ottawa to require nutrition information labelling on packaged foods. But the food industry was still refusing to tell consumers which products contained genetically modified (GM) products. Apparently the voters in the market-place need not be well informed.

Corporations are in some respects responsive to consumer concerns, though. In the early 1970s cereal-makers noticed a consumer backlash against sugar-loaded products as more and more shoppers turned to health-food stores to buy whole-grain cereals and granola made by independent companies. The big four cereal-makers quickly developed their own wholesome-sounding brands, advertising them with names and images like Country Morning and Nature Valley.

Yet in the new millennium Canadian children are still exposed to advertisements promoting sugary cereals. Pre-sweetened brands, with nearly a third of the cold-cereal market, dominate the grocery aisles. Supermarket management learned to place sugary cereals on the lower shelves so that children can see them. Manufacturers, aware of the negative image of these products, changed the names of some products. Sugar Corn Pops suddenly became Corn Pops and Sugar Frosted Flakes emerged as Frosted Flakes.

Most people now recognize that concentrations of sugar are not all that good for you. Sugar contributes not just to tooth decay but also to obesity and poor nutrition. But it is not the only ingredient that we might be consuming at higher rates than we imagine. A poll in 2001 found that the majority of North Americans were unaware that genetically modified foods were already being produced and sold in the United States and Canada. Indeed, as much as 60 per cent of the processed food in our shopping carts may now have "genetically engineered constituents."[20]

Although most of Canada's canola crop is genetically engineered, there are no labels indicating this feature on canola oil – nor do any other food products that contain GM food carry labels to this effect.[21] Genetically engineered crops, first planted in Canada in 1996, have quickly become part of our food system. In 1999 a quarter of the corn and the majority of the soybeans and canola grown in Canada consisted of genetically engineered strains.[22] These foods raise health, ecological, and ethical concerns, and long-term safety tests remain to be done on them. Proper labelling of the products (already carried out in about thirty European countries) would be a first step in controlling their development and use. Labels and advertising influence demand in a way that can be wildly out of sync with the way consumers would "vote" if they had the necessary information to make informed choices. And "freedom to choose" is the essence of free-market economics.

Advertising especially magnifies another distortion in the "voting" process – a distortion based on the condition that what is easiest and most profitable to sell is not necessarily what human beings need most. About one-third of all the vegetables consumed by children in the United States and Canada, for example, are in the form of potato chips and french fries.

Canada's highly productive food industry is not necessarily compatible with health. One of its results, obesity, is a serious problem in North America, where it is the second biggest killer after tobacco. Most overweight people are at risk of heart disease and diabetes, as well as tooth decay and poor nutrition. A highly productive food industry does not necessarily put an end to hunger and malnutrition: four out of five of the world's malnourished children live in countries that have food surpluses.[23]

Advertising promotes not only products like microwave ovens that promise to save you time, but also others like video games that help you spend the time you save. Consumer credit enables people to buy goods now and pay later. Canada's free market is full of paradoxes. It generates both wealth and poverty. The abundance of the supermarket contrasts with shortages at the food bank. We have healthy food but too much disease brought on by unhealthy eating. What can we learn from this about the laws of supply and demand?

> The present market is designed primarily to make profits, not to feed people. The supply and distribution of food are determined mainly by "effective demand," not human need. Effective demand is usually defined in terms of "ability to pay." Food supplies are often controlled in such a way as to drive up prices on the market. Furthermore, some food industries have gone so far as to destroy their produce when they could not get the market prices they wanted.
>
> — Canadian Conference of Catholic Bishops, "Sharing Daily Bread," in *Do Justice!* ed. E.F. Sheridan, 1987.

International Votes

When Canadians stroll down the aisles of the supermarket, they pass displays featuring such items as "English" tea and "Dutch" chocolate. But no tea is to be found growing on the moors of England, nor do cocoa trees bear fruit on Holland's damp polders. Advertising that emphasizes the European origins of fine foods masks the origins of raw ingredients grown in former colonies of the European powers.

Products like coffee and bananas that were once considered luxuries are now staples in Canadian supermarkets. They are produced in the tropical nations of the Third World, some of which were once better known as "banana republics." This label implied two things: dependence on one or two cash crops; and unstable, oppressive governments.

Such countries are typically poor in comparison to industrial nations like Canada and the United States. Inside a "banana republic" there is an oligarchy, or ruling elite of wealthy landowners and merchants, that tends to dominate the vast majority of peasants and urban poor. Since World War II those elites, together with the corporations that dominate the international food trade, have found it to be more profitable for tropical production to focus on export crops than to grow beans and corn for domestic consumption.

The act of placing a higher economic value on the production of bananas for export than on corn for local food reflects values of a different sort. It is, in a way, similar to Gross National Product measurements that count car accidents and oil spills but ignore caring for babies. Growing those bananas instead of beans reproduces internationally the kinds of values that dominate mainstream economic thinking the world over.

The price is paid unevenly. The bananas that Canadians find in their supermarkets were most likely grown, packed, and shipped by one of three firms that control two-thirds of the world's banana trade and 80 per cent of the banana trade in the North.[24] Chiquita, Dole, and Del Monte are not in the business of growing food to satisfy local hunger; the poor lack the cash to pay for that food. Return on investment is what matters. Thus, countries where people are literally dying of hunger actually export food. Human need does not count as a vote in the international supermarket, where the laws of profit and the growth of the money economy hold sway.

When returns seem threatened by reforms aimed at redistributing plantation land to the poor, a powerful company can arrange to have the offending government overthrown, as the United Fruit Company did in Guatemala in 1954. Or, if a banana republic attempts to get

---

Alternative Economic Indicators

Traditionally, economic growth has been equated with improved living standards and social progress. But often this is not the case and there are several social and environmental factors which are ignored in the conventional measure of economic growth. The main way of gauging economic prosperity until the 1990s was Gross National Product (GNP), a basic measure reflecting the prices for which a country sells its goods and services. Increases in GNP indicate economic growth, which is assumed to be good by definition. But GNP fails to take into account social and environmental costs. Disasters, automobile accidents, fires and environmental clean-ups are counted as good growth because they are given a financial value. . . .

In an attempt to measure more accurately the economic and social wealth (or poverty) of a nation, several alternative indices have been devised. These include the UN's Human Development Index, the Index of Sustainable Economic Welfare, the Physical Quality of Life Index, the Genuine Progress Indicator, the Per Capita Grain Consumption Index and the Elementary Living Conditions Index. The 1992 UN Conference on Environment and Development informally recognized the insufficiency of indicators such as GNP. The resulting blueprint for future action, Agenda 21, included a proposal to develop integrated systems of national accounts which would include social, economic and environmental aspects.

— *The A to Z of World Development*, compiled by Andy Crump, ed. Wayne Ellwood, 1998.

more money for its bananas by joining with others to impose an export tax, a big firm can break up the effort by bribing a local politician. This is what United Brands did in the early 1970s when it paid off the president of Honduras.

Unequal access to products of farm and field – poverty in the midst of affluence – does not occur only as the poor of Canada manoeuvre their carts down the supermarket aisles that are so well stocked with food. Gross disparities of income also exist on a world scale, where injustices between nations are duplicated by terrible inequalities and sufferings within them. While Canada and other countries produce surpluses of grain, people in many countries go without food as a matter of course. Yet in every so-called poor country, there are elites who live in conspicuous luxury. The patterns in poor countries and in the world economy are the same – relatively few people have more "votes" in the marketplace while the poor, who are the majority, have less.

Getting Started's first edition featured a 1979 pie chart showing the distribution of the world's wealth. At that time the richest fifth received 71.2 per cent of the income. By 1993 – after a decade in which the market was often praised as the key to economic development – the share of the rich had risen to 85 per cent. By 1998 it hit a new high of 89 per cent, with no signs of a reversal in the trend. "Markets may be impressive economically or technologically," concluded a United Nations report showing increasing world inequality. "But they are of little value if they do not serve human development. Markets are the means. Human development is the end."[25]

Another important aspect of the global economy is the international movement of capital. "Capital lacks loyalty – capital will go where the returns are most attractive," an official at the Royal Bank of Canada once said.[26] In a similar vein, the president of IBM World Trade Corporation expounded on the nature of free enterprise: "For business purposes, the boundaries that separate one nation from another are no more real than the equator. . . . Once management understands and accepts this world economy, its view of the marketplace – and its planning – necessarily expand."[27]

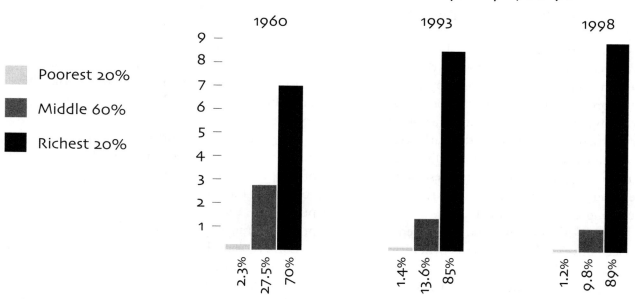

Increases in World Income Distribution Inequality 1960-98

Poorest 20%

Middle 60%

Richest 20%

1960 — 2.3% / 27.5% / 70%

1993 — 1.4% / 13.6% / 85%

1998 — 1.2% / 9.8% / 89%

Source: "Trickle down Trash, Squeeze Up Wealth" <www.richcity.org>. See also R.H. Wade, "The Rising Inequality of World Income Distribution," *Finance and Development*, vol.38, no.4 (December 2001); and Wayne Ellwood, *The No-Nonsense Guide to Globalization*, 2001, p.101.

Canadian capital and profits tend to leave the country, in part because of foreign, especially U.S., control of the economy. Although Canada has a surplus in its export of goods (pulp and paper, minerals, wheat), it also "exports" large amounts of money in the form of interest payments paid by the government and businesses on outstanding debts to large U.S. parent companies. On balance the country is a net exporter of capital.

At the Checkout

The trip to the supermarket nearly over, we reach the checkout counter. This is the site of changes in technology and labour that have been experienced not just in the grocery business but also by Canadians more generally. Since the 1970s, trends in unemployment, inflation, and declining real wages have put tremendous pressure on supermarket chains competing for market share. Megastores, which carry high volume, can operate on low markup, and they rely on a low-paid, non-unionized, predominantly part-time workforce. For example, most Costco and Sam's Club warehouse clubs operate with a non-unionized workforce that is 90 per cent part-time and paid at the minimum wage.[28]

Since, for supermarkets, labour is the most controllable expense, the cost of the fierce competition in this industry is borne by workers, who are disproportionately female. Gendered inequalities have always existed in this business, but rather than diminishing in the early years of the new millennium, these inequalities are being reinforced by the labour-force restructuring that the industry is introducing as a response to the prevailing economic climate.

The workforce is rigidly divided between service jobs (clerks and cashiers) held mainly by women and "production" jobs (such as meat packing and shelf-stocking) held mainly by men. Gender divisions are also visible in other aspects of the workforce organization. Management positions are almost exclusively male-occupied, and men also predominate in the category of full-time workers. With the exception of department manager positions, supermarkets have almost no remaining full-time, store-level jobs. This loss of full-time work is significant in an industry representing almost 4 per cent of total employment in Canada. Part-time workers receive lower rates of pay and fewer benefits than full-time employees do. As one industrial relations analyst observes, "To a large extent, the work organization of the food retail industry is built on low-paid, feminized and flexible labour."[29]

This segment of the labour force is particularly vulnerable to the kind of threats made by big industry players in recent years. Forcing a 1993 agreement in Alberta, which set the standard for retail food bargaining for years to come, Canada Safeway threatened to withdraw from the province unless workers accepted $45 million a year in wage cuts and benefits reductions. In the 1990s Loblaws also began making demands for wage reductions on the part of its employees. It started phasing out full-time cashier work.[30] Large supermarkets in general offered their high-seniority part-time employees one of two options: resign with a small severance package, or take a reduction in pay. For those who didn't want to join the ranks of the unemployed, this represented no choice at all.

Employment conditions are not the only thing to have changed at the checkout counter, and groceries are not the only things sold there. The checkout counter has become the site for a complex array of electronic transactions. Among these is the flow of information initiated by scanning the Universal Product Code (the small patch of stripes on nearly every product sold). The code's use means that cashiers no longer have to punch in each item, and customers can be processed more quickly. (Unfortunately for many customers, lengthy waits at the checkout persist because in most stores packers – a feature of early supermarkets – have been eliminated, their jobs handed over to cashiers or the customers themselves.) The electronic scanner records the sale of each item in the central computer, which automatically keeps inventory – and thereby decreases the number of people required to keep stock and affix price labels.

New information technology is more than a labour-saving device. It also makes it possible for supermarkets to buy consumer information in exchange for discounts and specials that used to be available to all shoppers without discrimination. The shopper who wants to take advantage of as many in-store specials as possible now needs to have "frequent shopper," "loyalty," or "bonus" cards. In return the information provided enables the supermarket to engage in consumer research and to act on its findings with targeted marketing.

As technology changes, so too does the extent of consumer surveillance (see also chapter eight). In a press release announcing the test marketing of a new K-Trac shopper monitoring system, the manufacturer enthused:

> In an age where consumers' shopping habits are tracked through ATM and credit card purchases, and one's Internet research patterns can be picked up through computer technology, it was only a matter of time before a shopper's actual traffic patterns inside of a retail store could be monitored and recorded for marketing purposes.[31]

Efforts have already begun to marry this kind of technology with shoppers' personal "loyalty cards" to generate customized audio advertising on "Klever-Karts" that direct the shopper to certain products, or which even trigger the products themselves to call out to the shopper from the shelf. In the money economy, shopping has become a "productive" activity.

Consuming Questions

Conventional economic wisdom says that as the big supermarkets compete with each other, customers should benefit. The winners of this cutthroat struggle for market share promise to provide Canadians with the best quality and cheapest food. But at what expense?

The organization of the food system raises substantial questions.

- Are there advantages in keeping smaller merchants and producers in business even if it means paying slightly higher prices at the checkout counter?
- Would it be better to ensure the survival of more decently paid, secure jobs but to choose from a narrower range of products?
- Is fair trade with farmers who produce cash crops in the Third World a good investment for Canadians even if it means a more expensive cup of coffee? (See chapters one and fourteen.)
- Do advertisers have an unlimited right to free speech in the market of ideas, or are they a threat to supermarket democracy?

These are only a few of the dilemmas we face, not only as consumers but as citizens participating in local and global markets and working to sustain the communities we live in and the more distant communities we depend on as well. There are no easy answers to dilemmas like these. They involve painful tradeoffs, especially for the worst-off among us. But they cannot be avoided. There are alternative ways of doing things in the food economy. Shoppers can buy organic produce where available. They can buy locally, buy in season, and try to buy fair trade products. If you have access to a plot of land, whether in your backyard or in a community garden, you could try growing your own produce (it's been done before). In some cities there is Community Shared Agriculture (CSA), where citizens, by buying shares, support local, environmentally friendly farming and in turn receive produce directly from the farm. If you eat conventionally produced fruits and vegetables, watch out for the ones that are most highly contaminated (apples, spinach, and peaches top a U.S. list). Try to avoid using pesticides around the home and in your garden.[32]

Choices are being made that have an impact on all of our lives. To remain lost in the supermarket is to leave these choices up to someone else.

"Diet Resolutions" from FoodShare

At FoodShare, we believe that food security is about more than people just having a minimum amount of money to get by – that is, it means creating a society where people have the knowledge and skills to prepare and eat healthy food, where food helps to build family and community and which supports a sustainable local food and global food supply. But we also believe that without a minimum income there can never be food security. To us, it's obvious: there must be affordable housing for everyone and welfare and minimum wage rates must be indexed to the actual cost of living.

These are our new year's "diet" resolutions for people who are interested in building food security.

1. Eat simply and locally: Support local farmers and protect the environment by eating seasonally and low on the food chain. Grains, beans, fresh fruit and vegetables, when purchased in season, are the least expensive and healthiest foods you can eat. The more we import, the less we know about the food we're getting and the way it was produced, and the less viable farming in Canada becomes.

2. Cook for yourself and your friends: save money, enjoy the company of others and know what you're eating by sitting down to more homecooked meals.

3. Grow your own: start your own garden or join a community garden to experience the fascination and satisfaction of planting, cultivating and harvesting food.

4. Buy outside the corporate food system: join a co-op, buy fair trade products, support your local corner store, buy organic, support a farmers market or field-to-table program. If you can afford it, spend more on your food – the drive for cheaper food is driving down wages for farmers everywhere and encouraging environmentally unsustainable agriculture.

5. Speak out to make the right to food a matter of justice, not charity. Food is as fundamental as water and air to our survival. Governments have a responsibility to ensure that everyone can get affordable and healthy food in a dignified manner.

– FoodShare Toronto, 2002.

Questions

❑ Take a look at the food advertising you see on TV and in newspapers and magazines. What kind of values do the commercials and ads promote? Health, convenience, family warmth, quantity? Do they really deliver? How healthy are the products that the advertisements sell?

❑ What do you think of the supermarket attitude to organic food, treating it as a "brand" as worthy of the same respect as Coke and Hostess?

❑ Do you know where your food comes from? Is locally grown food available in your community?

❑ Look at the packaging of the food you eat. Do you understand the list of ingredients? Are there additives? Were pesticides or herbicides used in the growing process? Does the food contain genetically modified organisms? Is there enough information available on the labels or in the stores?

❑ Does your community have a "good food box" program, food co-op, community kitchen, or other programs that make fresh produce available to community members at more affordable prices?

❑ The 1996 Rome Declaration on World Food Security states that food security exists when all people at all times have physical and economic access to sufficient safe and nutritious food to meet their dietary needs and food preferences for an active and healthy life. Do we have food security in Canada? Should food security be a national priority? What threatens and what sustains food security in Canada? How does Canada contribute to efforts to achieve global food security? Do we do anything to threaten that security?

❑ How has shopping changed in your community over the years? Do you have to go to one of the big supermarket chains to get your groceries? Are there any smaller independent retailers left? How have the changes affected retail workers, local small business people, and nearby producers?

❏ Where are the big stores in your area? Can you get to them easily and take your shopping home afterwards if you don't have a car?

❏ What considerations, in addition to the size of your final shopping bill, determine where you decide to shop and what you buy? Are there considerations, like avoiding pesticides or supporting local producers, that you would like to include in your shopping plans but can't because it seems that you just can't afford to? What are the costs, to you, your family, and community, of deciding to leave some of these values on the grocery store shelf?

❏ Have you ever worked in any part of the food industry? Were you in a unionized or non-unionized workplace? Were the workers mostly male or female? How were you treated by your employer? What kind of a perspective on food as a consumer product did you get from working in the industry? Share and compare your experiences.

Resources

• Deborah Barndt. *Tangled Routes: Women, Work and Globalization on the Tomato Trail*. Aurora, Ont.: Garamond Press, 2002. The book traces the tomato from a Mexican farm field to the Canadian market. Barndt examines the significance of fast-food chains and supermarket conglomerates and the lives of workers who serve the global food system – as well as the alternatives, including a framework for "the other globalization" through collective action and transnational coalitions.

• Jane Jacobs. *The Nature of Economies*. New York: Vintage Books, 2001. A conversation between five friends explores how economies work, comparing economic mechanisms and natural ecological processes. The book examines key economic concepts and controversies in a novel and engaging way.

• Andrew Kimbrell, ed. *Fatal Harvest: The Tragedy of Industrial Agriculture*. Washington, D.C.: Island Press, 2002. This international anthology explores the ecologically destructive agricultural system and offers a compelling vision for an organic and environmentally safer way of producing the food that people eat.

• Stella Lee, Caroline Liffman, and Cindy McCulligh. *The Supermarket Tour*. Hamilton, Ont.: OPIRG McMaster, 2001. A do-it-yourself kit that (like this chapter) accompanies you through the supermarket to explore food and economic issues: marketing methods, pesticides and additives, GM foods and biotechnology, meat production, and corporate control. Lots of resources, action tips, and a guide to leading your own supermarket tour. Available on-line and from OPIRG McMaster, Box 1013, McMaster University, 1280 Main Street West, Hamilton, Ont. L8S 1C0.

• Marion Nestle. *Food Politics: How the Food Industry Influences Nutrition and Health*. Berkeley: University of California Press, 2002. Nestle reveals how behind-the-scenes politicking and modern marketing strategies fatten the purses of corporate stockholders while threatening human health.

• Wayne Roberts, Rod MacRae, and Lori Stahlbrand. *Real Food for a Change*. Toronto: Random House of Canada, 1999. Discusses why and how to eat organic food; low cost foods that also deliver high value; the food system; and food security issues. This book connects individual health with the health of the community, the economy, and the planet.

• Eric Schlosser. *Fast Food Nation: The Dark Side of the All-American Meal*. New York: Perennial, 2002. An examination of the relation between the production processes and working conditions in the fast-food industry and issues of land loss, the growing gap between rich and poor, and the obesity epidemic.

• Marilyn Waring. *Counting for Nothing: What Men Value and What Women Are Worth*. Toronto: University of Toronto Press, 1999. Originally published in 1988, this updated book looks at the impact of economic measures that ignore the unpaid activity of child care, domestic labour, and subsistence farming, not to mention clean water, old growth forests, and other "undeveloped" land. Waring reveals the associations between these accounting systems and the economy of war.

• *The Ram's Horn: A Monthly Journal of Food Systems Analysis.* Available on-line <www.ramshorn.bc.ca> or from The Ram's Horn, RR#1, Sorrento, B.C. V0E 2W0.

• *Bacon: The Film.* Canada, 2002. Directed by Hugo Latulippe. NFB. Video. 82 min. When large-scale hog producers in Quebec got even bigger, so too did questions about the social and environmental impacts of this growth. The film shows how, in the face of soil sterility and contaminated water, citizens are fighting back to keep society on a human scale.

• *Deconstructing Supper.* Canada, 2002. Directed by Marianne Kaplan. MSK Productions Inc. Video. 48 min. Starting in his five star Vancouver restaurant, Canadian chef John Bishop sets out on an international journey interviewing farmers, scientists, and activists to investigate food safety in the age of GM foods and industrial agriculture.

• *The Genetic Takeover or Mutant Food.* Canada, 2000. Directed by Karl Parent and Louise Vandelac. NFB. Video. 52 min. Although genetically modified plants are already incorporated into about 75 per cent of what we eat in Canada, few Canadians are aware of what they are eating. The longer term effects on health and ecology are even less well-known. *Genetic Takeover* considers some of the possibilities and compares the more activist response of consumers in Europe and Asia to that in North America.

• *The Gleaners and I.* France, 2000. Directed by Agnes Varda. Zeitgeist Films. Video. 82 min. In this brilliant and highly personal documentary film, the veteran French new wave director trains her roving eye on "gleaners," people who go to fields and back streets and markets to find "produce" that others in society have determined they have no use for. Her investigation takes her from forgotten corners of the French countryside to off-hours at the green markets in Paris.

• *Who's Counting? Marilyn Waring on Sex, Lies and Global Economics.* Canada, 1995. Directed by Terre Nash. NFB. Video. 52 min. and 94 min. versions. Waring asks, "Why is the market economy all that counts?" An exploration of the human and environmental implications of market economics and the alternatives.

Websites:

The Who's Counting Project was formed after the Canadian premiere of Marilyn Waring's 1995 video. The video has inspired many people to work on human-scale economic alternatives, local currency exchanges, and more humane ways of measuring the quality of life. The Who's Counting Project website is a good place to start looking for suggestions on how to get involved in this work, with great action tips and resource links.

The Canadian Association of Food Banks maintains a website with links to food sharing resources and organizations as well as valuable research publications, including "Hunger Count," its annual report on Canada's emergency food programs.

FoodShare Toronto promotes policies – such as adequate social assistance rates, sustainable agriculture, universal funding of community-based programs, and nutrition education – that will make food a priority at all levels of society. Their website offers action tips, resources, and links.

Chapter Five
The Brave New World of Work

When people meet for the first time, conversation usually gets around to "What do you do?" The question refers not to their hobbies, of course, but to how they earn a living. "What do you do?" means "What's your job?" It is not considered polite to follow up that question with "How much do you make?" – which really means "What are you worth?"

In Canada our identities are strongly linked to the jobs we hold, and work is often considered the most important measure of worth. A person can have a good job, an important job, or a bad job. Shipping clerks working part-time and man-aging directors who put in extra long hours are rarely considered to be of equal stature. Yet both are a cut above someone who has no paid work at all. And many people, usually women, who are pulling their weight have vital jobs raising children, but those jobs are not paid at all.

When someone who is asked "What do you do?" answers, "Nothing . . . I'm unemployed," it is easy to imagine a dark cloud settling over the conversation. Active and capable people who have no paid work can feel – or be made to feel – that they are not pulling their weight.

In the distant past the main economic

problem used to be not how to employ people, but how to produce enough to meet their needs. Then the Industrial Revolution multiplied the output of material goods. Now productive capacity has developed to the point that coping with the garbage is a big problem. There is more than enough to go around. But access to the abundant goods and services varies. In a society in which a job is the usual source of income, access depends mainly on whether you have a job – and the kind of job you have.

A "good" job with high pay promises not only material comfort but also social status, a sense of personal worth, and the image of success. Like access to the supermarket, access to the job market is uneven, but now the question "What can you afford?" is replaced by "What do you do?"

"Nothing" – "Not Enough" – "Too Much"

Many Canadians – over 1.2 million in 2002 – answered "Nothing." They were the 7.1 per cent officially unemployed members of the labour force.[1] It was a good year for job creation, with the Canadian economy creating over half a million jobs. But despite the impressive job numbers, the unemployment rate remained stuck at over 7 per cent as large numbers of people entered the labour force. Losing a job means a decline in material living standards. Families are forced to cut back, first on luxuries, then on life's necessities. No wonder the monthly unemployment rate from Statistics Canada is a barometer of economic health.

Over a million jobless people sounds like a lot. But in 1984, when *Getting Started* was first published in the wake of a major recession, nearly 1.5 million Canadians were unemployed. Ten years later, when this book's third edition was published, the economy was struggling to recover from another downturn and there were 1.58 million jobless Canadians. So by those measures 1.2 million in 2002 does not sound too bad. It means many more Canadians were in the job market.

The unemployment rate moves up and down with the business cycle, masking larger changes.

The labour market is as complex and ever-changing as the supermarket. New technology, new employer strategies, and shifts in government policy all have an impact.

In 1984 the computer had yet to make its mark on the workplace. As employers downsized, contracted out, and developed more "flexible" strategies, part-time employment skyrocketed. Between 1989 and 1998, six out of ten new jobs created were part-time. Self-employment jumped by 40 per cent in the same period.[2] The federal government's changes to one of Canada's oldest social programs did more than alter the name from Unemployment Insurance to Employment Insurance. They meant that far fewer workers could collect benefits when they lost their jobs. The percentage of jobless people collecting regular benefits dropped from 87 per cent in 1990 to 42 per cent in 1997.[3]

At the same time that more people began working shorter hours in part-time, temporary, and contract jobs, more were working very long hours. Between 1976 and 1995 the number of workers who had less than thirty-four hours per week rose from 15.9 to 23.6 per cent of the labour force. Meanwhile, those working more than fifty hours increased from 11.7 to 14.8 per cent of employed people.[4]

People would rather work to support themselves – part-time, full-time, or on their own – than depend on the government. This has always been true, whether Employment Insurance and welfare were easier or harder to get. In the famous Great Depression of the 1930s, government support was minimal. It got more generous after World War II, only to shrink in recent years. But dependence on government programs can wear people down. "I don't cut welfare people up, you know, but I have my pride. To me, that's not my type of thing," one laid-off worker explained. "I want to go out and be a useful member of the community and say that I'm working and not freeloading."

People find it humiliating not to be able to earn their own living. "I'd like my children to see me as someone who can look after them the way other guys do."

I was down among the realities of modern life. And what are the realities of modern life? Well, the chief one is an everlasting, frantic struggle to sell things. With most people it takes the form of selling themselves – that is to say, getting a job and keeping it (and then) that feeling that you've got to be everlastingly fighting and hustling, that you'll never get anything unless you grab it from someone else, that there's always somebody after your job, that next month or the month after they'll be reducing staff and it's you that'll get the bird . . .

— George Orwell, *Coming Up for Air*, 1939.

"What's Your Number?"

How many Canadians are confronted with such feelings of purposelessness? It's hard to say, because Statistics Canada gives an incomplete answer. The federal information agency reports the number of "officially" unemployed. In 2000 things looked pretty good, at least in historical terms. The official unemployment rate was 6.8 per cent, lower than it had been since the early 1970s.

But the official rate represents only the people actively seeking work. If we add people whom Statistics Canada calls "discouraged" because they have abandoned the job search as futile, the rate rises to 7.1 per cent. If we add the "waiting group" – people on recall or with a long-term job starting in the future – the rate rises to 7.5 per cent. Add the partly unemployed – people who want full-time work but can only find part-time jobs – and the rate leaps to 9.1 per cent.[5]

Unemployment is also regionally uneven. Canadians in some parts of the country find it much more difficult to get a job than others who live in more prosperous areas. Atlantic Canada, some parts of Quebec, and Northern Canada always have much higher rates of joblessness than Toronto, Calgary, and Vancouver do. In 2001, official unemployment ranged from 4.8 per cent in Alberta to 17.3 per cent in Newfoundland.[6]

Fort McMurray, Alberta, is often called Newfoundland's third-largest city because so many Newfoundlanders have migrated there to work in the oil sands plants. Students in St. John's, where unemployment is chronically high, have a harder time finding part-time minimum wage work than students in Fort McMurray do. Workers are so scarce in the Alberta boom town that fast-food employers are forced to pay young people well above the province's modest minimum wage, and they still talk about the time they had to close the Tim Hortons drive-through because of a labour shortage.[7]

By unpacking the ways in which we normally look at things – or at least how they seem to be – social analysis questions our usual assumptions about whether unemployment is a bad thing. For whom is it bad?

Like other markets, the labour market fluctuates according to supply and demand. A tight job market and low unemployment tend to drive up labour costs, because workers are free to leave low-wage jobs, confident that there are plenty of positions out there. This is bad for employers who have fast-food franchises in Fort McMurray. But a high unemployment place like St. John's is bad for young people looking for work pouring coffee or flipping burgers. This simple fact of working life is not usually discussed in conversations about unemployment. It shows that unemployment has a different impact on different people.

The impact of unemployment is uneven in another way. The jobless rate is always higher for minority groups, the disabled, and young people. For Aboriginal people in Canada, unemployment rates are three times higher than the average for non-Aboriginal Canadians. Aboriginal people who are employed earn 34 per cent below the Canadian average. Visible minority workers earn on average 15 per cent less than all other workers.[8] As for young people aged fifteen to twenty-four, in 2000 their rate of unemployment was 12.6 per cent, compared to 6.8 per cent for the population as a whole.[9]

Decades of Unemployment

People frequently assume that the high levels of unemployment that accompany the regular downturns in the business cycle (recessions and depressions) will decline when the predictable recovery comes along and the economy expands. Those inclined to look at history through the lens of particular decades might refer back to the roaring twenties, a period of expansion and job growth. The 1960s are remembered not just for the Beatles but as another period of low unemployment.

But good times fade away. The 1920s gave way to the Depression of the 1930s: bread lines, work camps, and hard times. The eagerly awaited recovery was only ushered in by World War II, with its artificial demand based on terrible destruction. After the war, returning veterans, refugees, the baby boom, and the accompanied explosion in housing maintained the recovery. When the economy faltered in the late 1940s, along came the Korean War, ushering in the fabulous fifties. Jobs abounded until, late in that decade, another downturn drove unemployment up to 7 per cent.

This rate (which now seems low) seemed high back then, because joblessness had been hovering around 3 per cent since the end of World War II. With that low rate, employers were forced to give in to workers, who made steady gains. Things kept going in that direction as consumer demand and the war in Vietnam produced another boom. Among other things, the 1960s are remembered as a time of uninterrupted prosperity.

In the 1970s unemployment began to rise steadily, with halting recovery followed by decline. Many Canadians were sustained by government make-work programs and unemployment insurance (the system had been expanded in 1971 despite employer protests). Then came the severe recession of the early 1980s. There was no return to bread lines and soup kitchens, but that period will go down in history as the time when those symbols of the Hungry Thirties were replaced by a new phenomenon, the food bank (see chapter four).

Although the later 1980s saw an economic recovery, the food banks never did disappear. Instead, their numbers grew as unemployment declined. Indeed, they became a permanent feature on the social landscape, a metaphor for the fact that a rising tide does not lift all boats. In 1991 an Economic Council of Canada study pointed out that unemployment had risen steadily in the three decades since 1960, with the average for each decade surpassing that of the previous decade. By the end of the 1990s, the trend was confirmed. The average unemployment was above that of the 1980s.[10]

Surges of unemployment, then, have been frequent ever since people moved from farm to city and the country industrialized, ever since the majority of Canadians stopped working for themselves and needed a paying job to survive and to lend a purpose to life. There have always been periods when "What do you do?" could only be answered with a shrug about how hard it was to find work. Over time it has become clear that the economy is not primarily organized to provide jobs. Unemployment is not an irregularity, nor is it a temporary faltering in an otherwise steady march of progress based on economic growth. It is a chronic condition that worsens with every backward swing of the economic pendulum.

Canada is moving towards more – not less – unemployment. Canadians may look back on the 1990s as the decade in which they resigned themselves to high levels of unemployment as a fact of life rather than a passing phase. It was a time when more people had to choose part-time, contract, and other "contingent" work situations. More people than ever before became self-employed. As the chief economist of the Canadian Manufacturers Association noted at the start of the decade, "Right now, there is no job in Canada that is secure."[11]

The crisis of unemployment is certainly not peculiar to Canada, but is worldwide. It results partly from the emergence of the information society, and also from a growing service economy. These are two factors which move us toward an integrated global economy, and bring us closer to a borderless world. Transnational corporations, including banks and other financial institutions, today can shift information, capital, industrial design, and knowledge instantaneously around the world. They thereby out-manoeuvre not only workers' organizations but also domestic industry as well as government fiscal and monetary policies.

— Canadian Conference of Catholic Bishops,
"Widespread Unemployment: A Call to Mobilize the
Social Forces of Our Nation," 1993.

Who to Blame?

Unemployment, bound up as it is with complex economic questions, is bewildering. When people cast about for answers, they are really doing a rough sort of social analysis. Are the following comments typical?

- "Those shiftless young loafers hanging around at the mall . . . give them a pick and shovel!"
- "Too many people prefer to live off the government."
- "There are lots of jobs around, it's just that there aren't enough people trained on computers." Or "There's always work for anyone who wants a job. Just look at the want ads."
- "Immigrants are keen to work but Canadians have become lazy and uncompetitive." Or "There are too many immigrants taking jobs away from Canadians."
- "There's no such thing as a job for life anymore. Kids today have to learn to be flexible. They'll have several careers."

Such remarks, blaming unemployment on the unemployed, are common enough. They treat unemployment as an *individual* problem.

Sociologist C. Wright Mills, who wrote in the 1950s and 1960s, once pointed out that "troubles" are private matters. If a single person in a city of a million is unemployed, it makes sense to look closely at that person's character and skills. But, say, if fifteen million people are jobless in a nation of fifty million, does it make sense to look for a solution by focusing on those particular individuals? No, Mills argued: "That is an issue, and we may not hope to find its solution within the range of opportunities open to any one individual."[12]

Unlike private troubles, "issues" are public matters. Although saying that the unemployed are lazy or just need more training may be understandable — arising out of feelings of frustration, resentment, or powerlessness — it is not very helpful in understanding the factors that led to Canada's high levels of unemployment in the first place. These are economic, technological, and political factors.

Another reaction, similar to blaming individual unemployed people, is to place the weight of blame on the shoulders of individual employers. This is understandable, because it is individual bosses who decide to shut down plants, downsize offices, or introduce machines to replace workers. These highly visible people ("Neutron Jack" or "Chainsaw Al") can be painted as the villains, especially in the eyes of those harmed by their decisions. After all, a boss does not have to endure the loss of income and indignity accompanying unemployment, and can appear very callous in getting rid of workers.

Still, like blaming the unemployed themselves, blaming the immediate employer also fails to get at the basic causes of unemployment. These causes have little to do with the actions of individuals as such, whether they be bosses or workers. Both the small entrepreneur and the corporation manager operate within a specific system of priorities. The logic of private profit and corporate growth drives the market economy. This characteristic of the Canadian economic system limits the effective action of the individual. Bosses or managers who do not pay close attention to this rule of the market are likely to face bankruptcy or be dismissed themselves. And so both the laid-off worker and the manager are at the mercy of the structures of our market-based economy. This is an issue.

What Is to Blame?

In the market economy, which is organized primarily to grow and expand, generating profits and dividends, job creation is not a top priority. This simple fact of economic life was pointed out 225 years ago by Adam Smith, a Scottish thinker who was a strong supporter of free markets and manufacturing. There were no railroads or steam engines, and the industrial revolution was in its earliest stages. But this early analyst of capitalism was very clear on what lay ahead:

> The consideration of his own private profit is the sole motive which determines the owner of any capital to employ it either in agriculture, in manufactures, or in some particular branch of the wholesale or retail trade. The different quantities of productive labour which it may put into motion never enter his thoughts.[13]

The private-profit motive that Adam Smith celebrated spurred capitalists to mechanize agriculture and industrialize manufacturing. This first Industrial Revolution led to expanding job opportunities in fast-growing cities and absorbed labour displaced from agriculture. Instead of working for themselves on farms, people began working long hours for others in factories. The standard job was ten to twelve hours a day.

After World War II, when industry accelerated the replacement of people with machines and women entered the formal labour force in larger numbers, the increased labour supply of baby boomers was absorbed by job opportunities in the expanding service industries. The service sector includes repairing photocopiers, selling cell phones, and filling fast-food orders. It also fills needs for health care and education. Service work is done by office employees, consultants, retail clerks, social workers, teaching assistants, and so on. Although these activities do not produce concrete material products like cars, they form an ever more important part of the economy.

We all know that few Canadians work as farmers any more. Just as the Industrial Revolution made manufacturing grow, a second change has been underway. In 1951, when the baby boomers were being born, factory work accounted for one in four jobs. By the turn of the twenty-first century, fewer than one in seven Canadians worked in manufacturing. Before the 1980s, when employment tailed off in one area, there always seemed to be something else opening up. The unemployment of the 1980s and 1990s, however, was different from earlier downturns. Like jobs in agriculture and manufacturing, "standard" jobs – full-time positions working for large businesses or governments – started to evaporate.

Much of this change occurred in the rapidly expanding service sector, where seven of ten Canadians work. Nearly 90 per cent of the job growth since 1967 has been in this highly diversified sector. These service jobs differ dramatically. This reflects another important trend in the job market: polarization. Computer consultants sell their expensive services to business and government, while young people pour coffee at the drive-through. One government report that pointed this polarization out was called *Good Jobs, Bad Jobs: Employment in the Service Economy*.[14]

The lower-level work is often called "nonstandard," in reference to the old standard of

> The shadow of fear is nipping at your heels no matter how fast you go. Fear of losing your job, your money, your food, your home. No talisman can protect you from the curse of sudden bad luck. From one moment to the next, even the greatest winner can turn into a loser unworthy of forgiveness or compassion.
>
> Who is safe from the terror of unemployment? Who doesn't fear being shipwrecked by new technologies or by globalization or any other of the many storms whipping today's world? The waves pound furiously: the ruin or flight of local industries, competition with cheap labor from other latitudes, the implacable advance of machines that need no salary or vacation or bonus or pension or severance pay or anything but the electricity that feeds them.
>
> — Eduardo Galeano,
> *Upside Down: A Primer for the Looking-Glass World*, 2000.

regular, full-time work at thirty-five or forty hours per week. Many positions at the bottom of the service sector are part-time waitressing or security guard jobs. Other people do short-term telemarketing contracts on commission. Many, like one-truck movers, are self-employed. In the period from 1989 to 1998, part-time employment grew by 16.1 per cent, while full-time employment rose much more slowly, by 2.4 per cent. In the same period, self-employment rose by 39.6 per cent, accounting for 58 per cent of the new jobs created during this period.[15]

What do these changes mean for the world of work? For one thing, they offer people wider choices in when and how to work. Some people, particularly students and women with small children, want to work part-time. In fact, the majority of people who work part-time choose to do so. Even so, this choice may be dictated by other factors. For many women with children, lack of affordable child care often means that choices are made for them. Some young people might prefer to study full-time, but the rising cost of education makes this choice impossible.

Creating your own job and working for yourself offer intangible benefits. Being your own boss is an attractive idea. We live in an age when individual entrepreneurs are often admired for their steady, hard-working habits. Government programs aimed at dealing with unemployment emphasize the way that jobless people can become entrepreneurs. Of course, self-employment is nothing new. Most Canadian families — men, women, and children — were once self-employed in that they worked their own farms. Today, self-employment means anything from running your own legal or accounting practice to staying home to look after toddlers whose parents are out working.

Such trends in the job market lead to increased polarization. Whatever the mix of such work, it generally has several things in common. The pay is low. It is not unionized. It tends to go to women and young people. It offers little in the way of stability or benefits. Obviously, part-time jobs do not pay as well as full-time jobs because the hours of work are shorter. What's more, part-timers are paid less per hour than full-timers. In 1999 they earned an average of $11.84 per hour for 17.4 hours of work compared to $16.08 for full-time workers.[16]

The situation of self-employed Canadians, the category that saw such dramatic growth in the 1990s, stands out as a symbol of the polarization of the job market as a whole. Some self-employed people are at the very top of the income pyramid (doctors, owners of successful businesses both small and large), while others form the base of the pyramid (women who clean houses for other people). In 1995, 45 per cent of self-employed people earned less than $20,000, compared to 25 per cent of people working for others.

In the 1980s two-thirds of the increase in self-employment came in small businesses that employed other people. This changed in the following decade, when nine out of every ten people who started working for themselves were on their own. They had no employees. The 1990s also saw bigger increases in self-employment among women than men. But the wage gap between women and men is even wider among the self-employed than it is among employees. Self-employed women working full-time on contract for companies or government agencies all year round earn an average of 74 per cent of what men make. Self-employed women make only 64 per cent of the average earnings of self-employed men. Some 72 per cent of women who are self-employed earn less than $20,000, compared to 40 per cent of female employees.[17]

"Productive" Jobs and the Social Wage

The two trends – increasing polarization in the job market, and governments that are not inclined to offset the increasing differences in what people earn in the good jobs/bad jobs economy – raise important questions.

- How are millions of workers who are either *under*employed in non-standard jobs – or unemployed altogether – going to support themselves and their families?

- What jobs await young Canadians graduating from school and expecting something to do for a living? They want to earn their way, and they need money to support themselves. They want to contribute something to society. They want to feel useful.

- Is our society itself becoming increasingly polarized, with an ever-widening gap between the haves and the have-nots?

Back in 1983, a railway worker in Northern Ontario reflected on the changes in his industry. He was worried about the elimination of the cabooses that were attached to the end of every freight train in those days – as well as of the well-paid jobs like the one that had helped support his family. "They aren't making any provision for getting young people into the workforce because they don't know what to do with them in that workforce." Subsequently, with the privatization of Canadian National Railways and the emergence of a North American rail market, tens of thousands of Canadian railway jobs disappeared.

The surplus of idle and underemployed workers makes no sense when there are countless socially valuable jobs that need to be done. Many tasks, particularly those in which people help people, have been cut back severely. Governments have reduced spending on social services. Nursing jobs were eliminated and training for nurses cut back, and now Canada faces a crisis because there are not enough nurses. Parents find it hard to get suitable child care. The educational system falls victim to spending restraint, and class sizes increase. Universities and colleges scramble for dollars while laying off staff.

Scientists cannot find money for important research. Extensions for public transit systems stay on the drawing boards, while fares rise and highways are clogged with cars that spew toxic gases into the environment. Music, theatre, and other artistic endeavours are squeezed for lack of government support.

Some of these services are called the *social wage*, because they make benefits available to all members of society. Some of these benefits help to reduce hardship, while others make life more meaningful and pleasant, expanding our horizons.

Child care, research, and culture, however, are not seen as "productive" activities in the same way that the pure market economy treats mining zinc or growing wheat or producing automobiles, refrigerators, and weapons. But these "productive" jobs and others like them are becoming more capital-intensive (the proportion of machines increases) and less labour-intensive (fewer worker-hours are needed to produce a given quantity of goods). The notion of productivity, and the manner in which wealth and work are distributed in Canada, need rethinking.

What kinds of work *should* people be doing? A lot of creative but unemployed energy is being wasted, while human services are being diminished. Meanwhile, a lot of money, creativity and people-power is being used to market gas-guzzling SUVs, vehicles that are dangerous, squander non-renewable resources, and require fewer and fewer workers to build (see chapter seven). This is the sort of paradox that social analysis can examine. Cutbacks in people-oriented services like health care and education are questionable not just because of the loss of those services. There are also big job payoffs that come from investing in nurses and teachers. Far away at the other end of the scale is spending on the military, which generates comparatively few jobs for the money spent.

One argument against investing in social services is that they are not productive activities because nothing saleable or tradeable results. Such services do not, according to this argument, create wealth. But primary (mining, forest products) and secondary (manufacturing) industries need fewer workers to produce more goods. These goods are Canada's wealth. To spend some of this wealth on the social wage is not to waste it, but to use it in a socially conscious way to improve the quality of life for everyone.

Support for social service jobs in which people help people is by no means the only answer to the problems that plague Canada's job market. But a human-oriented society would opt for jobs that help people and provide creative opportunities rather than tolerate wasteful unemployment. Otherwise, the tragedy of the unemployed and the underemployed will inevitably become a permanent feature of Canadian life.

Just-in-Time

Clearly, unemployment makes little sense from a human or social perspective. But two questions underpin social analysis when we examine an issue like this. "Who wins?" and "Who loses?" There is only one social group that could be said to benefit from a lot of people being out of work or working too few hours to get by: employers. A high jobless rate tends to exert downward pressure on the wage demands of people who still have jobs. Workers have a basic instinct: when there are a lot of unemployed people ready to take any job, you are well advised not to make demands for higher wages.

This labour-market chill also affects on-the-job attitudes. If you are a student working part-time at a low-wage retail or restaurant job, there is no union, and no union rules about your rights. Perhaps the boss is being unfair about giving the best shifts to his or her favourite employees. Maybe a fellow worker is being harassed by suggestive comments from a manager who finds her attractive. If you are working in Fort McMurray, where there are lots of jobs for fast-food workers, you're more likely to feel free to quit than you are in St. John's, where you know you will have a hard time finding another job.

So when unemployment is high, the labour market becomes a buyer's market. The supply of workers outstrips the demand to the point where

"I worked at a pizza place for a couple of months, but I wanted to find another job. There was lots of pressure and the manager was always looking at you kind of dirty . . . he never touched me but he would say things that really make you feel uncomfortable. But I had to have a job . . . it was stressful. I was always afraid I might lose my job . . . it's not like you have a union." (Service sector worker, Saskatchewan)

"It's hard to find a job with my education. My experience has always been in retail . . . now there are only part-time jobs. I took evening courses in data processing because I thought I would have to need to know how to work with computers. But offices have changed a great deal since I was in school. . . It's hard to keep up." (An unemployed, single mother, in her mid-fifties, Ontario)

— from Morley Gunderson, Leon Muszynski, and Jennifer Keck, *Women and Labour Market Poverty*, 1990.

the price of labour, the commodity in question, declines. Workers are forced to put up with more difficult or unpleasant conditions on the job. The power of unions declines as management gains an extra advantage at the bargaining table.

As the balance has tilted in favour of employers, a new management watchword has become common: flexibility. This sounds like a common-sense notion. You have to be flexible, bending with the shifting winds that are changing the way the economy is organized. The opposite of being flexible is being rigid, and that sounds negative. If you are too rigid to take a poorly paid part-time job because you want (or need) full-time work that pays the bills, well, that's your problem. The world doesn't owe you a living.

With the growth of non-standard employment, more people work on a stand-by basis. They have to be flexible enough to be called in at any time. Gone are the days when only professionals like doctors carried beepers on their belts or in their purses. Many cost-cutting organizations have borrowed a Japanese management approach that emphasizes a "Just-in-Time"

system of inventory. The idea is to have the goods you need arrive at the factory just in time to be used when needed, rather than keeping a warehouse full of expensive parts and raw materials.

Similarly, managers now prefer "Just-in-Time" workers who can be brought in when needed and sent home when not required. This accounts in part for the rise of temporary and part-time work. It is also a reason that so many people are self-employed, selling their services on a short-term contract basis to institutions that have downsized and are replacing permanent workers with contractors.

This trend away from standard work and the standard workweek has increased the polarization in the labour market, with more people working shorter hours and more working longer hours. This trend started in the mid-1970s. The number of part-time workers rose by 120 per cent in the twenty years after 1976, while the number of full-time employees grew by just under 35 per cent. In the same period the proportion of workers with less than thirty-four hours a week rose from 15.9 per cent to 23.6 per cent. Meanwhile, the proportion of workers putting in very long hours (fifty or more) increased from 11.7 per cent to 14.8 per cent.[18]

Poorly paid part-time jobs are often occupied by women, young people, visible minorities, and new Canadians. "Because part-time jobs offer employers more flexibility and lower benefit costs, the increase was largely employer-driven," Statistics Canada observed just after the trend to non-standard work had become obvious.[19] Among young people, 42.2 per cent work part-time, and among women over twenty-five, the figure is 21.1 per cent.[20]

An economy that requires people to juggle one, two, or even three part-time jobs along with their family or school schedules is unprecedented – at least outside the home. For aside from their paid work, many women also bear most of the burden for work at home, looking after children and perhaps elderly parents. The job of housewife demands a high degree of flexibility: it can include chauffeur, cook, laundress, cleaner, childcare worker, nurse, schedule manager, crisis counsellor – the list seems limitless. A housewife, always on call, has to juggle a number of competing demands at once. Coincidentally, some of the new, non-standard jobs, such as teleworking and piecework sewing, are also done from the home.

The work of the "flexiworker," like that of the housewife, is undervalued in our society. Housewives receive no pay for all the skill, energy, and long hours that they bring to their ever-flexible work. Similarly, the new part-time, temporary, and self-employed workers are paid at the bottom end of the wage scale.

The trend towards more Canadians becoming "housewife-ized" is another piece of the social picture, a piece that helps us get a clearer picture of how society is changing – or is being changed.

Flexibility or Deregulation?

Business leaders urge government to privatize the economy, cut red tape, and get out of the way so that the private market can drive the economy. When it comes to the labour market, this movement takes the form of what the chief economist for a major Canadian brokerage firm calls the "creative destruction" of the market. She urges government to concentrate on supplying employers with trained workers and warns against interfering with the demand side of the labour market. Left alone, the market will create a demand for jobs. "The markets do not lie," says Sherri Cooper. "Government should foster an environment of creative destruction, of an ever-advancing labour force through education and training."[21]

Even though Adam Smith long ago pointed out that private capital is primarily committed not to job creation but to profitability and expansion, governments in Canada have, by and large, heeded the Canadian economist's advice (though political leaders hesitate to talk about creative destruction). The emphasis is on replacing "passive dependence" on supports like unemployment insurance and social welfare with "active" employment programs. In 1996, when the federal government made it so difficult to collect (much-reduced) benefits that less than half the contributors to the plan could use it, it changed the name of the former Unemployment Insurance program to Employment Insurance. The goals were to keep people who had paid insurance premiums from collecting and to concentrate on the supply side of the labour market by promoting skills training and upgrading. Job-skill upgrading, life skills, and job readiness programs place a major emphasis on self-employment assistance and "flexibility."

There is, however, another way for social analysis to look at these changes. Instead of an approach that stresses individual workers, their skills, and flexibility, this analysis looks at the labour market as a whole and emphasizes whether or not it is regulated or deregulated.

For an example of a deregulated job market, we can look to the United States, where unemployment insurance and welfare programs are weak and workers who want to form unions can be easily fired. Or we can look at Canada as it was a century ago. Back then, many people worked for themselves on the farm. Those who made the move to factories in the city had no protection from their employers if they tried to form unions, and the government offered no help to families whose breadwinners were out of work. There was no such thing as a minimum wage.

"In this type of labour market," explains an economist with a major Canadian union, "the terms and conditions of employment will be determined primarily through private contracts between employers and individual workers [so that] the incomes and economic prospects of workers will depend on what they are able to earn in that private, competitive labour market."[22]

Over the course of the twentieth century Canadian workers gained more on-the-job rights and protections. They formed unions to bargain collectively with their employers. During those decades government gradually moved to put publicly funded social programs in place, from medicare to public pensions to unemployment insurance. With such reforms, the public sector regulated the private market to moderate the hardships of sickness, old age, and joblessness.

More recently, with the return to a way of thinking in which the risks of unemployment are assigned to individuals, self-reliance once again overshadows social solidarity. Collective bargaining is more difficult because many provinces have made it harder to organize unions, and contracting out has returned more labour relations to the days of individual contracts between worker and employer. Government support of the trend to self-employment is particularly important here.

Against this background, the Canadian job market has made a U-turn in the direction of the individualism and polarization that prevailed at the turn of the twentieth century, when the gap between rich and poor had not yet been narrowed by interventions in the market and its regulation by governments and unions. The emphasis on job training is especially important here.

Employers and government emphasize the supply side of the labour market, concentrating on shortages of skilled workers. When the Canadian Federation of Independent Business surveyed its members, 45 per cent of the firms reported that they had difficulties finding "qualified labour to meet their employment needs." At the same time, three-quarters of the employers reporting skill shortages also complained that workers' wage demands were too high. The study that reported this also noted, "Employees are never sufficiently qualified according to their bosses."

While the number of jobs requiring a university diploma jumped 40 per cent in the 1970s and 1980s, the number of Canadian graduates in the labour market increased by 140 per cent. Between 1987 and 1997, when the demand for computer programmers and systems analysts grew as computers became cheaper and the Internet became a fixture, enrolment in university computer science courses rose by 21 per cent and in community colleges by 49 per cent.[23] Overall, a study for the Organization for Economic Cooperation and Development (OECD) showed that Canada's population was among the best-educated in the world and that it led the industrialized nations in the proportion of adults with post-secondary education.[24]

Canadians are told that tomorrow's prosperity will depend on a skilled workforce ready to deal with the information economy. They are already well-educated, but other countries have an even more advanced system. Scandinavian countries are noted for their "learning cultures," in which workers can easily take time off for adult education without suffering losses in income.

Clearly, training and education are important, especially as technological change alters many jobs. Yet government overemphasis on the supply of trained workers ignores the demand side of the labour market and the development of the good jobs/bad jobs polarization. That, in turn, influences how we think about unemployment, underemployment, and the growing gap between rich and poor – encouraging us to see them as private troubles, not public issues.

Poverty and Wealth – and Social Priorities

Canadians live in one of the richest countries in the world, in a society where there is more than enough to provide for their food, clothing, housing, and the rest of their material needs. If there is less work around, but just as much – if not more – wealth being generated by that work, why not share both the work and the wealth resulting from it? If less work is required to produce more wealth, perhaps it makes sense to consider reducing the hours that each person spends on the job while maintaining rates of pay.

At the turn of the twentieth century, when people routinely worked over fifty hours each week, employers resisted demands for a forty-hour week with the same vigour they showed in arguing against the abolition of child labour. Today, along with all the other improvements brought about through regulation of the job market, children no longer toil in factories and the workweek has been reduced.

In the not-too-distant future, people might be able to work two and a half days a week rather than five; or eleven days a month rather than twenty-two; or five and a half months a year instead of eleven. If people were adequately paid for this reduced work, they would have more time to spend with their families, pursue creative pastimes, enrol in courses that would enrich their lives and enhance their skills, or even do unpaid or volunteer work that they want to do. The time they do spend at work might also be more "productive."

A reduction in working hours would require redistributing the national income resulting from work. A twenty-hour week paid at a forty-hour rate – where would the money come from? Such an innovation could easily double the cost of labour in this country, possibly leading to a flight of capital as investors sought better returns elsewhere. Canadian products might rise in price, putting them at a competitive disadvantage in international markets.

The Canadian economy does not exist in a vacuum. This is the era of globalization and intense international competition. Capital can move around the world at the touch of a button. Free-trade agreements make it easy for businesses to relocate to countries where workers can be hired for a dollar a day (see chapter nine). But globalization is a process that involves not just markets and competition, but also trends towards insecurity and inequality, unemployment and underemployment.

As a rule, the people who control capital are interested not in the redistribution of wealth or working time but in the expansion of their own resources. Yet economic growth by itself, under present circumstances, promises little in the way of social justice for the jobless and the poor. Clearly, the problems of the labour market defy simple solutions. But it is equally obvious that the pattern thus far – limitless growth and the production of more goods by fewer corporations – is not leading to more good jobs for more people. On the contrary, it is leading to an increasingly polarized society.

What is new in this "postindustrial age" is the irreversible displacement of people from the economy. Blaming individual workers or managers sheds little light on this tragedy. A better analysis links the topsy-turvy job market to the structures within which decisions are routinely made. If a job market fractured between the haves and have-nots represents a critical problem to be solved – rather than the price to be paid for economic growth – then quite different, more creative, and human-centred priorities must guide economic decision-making in Canada.

The fundamental question concerns the use of capital. If the one and only motive for economic activity is to generate private profit and foster corporate growth, then by the logic of the market system the present trends will continue. Capital could, though, be used primarily to generate good jobs and foster people's creativity. That would involve more public control over capital. Such a path forward demands a break from the ways of the past. It means a redistribution of both wealth and work. It means mobilizing both resources and technology to serve social priorities.

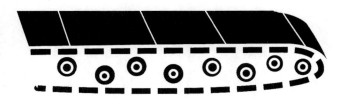

Questions

❏ Do you think a job is a basic human right? What is the public attitude towards people who are unemployed? Is it their fault or are they simply victims of larger circumstances?

❏ Do you or other people you know hold down part-time jobs while attending school? Is this common among students in your community? Do students who also work do so to pay for their education, to get some extra pocket money, or both? Do you feel that students regard part-time jobs as a temporary measure, or are they worried about the availability of good jobs upon graduation? Do you think that young Canadians worry about being stuck with no choice but a "McJob"?

❏ Is there anyone you know who is unemployed? Is there a family member who can't find a job? How long have they been looking for work? Have they had to think of relocating or revising their expectations downwards?

❏ Is there a group or association of the unemployed in your area? What are they doing? Are there ways of supporting such groups?

❏ When it comes to finding a job, do you think that the "YO-YO" ("You're on your own") approach is the most appropriate? Or do you rely on family contacts and friends to help you out? Do you think that the government has a role to play? What does the government already do to make sure that there are enough jobs out there? Should we depend on private enterprise to create jobs? Do ordinary people have the power to do anything about unemployment?

❏ What are your images of the "Dirty Thirties"? Do they come from your grandparents? From books, movies, or songs? Or from learning about the Great Depression in school? Do you think that 30 per cent unemployment could ever afflict Canada again?

Resources

• Linda Duxbury, Christopher Higgens, and Donna Coghill. *Voices of Canadians: Seeking Work-Life Balance.* Ottawa: Human Resources Development Canada, 2003. This report summarizes an exhaustive research study (31,571 Canadians working in organizations employing more than 500 people) and reveals that most organizations promote a work culture that fails to take family and personal life into account.

• Barbara Ehrenreich. *Nickel and Dimed: On (Not) Getting by in Boom-Time America.* New York: Metropolitan Books, 2001. Ehrenreich, a U.S. social critic, went to work as a waitress, hotel maid, cleaning woman, and Wal-Mart sales clerk to find out about the reality of working life at the bottom of a split-level economy. This book offers a different view of the meaning of "flexibility."

• Andrew Jackson and David Robinson. *Falling Behind: The State of Working in Canada.* Ottawa: Canadian Centre for Policy Alternatives, 2000. A close look at how the job market changed in the 1990s, documenting what has happened to jobs, income distribution, and working hours.

• Brian MacLean and Lars Osberg, eds. *The Unemployment Crisis: All for Nought?* Montreal and Kingston: McGill-Queen's University Press, 1996. A technical examination of the most recent period of high unemployment, this collection of essays argues that different government policy could have accomplished more to reduce joblessness.

• Bruce O'Hara. *Working Harder Isn't Working.* Vancouver: New Star Books, 1993. How we can return the Canadian economy — as well as ourselves and the environment — to balance by adopting shorter work hours.

• Jamie Swift. *Wheel of Fortune: Work and Life in the Age of Falling Expectations.* Toronto: Between the Lines, 1995. An examination of how the transformation of work and the job market affects the lives of ordinary people in Canada. The book questions the idea that the solution to unemployment is more training and education.

Websites:

Human Resources Development Canada (HRDC) maintains a website with other studies, including *Work-Life Compendium 2001: 150 Canadian Statistics on Work, Family and Well-Being.*

Provincial federations of labour provide information on the employment situation in each province; look at their websites. Check also the websites of the Canadian Labour Congress and the major national unions like the Canadian Union of Public Employees, Communications, Energy and Paperworkers, Canadian Autoworkers, and United Steelworkers.

The Vanier Institute for the Family website contains information about how the changing job market affects families, and includes links to other social policy groups. Look for links to research organizations and local unemployment help groups.

Chapter Six

Social Analysis Again

Social analysis starts with very normal concerns. Perhaps you are visiting with some friends from the United States, and you end up chatting about various ailments or the times the kids had to be taken to the doctor. The discussion soon turns to the differences between the health-care systems in Canada and the United States.

You might never have thought about the advantages of Canadian medicare, but your U.S. friends can't take medical care for granted. They are not assured of good medical care unless they can pay for it out of their own pockets. Their experience might leave you feeling thankful for Canadian medicare, but worried also about how secure it is. You might wonder how it can best be organized to recover from some of the setbacks it has already suffered while meeting rising health-care costs. You have questions for social analysis.

Or perhaps you have met some who arrived in Canada as a refugee from Africa but who cannot find work in her field because entrance requirements are different here. While taking the courses that will give her the Canadian credentials necessary to requalify, she is working at two part-time jobs, one for cash "under the table." Why is she subjected to harassment from people born here, who accuse her of taking work from "real" Canadians?

Increasing numbers of people living on the streets have made the housing crisis in Canada visible for citizens of cities and towns all across the country. Newspaper reports of deaths from exposure or fires in substandard rooming houses express the urgency of the situation. Many Canadians, alarmed by so much poverty amidst so much wealth, have responded by volunteering their services at local soup kitchens or donating to shelters for the homeless. A church opens up a "warming room" in an already overused recreation hall. Some people also ask critical questions about the causes of homelessness. Why do so many people have inadequate shelter? Can we find something better than a Band-aid solution for this problem?

Activists across the country gather information about the experiences of people who are on housing waiting lists, people who live in insecure housing, people on the streets. What they find out helps to counter the victim-blaming or poor-bashing stereotypes that enable politicians to avoid dealing with the issue. Sharing information with concerned individuals and organizations across the country makes it possible to construct policy proposals and leads to concerted efforts to lobby national, provincial, and municipal governments to take decisive action. It may be too soon to breathe a sigh of relief, but it looks as though these efforts are beginning to pay off.

A conversation, an experience, a newspaper story, a discussion, a personal or family crisis: these can all serve to bring urgent questions to the forefront. Something unfamiliar and unexamined – doctors' bills or rumours about rezoning to allow construction of a new megastore – can suddenly require examination. But this is an age that reveres experts and scientists. So, in addition to feeling concerned, people also need to become equipped to do the necessary analysis.

Experts may have an aura of objectivity, but they can also be used to support a specific position. They can intimidate citizens and the media or end up by simply confusing the issue. Experts can also have important and precise information to contribute. For example, an economist can analyze the relative costs of community-based nursing care and the savings to be reaped by closing hospital beds. Doctors can explain the medical benefits of using the new diagnostic technology that a for-profit medical institution could offer its patients. Still, specialists do not automatically hold a monopoly on correct interpretation, and they should not necessarily be allowed to sit in judgement over an entire issue. We can still ask about other costs and benefits that might have been overlooked. Will enough community-care services be offered when the hospital beds are closed? Who will have access to the new diagnostic technology?

That is why social analysis is often a matter of people developing their own expertise as well as learning to identify experts who can contribute to the solution of the community's problem.

The purpose of this chapter is to pause and reflect: What happens when we do social analysis? What kind of expertise has been acquired?

> Our wish for Canadian society is not for a nostalgic return to the 1950s when the nation's ambition was for one good job in every family (usually the husband's) and a suburban home. That vision of social bliss was flawed by its emphasis on conspicuous consumption and by its promotion of social invisibility for women. For many families it was never a reality, in any case.
>
> Our goals, which are today's and not yesterday's dreams, are more cooperative than those of the early post-World War II era. We want a society where all work and the work of all are valued. We want a society where people labour together to produce the housing, clothing, food, child care, and medical care which we all require. We strive for a sustainable society which values and protects the earth's non-human life.
>
> — Ecumenical Coalition for Economic Justice, *Reweaving Canada's Social Programs: From Shredded Safety Net to Social Solidarity*, 1993.

Learning to Read

Some people never have the opportunity of learning to read. About 22 per cent of Canadians over sixteen years old – about five million people – have serious problems dealing with any printed materials. Another 24 to 26 per cent have reading skills that enable them to "deal only with material that is simple and clearly laid out, and material in which the tasks involved are not too complex."[1] They get into trouble, for example, when they have to read a map, look for information in the classified ads, or fill out an order form. These limitations represent serious handicaps to participation in society. Functionally illiterate adults can't accurately read a label to determine the correct dose of medicine to give to a child, or can't fill out a bank deposit slip correctly. They can't compare the ingredients of breakfast cereal for their children.

What is illiteracy like in a country in which every adult is presumed to be literate? An Ottawa man spent most of his life unable to read and write. "Going shopping was a pain. I always got someone to go with me because I couldn't read the labels . . . I thought I was the only one in the world who couldn't read."

Reading and writing are, without question, critical to active participation in our society today. Illiteracy can present a barrier to full participation in life.

There is another, even more common, form of illiteracy that also prevents people from participating in society, and that is social illiteracy. For example, given the shortage of affordable housing in Canada:

■ How did the shortage arise?

■ What is its impact?

■ Why does it continue?

■ What can be done about it?

A person might recognize that the questions are important, but not know where to begin, what to ask or think or say. Not knowing where to begin is an experience of social illiteracy.

Social illiteracy means being unable to read – to interpret – the events that are going on in society. Unfortunately, few institutions teach Canadians to read social reality. A good percentage of our population remains unaware of how society works or where it is headed.

There is another interesting parallel between the understanding of language and society. Once upon a time, people thought of language as something forever fixed and unchanging, "a gift of the gods." But the study of linguistics makes it clear that every word is a human creation; language is inherited, and it evolves as it is used.

Similarly, people also used to think of human society as something God-given or eternal, as divinely created or the result of an age-old and unchangeable social contract. Today nearly everyone agrees that social institutions are human creations: the deliberate product of human ideas and the result of habitual human action. As evolving human creations, social structures and institutions are something people can learn about and understand – and change.

Learning to read – whether you are using a native language or a foreign one – is a somewhat mysterious process. What's involved? Certainly it doesn't mean memorizing a grammar text or dictionary. First of all, it means connecting sounds with letters, pictures with words. The learner grasps individual words, builds up a vocabulary, starts recognizing new words from their context. With time this process develops into expertise, which allows the newly literate person to understand the messages communicated by sentences and paragraphs.

To read tolerably well, you don't have to understand how language works, any more than driving a car requires an understanding of motor mechanics. Still, an acquaintance with how language works can make the learning more interesting and effective. The study that explains the building blocks (parts of speech) and the workings (rules) of language is grammar – the subject nearly everyone remembers as rather dull and forbidding.

Beginning to do social analysis is like learning

how to read: you learn by doing. The preceding chapters on health, housing, the marketplace, and unemployment are four introductory "readings" of social reality. This chapter goes on to present elements of the grammar of social literacy, some of the building blocks and workings of social analysis.

Four of these building blocks are symptoms, commodification, social costs, and structures. Although these "parts of speech" flow directly out of the discussion of the four previous chapters, they are also just as likely to emerge when we analyze other Canadian issues. Different parts and patterns will also emerge in the remaining chapters of the book – and still others will be found or invented as people go on to build their own social analysis.

Symptoms

Pain or malaise is often all too obvious. Good medical practice begins with a thorough description of the ailment, so we don't merely treat the symptoms with painkillers, but instead discover and remove the cause of the sickness. Anatomy and physiology provide an ideal picture of the whole body. The diagnostician can compare this picture with what has broken down and what is functioning properly.

Social malaise is also there on the surface for people to see: witness Canadians suffering from lack of access to adequate health care, affordable homes, nourishing food, or wages to pay for the necessities of life. Sometimes the malady, though perfectly obvious to those suffering from it, is hidden from those others who are well provided for. To note carefully, describe, categorize, and finally explore the symptoms – that is one task of social analysis.

Yet another link exists between medical diagnosis and social analysis. Bodily illness itself can be a symptom of social injustice. Infant mortality, reduced life expectancy, malnutrition, and many diseases are often symptoms of a social malaise, economic injustice, or political or cultural oppression. Moreover, these medical problems can be documented and quantified as proof that people's rights are being violated.

Commodification

The tendency to reduce a person or relationship to an object of economic value, a commodity to be bought and sold in the marketplace, is called commodification. Reification is the first step in this process. The word reification comes from the Latin word *res*, meaning thing or object. It refers here to the tendency to reduce a person or a relationship to the status of an object. Commodification is the next step, the step that transforms the object into an item of economic exchange, something whose purpose is to be bought and sold.

Chapters Two and Three, without mentioning these strange-sounding terms, brought them into play. People who say Canadians have the "right to choose" where to spend their "after-tax dollars" often use arguments that shift health care away from its position as a basic human right and into the realm of a commodity. "Healthy people might choose to purchase a new car. Those who need diagnosis and treatment for illness should be able to spend their money to secure it," one writer says – thus comparing health care to going out and buying a car.[2] Similarly, having decent, affordable shelter, which is a basic need and human right, has been commodified into a market-driven product, a consumer item available to those who can afford it.

Another, extreme example of this process would be to turn the fire department into a private business. What would citizens think of fire-fighters offering their services to individuals on a pay as you go basis? Obviously, at the moment of crisis everyone (except those who had private insurance) would feel held up to ransom by the firefighting company. The poor would not have the same access to fire protection as those who could afford the premiums.

Social analysis tries to make clear how basic necessities of life are transformed into commodities. It tries to show where a market mentality is intruding on relationships – with other people, with nature – that reflect respect for such fundamental rights as the right to adequate nutrition, health care, housing, and useful work. And it tries to indicate the responsibility of various social groups (government, investors, employers, labour, consumers) to protect these rights.

Social Costs

When big players in the food industry put small local producers and retailers out of business, the social costs often go unrecognized and end up being paid by the community at large, now or later. When developers choose to shift their money from housing to seemingly more lucrative shopping malls and office towers, their profits — and their losses — are not balanced by any accounting of the losses that Canadian taxpayers, tenants, and would-be tenants incur through this decision.

By themselves, profit-and-loss and other business categories fail to take long-term questions of health, aesthetics, culture, justice, or even jobs into account. Social analysis does take illness, pollution, and injustice into account, on the debit side. On the credit side it attends to human health and well-being, the flourishing of communities and their individual members. It analyzes these conditions as social costs and benefits that otherwise go unreckoned. Using this kind of analysis, citizens can see to it that the people who profit also repair the damages they cause, or pay for their repair, and that costs are not imposed on workers and communities without their knowledge and consent.

Structures

The word "structure" is familiar enough when it is being used as a reference to buildings — the Peace Tower, the Regina parliament buildings, a local hockey arena, or a high-rise apartment building. These become structures because a lot of parts — foundations, stairways, windows, rooftops — get set up in a certain pattern to form a whole.

It is the same with social structures. They are not so visible to the naked eye, but they are just as real as the prominent mass of the Château Frontenac or a grain elevator. We can identify social structures when we consider relationships, such as those involving:

- patient, health worker, doctor, hospital
- consumer (tenant or buyer), landlord, developer
- citizen, industry, regulator, newspaper.

Social analysis takes common relationships and considers them not as separate, isolated units but as parts of a whole, as parts of a structure. It unveils the more general structures that define and shape these common relationships, that construct the meaning and set the limits of our daily activities.

The structures can be beneficial or harmful in their effects on people. Too frequently they favour a few and damage the many. They may be invisible to the eye, but they are just as much "always there" — and apparently just as much beyond the power of the individual citizen to move as the Halifax Citadel.

There are structures of different kinds: social, economic, cultural, political, religious. Social analysis has to adapt its approach to each issue, to find out what kind of structures are most important in a given situation. In the case of the medical profession, financial interests (which are part of certain economic structures) play a decisive role. But cultural and political considerations also serve to determine the nature of the relationship between doctors and patients or attitudes towards pay-as-you-go services.

The word "structure," as it is used in social analysis, suggests that root causes are not individual, but rather institutional; not transitory, but solid and long-lasting. Social analysis involves discovering, describing, explaining, and ultimately challenging the structures that define social existence in Canada — dismantling the destructive structures and rebuilding according to sounder principles of social justice.

Ways of Reading

Learning to read is a fairly complex activity that can be broken down into a number of simpler components, like sounding out the letters in each word, recognizing whole words, recognizing how they work together with punctuation in

phrases, sentences, and larger grammatical structures like paragraphs or even chapters. The activities of social reading and interpretation can also be broken down into a number of simpler processes, which are eventually brought together in the complex we call social analysis.

Examining Commonly Accepted Beliefs

The economic and political structures of Canada are primarily – but not exclusively – responsible for giving the country its shape. Patterns of thought and belief also influence the shape of society.

The belief that real estate developers have the right to do what they want with their earnings, or that a competitive marketplace always results in the best readily available goods for meeting human needs, leads society in certain directions. Canadians can quickly march down an unknown path, for instance, if they believe that science always means progress or that the slogan "buyer beware" is all the protection we need from food industry applications of developments in genetic engineering. Staying alert to possible dangers lying further down the road calls for vigilant attention to new scientific developments and a careful reading of how they are represented to the public. It also requires looking carefully for reports and scientific research that avoid the particular biases that come into play when the attention of government and industry research is distracted by the potential for national or private economic growth.

If commonly accepted understandings of issues were always accurate, there would be little need to embark on social analysis. In fact, common notions about society, Canada, and the world often tend to be based on scattered bits of information or even misinformation.

Opinions are promoted as facts, at times unwittingly yet quite vigorously, by radio, television, newspapers, and magazines (see chapter ten). Problems with the labour market, for example, are more likely to be framed by discussions of

supply (lack of trained workers) than of demand (lack of good jobs). The media are more likely to put forward already accepted, official, or established points of view than to report on critical or innovative viewpoints. A critical questioning of commonly accepted beliefs asks whose interests are served by their widespread acceptance. It explores the relationships between the social power of those whose interests are being served and the power that those beliefs have in society.

Tracing History

Nearly every issue has a long history and has been examined many times before. In a historical analysis, the object is to view the past not with nostalgia for the good old days, but critically, with an eye for the effect on the present.

Even in the short lifetime of Canadian medicare there have been periodic crises, with a remarkably consistent pattern of complaints by the medical associations and of responses by people who use the health-care system. That struggle is an essential thread in the process whereby medicare became part of the Canadian social fabric, and in which it continues to evolve.

Chapter three looks at changes since the housing boom of the 1950s and the changes in the structure of housing development. If, for example, people were not aware of the accumulation and concentration of capital in real estate development and still believed that most landlords were small independent entrepreneurs, their analysis of this part of Canadian society would be seriously flawed.

If you were analyzing the relationships involved in the production of a cup of coffee, it would be important to consider what happened in the nineteenth century when indigenous peasants in Central America had their land taken away from them and turned into coffee estates – and what that means to today's coffee growers. Or, again, a great many of the problems posed by new technology today are similar to the ones that arose nearly two centuries ago (see chapter eight). Most social issues have a history that contributes to the problem at hand – and, if understood, can help to explain that problem.

Identifying Key Players and Perspectives

In our discussion of housing, a leading question is: "Who are the players?" From whose perspective shall we analyze this issue? Whose needs and whose interests shape how policy-makers and community members address this issue?

It is clear that some players make decisions and benefit from the choices made. Others, usually would-be tenants – and especially people with low incomes – have little say in what happens, even though they are often harmed in the process.

Perspective analysis is an important method of discovering how society divides into those with decision-making power and those who are powerless. Once the groups or classes have been identified, further questions help to sort them out. Who makes the decisions? Who benefits from the decisions? Who pays the cost of the decisions?[3] These questions clarify the social divisions that both surround an issue and are characteristic of society as a whole.

The questions of who the players are and how evenly the decision-making power is distributed apply easily to many issues besides housing. For example, what roles do the medical establishment, government, pharmaceutical companies, and investors in the growing private-sector "health-care industry" play in the structuring of Canada's health-care system? Who has a say in decisions about the regulation of the food industry? Who benefits from loose regulations?

Perspective analysis can also be applied not only to single issues but also to analysis of larger patterns and social structures. We will see this in the later chapters when we consider Canadian social issues as a whole from the perspectives of women, old people, and Aboriginal peoples.

Moving Back and Forth

We all experience a strong tendency to see individual problems as requiring individual solutions and to see social problems as insoluble. In response to this tendency, social analysis moves in two ways: from the individual case to the social structures in which that case is embedded, and back again; and from "someone's" vague problem

to "everybody's" concrete social issue. The four preceding chapters all provide examples.

- Illness at first appears to be a pre-eminently individual problem. Sick persons usually can't think of anything but their own misery. But going to a doctor would be difficult without medicare, which is a collective, social solution. At the widest social level, if government does not guarantee access to necessary health care or enforce (for instance) water pollution regulations, illness becomes an even more individual, apparently "private" matter.

- Housing is also a problem for every individual person or family. People with trouble finding housing they can afford may believe that they just need to get out and hustle for an appropriate apartment or house. Yet "the market" is not working for many of them. Any real solution to the problem of acquiring decent, affordable lodging must be sought on the social level – for example, by organizing an alternative structure such as a co-op to make housing available.

- The supermarket is a place to buy food for the family. The kind of in-store choices that shoppers can make are determined by market forces that they won't see unless they look beyond the supermarket shelves. At the same time, the choices they make have far-reaching implications for the lives of people who work in the production, processing, and sale of food products at home and all over the world.

- Unemployment can be one of the most socially isolating experiences a person can go through. Yet individual job losses are part of a much larger pattern. Looking at such patterns can raise new questions about how we think about work, how we use our time, energy, and skills, and how opportunities to contribute and to be rewarded for that contribution are distributed throughout society.

Focusing on the System

Many symptoms, many players, many issues, and many structures are interconnected to form a functioning unity. The word "system" suggests how these elements fit together in a set pattern at

There is a growing and widespread consensus emerging among the churches and faith communities that the current direction of public policy is wrong. This consensus is reflected in many public denunciations of federal and provincial policies that threaten the poor, the unemployed, the elderly, First Nations, newcomers to Canada, women, children, and youth.

These policies have resulted in a growing polarization of our society and country. It has resulted in divisiveness between the poor, the unemployed, the working poor, and middle class people. Economic mismanagement and failures in leadership have brought us to the current social crisis. This situation requires wider discussion and participation. Rather than an economics of prosperity, these choices have led to an economics of disparity and despair. There is another way. Canada needs an economics of hope.

— Canadian Conference of Catholic Bishops, "An Ecumenical Statement," February 1996.

a particular moment. "System" links apparently quite different issues and shows how very different groups are actually related.

For example, chapter two begins with symptoms and goes on to look at the root causes of those symptoms, which leads to a discussion of the structures of health-care delivery. The professional associations, medical and pharmaceutical industries, and insurance companies all interconnect. When looked at together these organizations or institutions, and relationships and structures, point towards a system that has to be understood in any effort to strengthen medicare or develop alternative health services.

The analysis in chapter two brings people up against this experience of system. Although the analysis may be partial and tentative, and although more information and analysis are surely necessary to provide a complete picture of the health-care system, still a good beginning can be made.

Getting Started does not speak much of the establishment or the system, as if there were a single grand pattern to explain every Canadian problem and injustice. Instead it acknowledges the complexity of Canadian society, without allowing that complexity to discourage people from beginning to do social analysis.

A clearer focus on a system that ties a whole social issue together provides a greater sense of what makes Canada tick, of how its social, economic, political, and cultural structures interweave and overlap.

Welcome to "The World Around Us"

People can learn how to read social reality without pausing to reflect on the grammar of social analysis. Similarly, people can continue to do social analysis simply by looking at one issue after another. Besides access to health care, better housing, decent nutrition, and meaningful work, other basic needs — such as education, culture, and recreation — are worth analyzing and could easily be added to the reading list.

But eventually it becomes clear that basic issues do not get resolved — or even fully understood — simply as human needs and basic human rights. Almost all social problems have an economic dimension. Health care and housing are treated not as human needs to be met but marketable commodities to be bought and sold. The supermarket is a place where food, another human need, is displayed and sold as a typical commodity. Supply and demand influence the job market, with unemployment levels having an impact on the price you can get for selling the commodity that is your labour.

"Issues in the Everyday" reveals the economic dimensions of our everyday lives on an issue by issue basis. The next part of the book continues to consider economic questions as well as the kinds of social costs and benefits often excluded from economic analysis. It considers the natural environment, the natural world that sustains all life on Earth — a world that has been continually reshaped by technologies, from the wheel to the modem. The newest technologies, we find, are deployed by the forces that both promote something called globalization and also struggle over its meaning. In "A World Around Us," our focus of social analysis widens in search of patterns connected to, or more visible on, a global level.

Chapter Seven

Energy and the Environment

M ost of us believe that we have basic rights: free speech, freedom from discrimination on the basis of sex, freedom of worship, freedom of assembly. Canada's constitution has a Charter of Rights and Freedoms that guarantees such freedoms. But a precious right not enshrined in the charter is seriously threatened: we should have the liberty to enjoy air, water, and the fruits of the earth without the threat of being poisoned.

Ancient peoples worshipped the sun, a source of life. Today we fear the sun as a potential source of deadly tumours. Weather reports include UV readings warning about the risk levels of ultra-violet radiation. Industrial activity has thinned the ozone layer, which once protected life on Earth from the sun's harmful rays. Industry in the rich countries now produces such a superabundance of goods that garbage disposal has become an enormous problem. Human communities have always generated waste. But back when people worshipped the sun, much of their garbage was naturally recycled, put back into the ecosystem to be "exploited by other organisms as part of a per-petual cycle of re-use."[1]

It is difficult, though, to reuse toxic wastes like PCBs and dioxins, not to mention the carbon dioxide that is the by-product of so many high-energy cars and furnaces. The way we use energy shapes society. Coal, the world's most plentiful fossil fuel, powered the industrial revolution, but burning it released unheard of amounts of carbon dioxide. That practice laid the groundwork for one of today's most urgent environmental problems – global climate change. In the age of steam, the problems caused by coal seemed local, and no one thought of the "greenhouse effect." As recently as the 1940s, people in London, England, routinely choked on the smog, but the development of clean-burning coal and tough regulations improved local air quality.

Hydroelectricity (called "white coal" back when they turned on the Niagara Falls generators in 1910) proved to be a cleaner energy source. Hydro megaprojects, however, often flood huge tracts of land, altering whole environments and displacing anyone who lives in the immediate area – which often means Aboriginal peoples. Nuclear power plants may not alter the climate in the way that fossil fuels do, but they are dangerous, unreliable, and extraordinarily expensive.

After World War II, cheap and abundant oil ushered in the transportation age. This form of energy also has its costs. Like coal, this fossil fuel releases carbon dioxide and accelerates climate change. As oil runs out – at present rates of consumption, the world's known reserves will be depleted in forty years – it will become more expensive. Natural gas is cheaper and is the fastest-growing energy source, producing about half the carbon dioxide that an equivalent amount of coal does.

The world has enough proven oil reserves to meet existing demand (73 million barrels per day) for forty years. If demand increases by 2 per cent annually, as predicted by the U.S. Department of Energy, the supply will last for twenty-five years. Even though new oil deposits will be discovered and exploited, significant shortages will emerge well before the middle of this new century. These foreseen shortages have prompted a race for resources, giving rise to wars in the Persian Gulf. Iraq has a tenth of the world's proven oil reserves. Neighbouring Saudi Arabia has a quarter of the oil.[2] The United States depends on imported petroleum, and control over supply is of primary importance to the Americans.

Sometimes the Americans import oil and gas from Canada, which, unlike the United States, is a petroleum exporter. But unlike the United States, Canada emits far more carbon dioxide per capita than do most other industrial countries – about 16.2 tonnes per person per year.[3] The kinds of energy we use and how we use them raise important social issues: control over the decisions regarding resource use; the distribution of power in society; how we use natural resources; how we alter the environment when we use those resources.

The natural environment is a marvellously balanced and self-healing system. Human communities share the global ecosystem with innumerable other animal and plant communities. The global environment is a web in the same way that the World Wide Web consists of uncountable "links" to everything else. Ecology, according to the basic definition, is the branch of science that is concerned with "the relationship between plants and animals and the environment in which they live."[4]

Canada should address the environmental sources of insecurity for current and future generations by establishing concrete and achievable objectives that would ensure the stewardship of natural resources. The present rate of overconsumption in Canada and other industrialized countries represents a squandering of nature that cannot be sustained. The principle of common security requires a commitment to collective responsibility to the earth and to those parts of humanity whose impact on the environment is minimal. Insofar as Canadian life is presently organized in a manner that makes our impact on the environment very large, Canada needs to offer leadership in reducing overconsumption.

— Ecumenical Statement on Canada's International Relations, *Peace with Justice in a Global Community*, 1994.

Indeed, the first rule of ecology is that everything is connected to everything else, so that we commonly refer to the "food chain" to show that life-giving fungi in the soil are linked to people who eat the grain that grows there or animals that eat that grain. This condition – that all creatures from the simplest organism to the most complex are linked in an interdependent fashion – means that the environment – their home, our home – is very much a social concern.

Idling at the Drive-Through

It is a familiar scene: a busy Canadian road dotted with car dealers, Big Box stores, and fast-food restaurants. Many of the vehicles on the road are driven by busy people, by themselves behind the wheel, on the way to work or school. Because they believe they have no time to get out to grab a coffee or a quick bite to eat, they head for one of the drive-through windows, only to find half a dozen vehicles in front of them. Engines idle while they wait to place their orders. There is a good chance that several of the idlers are sports utility vehicles (SUVs), the fastest-growing segment of the North American automotive market.

The scene is so ordinary that most of us would not give it a second look, or a second thought. Social analysis can explore the scene to unpack the meaning, revealing the links that connect it to both the global environment crisis and the ways in which society is organized.

Perhaps one of the vehicles in the lineup at the drive-through is a Discovery, made by Land Rover. Like the Jeeps that spawned the SUV boom, the original British Land Rover was a stripped-down, military-style vehicle designed for rough, off-road use on private estates in the Scottish highlands or on safari in Africa. Today's Land Rover is made by the Ford Motor Company, which bought up the smaller manufacturer. Although advertisements for the New Discovery claim that its huge eight-cylinder engine will "give you the courage to scale the Andes," the targets of that ad – affluent buyers – mainly live in the suburbs.

According to Ford engineer Stephen Ross, an SUV pioneer who designed the successful Explorer, the typical SUV buyer has a family but does not want a minivan because driving that vehicle sends out a "docile" message. Ford's market researchers found out that potential SUV customers were city people with desk jobs who wanted a product that made them feel carefree, bold enough to brave mountains. "What counted," explained Ross, "was the fantasy of what they might want to do."[5] The advertising people hired by Land Rover to promote the Discovery highlighted its wood and leather interior, 12-speaker, 220-watt audio system, and an optional DVD video player. If the drivers could not make it to the Andes, they were assured that at least they would be able to "storm the highway."

The automobile industry overwhelms all others in spending on advertising, supporting the television networks where most Canadians get their information. The SUV-makers are among the biggest, most powerful corporations in the world. What they do not advertise is that a large SUV can emit twice as much carbon dioxide as the average car. It was left to an environmental group to point out that choosing a big SUV over a mid-sized car means that you will burn as much extra energy as leaving the fridge door open for six years. Against this fact stands another reality: by 2002, General Motors had converted eight of its twenty-four North American assembly plants to make SUVs and the "light trucks" to which they are closely related; the world's largest automaker makes a $10,000 profit on its lucrative line of large SUVs.[6]

The image of the big vehicles spewing carbon dioxide and toxic waste as they idle at the drive-through raises important issues. Canadian cities – particularly the sprawling suburbs surrounding older downtown cores – are designed for people in cars. The scene is as common as the drive-through: large, low-density suburbs spreading horizontally across landscapes formerly occupied by farms and vital floodplains. The single-family dwellings have two- or three-door garages out front and extra driveway room to park two or

three cars. The design takes up a lot of land and makes it difficult for people to get around by public transit, because it is expensive to run bus and train lines to serve widely dispersed suburban populations. Canada is the only rich country whose national government does not routinely support public transit in its cities. People choose private automobiles not just because General Motors and Ford stimulate imaginations with catchy advertising campaigns; they choose them because the built environment encourages automobile use.

Anyone who has ever tried to walk to the mall will confirm what anti-smog advocates point out during the Canadian summers that are becoming hotter. Uncontrolled horizontal growth puts private transportation first. It discourages not only public transit but also low-tech, energy-efficient tools like the foot or the bicycle. The air is so polluted with ozone and harmful particulate matter that you can see it. Along with the UV warnings over cancer-causing solar rays, weather reports now include an air quality index warning city dwellers when it is unsafe to participate in risky behaviour, like outdoor breathing.

At the end of the summer of 2002, one of the hottest on record, the City of Toronto moved to ban drive-through restaurants in residential neighbourhoods, citing traffic and noise factors as well as air pollution. Ontario government estimates place the proportion of carbon monoxide emissions contributed by cars to the city's air at 93 per cent. Because pollution is greatest when a vehicle is standing or idling, Toronto had already passed a by-law requiring motorists to turn off their engines when the vehicles are standing for more than three minutes. The restriction on drive-throughs was prompted in part because the "stacking" of vehicles waiting for coffee and burgers often exceeded three minutes. Toronto planners also noted that drive-through-style urban designs require more paved surfaces, which generate more heat and more surface runoff.[7]

The way in which North American cities like Toronto and Los Angeles and countless others have taken shape owes much to how private automobiles and private choice have been allowed to take precedence over the public good, as represented by the environment we all share.

Few would question the basic rights to free speech and free assembly guaranteed by Canada's Charter of Rights. Few would question the right of the SUV to go anywhere, stop anywhere, and remain anywhere that its owner chooses. Of course, you may have trouble finding a parking place, but there is always one available if you have the money to pay for it. That's why some people find the suburbs and malls convenient – there is always ample parking. If you think you can't afford to take the time to park, there is always the drive-through.

Restrictions on drive-throughs not only meet resistance from fast-food chains (Toronto's efforts were opposed in court by McDonald's), but they also address only a tiny tip of the iceberg of the problem of global climate change. City governments do not have the power to deal with the issue. Coming to terms with it requires the co-operation of national governments, working together on an international basis.

In 1992 the world's governments set up the International Panel on Climate Change (IPCC), an organization of two thousand scientists from one hundred nations. The goal was to determine once and for all whether the world was on the brink of environmental disaster because green-house gases were changing the climate. There had already been reports that the ice cap at the North Pole was melting. President Maumoon Abdul Gayoom of the Maldives, a country made up of low-lying islands southwest of India, had already sounded the alarm. His country was in danger of being washed away.

It is in the interest of all the world that climatic changes are understood and the risks of irreversible damage to natural systems, and the threats to the very survival of man, be evaluated and allayed with the greatest urgency . . . it is not too late to save the world. It is not too late to save the Maldives.[8]

In 1995 the Panel reported back to President Gayoom and the rest of the world's leaders that global climate change is a reality and a threat and its most important cause is carbon dioxide released by the burning of fossil fuels – coal, oil, gasoline, and (to a lesser extent) natural gas. Carbon dioxide levels had remained relatively stable for ten thousand years but began to increase with the Industrial Revolution and took off dramatically in the twentieth century when industrialization accelerated. Ice cores drilled from the polar ice caps allow scientists to record the amount of carbon dioxide trapped in tiny bubbles that were embedded in the ice that first fell as snow so long ago.

The IPCC reported that the world is becoming warmer and, if nothing is done, temperatures could rise by up to three degrees Celsius within the next century if nothing is done. That may not sound like a lot, but a temperature drop of that amount brought on the last ice age. Nature's sensitivity is also explained by how our bodies react when our temperature rises even slightly. We feel quite well when our temperature is "normal" (36.7°C), but fever characterized by a small increase of half a degree sends us to bed with aches and chills. According to Canada's senior science advisor on climate change, the country is becoming hotter and wetter. Forest fires will

---

The Earth Charter

Preamble

We are Earth, the people, plants and animals
    rains and oceans
    breath of the forest and flow of the sea

We honour Earth as the home of all living things

We cherish Earth's beauty and diversity of life

We welcome Earth's ability to renew as being
    the basis of all life.

We recognize the special place of Earth's indigenous Peoples,
    their territories, their customs,
    and their unique relationship to Earth.

We are appalled at the human suffering, poverty,
    and damage to Earth
    caused by inequality of power.

We accept a shared responsibility to protect
    and restore Earth
    and to allow wise and equitable use of resources
    so as to achieve an ecological balance
    and new social, economic and spiritual values.

In all our diversity we are one.

Our common home is increasingly threatened.

— prepared by Non-Governmental Organizations gathered in Rio de Janeiro, Brazil, June 3-14, 1992.

---

increase as temperatures rise to unprecedented levels. The ice in the Arctic Ocean is becoming thinner and smaller in area. Sea levels will rise. Winter storms like the ice storm that devastated parts of Ontario and Quebec in 1998 will become more frequent and more intense. The cost of insurance against climate-related natural disasters in the Maldive Islands amounts to 34 per cent of that country's entire Gross Domestic Product. The Kyoto Protocol of 1997, which resulted from the IPCC findings, is only a small first step, and it will not solve the problem.[9]

Social analysis cannot explore the complex details of climate change, determining whether this "hottest summer on record" or that "devastating Prairie farm drought" is the direct result of so many people burning so much fossil fuel. It cannot link the arrival of the deadly West Nile virus to Canada's warmer climate. But it can help to understand the social causes and social costs of a crisis as immense as any that the Earth has ever faced. The picture of the SUV idling at the drive-through provides a starting point.

The Effects

The long boom that followed World War II, accompanied by an explosion of car ownership and suburban sprawl, was based in part on cheap fossil fuel. Baby boomers recall being driven around in huge, gas-guzzling station wagons. Big, wasteful vehicles were affordable because, from 1950 until 1973, the price of a barrel of oil from Saudi Arabia averaged less than two dollars. That all changed in 1973, when Arab states cut off oil exports to the United States to protest U.S. support of Israel in the Arab-Israeli conflict. At the same time OPEC (the Organization of Petroleum-Exporting Countries) announced a quadrupling of the price of oil. Although the embargo was lifted the next year and oil prices stabilized, the "oil shock" had a dramatic effect, underlining the dependence of the rich countries on imported petroleum.

Governments responded with new fuel-efficiency regulations, forcing automotive companies to make vehicles that used less fuel. Today's modern, fuel-efficient sedans are smaller and lighter. They run on a fraction of the fuel needed by the cars of the 1960s. Automakers learned so much that by 2002 big luxury cars like Ford's Lincoln were burning as little fuel as the Honda Civics that had become popular in the aftermath of the oil shock of the 1970s.

Still, overall carbon dioxide emissions continued to rise. In part this was because of the increasing "motorization" of the world. By the year 2020 transportation is expected to account for 52 per cent of world petroleum consumption, up from 46 per cent in 1996. Private automobile ownership is already high in the rich countries.

The United States leads the way, with nearly 775 vehicles per thousand people. Canada follows with 600 per thousand.[10] The rapid growth of a high-consumption economy has continued to be the highest ideal and main policy goal around the world. When poor countries start along the road to industrialization, car ownership quickly becomes the gold standard symbol of prosperity.

Another reason why carbon emissions have continued to rise has been the SUV boom. In the wake of the oil shock of 1973 the U.S. government ordered the auto industry to double the average fuel economy of cars by 1985. But because of lobbying from farmers and small contractors – and the motor industry – the regulations exempted most "light trucks," working vehicles like pickups and jeeps. The SUV boom followed when carmakers realized that they could cheaply convert existing truck factories, using old-fashioned pickup frames to support new, upmarket SUVs. Even though SUVs might have leather seats, DVD players, and never use their off-road capability, the U.S. government still classifies SUVs as light trucks.

The average fuel efficiency of U.S. vehicles peaked at 28 miles per gallon in 1988 and has declined since then despite technological improvements that offer the possibility of greater fuel efficiency.[11] The car industry and the United Automobile Workers have strongly opposed any further regulation of the amount of fuel used by vehicles they produce. With such measures on the back burner, the industry became free to produce more and bigger SUVs.

Ford's Michigan Truck Plant produces giant SUVs on underbodies that the company had already developed for full-sized pickups. Beginning in the mid-1990s, when menacing vehicles like the Lincoln Navigator and the Ford Expedition became popular among affluent families that once chose luxury sedans like Cadillacs and Lincolns, the Detroit-area factory became a key profit centre for Ford. Producing over a thousand vehicles every day, its 1998 production of nearly $11 billion gave this one plant sales greater than the entire world sales of companies like Nike and Honeywell. The Michigan Truck Plant's pretax profits of $3.7 billion that year gave it a profit margin nearly as great as Microsoft's.[12]

SUVs are not the only source of the carbon dioxide emissions that are threatening the global ecosystem, nor are they even the most important. Countries all over the world, including Canada, still burn coal to make electricity. This old technology generates far more greenhouse gas than all the SUVs that have rolled off the assembly line in the past twenty years. Global climate change is also caused by a host of other factors, including the clearing of forests (so-called "carbon sinks") which absorb carbon dioxide, and the use of chemical fertilizers in industrial agriculture. The nitrous oxide generated by fertilizer use is a far more potent greenhouse gas than carbon dioxide. Methane, another greenhouse gas more potent than carbon dioxide, is also generated when organic waste decomposes. Chlorofluorocarbons (CFCs), used until recently in refrigeration and air conditioning, are thousands of times more dangerous than carbon dioxide. Now being phased out, they will linger in the atmosphere for thousands of years.

The problem of climate change is intimately bound up with how humans interact with the natural environment. Since the coal-fired Industrial Revolution, greenhouse gas production has risen steadily, prompting the international conference at Kyoto to agree to take the first small steps to try to reverse the trend.

The reason to explore the issue of SUVs is that, just as concern over climate change mounted in the 1980s and 1990s, they were becoming the most important product of the biggest industry in the country that has the world's largest economy and uses up more of the world's resources than any other country. Two of the largest corporations with a vested interest in automobile and petroleum sales, General Motors and

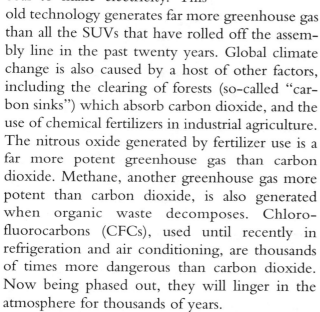

Exxon, were important backers of the Global Climate Coalition, an organization that downplayed the climate change problem and opposed the Kyoto Protocol.[13] Soon after George W. Bush took office in 2001, the new U.S. administration decided not to ratify the accord. In 2002 Robert Watson, head of the International Panel on Climate Change and a U.S. physicist supported by many pro-Kyoto European governments, was removed from his position after pressure from the U.S. government and Exxon.[14]

Decisions to oppose international efforts to cut greenhouse gases are based on economic considerations that put a higher priority on short-term profitability than on the long-term health of the environment. So too are decisions to convert factories from producing wasteful SUVs to producing energy-efficient cars. Such decisions are social and political, varying from country to country. The fuel economy of new vehicles sold in the United States in 2001 was 20 miles per gallon. Japan's stricter regulations meant that new vehicles averaged over 30 miles per gallon. European Union rules stipulated 33 miles per gallon in 2000, with Ford and General Motors agreeing to a new standard of 41 miles per gallon in Europe by 2008. Japan's per capita emissions of carbon dioxide are 9.2 metric tonnes. Each French citizen generates an average of 5.8 tonnes; each English citizen generates 8.9 tonnes. In contrast each American is responsible for 20.1 tonnes and each Canadian 16.2 tonnes. In 1997, the year these figures came out, Canada adopted U.S. standards for vehicular air pollution.[15]

The Costs

Although the benefits of improving automotive fuel efficiency are spread around globally — and may even help Maldive Islanders — the costs incurred by such improvements must be shouldered by big automotive companies and those who buy their products. The way such costs are allocated tells us a lot about the way different countries — and different societies — treat the natural environment.

Before the arrival of Europeans, the indigenous peoples of the Americas had low-tech societies based on the renewable productivity of the natural world. Their "ecological footprints" did not radically alter the ecosystem, while nature was often central to their spirituality and belief systems. European peoples who settled in the Americas tended to think that there would always be more than enough trees, pure air, fertile soil, and clean water. For people whose religious beliefs led them to consider themselves masters of the natural world, these were regarded as givens — free gifts of nature for society to use and enjoy.

According to conventional thinking, something that is "free" has, by definition, no cost or price tag attached to it. But as we use these resources without replenishing them, and as we pour waste products of industrial activity (like carbon dioxide) back into the environment without giving enough thought to the effects, society incurs a whole series of costs.

Some of these costs (like smog on a hot day) are tangible. You can see the brown haze hanging over a city and the air makes you cough. Others (like formaldehyde fumes emitted by building materials and synthetic carpets) are intangible; you can't see them and they are hard to measure. Whether tangible or not, these are what we call *social costs*. When serious pollution occurs, real damage is done. Ice caps melt, sea levels rise. Social costs deprive people in general of things (like clean air) they are entitled to — basic rights — and these losses are sustained by all members of society.

Air pollution, for example, causes lung disease and corrodes everything from the Parliament buildings to the vehicles that contribute to it. When smog descends, people get sick; the price

is paid by those who suffer and by society in the form of higher health-care costs. Contaminated lakes and rivers lose not only the fish and plant life that we can see, but also their ecological integrity. Also threatened are their aesthetic and recreational value, their ability to support tourism and fishing. Human illness and suffering, socio-economic losses, and irreparable harm to nature — all of these make up social costs.

Most pollution comes from industrial activity carried on by private corporations (like automobile manufacturers) striving to maximize short-term gains or profit; or by public agencies (like electrical utilities burning coal or splitting uranium atoms) with similarly narrow goals. When organizations confine their economic calculations to the values of the market (costs of production and sales), they ignore the social costs that cannot be expressed directly in monetary terms or can be sloughed off onto the public at large or the natural environment. Damages to people's health or the environment are treated as "externalities." When a company externalizes a cost, it means that it is never entered on the expense side of the ledger.

Other costs of doing business are visible. Building a Lincoln Navigator requires metal and plastic, the labour of engineers and assembly-line workers, electricity to power a factory. Social costs like more violent winter ice storms, hotter summers, and prairie droughts are more difficult to measure. But that does not mean that they are unreal or do not exist. Eventually the social costs of doing business are directly incurred (but not necessarily measured) by the community or the society at large. Perhaps they are passed on to the next generation. Maybe they are felt hundreds of kilometres away, or even on another continent. Yet no part of the original industrial product or the profit realized from its sale finds its way back to compensate the people whose health has been impaired or environment despoiled.

It is not easy for society to place a dollar value on the crisp, clean air of a spring morning or pristine lakes teeming with fish. Sometimes social costs can be expressed in monetary terms: health bills from cancer; or the social welfare costs to assist Newfoundland fishing communities when one of the world's most productive fisheries has been all but destroyed.

Sometimes, however, the costs cannot be expressed in dollars. What is the price of a dead lake or an ocean deprived of its normal fish stock? Of air not fit to breathe? Or a child whose learning abilities are impaired by lead? Or of three thousand needless highway deaths caused every day in the United States by the replacement of cars with SUVs that roll over, cause more smog, and kill more people in other cars? (This is about the same number of people who died in the attack on the World Trade Center on September 11, 2001.)[16]

Costs and Connections

If industry is profiting from "free" air, water, and soil, how can we stop it from doing damage? In most cases, the benefits appear on the balance sheet as profit (they are, in a sense, "privatized"), while the costs and risks are borne by society at large: that is, they are "socialized." How can we force private organizations to absorb the costs of the long-term damages usually sustained by the public? How can industry be made to include long-term, often faraway costs in its estimates, so that it has to make the right decision from the start, thus avoiding rather than cleaning up the damage?

In dealing with environmental issues, the first task of social analysis is to analyze the pollution.
■ What are the damages? The causes? The effects on people and the environment?
■ How does the natural environment suffer? What uses are being eliminated? How will communities be disrupted?

Following that, there are a number of other tasks.
■ Think about "uses" and "communities." What

do we mean when we use these terms? Do we immediately think of uses, such as recreation, by communities made of just of human beings? Or do we take into account the ways in which caterpillars and cardinals are part of communities that also use the natural environment?
■ Identify the social costs and determine their severity and distribution. Who is generating the pollution or misusing the land? Who is getting the benefit? Who is sustaining the losses in health, quality of life, environmental harm? Are these losses just confined to human communities?
■ Determine how the situation is controlled. Who is responsible for regulations, testing, monitoring, control, and rehabilitation? Who should be enforcing laws and standards? What are the rights of the public? What opportunities are there for the public to participate in decision-making and to ensure that something gets done?
■ Suggest a more just distribution of the costs and benefits. Will the people affected and the public at large be consulted and listened to? If there are conflicting interests or differing values involved, how can they be reconciled or resolved?

Citizens who want to ensure the health of their environment (even the global environment) and the safety of their communities (perhaps small neighbourhoods) enter into a system that is nearly as complex as the natural environment itself. The problems often seem unconnected. In 2001 residents of a downtown Toronto neighbourhood tried to stop McDonald's from building a drive-through because they were worried about noise, extra pollution, more traffic, and pedestrian safety. Some of those protestors may well be owners of SUVs. They may have little in common with the well-funded Washington lobbyists trying to get their government to clamp down on the wasteful vehicles. (Those lobbyists came up with the catchy point about choosing an SUV being the same as leaving your fridge open for six years.)

Both the women's movement and the ecology movement are sharply critical of the costs of competition, aggression and domination arising from the market economy's modus operandi in nature and society. Ecology has been a subversive science in its criticism of the consequences of uncontrolled growth associated with capitalism, technology, and progress – concepts that over the past two hundred years have been treated with reverence in Western culture. [The ecology movement] emphasized the need to live within the cycles of nature, as opposed to the exploitative, linear mentality of forward progress. It focuses on the costs of progress, the limits to growth, the deficiencies of technological decision making, and the urgency of the conservation and recycling of natural resources. Similarly, the women's movement has exposed the costs for all human beings of competition in the marketplace, the loss of meaningful productive economic roles for women in early capitalist society, and the view of both women and nature as psychological and recreational resources for the harried entrepreneur-husband.

— Carolyn Merchant, *The Death of Nature: Women, Ecology and the Scientific Revolution*, 1980.

But both groups are linked in the same way that ecology is all about relationships between living things. The solutions to the drive-through and SUV problems will be social and political. Even though the drive-through issue in that case is apparently about a neighbourhood's built environment and the SUV issue is a symbol of how excessive carbon dioxide threatens the global environment, both issues require asking the same questions about who wins and who loses under current conditions. A social analysis of environmental issues is essential if citizens are to effectively safeguard or repair the environment.

Energy to Burn

Canada, the second-largest country in the world, has fabulously rich energy resources: solids like coal and wood; liquids like oil; natural gas; sun for solar power; wind to power electric turbines; fast-flowing rivers that provide hydro-electricity;

uranium that fuels nuclear power stations. As a big country, we need energy to get around, although most of us live in sprawling cities whose design favours the private automobile over public transportation. As a Northern country, we need to stay warm in winter, although hotter weather brought on by the changing climate has pushed up summertime electricity use. Aside from our own needs, Canada also exports oil, gas, and electricity to the United States and coal to Japan.

How are energy and its benefits distributed? At the same time, how are the costs and risks distributed? Conventional economic wisdom tends to answer these questions by speaking about free markets and short-term profits. This analysis takes the example of an energy megaproject in a small province – nuclear development in New Brunswick – and asks, "Is it profitable?" and "Is it just?"

In 1974 the New Brunswick Electric Power Commission began constructing its first nuclear generating plant at Point Lepreau on the Bay of Fundy, 30 kilometres from Saint John.[17] The plant reached full power in 1983, several years later than planned. The cost had risen from an initial budget of $466 million, more than doubling to $1.4 billion.

To understand this kind of investment, recall the real estate market, where the "players" are the builders or developers, the institutions that lend the money to do the building, the government, and the consumers who buy or rent the houses (see chapter three). The final guarantee of financial success for both the developers and the money-lenders is the very need of people for housing and the ability of those people to buy or rent houses or apartments.

Corporations undertaking energy development like Point Lepreau are like house-builders. The nuclear power station carries certain "mortgage" payments. These mortgages are held by domestic and foreign bankers who lend money for such megaprojects. The government backs the loans. But the final guarantee of financial security for builder and banker is the ability of consumers to pay for their monthly electricity bills. From the point of view of the builders and bankers, a constantly increasing demand for energy and higher monthly bills are good things. From the perspective of consumers and the natural environment, this is not necessarily the case.

New Brunswick's government-owned utility chose nuclear power in anticipation of high growth rates in the consumption of electricity and because New Brunswick's geographic location allows it to sell excess power to U.S. markets. Point Lepreau was originally justified because NB Power expected electricity shortages in the province in the 1980s. But when the plant began operating at full capacity in 1983, the province was still a net exporter of electricity. Exports to other provinces and the United States were subsequently 25 per cent greater than the power generated at Point Lepreau. Meanwhile, consumption of electricity in New Brunswick was increasing more slowly than it had in the 1970s, when the utility decided to invest so heavily in nuclear power.[18] NB Power has consistently exported more than the total amount of the nuclear power generated and done little to encourage conservation. It even launched a campaign to encourage the use of electricity for residential space heating. Critics said this was an attempt to justify its billion-dollar nuclear investment.

Consumers were still supposed to benefit from nuclear power through a decreased reliance on the foreign oil that fuels New Brunswick's thermal generators. But once Point Lepreau came on stream, the nuclear electricity had to be exported to cover the costs and risks of Point Lepreau. NB Power was reluctant to phase out its oil-fired generators. By the early 1990s, 30 per cent of the utility's long-term debt was still in foreign currency. The money had been borrowed (or "imported") to produce energy, but the energy had to be exported to earn the foreign exchange needed to pay the debt.

Any large investment, particularly if it is well over a billion dollars, should provide much-needed employment. Sponsors of energy megaprojects argue that they are a powerful force for job creation. At the peak of construction in 1979 the Point Lepreau project employed 3,300 workers. By the 1990s, it was being operated by a staff of 425.

As far as safety goes, Point Lepreau has been a successful nuclear power plant. There have been no major environmental accidents, although there have been several heavy-water leaks, involving thousands of litres, and occasional conflicting reports from NB Power and the Canadian Nuclear Safety Commission (formerly the Atomic Energy Control Board). Although these incidents have thus far caused no perceptible damage to the environment, they do underscore the practical inevitability of human error. The potential social costs of accidents involving radioactive materials are incalculable. Those costs are one of the factors that, together with its history of multibillion-dollar cost overruns and heavy dependence on government subsidies, have made nuclear power a "sunset industry," according to The Economist, a conservative British business magazine.[19]

In light of all the costs and dangers, why have the provincial government and NB Power pursued a nuclear strategy? Among the motives were meeting the growing need for electricity, gaining independence from foreign oil, projecting the image of a modern progressive province, and, in the short term, providing construction jobs. But the utility's legal mandate is to provide inexpensive power for the residents of New Brunswick.

Another key motive was to help out the Canadian nuclear industry. As foreign sales of Candu reactors faltered, the federal government encouraged the construction of nuclear plants solely for the export of electricity, in order to help the industry through a slump and maintain a Candu export capability.

NB Power tried to go ahead with plans to build a second Candu reactor at Point Lepreau, despite widespread public opposition. With an installed overcapacity of 40 per cent in the early 1990s, NB Power was counting on the United States to buy additional electricity. Ironically, one reason for the potential U.S. market for Lepreau's power was that the U.S. anti-nuclear movement made the construction of reactors in nearby New England politically impossible. But Point Lepreau II was never built, as U.S. markets declined.

Nevertheless, NB Power kept up the pressure to stay nuclear. Planning for a projected winter-time electricity shortfall in 2006, when Lepreau reaches the end of the period in which it can be reliably operated with adequate safety margins, in 2002 the utility applied to reconstruct the station. Critics estimated the cost would be $1.2 billion for 635 megawatts, compared to $436 million for 400 megawatts if it built a new natural gas plant. NB Power argued that the price of gas would probably rise, making the operating costs unpredictable. Opponents of the nuclear option replied that since no one had ever rebuilt a Candu reactor from scratch or assessed the amount of work required to resurrect it for another twenty-five years, a repeat of Lepreau's original cost overruns was likely.

"To suggest that we will get 25 years from a salvage job," argued the critics, "is just not very prudent."[20]

Environmentalists often use something called the "precautionary principle." This means that we should err on the side of caution, not taking chances that our actions will cause damage, now or in the future. Nuclear energy is a serious threat to the environment because radiation is a threat to living things at every stage in the process. Canada is the world's biggest uranium exporter – 88 per cent of its refined uranium was shipped abroad in the 1990s. There are some 90,000 tonnes of radioactive mine tailings in places like Uranium City, Great Bear Lake, Elliot Lake, and Port Hope.[21] Nuclear workers must take constant precautions to avoid deadly contamination. The high cost of decommissioning old plants is one of the reasons that nuclear energy is so expensive.

More importantly, even though nuclear power has been with us for over thirty years, no one in the world has ever built a waste disposal site where the growing piles of high-level radioactive waste can be stored "permanently."

This waste remains deadly for at least 100,000 years. Imagine this: if societies that existed well before written history – perhaps the one that erected Stonehenge in England – had had the capability of using nuclear power, we would only now, some four thousand years later, be starting to deal with the problem. This raises a crucial issue. Can we rely on the short-term priorities (next year's profit, an election two years from now) that dominate the social institutions responsible for so many decisions that have an impact on the environment?

New Brunswick built Point Lepreau with little regard for the short-term economic costs, let alone the long-term environmental and social costs. Its electrical utility has been keen to go ahead and rebuild it, against all odds. An important reason for this has been that, like so many decisions about energy and the environment, this one has been guided by narrow, economic considerations: the market for electricity in New Brunswick and the New England states, and the "capital market," that is, the cost and availability of borrowed money. The main goal underlying all of this – and of both the Canada-U.S. Free Trade Agreement (1989) and the North American Free Trade Agreement (1994) – is growth: growth in the supply of power, in the power of the utility, in the economy as a whole.

The same priorities have governed how all of Canada's energy resources are developed and used. In the period after 1990 gas production in Canada increased by 69 per cent, and exports by 57 per cent. Oil production rose by 47 per cent, and exports by 59 per cent. These conditions had a major effect on greenhouse gas emissions from Canada.[22] The goal of an integrated North American energy market – with Canada and Mexico supplying energy to the United States – was a key free-trade goal. Even though Mexico insisted on keeping control over its energy resources and refused to go along, Canada agreed under the Canada-U.S. Free Trade Agreement and NAFTA to "accelerate the delivery of its non-renewable petroleum reserves at the lowest possible prices."[23]

Under its free-trade agreement with the United States, Canada gave up control of its energy resources. If an energy supply crunch were to happen, the Canadian government could no longer do as it did in the energy crises of the 1970s, when it brought in conservation policies that kept resources at home. It would have to keep selling the United States the same amount of energy as it sold over the previous three years. This makes it more difficult for Canadians to create the practical and affordable alternatives to the fossil fuel economy, which is the main cause of global climate change.

The Canadian oil and gas boom coincided exactly with the final realization that greenhouse gases were warming the earth's climate with potentially disastrous effects on natural ecosystems and human societies. The United Nations Framework Convention on Climate Change of 1992 led to the Kyoto Protocol of 1997 and increasing recognition by Canadians that their country had to do something because they were number two in the world in per capita emissions of greenhouse gases. Meanwhile, between 1990 and 2000, Canadian greenhouse gas emissions *increased* by over 15 per cent.

In addressing such issues, private corporations tend to favour free markets over government regulation, and voluntary guidelines over laws that require strict compliance. Canadian governments have in recent years gone along with this "deregulation." When the Kyoto Protocol attempted to reduce carbon dioxide emissions and other causes of climate change, Canada's fossil fuel industry agreed to sign on to a Voluntary Challenge and Registry, a new industry-government partnership under which participants voluntarily agreed to cut emissions. Still, emissions had grown by over 10 per cent by 2000. In 2002 environmental groups examined the Registry's reports and found that the largest corporate greenhouse gas emitters had recorded big increases. The list included Imperial Oil, owned by Exxon-Mobil, a leading Kyoto opponent and one of the world's most powerful corporations.[24]

The environmental effects of the energy free-for-all have not been confined to global climate change. Alberta, centre of the petroleum boom, has experienced massive environmental degradation. By 1995 the fossil fuel industry had cut 1.8 million kilometres (four times the distance from the Earth to the moon) of seismic lines through the province's rural and wilderness areas. Seismic lines are passages bulldozed through the bush so that oil and gas companies can plant dynamite, which is then detonated to help detect underground deposits. When found, natural gas is ever more frequently of the "sour" variety, containing a highly toxic hydrogen sulphide that has killed thirty-five petroleum workers in the past thirty years. During the late 1990s, 2.5 million cubic metres of "waste" gas were flared off every year in Alberta, sufficient to heat 150,000 homes for a month. One provincial report measured combustion efficiency at 66 to 84 per cent, compared to 98 per cent in Texas, where regulations are stricter. Alberta's Turner Valley has North America's oldest sour gas field as well as the highest rate of multiple sclerosis in the world.[25]

Environmental Values: Just, Sustainable, Participatory

Natural resource development – particularly when huge energy projects are involved – raises important issues: the environmental impacts of resource extraction itself; control over decision-making; the use to which natural resources are put; the distribution of power in society. Conflicts do not simply involve solar power versus non-renewable power, a billion dollars here or there. What is at stake for Canada, in its choice of resources for energy development, is the kind of society its citizens will live in, now and in future generations.

These broad objectives can be summed up in the ideal of a *just*, *participatory*, and *sustainable* society. Thinking about a society in this way helps to focus our analysis of the environment. These three *explicit* values can be used to question the *implicit* values contained in the decisions about energy. Such analysis questions values; it is an ethical reflection on economic policy. Such reflection is another useful technique of social analysis.

How are the benefits of energy development distributed? If Canada's high-energy approach continues, poor people far away stand to experience increasingly erratic weather. In Bangladesh, one of the world's poorest, most densely populated, and low-lying countries, people know that the seasonal floods are getting worse. In 2000 three million people were left homeless by flooding caused by torrential rains. What will happen if the fertile coastal plains sink beneath the sea within three or four generations? Where will the refugees go? Who will feed them?

Here in Canada the debate over ratifying the Kyoto Protocol pitted the Alberta government and the transnational energy corporations against Canadians worried about the long-term future of the planet. The Kyoto opponents warned of big job losses. The environmentalists warned of the loss of the natural world.

Largely unnoticed was the union representing energy workers. It argued for a "just transition" to an environmentally sustainable economy. The Communications, Energy and Paperworkers (CEP) union called for more government support for conservation and renewable energy industries like wind and solar power. It pointed out that the natural gas export boom was also a job export boom, because using gas as a "feedstock" to produce plastics and petrochemicals in Canada creates more jobs than piping it to Chicago. The union's just transition proposal argued for a transition fund (1 per cent of all fossil fuel and uranium sales) to assist workers hurt by the shift to an economy based on environmental sustainability and renewable resources.[26] There is evidently money for the energy industry. From 1977 to 1999 the federal government alone gave the oil and gas industries $40 billion in subsidies.[27] The question remains: is the money distributed in a just manner?

Environmental justice requires a fairer distribution of the world's resources. In 1960 the 20 per cent of the world's people living in the richest countries had thirty times the income of the poorest 20 per cent. By 1995 they had eighty-two times as much and were consuming 58 per cent of the world's energy.[28] Clearly, those of us in the rich countries make a deeper ecological footprint than the people in poor countries. But should the poor follow the high-consumption path of the rich countries, with Bangladeshi families idling at the drive-through in SUVs? That would hardly be sustainable. Although many poor people need to consume more, their countries could leapfrog the growth pattern of the rich with its huge legacy of wasteful

---

Energy is the source of vital human needs like warmth, light, and transportation. Energy is an economic necessity required for the production of goods, and energy industries employ millions of people. . . . There can be no successful, meaningful or viable energy policy for Canada that does not respect the views and interests of the working people who produce, distribute, and process this country's energy resources. It is the exclusion of these interests that allows the world's largest corporations and the enormous bureaucracies of public utilities and regulatory boards to continue the policies that have brought the world to the brink of environmental disaster and alarmingly depleted this country's energy resources. . . .

We have a positive vision of a sustainable environment and a prosperous economy that requires a stable energy supply. The energy industries of the future will be increasingly diversified, renewable, and smaller scale. . . . The key to this positive future is democratic public control and regulation of our energy resources, and just transition measures to ensure that today's working families and communities are included in tomorrow's energy industries.

— Communications, Energy and Paperworkers Union of Canada, *National Energy Policy*, 2002

consumption and environmental destruction. Taking a lesson from the mistakes of the North, poor countries can choose a more sustainable path featuring smaller-scale industries using renewable resources, producing for local needs. Rather than eight-cylinder SUVs, a better choice is the clean, four-stroke engine now compulsory in Thailand for motorcycles and three-wheelers.

The notion of *sustainable development* has been much discussed and often abused since it was coined by the United Nations' World Commission on Environment and Development in 1987. But it is still straightforward enough to have real meaning: "development that meets the needs of the future without compromising the ability of future generations to meet their own needs."[29] Is Canada's energy strategy environmentally sustainable? Burning coal and gas to produce electricity produces climate-disrupting carbon dioxide. There is no safe method for the disposal of nuclear waste, cancer-causing garbage that will still be deadly in a hundred thousand years.

People want to participate in the future of their society. Access to energy and methods of energy production need to be discussed as widely and as frankly as possible. Does everyone have a say? The very size and shape of megaprojects like nuclear power stations and the Alberta oil sands make them difficult to grasp. They are the products of the collaboration of physicists, geologists, chemists, and engineers. The financial press publishes notices of bond issues listing international banks that get together to lend enormous sums of money for energy-related projects. These complex transactions and all the technical decisions make it very difficult for the public to get involved in the debate.

The problem is that these decisions are made within very narrow financial and scientific perspectives. The human, social, and environmental costs that emerge in the long term are downplayed or ignored.

Participation is something that people have to work to achieve. One approach is to win autonomy from outside forces like provincial utilities and transnational oil companies through conservation and the use of renewable resources. People add insulation and redesign their homes to save energy, adding special lighting and efficient windows that cut heat loss. Approaches that emphasize conservation and renewable energy tend to be small-scale and decentralized. It is far easier for people to exercise control over a comprehensive district heating plan, local conservation program, or a small hydroelectric generator than it is to have input into a nuclear power station or an offshore oil rig. Why does government give its massive support to the huge projects and not to local initiatives?

Non-participation has become "normal" and acceptable. Citizens are usually excluded from decisions that have the biggest effects on the

Security Requires Environmental and Social Justice

The most profound danger to world peace in the coming years will stem not from the irrational acts of states or individuals but from the legitimate demands of the world's dispossessed. Of these poor and disenfranchised, the majority live a marginal existence in equatorial climates. Global warming, not of their making but originating with the wealthy few, will affect their fragile ecologies most. Their situation will be desperate and manifestly unjust.

It cannot be expected, therefore, that in all cases they will be content to await the beneficence of the rich. If then we permit the devastating power of modern weaponry to spread throughout this combustible human landscape, we invite a conflagration that can engulf both rich and poor. The only hope for the future lies in co-operative international action, legitimized by democracy.

It is time to turn our backs on the universal search for security, in which we seek shelter behind walls. Instead, we must persist in the quest for united action to counter both global warming and a weaponized world. . . . To survive in the world we have transformed, we must learn to think in a new way. As never before, the future of each depends on the good of all.

— Statement by one hundred Nobel laureates on the hundredth anniversary of the Nobel Prize, 2001.

environment. Should they have the opportunity to consider the full range of risks and benefits of different options? The idea is not to shirk all risks or condemn all development, but to prevent costly decisions from being imposed without people having a say. Participation is the key to ensuring environmental policies that are more just and sustainable. Participation is also at the heart of the democratic ideal. It is an end, or a value, in itself.

Questions

❏ What is the source of the water you drink? Is it tested for contaminants? If it is, are the tests aimed at finding bacteria alone, or do they cover a broader range of potentially hazardous substances? Who does the testing? To whom do they report? Is it easy for ordinary citizens to find out the answers to these questions – and to participate in confronting these and other environmental challenges?

❏ How clean is the air where you live? To what extent do local industries and electrical utilities emit dangerous pollutants? What about automobiles? How do you react if you can see the air on hot, smoggy summer days? Do people – yourself included – see it as part of the weather, something that no one can do anything about? Or do you respond by trying to change your individual lifestyle by walking, cycling, or taking public transportation instead of driving? And are you inclined to get involved in public issues, such as determining how cities are designed and the extent to which industry emissions are regulated?

❏ China, with over a billion people, has a strict, one-child-per family policy for the sake of the country's future. Most Canadians would approve of this effort to control the human impact on the Earth. Resources are limited. But Canadian physicist Ursula Franklin has asked an important question: why have Canadians, and people in other rich countries, not addressed the possibility of a one-car-per-family policy for the sake of the country's – and the world's – future?

❏ Do you take cars for granted, as a natural way of getting around? Do you know many people who see their vehicles as status symbols as well as tools? What is the effect of advertising on how we view the relationship between the way we live and the issue of environmental degradation? How would you or your family and friends react if the government passed a law restricting car ownership?

❏ Highly trained experts employed by government and industry are used to working with reports, statistics, flow charts, and obscure technical terminology. Their experience can easily lead them to doubt the ability of most citizens to assimilate and understand complex data. But without the facts about energy use and pollution, how can ordinary people make informed judgements about issues like dioxins in the aquifers and particulate matter in the air? What responsibility to the public do experts have? Are there alternative sources of expertise upon which citizens can rely?

Resources

• Gordon Laird. *Power: Journeys Across an Energy Nation*. Toronto: Penguin, 2002. Canada is richly endowed with energy resources, but extraction comes at a cost. Laird examines Canada's energy frontiers, from offshore Atlantic petroleum and the Alberta tar sands to the Arctic, where ice is thinning and ozone depletion is on the rise.

• Jeremy Legget. *Carbon War: Global Warming at the End of the Oil Era*. London: Penguin, 2000. A comprehensive overview of the debates and conflicts over global climate change. The book describes the events that unfolded between the late 1980s and the turn of the century.

• David Suzuki and Holly Dressel. *Good News for a Change: Hope for a Troubled Planet*. Toronto: Stoddart, 2002. Canadian geneticist and environmentalist Suzuki has often been accused of being a naysayer, with his warnings of ecological catastrophe. In this book he and his co-author describe the worldwide efforts of citizens, groups, and businesses to change the way they work and live as part of helping to create a sustainable environment.

• *Isuma – Canadian Journal of Policy Research*, vol.2, no.4 (Winter 2001), features articles on climate change. According to the journal, "Isuma" is Inuktitut for "idea" or "thought" and encompasses a sense of responsibility towards the community. Unlike most scientific or academic journals, Isuma is available on-line free at <www.isuma.net>.

• *"Ah . . . the Money, the Money, the Money": The Battle for Saltspring*. Canada, 2001. Directed by Mort Ransen. NFB. Video. 51 min. Local resident and documentary filmmaker Mort Ransen presents debates with developers and the actions taken by community members against threats to the community and the environment when a logging operation arrives in the pristine wilderness of the Southern Gulf Islands off the coast of British Columbia.

• *Turning Down the Heat: The New Energy Revolution*. Canada, 1999. Directed by Jim Hamm. Narrated by David Suzuki. NFB. Video. 49 min. Addresses the crisis of global warming and takes a look at examples of renewable energy and energy conservation, from around the world, as viable solutions.

Websites:

Environmental organizations were among the first to use the Internet for communication and organizing. Check the websites of groups like Alberta's Pembina Institute and the Conservation Council of New Brunswick. National organizations, from the Sierra Club of Canada and Greenpeace to the World Wildlife Fund and the Canadian Nature Federation, maintain comprehensive sites that provide links to everything from global climate issues to local efforts to restrict lawn pesticides.

The website of the United Nations Framework Convention on Climate Change (UNFCCC) provides the basic documents and text of the Kyoto Protocol, news about the ratification process, arguments, and information.

A global non-profit organization, the International Institute for Energy Conservation (CERF/IIEC), works with developing countries to provide assistance in implementing energy efficiency, renewable energy, and integrated transport planning. Its website can also be useful.

Technology from Past to Future

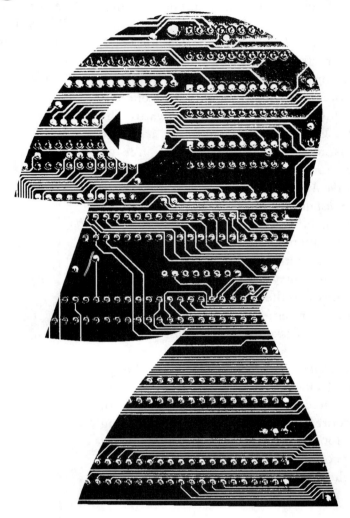

There is a French expression, commonly used in English, that starts *"plus ça change . . ."* Often it is enough to say just that, "The more things change . . ." and people will know what you mean even if you don't complete the old saying: *"Plus ça change, plus ça reste la même chose"* – "the more things change, the more they stay the same."

What is changing? And what is staying the same? Rapid changes in computer technology offer the latest fads in consumer goods. Cell phones double as cameras and e-mail devices, while video games boast the production values of Hollywood movies. The number of households with at least one member using the Internet regularly at home has continued to increase. In 2001 it rose to about half the population – 49 per cent, jumping up from 26 per cent just a year previously.[1] Computers have altered how Canadians work and communicate, two of the most important things done by people in any society.

Amidst all of this, though, we need to consider what is merely changing superficially – and what is changing more profoundly. At the same time, what is failing to change? To grapple with these questions, let's take a look at some of the technological changes that are happening with such speed. After all, in 1984, when they were preparing the first edition of *Getting Started*, its authors were surprised and puzzled because they had never before used a computer . . . let alone pondered the possibility of carrying one around in their pockets.

Plus Ça Change

Another thing that struck the original authors as odd was a headline that read: "ROBOT JUST DOING ITS JOB: MAN GETS IN THE WAY!" In 1983 the headline appeared over a newspaper article about a Canadian autoworker who needed several dozen stitches after being lacerated by an industrial robot. Now, two decades later, robots have since become commonplace in factories, and a worker getting hurt by one of them would scarcely generate any notice at all, much less a headline with an exclamation mark.

In computer-controlled factories and offices, the speed and power of data processing keep on growing, and growing, so that Moore's Law seems as inevitable as the law of gravity. In 1964 Gordon Moore, co-founder of the computer-chip manufacturer Intel, noticed that the speed and power of chips seemed to be doubling every year. He predicted that the trend would continue and, by and large, it has. As a result, its applications to everyday work and life are said to be the greatest set of innovations since the development of steam power and the spinning jenny during the Industrial Revolution of the nineteenth century.

The changes do seem revolutionary. Computers became faster, smaller, and cheaper in record time. When it was first switched on in 1946, the Electronic Numerical Integrator and Calculator (ENIAC) had 18,000 vacuum tubes (which failed on average at the rate of one every seven minutes). ENIAC eventually became as famous for its size (its nine-foot-high metal cabinets weighing thirty tons) as it was for its distinction of being the world's first large-scale, general-purpose computer.

> The introduction of computers and robots in industries and offices has begun to create what may become a new class of people, namely, the so-called "techno-peasants." These are the men and women who are being shut-out or marginalized by their functional illiteracy in the new technologies. The more affected are expected to be workers in manufacturing, agriculture, and resource industries. Indeed, it is the middle classes which are most vulnerable to increasing marginalization, due to the new technologies. The upward social mobility of the post-war years is rapidly giving way to the new trend of downward social mobility for many people. This is likely to contribute to an enlargement of the sectors of poverty and powerlessness in our society.
>
> — Canadian Conference of Catholic Bishops, *Ethical Choices and Political Challenges*, 1984.

By 1977 another Intel founder was able to claim that a typical microcomputer of the day was twenty times faster than ENIAC, as well as being one-thirty-thousandth the size and one-ten-thousandth the cost. As another observer of the computer revolution explained it, if the automobile business had developed like the computer industry, by 1987 a Rolls-Royce would have cost $2.75 and travelled for five million kilometres on five litres of gasoline.[2]

Tiny microchips began appearing not just in computers but also in everything from wrist watches to jumbo jets. Typewriters became obsolete in the short space of ten years. For some time now banks have used computerized banking machines (ATMs) to replace tellers. They have also started to encourage customers to do their banking on-line. Both moves improved bank productivity and profits dramatically. Machines have no need for wages and benefits, and never go on strike for improvements in either.

Another crucial development was the convergence of computer and communications technologies, resulting in the expansion of the Internet and a new application called the World Wide Web in the early 1990s. Again, within ten years something that had been virtually unknown had become a familiar tool for hundreds of millions of people. In 1995 there were 17.5 Internet hosts for every thousand Canadians. By 2000 the number had risen more than sixfold to 108.[3]

When "high" technology first invaded the factory and the office, there were worries that people would be replaced by machines. Some of those worries turned out to be true, although new jobs were created in the information technology (IT) sector.

The enormity and speed of technological change affect everyone. To survive as a worker, consumer, or citizen, must each one of us become a computer expert? Perhaps not, but people who have little interest in the intricate details of technology do have to become familiar enough with computers and communications that they won't be intimidated or overwhelmed by the changes.

Our social analysis here is an initial overview of this immense, complex, and exciting issue. The first step is to look at how new machines and technologies were introduced and perceived in days gone by. The historical context provides a clue to what, exactly, is changing – and what remains the same.

The Parable of the Teaspoons

IBM is one of the oldest and still the largest producer of computer technologies in the world. It is also one of the world's biggest corporations. The computer giant once ran this advertisement:

> Two men were watching a mechanical excavator on a building site. "If it wasn't for that machine," said one, "twelve men could be doing that job." "Yes," replied the other, "and if it weren't for your twelve shovels, two hundred men with teaspoons could be doing that job."

A construction company can buy an excavator that uses diesel and hydraulic technology and then hire an operator much more cheaply than it can employ twelve shovellers or two hundred workers, even if they bring their own teaspoons.

> The old concept of labour as a commodity simply will not suffice; it is at once wrong and dangerous. Hence there is a responsibility upon the entrepreneur who introduces technological change to see that it is not effected at the expense of his working force. This is the human aspect of the technological challenge, and it must not be ignored.
>
> — Samuel Freedman,
> *Report of the Industrial Inquiry Commission on Canadian National Railways "Run-Throughs",*
> Ottawa, 1965.

Given the cost advantages accruing to owners of firms and factories, automation is sure to come and replace more workers. To denounce this sort of innovation without considering its implications and who controls it is of little help. To embrace technological change as inevitable – the only sensible option because "you can't stand in the way of progress" – seems just as foolish.

In the teaspoon parable, the first man, cast in a pessimistic light, worries about the negative effect of technology on employment. He hesitates to jump on the IBM bandwagon. He seems to doubt the happy times promised by new technologies. Apparently enough people shared such worries to warrant an expensive ad designed to present technology in a warm, optimistic light.

Doubts and concerns have also been voiced in high places. In 1983, when IBM had taken an early lead in the new field of personal computers, the federal employment minister admitted to the Canadian Advanced Technology Association that he was afraid workers might react violently to innovations beyond their control. Too often, he told the employers, workers have been casually informed that they were no longer needed. When this happens, employers often worry about machines being "sabotaged." The word comes from the French for "clogs," or sabots, heavy wooden shoes used to destroy machinery. Sabotage has a long history.

A 200-Year-Old Story

People who seriously question the application of new technologies often get labelled, usually with contempt, as modern-day "Luddites" – as people standing in the way of progress. The Luddites were a group of English artisans and other skilled craft workers whose livelihoods were threatened in the early years of the Industrial Revolution. They valued their skills and their freedom to control when and where they worked. They did not want to become servants, hired wage-workers subject to the discipline of the factory. As it turned out, in the factory system that eventually took root the new machines were often tended by unskilled women and children who laboured in virtual slavery under prison-like conditions.

The Luddites attacked and destroyed some of the machines threatening to replace them, especially in the textile trade. They were not blindly resisting progress. At various times they pushed for a minimum wage, control of the "sweating" of women and children in factories, the prohibition of shoddy work, and the right to form trade unions. They even demanded that employers be obliged to find work for skilled workers displaced by machinery.[4]

From an early twenty-first century perspective, the Luddite resistance seems remarkable (and, for some, ridiculous). But equally remarkable is the sympathy that most people in the English Midlands in the early nineteenth century had for the machine-wreckers. No Nottinghamshire Luddite was turned in to the authorities, although many people in the community knew who was attacking the machines. In Wiltshire the authorities could not discover who was destroying the new mills. For many people it made sense to resist what others regarded as progress.[5]

Because workers had no control over the introduction of new technology, the Luddites knew how unlikely they were to benefit from its application. As early casualties of the Industrial Revolution, they would probably have been sympathetic to the sentiments of a Canadian trade unionist speaking 170 years later: "You cannot stop the new technology, but there's no reason that people should suffer from it. We want some of the benefits of technology, not just the adverse effects."[6]

The development of steam-powered machinery and the growth of iron and steel production were two of the driving forces behind the Industrial Revolution of the nineteenth century. With the centralization of production in factories, the jealously guarded skills of artisans and craftspeople – weavers, shoemakers, stockingers, and other textile workers – were gradually made obsolete. Although modern industries could produce more goods, the Luddites resisted out of fear that these changes would turn their world upside down. Displaced workers could either migrate to the growing city slums to work in the factories, or they could emigrate to the colonies. Given the dilemma they faced, either way the familiar security of their work and lives would be destroyed.

Almost two centuries later, how do people view the resistance of the Luddites? It all depends on how they interpret the tremendous mechanical, economic, and social changes of the Industrial Revolution. If these are seen as entirely inevitable, "progressive," and of unquestionable advantage to society, the Luddite resistance was indeed blind and futile. If some of the costs and consequences of "progress" are questionable, the Luddites appear to be more prophetic than hysterical.

In 1993 loggers in Northern New Brunswick were confronted by a challenge similar to that faced by the Luddites. Logging machines that shear off trees using diesel-hydraulic power were eliminating the need for loggers who used chain saws – and whose seasonal jobs barely provided the necessary weeks to secure employment insurance. As a result, at least one logging machine was burned.

What happens to a society that does not adapt to changing technologies? Could Britain have remained a nation of cottage industries? What happens to industries that are slow to embrace the rapid advance of computerization? If Canada slowed down in this way, industries could be bypassed in a frenzy of international competition as other nations captured new markets, which would lead to even harder economic times. Yet leaping onto the bandwagon represents a leap of faith that technology will help all people equally and give rise to a general increase in the common good.

These dilemmas spark another question for the social analyst. Maybe it is not just the technology alone – the steam engine in the nineteenth century or the microprocessor in the twenty-first – that accounts for the revolution, but also the economic context into which the technology is introduced: the social relationships of production and distribution, the patterns of decision-making, the forms of control over how technologies are built and introduced.

Canada's High-Tech Success Story

Canada's telephone system is regarded as a model of efficiency. Bell Canada, the firm that provides much of Central Canada with phone service, was the country's fourth most profitable corporation in 2001, ranking number eight in revenues. Nortel Networks, once a Bell subsidiary called Northern Electric, used to make heavy, black, rotary dial telephones. Now an independent company, it makes all the computerized components that form the skeleton of any modern telecommunications network.

In 1976 Northern/Nortel launched its Digital World line of computerized switching equipment and in the next ten years its revenues jumped six-fold, largely because of its success in the U.S. market. Over those years the number of workers who made the equipment declined and the nature of their work changed as labour became a less important factor of production. In London, Ontario, the company's workforce fell from 2,300 in the 1970s to 700 in 1993. The Canadian Autoworkers (CAW) represented 6,000 Nortel production workers in Canada in the early 1980s. Some twenty years later they represented 350.[7]

At the same time as the number of jobs declined, the nature of work changed. The remaining jobs were divided between complex tasks and repetitive jobs that required little skill. Standardized sub-assemblies arrived "Just in Time," often from low-wage countries. Corporate managers were frank about the factory-floor workforce they needed to test the new equipment: "We want to reduce tests to their lowest common denominator. It increases our control and our flexibility with labour. It's easier to find lower skilled people."[8]

Workers who had taken years to learn how to produce parts for phone systems had to adapt to new automated systems in which they had no control over systems designed by far-off software engineers. Both kinds of work are described with the lofty label of "high tech," but that does not mean that the lower-skilled jobs at the bottom of the pyramid are challenging or interesting. There is most often little or no participation in the planning or control of the work.

Computers have certainly provided the basis for new industries and jobs. They have also contributed to a new scenario: the separation between a small top layer of managers and analysts who perform creative tasks and a large pool of job holders and job seekers. The latter group may be familiar with computers, but their tasks are determined by and depend on technology over which they have no control.[9] The people making the equipment in London were not necessarily content with how technology was altering their working lives:

> It wouldn't be so bad if they came in and said a year down the road "This is what we are going to do." But they don't. They tell you after they do it. We are not going to be able to stop technology. We are not going to stop change. But at least they could tell us what is going on.[10]

In the end the flexibility and adaptation did the workforce little good. In 1993 Nortel closed the operation and moved production elsewhere. Its globalization strategy, together with its leading role in the high-tech boom of the late 1990s, made the company a favourite among business observers who believed that computer and communications technologies were laying the foundation for a "new economy." When the technology bubble burst in 2000-2001, Nortel laid off 30,000 people, a third of its entire workforce.

Technological Turnaround at the Phone Company

Meanwhile, Nortel's former parent company was busy streamlining its operations for the wireless information age. Bell purchased CTV and *The Globe and Mail*. It offered digital television via satellite, mobile phone service, and Internet access. Of course, it did not abandon its basic business of providing ordinary telephone service in Central Canada. But all the changes did have huge implications for women workers at Bell.

The telephone operator was once the most readily identifiable representative of the phone company. The position was most always held by women. In the old days, sitting shoulder to shoulder, operators would plug in jacks whenever a light on the switchboard flashed. As technology evolved, calls were switched automatically, and phone companies needed fewer operators. Jobs disappeared as phone service became faster and more efficient.

The digital switching equipment provided more than just customer convenience. The operators believed that, more and more, they were serving machines under conditions dictated by the company that owned the machines. Nevertheless, management at both Bell Canada and Northern Telecom (as it was still known then) waxed enthusiastic about the benefits of the new technology to the workers who sat in front of the new video terminals: "Extensive research led to a position that offered a new prestige and in turn, greater job satisfaction and efficiency."[11]

Yet what looked like efficiency to management appeared to the operators as a loss of the minimal control they had once had over their jobs. Workers in a host of other industries, from typesetting to the production of machine tools, have suffered a similar loss of control over even the most incidental details of their jobs.

Still, few people would want to return to the old days when they shared a "party line" with the neighbours. We all benefit from a more advanced and efficient telephone service. Moreover, technological change provides enormous cost advantages to the owners of firms. Managers would never consider the possibility of not bringing in new technologies, because their competitors at home and abroad are rushing to keep up with the latest advances.

Technological innovation is most often introduced unilaterally by management. The phrase "top-down insertion" describes how new technology comes to the workplace, without participation by the people who are most affected. In some cases new machines are designed so that workers need only to monitor a few gauges or screens. Along the way, skills that were formerly highly valued are replaced. Even if it does not result in direct job loss, this *de-skilling* is frustrating for people who take pride in the experience they have gained and their ability to conceive and carry out a task. When this experience is replaced by a pre-programmed computer, the "need to know" disappears. Technical systems gain in efficiency by reducing the human factor to a minimum.

During the first Industrial Revolution, it took the strenuous efforts of workers and their unions to change the situation so that labour could gain a partial share in the benefits of industrialization. Now, with a new, microelectronic revolution in place, are the owners of the new technology appropriating all the benefits, leaving the workers to shoulder the costs? Are those affected consulted at all? Canadians seem to have reached a new threshold.

The labour movement is worried about the effects of technological change on workers. It urges consultation about new technology before changes are introduced. Just like the Luddites of old, labour wants some guarantee of work for those displaced by machines. Some unions have managed to get clauses in their contracts calling for companies to provide notification and consultation prior to the introduction of the latest systems.

However, a huge number of office and other service-sector workers – primarily women – do not have union protection. At the same time, many planning and supervisory jobs have vanished – layer upon layer of management has been removed as "intelligent" networks allow managers at the top of the hierarchy to monitor the performance and output of people below them, with less assistance from those who once had jobs in the middle.

Bell Canada has experienced a dramatic loss of operator jobs. The operator workforce shrank from 12,000 in 1969 to 4,542 in 1985. Employment in both craft and operator services declined another 14 per cent between 1990 and 1993, when an operator attending a union educational session on work reorganization told her fellow workers, "Nobody knows what's going on."[12] A few months later Bell announced the elimination of five thousand jobs in Ontario and Quebec, and by 2002 only a handful of operators remained with the company. The rest of the jobs had been eliminated by a combination of technological change and contracting out.

Just as the early effect of the digitalization of the phone company was becoming apparent, a Bell manager explained the employer perspective: "Operators represent expense . . . and in order to cut costs in any organization, perhaps part of the way you do that is by reducing expense." An operator summed the situation up differently: "The villain is not really the technology. It is the employer who does not recognize that the people sitting on the machines are not just a piece of technology or a commodity."[13]

The Bell case is a classic example of what often happens when new technologies are introduced. Profits are based on productivity, productivity can be enhanced by new technology, and that technology displaces workers. The technology is labour-saving, efficient, and profitable. There is no reason, however, why its introduction must always cause hardship – unless the economic and political structures into which it is introduced are unjust.

Tools: The Surveillance Society

Nineteen Eighty-Four, George Orwell's frightening novel about an all-seeing, all-powerful dictatorial state, anticipates a time when "Big Brother is watching you." The book gave rise to the use of its author's name as an adjective that we use to describe a society in which surveillance is the order of the day. In an "Orwellian" society, the citizens are constantly spied upon by video cameras and wiretaps. With the marriage of computer and communications technologies fifty years after the publication of *Nineteen Eighty-Four*, the type of surveillance Orwell imagined is now in place.

Social analysis raises serious questions about who is watching and how. Why are they doing it? Do they have our permission? Do we even know we are being watched? To what extent is our privacy being invaded?

Not only do new technologies, new ways of doing things, eliminate specific tasks and workplaces – telephone operators and their switchboards, statisticians and their files – but the remaining work is frequently done asynchronously in terms of both times and space.

But how and where . . . is discernment, trust, and collaboration learned, experience and caution passed on, when people no longer work, build, create and learn together or share sequence and consequence in the course of a common task? . . . When people no longer work together in the same place – the shop floor, the typing pool, the warehouse or the factory – opportunities for social interactions, for social learning and community building disappear, just as the implicit learning opportunities in the classroom can vanish when the cohesion of learning in a group is eclipsed by the device-assisted, individually paced acquisition of knowledge. But where, if not in school and workplace, is society built and changed?

— Ursula Franklin,
The Real World of Technology, 1999.

Since the Industrial Revolution began, employers have tried to monitor and control what workers are doing. The image of a manager conducting a time and motion study, stopwatch in hand as he calculates whether his employees are working fast enough, is a potent reminder of how the factory system was organized. Frank Gilbreth, an early time and motion theorist who spent years observing bricklayers at work, even divided the movements of the human body into minute motions that he called *therbligs*, a variant of his name spelled backwards.

The idea was to divide each job into fractions and hire less skilled people to do them – and pay them less money. Workers responded, though, by attempting to preserve their skills. They took pride in their work. Besides, high skill levels allowed them more bargaining power when dealing with employers. Workers are well aware that the more the employers know about how they conceive and plan their jobs, the less control the workers have over the work itself. So they have always feared and resented surveillance by time and motion experts.

Computer technology has not only allowed employers to replace workers with machines, but also opened up new vistas of surveillance. Employers can now investigate exactly what their workers are doing and how fast they are doing it . . . often without the knowledge of those being watched. Millions of workers now have their every activity quietly monitored by their employers. The operators who still have jobs at Bell Canada are subject to sixty-five different forms of electronic surveillance as their employer attempts to evaluate their work and their relations with customers.[14]

With the spread of cheaper hardware and software, more and more people routinely use computers on the job. As a result an entire new industry has sprung up, and managers have come to accept "Employee Internet Management" as a routine part of overseeing the work of others. One factor behind EIM is the goal of preventing employees from using their time at work to surf the Internet and send personal e-mails on company time. While there is indeed evidence that employees working with computers do exchange personal correspondence, shop, and inspect photos of naked people cavorting in interesting postures, the monitoring of their computer use has other, much more traditional, advantages for employers.

Using programs with names like *Superscout, Silent Watch,* and *FastTracker,* employers have increased their surveillance activities dramatically in the brief period since individual computers became linked by modems, phone lines, and cable hook-ups. One study reported that active monitoring has "skyrocketed," rising from 35 per cent of firms surveyed in 1997 to 78 per cent in 2001. This prompted an official of the American Management Association, the organization that carries out the annual survey, to conclude, "Privacy in today's workplace is largely illusory."[15]

It can be argued that employers have every right to inspect what their employees are doing on company time using company computers. While this may be true, it is equally true that, going back to the time of Frank Gilbreth, employers have other motives. Not all the electronic monitoring programs are aimed at surveillance of on-line activity. So-called "client-based programs" generate detailed logs of employee activity so that managers can inspect what staff do, when, and for how long. When a corporation or government agency installs *WinWhatWhere Investigator* on your computer, you must keep in mind that, at the end of the day, supervisors can print out a record of the software you used, the names of the windows that were opened on your computer, the number of keystrokes you made while you were at work — even the number of times you hit "delete."

Such programs can be installed on employee computers with or without their knowledge. *WinWhatWhere* offers a "stealth mode" feature that conceals the program in the background so that the computer user has no idea of being monitored. *PcAnywhere* permits an employer to connect with any personal computer on its network, anonymously. Other products allow supervisors not only to monitor the number of keystrokes but also to compare a worker's performance with the company average. Still others give the employer the ability to monitor the amount of time that employees are absent from their work stations and how long their computers remain idle. Products like *FastTracker* allow employees to look at each other's work electronically.[16]

Another new form of workplace surveillance, the "awareness monitoring system," allows isolated employees to look at each other while they work. (It also enables managers to look at their subordinates.) These systems, consisting of a voice hook-up and video cameras pointed at the worker's chair, are sold as a means of facilitating communication between employees and managers working in different places. More people are working from home using computer technology supplied by their employers, and large corporations have employees scattered around the globe. Employers hoping for better productivity through more face-to-face interaction find awareness monitoring attractive, particularly if they are insisting that isolated workers are part of a "team."

Canadian researchers who questioned employees in general and teleworkers in particular found a belief that this technology intrudes on the workers' privacy and violates their psychological barriers. The negative assessments even persisted when participants were told that awareness monitoring systems could be adjusted to give them more control over when and how they would be observed. Many pointed out that supervisors would probably evaluate them negatively whenever the camera revealed that they were not at their work stations.[17]

"It was no surprise that, overall, people found these systems to be highly invasive and unfair," said researcher David Zweig. "People questioned the usefulness of the technology and even suggested that they would not want to work for an organization that implements awareness monitoring techniques."[18]

Pharaohs and the Social Nature of Tools

When we consider the role of technology in society — and the word technology itself — we might be tempted to think just of tools. Technology does indeed include tools, from the simplest stone axes and clay pots used by ancient peoples to the palm pilots and power saws of our own era.

An exclusive focus on the tools, however, ignores the social context in which tools are used — who designs them, who controls their use, and what kind of tools are designed and chosen in the first place. This point applies to all machines, big and small. To convey his understanding of this social nature of tools, historian of technology Lewis Mumford reached back to the Egyptian pyramids and explained them as the product of what he called "the first megamachine."

It was not simply levers, ropes, and slaves that allowed Egyptian society, just emerging from the Stone Age, to build such immense, complex structures. It was also the result of a centrally directed hierarchy that was able to plan and execute the construction of huge, symmetrical mountains of stone. "Was it possible to create such a structure without the aid of a machine? Emphatically not."

For Mumford, this first megamachine was a labour mechanism comprising an army of slaves who endured grinding poverty and forced labour for the glory of the king. The Pharaoh's bureaucracy organized "the first large-scale power machine":

a machine of a hundred thousand manpower . . . composed of a multitude of uniform, specialized, interchangeable, but functionally differentiated parts, rigorously marshalled together and coordinated in a process centrally organized and centrally directed: each part behaving as a mechanical component of the mechanized whole.[19]

This emphasis on social control and power – the social apparatus itself as a kind of machine – underlines the importance of understanding technology not simply as a matter of things but as a way of organizing those things. Those things can be anything from the stone blocks that form the pyramids at Giza to today's massive data banks that get more massive as computers become ever faster, more powerful, and more capable of communicating with each other.

Monitoring and Social Sorting

Canadians hear a lot about "transparency". The word is usually used in discussions of the need for governments to become more open about how they make decisions about public affairs. The reasoning is that citizens have a right to full information about the conduct of public business. Similarly, corporations are urged to be transparent with respect to their dealings with customers and shareholders. The idea is that large institutions should make information freely available because people need information to make informed decisions.

But the technologies now available to such institutions mean that the information flow is likely to be in the opposite direction. Information is gathered, combined, and sold in ways that few people outside the world of science fiction might have imagined a generation ago.

Data and information are extracted from people when they make cell phone calls and use their bank cards to make everyday purchases. Every time you click your mouse while you are logged onto the Internet, a government agency or company can track your electronic activity, keeping a record of the websites you looked at and possibly reading your e-mail. The growing field of electronic surveillance has a new term – "clickstream monitoring." PIN numbers, smart cards, genetic databases, and closed circuit television all contribute to a "surveillance society" in which more institutions file more information on more people than ever before.

The marriage of communication and computer technologies means that the nature of surveillance is changing. Just as time and motion experts with stopwatches have given way to electronic monitoring and data-gathering at the workplace, society at large has witnessed a shift. "Surveillance" at one time suggested police wiretaps and spy novels, with security agents following foreign spies to see where microfilm would be dropped off. Surveillance today happens at the local store and on the global Internet. Defined as the "collection, use and retention of personal information," it is now carried out by organizations far beyond the Big Brother government that worried George Orwell. As former B.C. information and privacy commissioner David Flaherty put it, these bodies

> include telephone companies, banks, trust companies, credit unions, employer associations, labour unions, transportation and telecommunication companies, large and small retailers, grocery stores, pharmacies, direct marketers, telemarketers, credit reporting bureaus, insurance companies and brokers, physicians, dentists, lawyers, accountants, therapists, psychologists, travel agencies, charitable organizations, associations, churches, hotels, investment dealers, the media and video rental shops.

Flaherty explained that he made his list so long to illustrate the extent to which the private sector in Canada is virtually unregulated when it comes to the collection and use of personal information.[20]

In addition, the government collection of information on citizens continues with more zeal than ever. Sometimes the data is gathered for reasons of efficiency, as in a proposal for centralizing health records electronically. Sometimes, as in the aftermath of the 9/11 attacks on the symbols of corporate and government power in the United States, "national security" is given as a concern.

Pressure for mandatory, machine-readable "smart cards" that would contain personal information increased. After 9/11, the Canadian Customs and Revenue Agency (already the custodian of vast files on personal incomes) began keeping track of people's travel habits – even though Canada's privacy commissioner objected.

Civil liberties, always vulnerable in wartime, are doubly threatened by the use of new technologies. During World War II thousands of innocent Canadians were herded into detention camps for being of Japanese ancestry or for their political beliefs. Today, "national security" can override privacy and civil liberties. Innocent Canadians become vulnerable with the convergence of private-sector and government surveillance systems.

During World War II the authorities could learn little or nothing about citizens through their telephone numbers. Some sixty years later, Internet Service Providers came under increasing pressure to provide the authorities with surfing data as part of a "war on terrorism." A URL is far more useful than a telephone number because of what it reveals about personal interests, personal contacts, and buying habits.[21] All of this activity makes our private lives, habits, and thoughts that much more transparent in an era of networked surveillance.

There is a paradox here. The deregulation of the private sector and privatization of government services have been based on the idea that "the market" is the best way of providing services (garbage collection, health care, transportation) that have long been public responsibilities. This trend has blurred the lines between the public and private sectors, making it difficult to determine where one ends and the other begins. At the same time, the collection and exchange of private, personal information by both governments and corporations threaten to expose the most private details of our lives to scrutiny.

In 2001 the Toronto police adopted "e-Cops" (Enterprise Case and Occurrence Processing Systems), a wireless data communication system that connected patrol car laptops not only to drivers' licences, vehicle registrations, and the Canadian

Police Information Centre, but also to an IBM database and business intelligence software.[22] What does this say about the ways in which personal privacy is – or is not – safeguarded in the era of privatization?

Although the new electronic tools have an impact on individual privacy, they remain essentially social. They result from human decisions made within economic and political institutions that are rooted in society at large. As much as networked surveillance can be used to watch people, collecting information in searchable databases, it can also be used to influence and manage people, sorting society into groups that the marketers or police and welfare agencies see as being worthy of special attention.

A new industry that categorizes Canadians for marketing purposes has grown dramatically in lockstep with computer and communications technology. Canada is now organized by "geo-demographic" categories, according to age, race, gender, and class. CompuSearch sells its lists of groups (urban, suburban, and rural) and subdivides them into clusters.

The Suburban Affluent group includes both "bureaucrats and technocrats" and "Asian heights." The Rural and Comfortable Families take in "pickups and dirt bikes." Big cities are sorted not only into Urban Elite and High-Rise Melting Pot but also Urban Downscale. That last category includes Cluster 59, codenamed Big City Stress:

> Inner city urban neighbourhoods with second lowest average household income. Probably the most disadvantaged areas of the country. Predominant age skew is young and almost everyone rents. Dwellings are older, low-rise with some newer, high-rise. Household types include singles, couples and lone parent families. A significant but mixed "ethnic" presence. Unemployment levels are very high.[23]

Although the affluent groups are more likely to attract the attention of SUV advertisers, people sorted into the Big City Stress cluster are subjected to strict government surveillance. In 1996

Quebec changed its Social Welfare Act to allow for extensive data searches of welfare applicants and recipients, thus tightening surveillance over an entire section of the population.[24] Those in serious need of income assistance due to joblessness, sickness, poverty, or single parenthood fall under intense surveillance. There is very little about their personal lives that the state does not want to know.

Surveillance as social sorting places a different value on different people according to class, race, and gender. People of colour have objected to the tendency of police to do racial profiling, which stigmatizes certain groups as being more likely to break the law.

Surveillance for social sorting has not increased just because there are new tools available to do the job. It has also grown because of other changes, such as the gradual unravelling of the social safety net. The idea behind the construction of the welfare state was that the risks of poverty, illness, and disability could be socially shared. Reducing social programs tends to individualize risks, placing them on the shoulders of individuals and families rather than society at large. This in turn creates market opportunities for organizations like insurance companies that will take advantage of every available tool to investigate the health, job, and other risks faced by each applicant.[25]

The Technological Mindset: A Change for the Better?

We often learn in high school history class that the crucial machine during the Industrial Revolution was the steam engine. But a more important instrument, still very much with us long after steam engines were relegated to museums, is the mechanical clock. Most houses have a clock beside the bed, on kitchen walls, or in VCRs and the microwave ovens. Every computer has one. People still wear a watch on their wrist.

The clock came along well before the Industrial Revolution, when European monks

> The Internet age is passing by substantial numbers of people who do not have the money or opportunity to participate. In 2000, 77% of households with the highest 10% of incomes used the Internet, five times the rate of 15% among those with the lowest 10% of incomes. The proportion of new users coming from households with lower incomes has been increasing. However, from 1996 to 2000, it was actually middle-income groups who picked up share and accounted for proportionately more Internet users.
>
> In 1997, 25% of all new Internet users came from households with the top 10% of incomes. By 2000, only 11% of all new Internet users were from the top income bracket. However, households in the bottom two income brackets accounted for about 7% of new Internet uses in 2000, up from only 4% four years earlier. Overall, the relative digital divide is closing. However, this has been entirely because of these households in the upper-middle of the income scale. Households in the three bottom income groups are continuing to lose ground compared with households in the top income group.
>
> — Statistics Canada, *The Digital Divide in Canada,* 2002.

(there were once 40,000 Benedictine monasteries) built them to regulate their times of work and prayer.[26] Today no machine is more important in regulating social life. Our lives are organized according to schedules and appointments. Significantly for social analysis, the mechanical clock emerged from one of the most powerful social institutions of its day, the Christian church.

Similarly, the computer and the Internet were products of an institution that, for over a half-century, has been one of the most powerful in the world: the U.S. military. The U.S. computer industry owes its rapid growth to U.S. Department of Defense funding for research and development as well as procurement contracts. The Internet and its predessessor (ARPANET) were created by the department's Advanced Research Products Agency (ARPA).[27]

Technology is social, not just because new tools spring from social institutions like the church and the military, but also because they reflect the priorities of those institutions and how they organize people and the work they do. This remains true whether the technology involves weaving cloth in the early nineteenth century or driving computer systems in the early twenty-first. Above all, warns Canadian physicist Ursula Franklin, we must be aware of how the technology involves a "mindset" and becomes "an agent of power and control" that dictates the ways in which tools are used.[28]

The Luddite weavers challenged that mindset and control. We face similar challenges today. Steam-driven mills may seem a far cry from electronic telephone switching systems or remote surveillance programs. Yet rapid technological change without adequate social safeguards echoes what happened to English workers in the nineteenth century. Those whose lives are altered by changes in technology are rarely, if ever, those who make the decisions about what tools are introduced, and how. Still, many people in Canada and around the world are picking up the new tools and controlling them and using them for their own purposes (see chapter ten).

Plus ça change. The changes resulting from new technologies have brought society to a crossroads. If the future is to mirror the past – *plus ça change, plus ça reste la même chose* – the structural unemployment wrought by technological change will continue, as will increased surveillance on the job and off. The existing structures are not equitable in their distribution of work, costs, benefits, responsibility, and control. Many people are simply instructed to adapt without being consulted.

The message of the Parable of the Teaspoons is that you cannot stand in the way of progress. If new technologies were to lead to a life freer from hardship and insecurity, with lots more leisure time for everyone, that would be progress – but progress of a different kind.

Questions

❏ How have you and people you know been affected by new technology? Have its effects been felt at home, in the workplace?

❏ Do you think that new technology offers hope for a better world? Or do you think it will create more problems than it solves? In Canada? In poorer countries?

❏ Industry, government, and educational institutions place great emphasis on information technology. To what extent has your exposure to and education about such technology included questions about the economic and social changes that accompany it? To what extent do you feel in control when new technologies are introduced?

❏ People often assume that the economic system will remain fundamentally the same, despite the introduction of new technologies. How does the revolution in technology relate to economic and social change? Does an alternative way of organizing the economy necessarily put a halt to technological progress? How would you suggest that the increased productivity be used? What obstacles built into society prevent technology from benefiting people and representing true progress?

❏ Some thinkers argue that differing values like privatizing knowledge or sharing knowledge are embedded in different technologies. To what extent do "proprietary" systems (Microsoft) and "open source" systems (GNU/Linux) represent different values?

Resources

• Janet Abbate. *Inventing the Internet*. Cambridge, Mass.: MIT Press, 2000. Although the Internet only came into common use in the early 1990s with the advent of the World Wide Web, its development reaches back to the 1960s. This book locates the people, institutions, and technologies that contributed to the inventions of the Internet. More importantly, it focuses on the social and cultural factors that guided the Internet's design and use.

• Ursula Franklin. *The Real World of Technology*. rev. ed. Toronto: Anansi, 1999. This is an updated version of the original book based on the renowned Canadian scientist's 1989 Massey lectures. The first edition explored how technology gave rise to a "culture of compliance" in which we accept external management as normal. The revised edition discusses how the marriage of computer and communications technologies affects time, space, and how we relate to each other.

• Heather Menzies. *Whose Brave New World? The Information Highway and the New Economy*. Toronto: Between the Lines, 1996. A succinct, provocative critique of the impact of computerization on society and the workplace. A book that "could well be subtitled 'Economics when people no longer matter'" (Ursula Franklin).

• David Noble. *Progress without People: New Technology, Unemployment, and the Message of Resistance*. Toronto: Between the Lines, 1995. This analysis of the effects of automation reaches back into history to put the struggles of the Luddites into perspective. The author questions the idea of the inevitability of progress through ever more machine innovations.

• Langdon Winner. *The Whale and the Reactor: A Search for Limits in an Age of High Technology*. Chicago: University of Chicago Press, 1986. An examination of the way we think about technology, this book focuses on the moral and political implications of technical systems rather than the systems themselves. The argument that power and authority, and freedom and social justice, are "embedded" in technical devices leads to the conclusion that they lend important meaning and direction to individual people and societies in general.

• *McLuhan's Wake*. Canada, 2002. Directed by Kevin McMahon. NFB. Video. 94 min. Explores the legacy of Marshall McLuhan, the influential Canadian thinker who viewed media as environments that shape human life. Fascinated by the role that technology played in transforming our lives, McLuhan foresaw the impact of the digital age on our social, spiritual, economic, and ideological selves.

Websites:

The Nature Institute provides a good gateway into Internet sources that contain critical examinations of science and technology. It publishes *NetFuture*, an electronic newsletter that probes the ways in which we shape technology and are in turn shaped by it. There is a strong emphasis on ethical issues in science and technology <www.netfuture.org>.

Chapter Nine

Globalization and Development

One World, Ready or Not: the title of just one of the hundreds, perhaps thousands, of books dealing with globalization published in the 1990s and into the present century. Two even shared the same suggestive title, *Globalization and Its Discontents*. Most described something apparently inevitable: the ever-increasing integration of the planet. Money flows faster, goods move faster, information travels at the speed of light. People travel faster and more often. The very nature of human contact has been transformed.

Transnational corporations can now manage their production and marketing operations in different corners of the world. Clothing at The Gap is manufactured by hundreds of subcontractors in dozens of tropical countries. Made-in-USA images of the good life are projected by a company with a name hard-wired to the notion of globalization – Planet Hollywood.

When fire ravaged the Kader toy factory outside Bangkok, Thailand, in 1993, it left at least 188 workers dead and thousands of charred Bart Simpson and Big Bird dolls scattered in the wreckage. The actual number of people killed will never be known, because only a hundred of the three thousand workers, mostly women, were legally designated employees. The same employment system common in Canada was in effect at Kader, which means that the other 2,900 were contract workers. No one kept track of them. They had few rights or benefits. Many had migrated from rural Thailand, where small farmers were being pushed from their ancient plots of land by debt and large-scale rice producers and forestry and dam projects.

It was, in a way, a familiar story, a replay of the old pattern that had been witnessed first in Europe, then in North America, and more recently in the poor countries of the South. During the Industrial Revolution, farmers displaced from their land migrated to cities, where they took whatever factory jobs they could find, whatever the conditions. Today, in the rich countries of the North, children no longer toil in deadly factories. Things have changed since the nineteenth century, and laws, unions, and public attitudes no longer tolerate the unchecked power of employers to do whatever they want.

Why, then, asked the author of *One World, Ready or Not*, are corporations that can run complex global operations — buying and selling Big Bird and Bart Simpson puppets on a world scale — unable, or unwilling, to take care of ordinary tasks like fire safety? The easy answer was profit, "but the deeper answer was about power," William Greider says. "Firms behaved this way because they could, because nobody would stop them. When law and social values retreated before the power of markets, then capitalism's natural drive to maximize returns had no internal governor to check its social behaviour."[1]

If every action prompts a reaction, the face of globalization represented by the Thai toy fire provoked a sense of outrage. Market values were challenged by people with different social values, like human rights. Groups like Students Against Sweatshops organized to improve working conditions on the other side of the world. An "anti-globalization" movement began to take to the streets in cities like Seattle, Prague, and Quebec City. The question was straightforward. Instead of a deregulated market that erodes the rights of citizens, communities, and nations, why not control capitalism's social behaviour? That way, the fruits of the most productive age in the history of humanity could be distributed more equally, while minimizing harm to the natural environment.

Social analysis asks, "What's new about globalization?" How is our era different from others? Who's in control? What are the social forces at play? What values take priority? Why?

The Third World?

The notion of a "Third World" originated after World War II, with the division of the planet between the industrial countries of North America and Europe (the First World, or the "West") and a Soviet-led Eastern bloc (or Second World). What remained after this division was the so-called Third World, those other countries that were closer to the equator and poorer. Many were only just throwing off the shackles of colonial rule. Since then, and particularly since the collapse of the Soviet bloc in the early 1990s, the Third World concept has had less meaning. But its use persists, so much so that poor people in the affluent Northern countries are often described as living in "Third World conditions." Meanwhile, various other terms have been used to describe the poor or marginalized peoples or regions: the South; the Majority World; underdeveloped countries. But none effectively captures the complexity of a world in which we can use our bank cards to withdraw Indonesian rupiahs from an automated teller in Jakarta or Canadian dollars from a similar machine in Toronto, but still pass by the same excluded people begging as we step out the bank door.

Change and Exchange in a "New Era"

Thai food – lemon grass, *phad thai* – was a novelty in Canada twenty years ago. But since the 1980s it has become commonplace in Canadian cities. Globalization is often said to be stimulating culinary and many other forms of cultural cross-fertilization, and songs from other lands have now gained a section of their very own in the record stores – "World Music."

This is the natural extension of a global exchange of ideas about everything from food and music to religion and philosophy, an exchange that has been going on since the days of the first spice traders and missionaries. Trade unionists have been talking about "international solidarity" since the nineteenth century. In our time, however, the natural desire for capitalism to put everything on the market has given rise to a situation in which money, markets, and corporate logos have slipped into many corners of everyday life. In another book about globalization, *No Logo*, Canadian writer Naomi Klein describes how the marketing efforts of transnational corporations have attempted to get people to identify with products and logos, not the workers who produced those products.[2]

If we are to believe the advertising, Canada's Second Cup now has "close relationships" with coffee growers around the world and serves up a brew that is "similar to vintage wine." Some people refer to coffee as "Java," in reference to Indonesia's most populous island. Yet almost half of the world's coffee beans, originally from Ethiopia, are today grown in Latin America,

where they were introduced by Spanish colonizers. Similarly, people from Africa were enslaved by Europeans to produce cane-sugar, which originally came from India. Potatoes, identified as the staple food in Ireland, originated in Peru.

This sort of exchange has been going on for over five hundred years. It accelerated during the colonial period, when European kingdoms expanded their control over foreign lands, whose raw materials enriched international traders. Canada supplied furs, fish, and lumber. Gradually, in the years after World War II, factories specializing in goods for export began to spring up in poor countries. Asian countries that once specialized in tea and spices now export computer chips and nearly everything in every dollar store.

Conventional economic theory assumes that all of this global trade and commerce will generate the economic growth necessary for "development." And if globalization is a new word for a phenomenon as old as the galleons and clipper ships that carried the raw materials from the New World to the Old, "development" only came into use with the age of the Cold War and the jet plane. Development, a word hinting always at positive changes, found its way into popular use after 1949. It was in that year that the U.S. president announced a program to make the benefits of scientific and industrial progress available "for the improvement and growth of underdeveloped areas . . . a program of development based on the concepts of democratic fair dealing."[3]

Democracy, fairness . . . development: the future seemed bright. Within fifty years the Cold War was over and the "underdeveloped" countries had freed themselves from control by European powers. But although the Soviet Union had collapsed, the Us and Them of the Cold War period was replaced by a persistent and growing gap between rich and poor. In 1960, as the era of formal colonialism was ending, the 20 per cent of the people in the richest countries had thirty times the income of the poorest 20 per cent. By 1997 the richest had seventy-four times as much as the poorest. The assets of the world's three richest people were more than the com-

> "Developing countries" is the name that experts use to designate countries trampled by someone else's development. According to the United Nations, developing countries send developed countries ten times as much money through unequal trade and financial relations as they receive in foreign aid.
>
> — Eduardo Galeano,
> *Upside Down: A Primer for the Looking-Glass World*, 2000.

bined Gross National Product of the poorest forty-eight countries.[4] Between 1990 and 1997 the underdeveloped countries paid out more in debt service than they received from new loans, resulting in a $77-billion transfer of wealth from South to North.[5]

Colonialism, it seemed, had not gone away but had simply taken on a new form. The missionaries of old who had accompanied the traders and the king's soldiers had been replaced by a new breed of believers whose faith in the market was every bit as unshakeable as that of priests seeking converts. If only the poor countries would let the free market work, they believed, the economy would grow and everyone would benefit. In 2002 Joseph Stiglitz, the former chief economist of the World Bank described the International Monetary Fund (IMF) and his ex-employer as "the new missionary institutions" who pushed their ideology on poor countries that needed the loans that these institutions had to offer. Stiglitz, who had just won the Nobel Prize for economics, underlined what IMF and World Bank critics had been arguing for years.

According to the new missionaries, governments were the problem and free-market capitalism was the solution to the problems of developing countries. Stiglitz found out how this theory worked in practice when he paid a visit to Ethiopia in 1997. At the time Canada was ranked as number one in the United Nations' human development index. Ethiopia, just emerging from years of drought, famine, and military rule, was number 170 on the UN list – sixth to last.

Stiglitz reported that Ethiopia, a desperately poor country, was cutting military spending in favour of fighting poverty in the rural areas, where 85 per cent of Ethiopians lived. Ethiopia was also paying back its foreign loans as fast as it could, because the interest rate was much higher than the rate it was receiving on its modest reserves of foreign currency.

The IMF and the United States (by far the most influential of the Fund's donors) objected to the early loan repayment. They objected not on the grounds that early repayment was a bad idea – they agreed that it made good economic sense

– but because the Ethiopians had not asked the IMF's permission before writing the cheques. "To the Ethiopians," Stiglitz explained, "such intrusiveness smacked of a new form of colonialism; to the IMF, it was standard operating procedure."[6]

The Ethiopians were also confronted with another IMF demand. The powerful Washington-based organization told them that they had to undertake a program of "financial market liberalization." Because of the IMF's origins – it was established by the United Nations in 1944 to help stabilize a world economy that would soon emerge from World War II – it supports a liberal, or "free," trading system. This kind of system strives to avoid the protectionist measures that its advocates believe had contributed to the Great Depression of the pre-war years of the 1930s. In recent years the original mandate has evolved into a commitment to free-market economics at all costs.

In Ethiopia's case, the IMF demand for financial market liberalization meant opening the country's banking sector to competition from Western banks like Citibank, Credit Suisse First Boston, or the RBC Financial Group (formerly the Royal Bank of Canada). The IMF also wanted Ethiopia to break its largest bank into several pieces and to allow interest rates to be determined not by the national government but by the free play of market forces.

Opening the country's vulnerable domestic banks to foreign competition and allowing international megabanks to compete with Ethiopia's home-grown institutions flew in the face of the successful experience of from-the-ground-up solutions to the problems of development. The assets of that country's entire financial system were no larger than those of Regina, Moncton, or any other medium-sized Canadian city. Allowing big operators in to compete freely with tiny local banks meant that they would easily attract depositors with higher interest rates. Or they would simply buy up the local competition. Global financial institutions are also much more interested in providing loans and services to really big customers like transnational corporations than they are in lending small amounts to farmers for ploughs and bags of seeds.[7]

What's more, even hugely rich economies like the United States and Western Europe did not "liberalize" their financial systems, allowing market forces to set interest rates, until after 1970. By this time their economies were well established.

The Ethiopian farmers who need money for seed, tools, and fertilizer are poor people. So are small business people who fashion metal cooking implements or fix motorcycle engines. So important is credit for small farmers and micro-enterprises that entire development aid projects are routinely devoted to coming up with simple methods of lending money to poor people in poor countries. The Grameen Bank of Bangladesh is the best-known credit provider in the South, with over two million customers, mostly women, and a default rate of 2 to 3 per cent. After World War II the Japanese government helped to rebuild its devastated economy with easy credit and loan guarantees through the People's Finance and Small Business Finance corporations. In South Korea, Malaysia, and Singapore – among the most successful "developing" countries – governments followed Japan's example by introducing savings offices in its post offices. This gave poor people access to services and credit they needed to take advantage of market opportunities.

Nevertheless, the IMF had a one-size-fits-all development model for a vulnerable country like Ethiopia, telling it to get on with the job of letting the market decide who should get credit and at what rate of interest. It was a prescription that had little to do with the actual conditions in the country and everything to do with what Stiglitz described as a "naive faith in markets." The Ethiopian government, which did not share this faith, refused to go along because it worried that farmers who needed credit for seed and fertilizer would be unable to get it. Or they could be forced to pay higher interest rates that they could not afford. As a result, the IMF suspended its assistance program. The help was only restored after high-level pressure in Washington, where Stiglitz had been a close advisor to U.S. president Bill Clinton.

In another case, a non-governmental organization (NGO) concluded that village women in Morocco could both earn money and produce more food by running a new business alongside their traditional activities. The community-based project settled on raising chickens. The NGO provided funding support and training, and a public agency supplied week-old chicks. Then the IMF stepped in and told the Moroccan government that it should not be in the chick business. The government obeyed. A market-based solution seemed to be at hand when a private supplier began to provide the chicks, but the death rate of the birds tends to be high and the private company would not provide guarantees. The village women, in turn, could not risk spending their scarce resources on vulnerable chicks, so the whole project was shut down.

It was, concluded Stiglitz, yet another example of market fundamentalism applied with little understanding of the reality of the challenges of development faced by poor people. "The assumption underlying this failure is one I saw

> As the commodification of food is intensified nearly everywhere, more and more people in Mexico and other countries around the world, many of them from peasant communities, work to produce food that they may not ever eat themselves. Instead, they are supplying world markets and often eat what comes back to them from world markets. Tomato workers in Mexico cannot afford to eat the fruit they pick and pack for US and Canadian markets. . . . As cheaper US corn moves into the Mexican market, they will likely buy it, even though it tastes different and makes a different type of tortilla from what they have eaten in the past. . . . Taco Bell has opened branches in Mexico to serve industrial tortillas to Mexicans uprooted from their villages.
>
> — Harriet Friedmann,
> *How We Eat, What We Eat, and the Changing Political Economy of Food*, 2000.

made repeatedly," he said. "The IMF simply assumed that markets arise quickly to meet every need, when in fact, many government activities arise because markets have failed to provide essential services."[8]

Despite such experiences, let-the-market-decide programs of privatization and liberalization have been the hallmark of the new era of globalization. Whether they have given rise to development is questionable, particularly because this period has coincided with the growing gap between rich and poor. Rather, the emphasis on open markets and less interference is a throwback to a previous era when governments did little to protect and assist their citizens, particularly the poorest and weakest among them.

The Market – Place or Principle?

Ethiopian grain farmers, like Canadian apple producers, are familiar with markets.

Canadians interested in buying apples from people who grow them go to the "farmers' markets" held in city parking lots and fairgrounds. Otherwise they must go to the chain food stores dominated by the handful of powerful corporations that in turn dominate the retail food system (see chapter four). In Ethiopia, farmers with goods to sell will travel to markets in towns like Negeli and Gondar, carrying their produce on their heads or, if they are doing well, using a draught animal to pull a cart.

The Canadian farmers' market and the Ethiopian town market are close to the original idea of the market as a *place*. This is where buyers and sellers meet, exchange goods for money, and swap information – sometimes with strangers, sometimes with people who customarily gather for both economic and social reasons. This older view of the market is still familar to Ethiopians today, as it was to Europeans who gathered at the town square during the Middle Ages to sell any extra produce they had. It is possible to idealize this conception of the market, because to participate one must possess certain resources (money, goods). At the same time, it is a useful tool of social analysis that allows us to better understand different uses of the notion of *market*.

Today's idea of the market tends to be abstract, more *principle* than place. In the era of globalization, we hear about the world market for coffee, or hog belly futures, or financial derivatives. The latest reports flash endlessly across our television screens, signalling the ups and downs of the Canadian dollar and the Japanese yen. This market is not a place you can visit, except perhaps electronically. As a principle, it is invoked to govern social relations – between people, countries, corporations. It is, we're told, ruled by supply and demand, competition and price. Governments and corporations regard it as the best way to get things done, to get the economy to grow, to provide for the good of all.

According to this way of thinking, the common good is best served when there are few if any restrictions on the flow of money, either inside countries or between them. Yet deregulation of the U.S. banking system during the 1980s helped to trigger a recession and cost taxpayers $200 billion in what became know as the S&L (or savings-and-loan) scandal. The government bailed out floundering banks, with the result that big banks took over smaller, weaker ones.

Although the IMF and the World Bank were established in the wake of the Second World War, amidst fresh memories of the Depression of the 1930s, to promote stability in the international economy, their support for market deregulation has made that economy much more unstable.

Deregulation stimulated the growth of the global currency trading market. Most often described as a "casino," it is a market that has grown by some 600 per cent since the early 1980s, with $1.2 trillion changing hands every day in 2001.[9] Large global banks profit by speculating (or betting) on the value of a country's currency – the Thai baht, the Mexican peso, the Canadian dollar. Well over a trillion dollars changes hands *every day* in this sort of activity as currency traders shift "hot money" around the world, searching for tiny increases in interest rates.

These shifts are not investments in factories or other real things. The capital is not patient; nor is it rooted in a country's economy. Money enters a country and leaves again within days and even hours, the quick round trip resulting in fast profit for the speculator. According to the principle of the free market, a country should do nothing to restrict or regulate these currency flows, even though they can have destabilizing or even disastrous effects.

Before it relaxed its capital controls, Thailand had strict rules against bank lending for speculative real estate developments. When that market was deregulated, there was a frenzied boom in office contruction followed by a real estate crash. When the Thai baht collapsed on July 2, 1997, it was the start of the biggest economic collapse since the Great Depression. Currency speculation hit much of East Asia. Unemployment tripled in Thailand. The country's Gross Domestic Product (GDP) plunged rapidly, as did the value of the baht – 25 per cent overnight. When a currency plummets, not everyone loses. Stiglitz states:

> Assume a speculator goes into a Thai bank, borrows 24 billion baht, which, at the original exchange rate, can be converted into $1 billion. A week later the exchange rate falls; instead of there being 24 baht to the dollar, there are now 40 baht to the dollar. He takes $600 million, converting it back to baht, getting 24 billion baht to repay the loan. The remaining $400 million is his profit – a tidy return for one week's work, and the investment of little of his own money.[10]

This sort of unproductive – but highly profitable – activity became commonplace as the power of unrestricted global financial markets overwhelmed many governments, especially in poor countries. When exchange rates are increasingly influenced by currency speculators who have no knowledge of – or interest in – a country's economic fundamentals, governments lose the capacity to pursue independent policies tailored to their particular circumstances. Countries no longer have the ability to influence exchange rates that in turn influence the price of imports and exports, productivity, and jobs.

According to the logic of the globalized market, the principle of free, unrestricted movement of capital is sacred. James Tobin, a Nobel laureate, advocated controlling hot money with an international tax on speculative financial transactions. For Tobin, today's globalization with its devotion to pure free-market principles and rejection of government regulation is nothing new:

> The doctrines of the day have been accepted all over the world – that the thing to do is to free up your financial markets so that there are no limits on what can be done. The ideology, after all, is an old one which goes back a long way, long before the present financial technologies. It's just a spin-off of "the-free-market-does-everything-right" ideas that are prominent all over the world today.[11]

Theory, however, does not always correspond to reality, particularly in the real world of the market. The transnational corporations that increasingly dominate the global economy saw their share of world markets rise from a quarter in the mid-1980s to a third ten years later. It has become almost a cliché of globalization analysis to observe that the biggest corporations are bigger in economic terms than entire medium-sized countries: General Motors' sales are larger than the GDP of either Thailand or Norway; Shell is bigger than Greece, Wal-Mart bigger than Israel. From 1990 to 1997 the annual number of mergers and acquisitions more than doubled. The biggest industries became ever more concentrated into fewer corporate hands. Daimler-Benz (cars) bought Chrysler; Sandoz (drugs) bought CIBA-Geigy; Exxon (petroleum) merged with Mobil; American Home Products (drugs/chemicals) acquired Monsanto; America Online (communication) merged with Time Warner.[12]

The Canadian government had, at least until 2003, refused to allow mergers in the country's highly concentrated banking sector. But the politically influential banks have kept insisting that they need to be "globally competitive." Coupled with the belief in the principle of the unrestricted free market, this insistence means that pressure to lift restrictions has continued. Yet mergers and acquisitions in Western Europe in the 1990s resulted in the disappearance of at least 130,000 financial-sector jobs. Between 1995 and 2001, banking jobs in the Czech Republic fell by 42 per cent, while a single merger of two Thai banks resulted in the layoff of six thousand out of nine thousand workers.[13]

Like the deadly toy factory fire in Thailand, the elimination of bank jobs is an example of what so often happens when market principles overwhelm social values. The new steam-driven machinery of Europe's Industrial Revolution resulted in fantastic increases in production and created vast fortunes for employers. It also meant that undernourished children became chained to those machines. Similarly, reaping the benefits of today's globalization – with its shrinking time, shrinking space, and disappearing borders – depends on where you are in the global hierarchy. *Plus ça change.*

We apparently live in a time of increased mobility and freedom of movement. Frequent business-class flyers can have their irises scanned to avoid the hassles of increased airport security when they fly around the world. Transnational corporations roam the globe in search of new markets and cheaper labour.

On the one hand, highly skilled people travel easily, so that more than a quarter of a million African professionals work in Europe and the United States while Africa suffers from acute shortages of skilled labour. On the other hand, hundreds of millions of people in poor countries lack passports, let alone the visas necessary to travel to find work in a security-obsessed world. Rich countries place tight restrictions on unskilled workers, and those who do find work in the North – legally or illegally – find themselves separated from their families. Over a billion dollars a year flow into Nigeria from Nigerians working abroad – more than the country receives in foreign direct investment.

"The collapse of space, time and borders may be creating a global village," concluded the United Nations Development Programme, "but not everyone can be a citizen. The global, professional elite faces low borders, but billions of others find borders as high as ever."[14]

How can we understand a global system that has changed so much, so quickly, yet has remained the same since the nineteenth century? Is it indeed anything new that global capitalism is capable of generating so much growth without development? And what of the notion of "development" itself?

The Push and Pull of the "Double Movement"

In the decades since U.S. president Harry Truman announced his optimistic plan for a program of development and improvement of underdeveloped areas, global economic output has increased by five times. Humans have consumed more of the world's natural resources during this short period than we did throughout the previous thousands of years of recorded history.[15]

We live in an era of abundance, at a time when human beings have the capacity to produce more than enough to meet the needs of all the world's people. And we do. The market system is so good at producing such a cornucopia that the places in which we buy our food – stores with quantities and varieties unknown to the very richest kings and merchants of yesteryear – are called supermarkets.

To appreciate the enormity of this achievement, we only have to consider one simple fact: one of the most urgent problems confronting rich countries is how to dispose of what we waste, whether it is too much packaging and other garbage or too much carbon dioxide and other gases (see chapter seven).

We distribute the gas into the upper atmosphere, where it alters climates and has an impact on everyone on the planet. But we produce it unevenly, and its global effects are similarly uneven. While every Canadian generates 16.2 tonnes of carbon dioxide annually, each resident of the Maldive Islands, a country threatened with virtual extinction by climate change, produces 1.2 tonnes.[16]

Capitalism's self-regulating market (or unrestrained capitalism) is a double-edged sword. It generates ample goods and services, but distributes them unevenly. It produces negative social and environmental costs, like poverty and pollution, and these too are distributed unevenly. It also produces something else – a response from people concerned about its effects.

Industrial capitalism first took hold in the North in the eighteenth century, spreading and growing in the nineteenth. Along the way it harnessed peoples of the South to the expanding empires of the day. The Industrial Revolution and its accompanying global thrust for imperial power provoked an inevitable reaction. People rebelled against child factory labour in the North and colonialism in the South, and in time these conditions came to an end. As a result, in places like Canada, men without property and women – who had also been banned from voting – gained the right to participate in the political process. The former colonies of the South gained the right to form their own nations.

The people who agitated against the harmful effects of market capitalism most often employed the language of rights: the right to speak out, the right to vote, the right to self-determination. They were using concepts rooted in *liberalism* (from the Latin *liber*, or free; *libertas*, or freedom). Political ideas about rights and freedom, about how every human being should enjoy a good

measure of each, only began to take root slowly, and in a limited way (women and colonial subjects were generally excluded), in the seventeenth and eighteenth centuries in tandem with market capitalism as a principle of social organization. (See also "Liberal Capitalism," chapter ten.)

Early liberal doctrine did not by any means call for everyone to have the right to vote, to participate in making decisions that affected their lives. That only came later, although it was in 1792, at the height of the French Revolution (with its slogan, "liberty, equality, and fraternity") that the English writer Mary Wollstonecraft put forth the idea that women were rational beings who should reject the male-imposed order that kept them under the control of husbands and fathers. Her book was called *A Vindication of the Rights of Women*.

In its early years, advocates of liberalism – a complex and nuanced set of beliefs – were concerned mainly with the rights of individual property owners in the face of the power of kings and government. They were concerned about freedom from state interference in trade and commerce. They called for constitutions, laws, and charters to guarantee individual rights against interference from government. They believed in the supremacy of the individual, *his* rights and freedoms. Powerful property owners, who rejected government interference in their business affairs, also opposed the labour organizers who argued that they had the right to free association and, therefore, the right to form unions. For a long time unions in Canada were illegal, just as political parties advocating independence were banned in the colonial world.

People who, like Mary Wollstonecraft, wanted to broaden notions of rights and freedoms turned classical conceptions of liberalism into contested terrain. They pushed the boundaries to include human rights, more broadly defined. Gradually, during the twentieth century, governments began to regulate the market, responding to popular pressure for laws controlling pollution, promoting public health, or mandating safer and cleaner workplaces. Similarly, after World War II governments in most industrialized countries

began to provide public services, free of charge: health care and education, unemployment insurance and social welfare, public pensions, support for non-profit housing.

The idea was that the market, by itself, was efficient at providing material goods like cars and electric-garage-door openers. But in other areas the government had to step in to make sure that all citizens had access to basic services. Similarly, protecting the natural environment and looking out for workers on the job were not initiatives that private businesses were likely to undertake. Indeed, private-enterprise activity often polluted the air and caused workplace illnesses. It was up to the public authorities to regulate the behaviour of the market – although it was not easy to convince governments, often reluctant to interfere with the workings of the free market, of that need.

It took decades to build the movement towards a more humane society in which people did not die of curable diseases and everyone could be confident that their children could go to school. It was all part of what Karl Polanyi, one of the twentieth century's clearest voices on such matters, called the "double movement." Polanyi described "two organizing principles of society," each with different – and often opposing – goals. These conflicting ideas emerged when capitalists threw aside the trade restrictions of kings and their governments:

> The one was the principle of economic liberalism, aiming at the establishment of a self-regulating market, relying on the support of the trading classes, and using largely *laissez-faire* and free trade as its methods; the other was the principle of social protection aiming at the conservation of man and nature as well as productive organization, relying on the varying support of those most immediately affected by the deleterious action of the market.[17]

Polanyi argued that the market had an inevitable tendency to ignore its social and environmental effects, to become "disembedded," or separated, from society. Society could only be protected by social forces that were constantly defending people, land, and culture. His double movement is the tug-of-war between the negative effects of an unfettered free market and the countervailing forces thrown up by society.

Today's globalization – critics call it "corporate globalization" – is characterized by a push for free trade, deregulated markets, and privatization of government services. Powerful institutions like the International Monetary Fund and the World Trade Organization subscribe to what Polanyi described as a "veritable faith in man's secular salvation through the self-regulating market."[18] According to the dominant view, the role of the public sector should be reduced to enhancing the market's efficiency. Otherwise, government should get out of the way and privatize services to allow commercial operators to run the health-care system. In the poor nations of the South, conventional IMF loan conditions have typically included the elimination of government subsidies on food for poor people and the implementation of higher fees for parents who want to send their children to school.

Such attempts to roll back social gains designed to protect people have often been called *neo-liberalism*. The use of this term suggests that globalization constitutes a return to an earlier period, before people had succeeded in instituting social protections like medicare, unemployment insurance, and the array of programs that benefit everyone, particularly the most vulnerable. While

Neo-liberalism

Confusing when used interchangeably with "neo-conservatism," the notion of "neo-liberalism" refers back in time to the classical liberalism of seventeenth- and eighteenth-century Europe. Philosophers and merchants put forward the idea of liberation from the restrictions of kings and their governments. At the same time, reformers and revolutionaries promoted doctrines of a citizenry endowed with democratic freedoms. What emerged was a tangled philosophical thicket that includes the ideal of limited government, the rights and freedoms of the individual, and tolerance in matters of religion and morality.

Liberty – individual freedom – was clearly the defining ideal. Less clear back then were the conditions necessary to ensure individual freedom. Does freedom mean guaranteed non-interference with an individual's pursuit of his or her goals? Does the possibility of a free citizenry presuppose guaranteed access to a few fundamentals like basic shelter, nutrition, and education? And what if any rules are necessary to protect freedoms?

While liberals and neo-liberals are both concerned with freedom, liberals have sometimes focused on social changes that will recognize the rights of larger numbers of people formerly excluded from the club: for example, women, non-whites, and wage-labourers. They have also paid attention to how social wealth is distributed and how that distribution can limit political freedom. By contrast, neo-liberals (or libertarians, as they are sometimes called) emphasize freedom in market exchanges, even to the extent of extending rights to business corporations. Paradoxically, the emphasis on the rights and freedoms of corporations and other economic agents has resulted in replacing the domination of social life by governments with its domination by large business interests.

The neo-liberalism of today is less concerned with extending the frontiers of human freedom generally (especially freedom from hunger and want) and more with ensuring a market free from regulation by government.

the liberals of old wanted to be free of the king's restrictive tariffs, the neo-liberals (particularly the most powerful corporations) want to rid themselves of any and all barriers to investment. Corporations argue that they have obligations not to society at large but to their shareholders. If, for example, international banks can profit from speculating on the Thai baht on unregulated international currency markets, that is a good thing – no matter how it may hurt people in Thailand.

The double movement's tug-of-war, however, is never over. While one side may have the upper hand, the other is still there on the field. On the international front, the opposition gained strength in the middle of the last century. After World War II, when members of the new United Nations set up the IMF to stabilize the world economy, they also passed the Universal Declaration of Human Rights as a statement of principles: that people have the right to life, liberty, and education, and to freedom of movement, religion, and association. That was before there was anything like Amnesty International or any of the other networks of non-governmental organizations that have sprung up to push for an end to human rights abuses. These efforts can be narrowly defined, such as Amnesty International campaigns to free individual prisoners of conscience; or they can be aimed at broader goals, like a world ban on land mines or to provide African AIDS patients with antiretroviral drugs.

The growth of such networks is another aspect of globalization. By 1993, just as concern about the inequality wrought by the growth of neo-liberalism was rising, human rights campaigners at the 1993 World Conference on Human Rights in Vienna were seeking to expand the horizons of freedom in new ways. They succeeded in broadening the concept of human rights yet again. Article 25 of the Vienna Declaration, ratified by Canada, declares, "It is for states to foster participation by the poorest people in the decision-making process [and in] the promotion of human rights and efforts to combat extreme poverty."[19]

Taking this broad commitment to human rights seriously, by the turn of the century an energetic "anti-globalization movement" had emerged. Whenever the IMF or the World Trade Organization held meetings, the surrounding streets would be full of demonstrators with puppets and protest signs. The movement would also stage counterconferences, where people from around the world exchange information and planned campaigns. The same technologies that permit currency speculators to send money around the world instantaneously also gave globalization's opponents the ability to establish websites where they could learn, for example, about the effort to control speculation with an international tax named after James Tobin. Similar networks abound, organizing campaigns to curtail greenhouse gas emissions and promote Third World debt relief. (For more on the Quebec Summit of the Americas, see chapter fourteen; and for an Aboriginal perspective, see chapter twelve.)

Global Constitutions: Contested Terrain

A constitution is a formal system, established by law, of principles and rules by which the people of a state are governed. It establishes and limits the basic options available to governments and citizens, to individual and corporate persons. Ideally, people agree to conduct their affairs according to the constitution, in a way that ensures respect for everyone's rights and freedoms.

In a way, a country's constitution is the equivalent of the Ten Commandments, rules to live by. A constitution formalizes the institutions that make decisions and sets limits on the powers of government. Canadians have the right to free association, which means that the government cannot ban organizations that organize against its activities, as long as they do so by lawful means.

Just as political constitutions establish basic frameworks that govern civic behaviour, the notion of "constitution" also extends to the equally basic principles and rules governing the economy. Various economic charters, recently established, govern a country's business, finance,

production, and trade, particularly as they relate to the international arena. The rules affect everyone who makes a living and buys goods and services. They affect all businesses and each level of government.

Canada has adopted several international economic agreements that are, in effect, neo-liberal constitutions. On the surface, they deal with "trade." In practice, however, the Canada-U.S. Free Trade Agreement (1989), the North American Free Trade Agreement (1994), and the World Trade Organization (1994) have established strict limits on the powers of government to regulate business and the economy, even if such regulations benefit Canadians as a whole.

NAFTA prevents Canada from benefiting from the lucky fact that it has abundant energy resources, forbidding the Canadian government from pricing oil and gas prices differently in its home and export markets. People in Regina heating their homes with gas must pay the same price for that gas as do people in Phoenix who rely on it to power their air conditioners and clean their swimming pools. The WTO prevents governments around the world from adopting rules aimed at promoting local processing of natural resources (which would generate more jobs at home). Canada has long attempted to stimulate its forest products industries by banning the export of raw logs and encouraging the growth of sawmilling and fine-papermaking industries. These are now contested terrains under WTO rules.

These new economic constitutions make it more difficult for the public authorities to protect their citizens against health and environmental threats. France banned the import of asbestos from Canada because it is a deadly carcinogen. Even though Canadian health and safety rules recognize this fact, Canada appealed to the WTO because it has an asbestos mining industry. Similarly, Canada and the United States contested a European Union ban on beef from cattle raised with growth hormones. The hormones are not allowed in Europe because of fears of their health effects. Such "technical" barriers to trade have increasingly been used to attack health, food safety, and environmental rules because, argue neo-liberals, they interfere with the free play of market forces.

NAFTA's Chapter 11 gives corporations what amounts to a new constitutional right to challenge government laws on the grounds that those laws might "expropriate" their future earnings. The Ethyl Corporation was disappointed when the U.S. Environmental Protection Agency banned the gasoline additive MMT, a poison affecting the nervous system. When Canada banned MMT, the Ethyl Corporation used Chapter 11 to claim that it had suffered a loss of $250 million in business and future profits. Canada retreated, apologizing and paying the company U.S.$13 million. Ethyl used Canada's capitulation as part of a global marketing strategy claiming that its product was safe.[20]

The neo-liberal constitutions underpinning globalization are similar to the formal political constitutions that countries adopt. Canada's Charter of Rights and Freedoms guarantees citizens certain rights that politicians, parties, and governments cannot easily change. The economic constitutions provide similar rights and freedoms to private businesses, particularly the transnational corporations that dominate global commerce.

When freedom from regulation by government becomes legally "constitutionalized" in this way, market forces regain freedom from public control — a freedom that had gradually eroded since the days of the Industrial Revolution. The first trade complaint filed with the WTO was a challenge to U.S. Clean Air Act regulations banning the importation of dirty gasoline. Appeals to the WTO are held in secret. The decisions are made by unelected officials who are unaccountable to those harmed by their rulings. The new global order may also be doing its most serious damage quietly, behind closed doors, as governments, wary of getting involved in international trade disputes, retreat from commitments to worker and consumer protection, and environmental regulations.

The double movement continues in the face of globalization. Street protestors at anti-globalization rallies have often dressed up as sea turtles because the WTO decided that regulations banning fishing nets that also endanger the turtles constitute a violation of the principles of free trade. Students have organized networks like Students Against Sweatshops to improve workers' rights in the worldwide garment industry. They use negotiation and direct action to push for anti-sweatshop codes of conduct guaranteeing that university merchandise is made under ethical and fair conditions. Canada's Maquila Solidarity Network promotes solidarity with groups organizing in *maquiladora* factories and export-processing zones in Mexico, Central America, and Asia to improve conditions and win a living wage.

Similarly, TRIPS (Trade-Related Aspects of Intellectual Property Rights) became hotly contested terrain in the late 1990s with a noisy international campaign to make HIV/AIDS medicines available to poor people in Africa, where the pandemic is at its worst. At that time antiretroviral drugs, capable of reducing AIDS deaths dramatically, were widely available in industrial countries but were priced globally at over $10,000 per year. At that rate it would have cost badly afflicted Zambia three times its entire national income to treat people ill with AIDS. The campaign sparked international outrage over a system that was putting the rights of patent-holding corporations to charge what the market would bear over the rights of sick people to survive. It soon forced the transnational drug companies to back down from their high prices.

According to free-market economic theory, competition keeps prices down. In the pharmaceutical business, according to this theory, once a company's patent expires the cost of the drug to individual patients or public health and private benefit plans should decline as competitors move into the market with cheaper "generic" versions of the drug. The Canadian government long ago recognized the importance of affordable pharmaceuticals. In 1923 it amended the Patent Act to allow domestic firms to make patented drugs in Canada even before the patent had expired. The idea was to stimulate competition, although the size of the Canadian drug business limited the measure's effectiveness.

The Pharmaceutical Manufacturers' Association of Canada, representing the transnational drug firms, lobbied unsuccessfully against a 1969 Canadian law that allowed the import of generic drugs from abroad. The goal of the legislation was to keep drug prices down. When a U.S.-based company mounted a legal challenge, the change was upheld by the Canadian courts. But this kind of protection was abandoned with the rise of global trade liberalization and the new constitutions enforcing it. In 1986 a Canadian government with a different ideological bent (see chapter ten) was convinced that the United States needed an incentive to agree to liberalized trade. One incentive offered was an agreement to overhaul Canada's drug patent legislation in favour of the international pharmaceutical firms.

As a result, competition in the Canadian drug market declined. In 1993, to conform to NAFTA and the General Agreement on Tariffs and Trade (soon to be the WTO), Canada abolished the licensing system that had boosted the growth of a Canadian generic drug industry. International drug firms now had guaranteed market exclusivity for the entire patent term. In 1999 the United States and the European Union — home

to the dominant drug firms — attacked Canada's drug patent system. This time the challenge was not in Canadian courts but at the WTO. In 2000 Canada lost at the WTO and was forced once again to change its laws in favour of the brand-name drug transnationals.[21]

> Not that long ago, slavery was a well-established fact of life. To fight against it seemed futile. Powerful economic interests, after all, not only supported slavery, but also benefited from it. Fortunately, the scope of that struggle didn't deter those who believed that ownership of one human being by another was morally unconscionable. . . . Woven deeply within the drama of life on this planet are the themes of interdependence and interconnectedness. The nineteenth century abolitionists knew this, and in their struggle to end slavery, they celebrated them. By fighting to eradicate poverty, we would do the same.
>
> — Betty Plewes, Canadian Council for International Co-operation, *What We Can Do: A 10-Point Agenda for Global Action against Poverty*, 1998.

To understand the forces at play in this conflict, social analysis has to examine competing claims. Public health groups, seniors' organizations, and generic drug companies argue that the price of drugs is high and is eating up more and more of government and individual budgets. The international drug companies argue that they need to have their patents and intellectual property rights protected so that they can recover their high research costs and invest the profit on expensive research and development programs for new medicines.

What to make of these claims? In 1998 the world spent $70 billion on health research, of which only $100 million was spent on malaria research. That means .14 cent out of every health research dollar was invested in countering a disease that is a major killer in poor countries.[22] Meanwhile, brand-name drug companies invested heavily in developing and advertising highly profitable brands like Prozac and Viagra, targeting anxieties and erections in rich countries.

What about Development?

The protest and action campaigns call into question the very idea of the economic constitutions that have been put into place without consulting those who will be constricted or harmed by the new international rule book. They also point out how "development" cannot simply be limited to economic growth. To be at all successful, development should share the characteristics – just, sustainable, and participatory – that underpin social analysis geared to social justice.

For this to happen, development has to spring from the self-generating notion of *se développer*. The French verb is often reflexive: to "develop oneself." This implies a measure of democracy in which people decide for themselves what development really means. Development is a word that has itself become contested terrain, perhaps because it is rarely used negatively. As Mexican writer Gustavo Esteva puts it:

> The word always implies a favourable change, a step from the simple to the complex, from the inferior to the superior, from worse to better. . . . But for two-thirds of the people on earth, this positive meaning of the word "development" – profoundly rooted after two centuries of its social construction – is a reminder of what they are not. It is a reminder of an undesirable, undignified condition.[23]

Esteva describes a mindset in which people from the South are encouraged to believe in Planet Hollywood, to look down upon what their own societies have as being somehow inferior to what the rich countries have to offer. Indigenous cultures and societies, many of them colonized centuries ago, are increasingly integrated into the world market. Ever more subject to its new economic constitutions, they are subject to the inroads of international commerce, devalued in favour of everything new and modern that "McWorld" has to offer under the guise of "development."[24]

But the new and the modern may bring work in firetrap toy factories, growth without development. Economic growth is not necessarily accompanied by an expansion in personal and political freedom, even though the U.S. president repeated the phrase "democratic markets" during his historic visit to Russia soon after the fall of communism. In the years that followed, Russia witnessed the unchecked expansion of the market, unaccompanied by the expansion of political freedom. This "development" gave rise to a form of gangster capitalism in which a tiny elite became super-rich while more and more Russian people slipped into poverty. In 1989, 2 per cent of Russians were living in poverty; by 1998 the number had risen to 28.3 per cent, with half the country's children living in poor families.[25]

Significant development requires the removal of what Indian economist Amartya Sen calls the major sources of "unfreedom" – poverty and tyranny, poor economic opportunities and systematic social deprivation, and the neglect of health, education, and other public facilities.[26] A focus on freedom – for poor people, not international investors – defines worthwhile development. Confusing the expansion of GNP with the growth of freedom is to confuse means with ends. Economic growth may provide the wherewithal to put in place better public facilities, but it provides no guarantees. The liberty to participate effectively in public decision-making is a prerequisite for ensuring that the benefits get spread around equally. (See also chapter twelve, "Development and Self-Determination.")

In days gone by, in rich countries like Canada or poor ones like Pakistan, debates over the changes wrought by economic growth and industrialization were not much informed by democratic participation.

The same holds true with changes to our political constitution. When Canada entered World War I, in which over sixty thousand Canadians were killed, it did so by constitutional convention because the British government had declared war on Germany. There was little popular debate. Later, when it came time to change the constitutional arrangements between Britain and Canada, the groundwork was laid at Imperial

Conferences. The 1931 Statute of Westminster, which changed Canada's Constitution to allow it virtual autonomy from Britain, was passed in London. All of these matters were left to political and bureaucratic elites.

Before Canada's Constitution became truly Canadian, being "patriated" from Britain in 1982, citizen groups representing Aboriginal peoples, the disabled, linguistic communities, and women agitated for changes in the draft text. Our Constitution establishes basic institutions such as parliament and the courts, recognizes the two official languages, and includes the Charter of Rights and Freedoms. But it also enshrines Aboriginal rights and gender equality. The increased participation in constitution-making resulted from frustration with top-down politics and negotiations behind closed doors.

Similarly, the impulse to have a voice in decisions that have an impact on people's lives animates citizens concerned about the harmful effects of globalization. Significant development, they argue, requires ordinary citizens to play a role when they are told that free trade is all about establishing a level playing field between countries. Critics have proposed that tariffs be lowered for countries with social protections similar to Canada's – effective social programs, environmental standards, the right to form trade unions. In essence, what this means is that those who experience the impact of globalization's new economic constitutions should help design the playing field and make up the ground rules.

Democratic development, locally or globally, requires that ordinary citizens play a role in addressing poverty and inequality. When Canadians first became involved in the attack on global poverty, they formed non-governmental organizations that sent money to the South to feed children and dig wells. More recently they have realized the importance of building equal relationships with the organizations they support in other countries, making sure that decisions get made democratically. Democratic development and real change cannot be sustained unless people are participating directly in the decisions that have an impact on their lives.

Questions

❏ Canada's Charter of Rights and Freedoms protects the civil rights of individual citizens. How should the new economic constitutions protect and promote the civil rights of individuals and the economic rights of citizens as well as corporations?

❏ A United Nations Declaration states that development must aim "at the constant improvement of the well-being of all individuals on the basis of their active, free, and meaningful participation in development and in the fair distribution of the benefits resulting therefrom." How do Canadian policies on trade arrangements, aid, and development contribute to these conditions? Or how do they fall short?

❏ What do you know about the international organizations that govern the global economy – the International Monetary Fund, World Bank, World Trade Organization? What role does Canada play in each of them? What is their stated purpose? Does it correspond with what they do in practice? Whose interests do they serve?

Growing awareness of our inevitable interdependence must be transformed into international solidarity. According to the basic principle that the goods of creation are destined for all people, whatever goods or services industry produces must serve the good of everyone. Canada has earned a reputation as a nation which is compassionate towards the poor and defenceless both at home and abroad. However, we must now be vigilant lest our immediate concerns at home overshadow our international obligations of social justice.

— "Widespread Unemployment: A Call to Mobilize the Social Forces of Our Nation," Canadian Conference of Catholic Bishops, Ottawa, April 14, 1993.

❏ When the word "market" comes up, what do you think of? Is it an open public place that you can visit, where the apples are grown or the clothing is made by the people selling them? Or is it a virtual electronic space where traders who cannot see one another buy and sell derivatives, currencies, stocks, and hog belly futures? What rules govern each of these two versions of an idea that is nearly as old as humankind? Who sets the rules? Who benefits from them?

❏ Jet travel, film and video, and television have made the painful injustices of huge global inequalities in living conditions more widely apparent than ever before. How do you think this awareness has influenced the relations between the poor South and the rich North? Has the danger of terrorism increased as the great global divide becomes more obvious to more people, even if they are not themselves suffering from poverty? Do you think citizen action and autonomous development can address the divide? Since such efforts tend to challenge the status quo, how is the "war on terrorism" likely to affect them?

Resources

• Deborah Barndt, ed. *Women Working the NAFTA Food Chain: Women, Food and Globalization*. Toronto: Sumach Press, 2000. Food is both commodity and one of life's necessities. It has most always been prepared by women, who have also traditionally grown it. This book is the result of a unique research project conducted by Canadian and Mexican women who probed the global production and distribution system that depends on women's labour.
• Wayne Ellwood. *The No-Nonsense Guide to Globalization*. Toronto: Between the Lines, 2001. Globalization is a word used to describe everything from lightning-quick international currency transactions to changing tastes in food. This book provides concise insights into what it really means.
• Naomi Klein. *No Logo: Taking Aim at the Brand Bullies*. Toronto: Alfred A. Knopf Canada, 2000. Klein explores the corporate world of "branding," from sweatshops in Indonesia and the Philippines to North American malls, and tracks and explains the anti-corporate activism, the growing global protest movement, that has begun to confront the "brand bullies."
• John McMurtry. *Unequal Freedoms: The Global Market as an Ethical System*. Toronto: Garamond Press, 1998. An overview of the ethical underpinnings of the world economic system, this book questions the belief system that has come to be called "neo-liberalism."
• Wolfgang Sachs, ed. *The Development Dictionary: A Guide to Knowledge as Power*. London: Zed Books, 1992. This collection of essays explores many of the concepts associated with the idea of development – a particular worldview, not simply an economic project. Writers from North and South offer critical perspectives on "helping," "needs," "science," and "standard of living."
• *Turbulences*. Canada, 1998. Directed by Carole Poliquin. NFB. Video. 52 min. A film that explores the interconnections and interdependence of the global market – from squatters in Paris, factory workers in Thailand, and fish processors in Senegal to families living on welfare in Quebec and teachers in Ontario. Poliquin also interviews market speculators and fund managers who help dictate economies worldwide.

Websites:
The WebActive! site, a project of RealNetworks, Inc. of Seattle, Wash., provides links to thousands of activist-related sites. It is updated regularly, which means that it has very few dead links. It is also easily searchable alphabetically or by topic area. A useful tool for finding resources on the World Wide Web and connecting to other organizations and people with similar values and interests. Go to <www.webactive.com>.

Another useful tool .is the site of the International Forum on Globalization (IFG), an international alliance of activists, economists, researchers, and writers, formed specifically to stimulate new thinking on global economic issues. Its goal is to direct public and media attention to the effects of economic globalization.

Chapter Ten
Media and Ideology

There is an old saying about looking at the world through rose-coloured glasses. It brings to mind someone whose outlook is overly optimistic, rosy. It also hints that everyone looks at the world through glasses of one colour or another.

Communications media – television, radio, newspapers, the Internet – provide one very important set of glasses that we use to view the world. And those particular glasses influence the understanding of every issue treated in *Getting Started*. The first part of this chapter focuses on one aspect of the media, the information industry,

to see how its corporate structures and market approach influence the information that filters down to us.

The notion of using a particular set of glasses, a particular tint colouring our world view, illustrates a rather difficult concept, "ideology." The second part of this chapter considers ideology, looking back over issues in everyday life and the world around us analyzed in the first two parts of this book. Our goal is to identify some of the ideological factors shaping Canadian society. This work helps us to prepare for the analysis in the third part of the book, "People and Perspectives."

The Information Industry

In a world shaped by a flow of information that is getting faster and heavier every day, Canada holds a respectable position. We have freedom of the press, which is not as common elsewhere as it ought to be. Not many among us now remember the days before radio, and most of us grew up with television. Today's young Canadians grow up with computers and the Internet.

Years ago – when the telephone was a novelty restricted to wealthy homes – people relied on face-to-face communication to get the news. They absorbed information (and ideology) through family, workplace, neighbourhood, and church. Even though literacy levels were not as high as they are today, local newspapers were also important At one time most people got their news from the independent papers established in every city.

Canada now has more television stations than it does daily newspapers. Nearly two out of every three Canadian homes with television have at least basic cable service, giving them access to dozens of stations.[1] More and more people, especially in areas without cable, have satellite dishes and the "five hundred channel universe." Canada has three "national newspapers," two in English Canada and one in Quebec. The newsstands are packed with hundreds of magazines. The airwaves are crammed with so many radio signals that there is no more transmitting space left in the biggest cities.

Computer communications are growing with breathtaking speed. By 2001, over 5.8 million Canadian households (or 49 per cent of all households) included at least one member who regularly used the Internet from home, up 23 per cent from 2000 – although this is less than the increase of 42 per cent from 1999 to 2000.[2] More and more households used the Internet as an information source, using news sites or searching for government information on-line. In 2001, 87 per cent of the one-quarter of households in the highest income bracket used the Internet, up from 58 per cent in 1997. Only 32 per cent of the one-quarter of households with the lowest income level regularly used the Internet in that year. Still, this was nearly triple the rate of 12 per cent five years earlier.[3]

Despite this seeming abundance of communications media, the information industry consists of a few large corporations. Continuing worries over the demise of stand-alone media outlets – those not part of a chain – were enough to provoke Ottawa to launch two major inquiries into media ownership. Both the Special Senate Committee on Mass Media (1970) and the Royal Commission on Newspapers (1981) focused on increased concentration of newspaper ownership and decreased competition. The 1981 Royal Commission emphasized the importance of decreasing the power of the companies that own newspapers and television stations so that they would have less influence on how the information is presented. It also expressed concern over the integration of newspapers with other businesses.

Worries over more control of more information by fewer corporations were stimulated by the recognition that those who control the distribution of messages through the media can shape society. Companies owning huge media outlets reach huge numbers of viewers, audiences, and readers. This influence carries with it political, cultural, and social power. Social groups (for instance, racial minorities and poor people) without access to the media are deprived of that sort of vital influence.

The dangers of concentrated corporate control of the media are widely recognized. In the United States (where in other respects government is unwilling to interfere with market activity) the same company is not allowed to own a television station and a newspaper in the same market – city, state, and so on. In Canada the situation is different. Here two of the three national television networks are owned by major communications firms, and each of those companies also owns the two newspapers that claim to be national in scope. Bell Globemedia controls both the *Globe and Mail* newspaper and the CTV television network. CanWest Global controls the *National Post* newspaper and the Global television network. Moreover, in several important big-city media markets (Ottawa, Calgary, Vancouver), CanWest Global owns the leading newspapers as well as a television station.

> Journalism is arguably the most important form of public knowledge in contemporary society. The mass media — of which journalism is one, key, news-spreading part — have become the leading institution of the public sphere — "that realm of social life where the exchange of information and views on questions of common concern can take place so that public opinion can be formed."
>
> — Robert A. Hackett and Yuezhi Zhao, *Sustaining Democracy? Journalism and the Politics of Objectivity*, 1998. The quote is from Peter Dalhgren, *Television and the Public Sphere: Citizenship, Democracy and the Media*, 1995.

A Canadian Media Uproar

How does such ownership influence the flow of information? In 2000 CanWest Global paid $3.5 billion to Conrad Black's Hollinger Inc. to acquire the newspapers formerly owned by Hollinger and the venerable Southam chain. After that deal, journalists and media observers once again expressed long-standing concerns about excessive concentration in the media sector. These alarm bells might since have faded if several events had not brought into focus the way that such control can work.

Winnipeg's Asper family controls CanWest Global. In 2002 CanWest chair Israel Asper told the shareholders at his company's annual general meeting that his fourteen large-city newspapers should have a single editorial position – not fourteen distinct positions – on important national and international issues. This was contrary to the position that the Southam chain had maintained even when it was controlled by the controversial Conrad Black. In 1995 Southam's Annual Report was still proclaiming a Statement of Editorial Independence declaring, "For more than a century, Southam has proudly upheld its policy of editorial independence on all matters involving news and opinion. In the widely different environments in which Southam operates across the country, publishers and editors make their own editorial decisions."[4]

When the former Southam papers began publishing single "national" editorials that they received from CanWest's Winnipeg head office, the practice produced loud protests from journalists, including many at the company's own papers. They were particularly upset by the company stipulation that locally written material should not contradict the positions taken by head office. The furor increased when CanWest fired the publisher of the *Ottawa Citizen* after that paper published editorials sharply critical of Prime Minister Jean Chrétien. The wealthy Aspers are strong supporters of the Liberal Party.

In Regina, where CanWest owns the only newspaper along with all the other daily papers in Saskatchewan, reporters for the *Leader Post* were suspended and reprimanded after withdrawing their bylines to protest censorship of the news. This took place after Haroon Siddiqui, an emeritus editor at *The Toronto Star* (itself part of a major media empire that owns seven Ontario dailies, including the largest paper in Canada), spoke in Regina. The *Leader Post* journalist who covered Siddiqui's lecture at the University of Regina began her report with a "lead" that emphasized what she felt was the most important point: "CanWest Global performed 'chilling' acts of censorship when it refused to publish several columns containing viewpoints other than those held by the media empire, a *Toronto Star* columnist said Monday."[5]

When the newspaper appeared the next day her report had been changed to read: "A *Toronto Star* columnist says it's OK for CanWest Global to publish its owners' views as long as the company is prepared to give equal play to opposing opinions." Critics were quick to point out that the second version was not completely accurate. When Aboriginal writer Doug Cuthand wrote a column for CanWest's Regina and Saskatoon papers in which he compared the plight of Aboriginal Canadians to the condition of Palestinians, the papers refused to publish it.[6] The Asper family is well known for its militant support of the Israeli side in the Palestinian-Israeli dispute.

Convergence, Advertising, and the Good Old Days?

Quebecor is a Canadian company with a convergence strategy. The company publishes the tabloid-style *Sun* newspapers in Winnipeg, Calgary, Ottawa, Toronto, and Edmonton, along with eleven others, like *The London Free Press*, which are the only daily newspapers in their home cities. It runs *Le Journal de Montréal* and *Le Journal de Québec*, hugely popular tabloids in Quebec. It owns the biggest commercial printing company in the world. All in all, it publishes 190 regional newspapers and magazines. Quebecor owns TVA, Quebec's largest private television network as well as Vidéotron, the largest Quebec cable company. It runs Netgraphe Internet portals and Canoe.ca. It controls the Nurun web agency offering site design, e-commerce and transaction processing systems, automated publishing, and on-line marketing.

Given this sort of "convergence" — or cross-media ownership of Internet, newspapers, and television — what happens to the public's right to get information from independent voices? What are the implications of a company like Quebecor that owns so much? Or of a giant like AOL Time Warner? In 2001 America Online, the dominant Internet company in the United States, joined forces with the huge movie and publishing company Time Warner in one of the largest mergers in corporate history. As a result, the same company now provides nearly thirty million Americans with Internet service and offers cable service from Poland to Brazil. It presents the news on CNN and through the pages of *Time*. It sells record albums by Madonna, publishes books, shows cartoons (*Bugs Bunny* and *Scooby Doo*), runs theme parks and Warner Bros studio stores, and

owns a vast vault of American music and movies.

Although convergence alarmed critics concerned about too few corporations controlling too many media outlets, it seemed like a good idea at the time to the businessmen who did the deals. But it was not long before the consolidations began to lose their business-sense glow. In 2002 AOL Time Warner recorded the largest loss in U.S. corporate history — $99 billion. In Canada, CanWest-Global was still staggering under an unsustainable debt load brought about in part by its media acquisitions.

Still. with convergence, companies hold out hopes of more efficiency and higher profits. Takeovers and concentration in the newspaper sector always caused concern among citizens who believed that too much control over information by too few people constitutes a new threat to freedom. Now that the process has accelerated with electronic, print, and on-line media being grouped together under a few corporate roofs, those worries have become even more pronounced.

The concerns are certainly valid. Freedom of information is crucial for democracy. Culture — the stories we tell each other and that give us the sense of who we are and how we understand the world — should not be reduced to Disney-style entertainment. Democracy and culture are too important to be left to the market. But it is important to remember that today's convergence is, in one important way, not that different from how Canadians have always received the news of the world.

Nineteenth-century newspapers were closely tied to political parties, to the extent that the description "political organ" is often used to describe them. The Toronto *Globe* served as the personal podium for its owner, George Brown, a Reform politician. On the other side of the fence, the Conservatives set up the Toronto *Mail*, a vehicle for John A. Macdonald. (The papers later merged into *The Globe and Mail*.) Newspaper partisanship — there was no hint of balance in reporting — was cemented in the papers' dependence on money from political parties as well as on circulation to pay their way.

With increasing literacy and higher circulation came the rise of advertising. In the twentieth century, those who sold the news came to depend not on political parties in search of votes but on stores and soap producers in search of customers. Despite paying more attention to balance and getting both sides of a story, the information dealers — including new media like radio and television — did not often challenge the status quo, particularly when it came to criticizing those who paid the bills. Owners of media outlets often shared the values of their advertisers, whose interests they were unlikely to challenge through their media "properties."

In the 1930s and 1940s, under the ownership of Victor Sifton, the *Winnipeg Free Press* made a deal with Eaton's department store, which advertised heavily in the paper. Before running any article that mentioned Eaton's, the paper would clear the story with the company. This situation had arisen because Eaton's had pulled its advertising when the paper ran an item casting the store in an unfavourable light. On one occasion a man committed suicide by jumping from the roof of Eaton's in Winnipeg. On orders from the owner, the story in the city's biggest newspaper did not mention that the event had taken place at its biggest department store.[7]

In 1990 the independently owned *Kingston Whig-Standard* featured a story in its Saturday edition about people who sold their own homes and were thus able to save on real estate agency commissions. Local realtors who advertised in the Saturday paper were outraged and shifted their business to a twice-weekly paper that was part of the *Toronto Star* chain. Along with a recession, this was one of the factors that prompted the long-time owner of the *Whig-Standard* to sell the paper to the Southam chain. Under chain ownership, staff was cut, along with coverage of the day's news.

Newspapers are certainly not alone in being in business to sell advertising. Television, radio, and Internet commerce all provide news and entertainment liberally sprinkled with commer-

cials. The automobile industry is the biggest source of advertising revenue for television stations and networks. Just as you would not expect a publication run by environmentalists to feature articles denying that the greenhouse effect is caused by carbon dioxide emissions, neither is it surprising that the safety and pollution records of automakers are not subject to sustained critical scrutiny by broadcasters.

The pattern of corporate concentration in the news and entertainment media is similar to the pattern in the housing, food, and energy industries. Perhaps news is not distorted outright as it was when the Regina reporter tried to report what was really said about CanWest. But events are often distorted or downplayed in the course of normal, daily relationships between editors, producers, and reporters, on the one hand, and media owners and other members of the business community on the other. While media outlets controlled by large chains are unlikely to unearth hard-to-get stories that run contrary to their interests, they are usually ready to protect their allies.

The coincidence of media ownership with concentration in the food industry is illuminating. A Canadian university researcher found that the press had consistently joined with the food industry in attacking the role of the marketing boards that manage the supply of farm products. Supply management was blamed for high food costs and Canada's alleged inability to compete internationally in the food sector. The study cited a series of articles and editorials that appeared in *The Globe and Mail* and were "echoed in much of the Canadian business press." (Although most people get their news from television, most television and radio producers and reporters still take their cues from newspapers, particularly national "papers of record.") The critics characterized the supply-management system as "wretched" and as damaging "the competitive advantage of an entire sector of the economy."[8]

This analysis attributed higher food prices to corporate concentration in the retail food sector, not farm marketing boards. Big food retailers have captured a greater share of the food dollar than have farmers. The study concluded:

> Perhaps the more interesting question is: why have the giant food retailers attracted virtually no attention from the major media on this question? Instead, the media have chosen to focus their attention elsewhere in the food chain, that is, on the institutional arrangements protecting primary producers – the sector that is least organized, [and] most fragmented.[9]

Community-access television – once a mandatory obligation of all cable licensees – has been steadily eroding across the country since 1997, when the Canadian Radio-television and Telecommunications Commission (CRTC) lifted the requirement that cable companies must operate a community channel as a condition of their license. In anticipation of the CRTC's 1997 decision, Rogers Cable (Vancouver's former cable supplier prior to Shaw) closed three of its four neighbourhood T.V. production facilities in the city in 1996. . . . That's when ICTV [Independent Community Television Co-operative] was born, along with its sister organization, the Community Media Education Society. . . . A truly democratic society requires some vehicle for democratic communication – a vehicle that allows citizens and underrepresented groups to tell their stories, express their views and information, and present their art, unfiltered by corporate bias.

— Kim Goldberg, "Reclaiming the Airwaves," *Canadian Dimension*, September/October 2001.

A partial answer to this question rests in the business relationship between the media and the food industry. Simply put, farmers don't often advertise in the media. Other parts of the food business do.

The real world of journalism has never been a place free of censorship, free of management interference in editorial matters or in crucial decision-making about which stories are covered and how they are presented. According to journalist Linda McQuaig, "Most journalists have no say in their newspapers' editorial positions, no input into what news stories are given prominence, nor any guarantee that their own stories – no matter how accurate and important – will even be published. All these things are ultimately determined by the newspaper's owner."[10]

News for Sale

"You can't believe everything you hear" is true of neighbourhood gossip, and it is best to apply the same scepticism to the news we see, hear, and read. But no matter how sceptical we try to be, the daily barrage of information has an inevitable influence. The mass media remain our primary source of information about a very complex world. The matter-of-fact prose of *Maclean's* magazine and the reassuring tone of CBC news readers exude credibility. The CTV network got to the heart of the matter when it began to use two unrelated words to describe its newscast: "Trust and Tradition."

In 1925 the editor of *The Wall Street Journal* made an observation that is still relevant in the era of the Internet: "A newspaper is a private enterprise, owing nothing to the public which grants it no franchise. It is therefore affected with no public interest. It is emphatically the property of its owner, who is selling a manufactured product at his own risk."[11]

Indeed, the media are structured and controlled like any other Canadian industry. Their products are news and entertainment, delivered in greater quantity and more quickly as the years pass. Events are skilfully refined before they are served up with our morning coffee or broadcast into our houses at prime time. Many of us have access to "all news/all the time" television and radio stations, as well as news on-line all the time. Each day thousands of raw events are readied for Canadians to consume as news.

What happens to the events covered in this "manufacturing" process? They get turned into items that are *intense, unambiguous and balanced, familiar and marketable*. To better interpret the news that is produced, let's consider these criteria.

"Intense"

For an audience accustomed to high-speed movie and video-game car chases, the fast cutting of music videos, and prime-time "real life" TV shows, intensity is a must ingredient. Journalists and editors either choose events for their drama or focus selectively on the dramatic elements within items.

Protest marches get covered (they make good pictures), but the news will concentrate on any scuffles or arrests to the virtual exclusion of other aspects of the story, including the issues involved. The news coverage of the 2001 Summit of the Americas anti-globalization protests in Quebec City, with its symbolic fence and tear-gas attacks on demonstrators by the authorities, received blanket coverage. Similar protests occurred in Calgary at the G-8 summit a year later, when the concerns were the same, but those demonstrations received far less attention – the protests were by and large peaceful. The world leaders were at a distant resort in Kananaskis. The police were more restrained.

In local news the need for intensity results in a constant stream of images of accused criminals, trials, and stories about violent crime. The media pay far less attention to non-violent corporate or white-collar crime, even though corporate crime costs society far more than the activities of violent thugs. Price-fixing by Canada's major petroleum companies from the 1950s to the 1970s took an extra $12 billion from consumers, but those firms are rarely if ever portrayed as criminals.[12] Similarly, the media – particularly Internet-based services – emphasize the drama of personality and celebrity (the death of Lady Di is the most striking example) at the expense of political issues.

In international coverage, events in Third World countries make the news fleetingly when there are coups, earthquakes, or famines. In reports from Latin America and Africa, national strikes, violent demonstrations, and "bloodless" coups blur into one another. One study of the "story geography" of Canadian TV news concluded, "The outbreak of war guarantees a steady supply of visually fulfilling stories."[13] Less intense stories – an election or the struggle to survive of children living in poverty – appear from time to time, but without the same regularity or high profile.

TV news crews find it easier to cover a volcano eruption in Brazil's Amazon basin than the daily suffering caused by that country's heavy foreign debt. One TV news producer explained the reasoning: "You can't show the deaths caused by the debt. The volcano wasn't there yesterday and is there today – that's new, that's television news. . . . People in the morning say, 'Gee, did you see the footage of that volcano last night on the news?' But nobody gets up in the morning and says, 'Gee, did you hear about that debt in Brazil?'"[14]

Stories pop into the news, evolve at alarming speed, and – scarcely digested by the public – pop out again to make room for fresh events. The American anthrax scare immediately after the 9/11 attack on the World Trade Center is an example. Fresh, novel items are always being served up, but often at the cost of missing the truth behind them. The coverage is too brief, too fleeting to provide much of an idea of what led up to events or caused them, or what might flow from them in the long run.

"Unambiguous" and "Balanced"

Another criterion establishing newsworthiness is that the information be cut and dried, without much ambiguity, and presented from a "balanced" or "objective" viewpoint.

When TV and print media cover a political story they usually present both the government and the opposition sides. In environmental stories there are the industry and the activist sides. Some people are in favour of globalization, some are opposed to it, many are still confused by what it all means. In reports on the nuclear power industry there are "good news" stories (when the nuclear industry is successful in meeting its objectives) and "bad news" stories (when the industry has to pay billions of dollars extra to repair a reactor).[15] There is the "status quo" and there are "interest groups" trying to change it.

Aside from the odd opinion piece that may carry a more complex or nuanced picture of an issue, most TV news and newspaper coverage follow this pattern. As a result, a black and white picture tends to become common knowledge, common sense. Overly simple news items, laced with intensity to attract attention, draw the audiences required to attract advertisers. But they often distort or ignore what is really going on.

Canada went through long constitutional debates in the 1980s and early 1990s, as the constitution was patriated from Great Britain and the federal government attempted to get Quebec to sign on. For the first time in Canadian history the Aboriginal issue became central to the debates. In Quebec there were — and are — separatists and federalists. The media formula can easily handle this, adapting to allow for the "undecideds." But with the Aboriginal issue, things became a bit more nuanced — as journalist Henry F. Heald points out, "too complex to be dealt with in the single-issue context that reporters customarily work in."

> With aboriginal people . . . there are more than 50 nations comprising some 600 bands or groups. There are Inuit, Indians, and Metis. There are sophisticated people holding down good jobs and living comfortable lives in the urban milieu. There are people living comfortably off the land the way their ancestors did, living on reservations where rich natural resources have been developed to provide a high standard of living for the inhabitants. There are also people rotting in urban slums. There are people living on reservations in poverty, vice and squalor.[16]

Journalists did become more sensitive to the "Native side" of things as the constitutional debates unfolded. The availability of a national chief of the Assembly of First Nations allowed them to provide an Aboriginal perspective on the constitutional negotiations. But reporters often found out that their sources, leaders like National Chief Ovide Mercredi, did not necessarily speak for all Aboriginal peoples. There was no single definition of what Native peoples wanted from constitutional reform. (See chapter twelve.)

"Familiar" and "Marketable"

In order to become news, an event must be culturally familiar and socially recognizable.

A car accident in which someone is killed or badly injured will always feature on the local news. But on big, national newspapers there is a kind of story we call "the bus plunge." The event can occur anywhere — a bus goes off the road and over a cliff, killing dozens of passengers; a crowded train is derailed, catching fire. "Bus-plunge" stories employ repetitive phrases and images that have a cumulative effect, reinforcing prejudices and stereotypes. But the "marketability" of the story — the extent and depth of the coverage — depends greatly on where it happens.

One Saturday in early 2003, two news stories captivated the Canadian media. Both involved the sudden violent deaths of seven people. Within hours of the space shuttle Columbia exploding over Texas, with the loss of its astronauts, seven students from an elite private school in Alberta were killed by an avalanche while they were out on a back-country ski trip in British Columbia. Both events received massive media coverage. This is not so surprising, because both were familiar and recognizable; Canadians had learned of a similar ski accident in the same region only weeks before and, of course, the high technologies and dangers and discoveries of space travel have long held a general fascination.

That same Saturday a fiery train collision in Zimbabwe killed at least forty-six people. That, too, was news. But in contrast to the blizzard of stories and miles of videotape produced by the tragedies in the B.C. mountains and the sky over the United States, the African incident was mentioned only briefly. The event, equally tragic, was covered, for example, by a four-sentence story in *The Globe and Mail*. There was no follow-up, no exploration of how such a terrible thing could have happened.[17]

Repetition, combined with the limitations of news-gathering capabilities, ensures that what we see is largely limited to the familiar. International news coverage by Canadian TV networks is concentrated in a few countries that receive the bulk of the coverage, with the rest of the world largely ignored.[18]

In 1989-90, for instance, the media, understandably, were filled with news of the fall of the Berlin Wall and the end of the Cold War. These events had immense historical importance. For thirty-five years the Cold War and the Soviet Union's control over an entire region had been a familiar news theme, and now the collapse of Communism and the democratic revival in Eastern Europe dominated the headlines. At the same time the news downplayed — "completely overlooked," according to one media analysis — crucial historical changes taking place in South America.[19] That region also had a dominant superpower that had long backed military dictatorships there. The U.S. media virtually ignored the first free elections held in Chile and Brazil in sixteen and twenty-five years respectively.

Other familiar images come up when famine strikes places like Bangladesh, Ethiopia, or Somalia. We have often seen pictures of Black children with distended bellies, flies in their eyes. Haunting, heart-rending images bring home the effects of famine but not the human and political causes. The images do not inform, much less provide, a critical point of view. When the media employ certain familiar (racial, sexual, economic, or political) stereotypes again and again, each use reinforces them. According to a Zimbabwean media analyst, "News reports show outside white people feeding and helping black people. They never show black people helping themselves."[20]

To attract the largest audiences — or to capture "market share" — the media companies attempt to provide coverage that is intense, unambiguous, and familiar. Television networks produce prime-time dramas and "reality-based" survivor shows that feature unfamiliar, exotic settings with familiar-looking people indulging in intense competitions. Similarly, the news is geared to consumer taste. This may mean something as apparently innocuous as pampering Canadians' sweet tooth for royalty. It also gives rise to the *Sun* tabloids. Like the mainstream Internet, the tabloids emphasize celebrities, sports, and sensational, often violent stories — neatly packaged with Sunshine Girls and Boys.

Invasions always make good copy. The U.S.-led invasion of Afghanistan following the attacks of September 11, 2001, received saturation coverage as the mass bombing of one of the world's poorest countries was followed by ground attacks that toppled the Taliban government. Canadian involvement added an element of familiarity, although the lines between the good guys and the bad guys became more blurred when Canadian personnel were killed not by terrorists or the Taliban but by U.S. "friendly fire." A year later the terrorists responsible for the 9/11 attacks had not yet been found, and the media focus had shifted to Iraq. Some twelve years earlier Iraq had invaded Kuwait, and had itself been invaded in 1991. Would Iraq be invaded again?

The invasions come and go, and the media come and go with them. What happens afterward is not covered with anything approaching the same intensity. Did the people of Afghanistan fare any better in the wake of the U.S. invasion than they had after a Soviet Union invasion twenty years before? In facing another invasion, would the Iraqis suffer the same fate (at least a half-million dead as a result of international sanctions) that they experienced after the invasion of 1991? The more complex questions and issues are less marketable than the cut and dried intensity of an invasion. As a result, they receive far less attention.

Analysis

Events are always being refined and made intense, unambiguous and balanced, familiar and marketable. Contrary facts, prior conditions, long-term causes, and underlying structures that explain events tend to be downplayed or crowded out, not because of ill will, but because of bias built into the manufacturing process. Given the ownership and structure of the information industry — as well as the pressure from its entertainment arm — this conclusion should come as no surprise.

Some things have changed rapidly — with cable, satellite, and the Internet, the media are becoming more fragmented, with consumers offered a dizzying array of choice — but what has not changed is the expectation that the media reflect the big-business values that maintain the Canadian economy and the social order based on it.

The coverage of issues related to nuclear power provides a good example of this tendency. A study of newspaper reporting on nuclear power issues found that the accounts tended to favour the supporters of nuclear energy. Reports were "overwhelmingly dominated by the proponents of nuclear power," while the case against this particular form of electricity generation was "virtually invisible." The explanation is that the owners and managers of the newspapers identify closely with the world view of the industry itself.[21] (See chapter seven.) The media do cover issues related to racism, sexism, violence against women, and the plight of the poor. But women, minorities, and poor people are most often represented as people with problems, or as people who are themselves problems. Such stereotyping sets them apart from what is generally considered to be "normal." And the media implicitly portray white, middle-class men as the norm in Canadian society — they speak loudest and most frequently. The voices of the "other" are far more muted in the mainstream media.

Media analysts find that women are grossly under-represented in the mass media as people who might have something interesting to say, whether as journalists, interviewees, or newsmakers. One study of global media found that women made up only 17 per cent of interviewees in newspapers, radio, and television. Among North American sources the figure only rose to 27 per cent for women. North American figures for the percentage of female journalists (38 per cent) were actually lower than the worldwide incidence (43 per cent). The numbers were even more startling in a 1998 study of Canada's national newspapers, which had male reporters, photographers, and newsmakers outnumbering their female counterparts at a rate of three to one. The *National Post* featured women as newsmakers only 10 per cent of the time, while the figure for *The Globe and Mail* was 22 per cent.[22]

The media tend to stereotype particular visible minorities in particular ways. For instance, rather than focusing on Jamaican Canadians as the norm in an increasingly diverse society, news stories are slanted in other directions. A study of 2,622 articles mentioning Jamaican Canadians in three Toronto newspapers found that 45 per cent were about sports and entertainment and 39 per cent about crime. Some 2 per cent were individual or community success stories.[23]

Similarly, an event like the 9/11 attacks on New York and Washington can bring more direct stereotyping to the surface. Although the Canadian media often attempted to explain that the terrorists who flew the planes had little to do with the teachings of Islam, such analyses took a back seat to more sensationalist images and opinions. A front-page column in *The Globe and Mail* the day after the attacks referred to the "men from remote desert lands . . . ancient tribal cultures built on blood and revenge." Krishna Rau, a former editor of a media monitoring publication, *Diversity Watch*, pointed out that Judaism, Christianity, and Islam all emerged from the same region and cultures, but that Islam was a regular target in the aftermath of September 11.[24]

The media are the glasses, and as we've seen they take on a certain tint. They promote a particular view of things that in a camouflaged but effective way helps to give a certain shape to Canadian society.

The Information Flow

An old expression describes what happens when you're removed from the environment you're used to. You feel "like a fish out of water." Another says that the first species to discover water could not have been a fish — "To the fish, the water is invisible," says an old proverb. Together, these sayings get at the idea that your surroundings are both important and pervasive. We become so used to the things around us that we take them for granted and often don't even notice them.

This is the case in Canada today. Information washes across us all day, every day. A high-speed Internet connection is something to be sought after. We are immersed in urgent-sounding televised reports of crisis and crime, as well-groomed "anchors" tell us breathlessly, "This just in!" Our friends become impatient if we do not answer their e-mails right away or if something keeps us from getting back to them about that message they left on our voice-mail. Our phone conversations are interrupted by call waiting. Eating habits have changed to the extent that on-the-run people feel that their cars are mobile houses; hence the popularity of grabbing fast food at the drive-through. Tim Hortons, having overtaken McDonald's as the top fast-food outlet in Canada, has its time per car down to twenty seconds. Statistics Canada reports a steady increase in the number of people feeling time-stressed.[25]

In 2001 a Pickering, Ontario, man was talk-ing on his cell phone and drove into the path of a speeding train. The man was killed, along with his two-year-old daughter. Police concluded that he was so distracted by his call that he did not notice the flashing lights and the gate arm at the level crossing. The subsequent coroner's inquest renewed the call for a ban on cell-phone use while driving. The whole incident also raises the issue of how the increasingly massive flow of information alters our lives. Do the feelings we experience — on-line, on the cell phone, listening to the radio or the stereo at home, on the bus or in the car or out jogging, punching the buttons of the TV remote, using call-answering and call-forwarding, playing video games — entertain us? Do they make us feel more connected? Do they distract us?

Certainly, we pass more time looking at screens, from automated bank tellers to home computers to computers at work to television. The screens seem to be everywhere — in banks, train stations, at the gym. In large cities, old-style billboards are being replaced by giant video screens with fast-paced advertising visible from blocks away. At stadiums and large concerts, giant screens supplement (or displace) the live action. Our culture is increasingly a market culture, geared to producing things that will sell, from palm pilots to the thrill of "driving" in a video-game car chase. We seem to feel connected, with the person at the other end of the messaging systems or with a sense of fun and excitement as new sets of images rush by. All-news channels offer not just a report from the Middle East but the time and the local weather. A ribbon of stock-market data flows across the bottom of the screen, although only a small minority of viewers own shares directly. Sports networks feature constant highlights of the latest games, coupled with an endless parade of the scores below. Among the pop-up ads, the Internet allows you to chat, check the sports scores, click, download, and, of course, shop.

Although many critics focus on the companies that own the information networks and how the news is biased in favour of the political status quo, there is something else going on here. The popular phrase "couch potato" comes to mind. Even though the notion of "surfing" the Internet hints at more active participation – and it is certainly possible to sign on-line petitions and visit anti-globalization websites – surfing more often resembles channel-hopping. According to sociologist Todd Gitlin, our time-starved era does not just make people stressed because they have too many things to do in the day.

> While our eyes and ears are taking in images and sounds in all their abundance, we are usually sitting down to receive them. The torrent speeds by, but we ourselves – despite the treadmills, the Walkmen, the sports radios – are mainly immobilized. . . . In the age of unceasing image flow, there is no social anxiety that cannot be addressed with a commodity, a craze, and a news exposé – none of which quite dispels the anxiety.[26]

Much of the torrent is consumed privately, or at least passively. Consuming it all can be distracting, absorbing the attention of people who have that much less of an opportunity to see the world through different-coloured glasses. That is where the notion of ideology comes in.

Up against the Wall

How would you react if a mentally ill man lurched into your kitchen, dug his hand into your supper, and wolfed down a generous portion? Your emotions might run through shock, fear, and outrage before you called the police to haul the intruder away.

But in this incident from *The Tree of Wooden Clogs*, a movie about an Italian peasant family, the mother who had prepared the food welcomed the man as a guest. She let him help himself to the food and warned her children to be polite to him. She believed that people with mental disabilities, because of their simplicity, were especially close to God. This belief, right or wrong, guided her reaction.

Many of our reactions to daily events and circumstances – using these glasses of ours – do not spring from a deliberate position or well-thought-out theory, but rather reflect semi-conscious beliefs and values. These built-in attitudes do a lot to shape how we see ourselves, society and the world – and they point to what is called ideology.

The scene from *The Tree of Wooden Clogs* raises questions. Why do people in different societies react differently to similar situations? Where do our social attitudes and responses come from?

In the first instance, our attitudes are formed by the influences of our parents, friends, and peers, teachers at school, our religious upbringing, and the neighbourhoods and communities we share with our fellow citizens. These attitudes – about what's worthwhile, how society works, who the heroes and villains are – continue to be moulded by the people and institutions around us. The mass media – advertising, television, the Internet, the whole torrent – are another very important influence. (The average American is estimated to see 150,000 television commercials in a lifetime; globally spending on advertising is approaching $500 billion annually.[27]) These factors are all sources and reinforcers of ideology, and they deserve careful analysis.

Ideology is a complex topic. *Webster's* defines it as "the doctrines, opinions, or way of thinking of an individual, class, etc.; specif., the body of ideas on which a particular political, economic or social system is based." One student of the word found over a dozen different meanings given to it. Here we touch on ideology in an introductory way, by describing it rather than defining it, and in particular look at the role of ideology in everyday experiences.

People who confront the kinds of problems analyzed in this book often find themselves at a total impasse. They're "up against the wall," as the phrase goes. What is "the wall"? The word refers at first to a mass of problems that people face (for instance, unemployment, substandard housing, problems getting health care, environmental degradation). As social analysis sorts out the problems, "the wall" begins to be broken down into the issues, structures, and systems that are gradually uncovered.

"The wall" exists not just out there in society, but also inside our own heads. The word ideology describes the interaction between what goes on in our heads and what is going on outside, in society. It's all about ways of seeing. It refers to a whole complex of dominant *ideas* that both form the basis of an economic and political system and shape the manner of thinking of groups or classes of people within that system.

Although it is a way of seeing, ideology can be *blinding*. People's blind spots are based on their class, sex, language, ethnic and religious origin, education, and work experience. Ideology also *preserves* structures and systems by making them appear legitimate, normal, and unchangeable.

People are usually unaware of their own ideological assumptions, regarding them as common sense. At the same time, they make statements like these:

- "Government should stick to governing and stay out of the economy."
- "Those people make more money on employment insurance and welfare than I do in my job – and I work plenty of hours. They've got to stop people being paid for doing nothing."
- "Our immigration laws stink. Just watch the news and you see all the crime. And they're taking our jobs."
- "I'm against prejudice, but employment equity is carrying it too far – why can't those minority groups compete for jobs like the rest of us?"
- "User fees make sense. If people had to pay, they'd stop running off to the doctor every time they got a cold. Why should everybody have to pay for that?"

Everyone has ideological beliefs that govern their opinions and judgements about the world around them. Those who deny that they have a bias are apt to accept wholesale the dominant values of their society.

The role of ideology has been a concern of the analysis in *Getting Started* right from the first. In "Issues in the Everyday," the analyses of health, housing, food delivery, and the job mar-

ket hinted at sharp differences in attitudes and values. In "Lost in the Supermarket," for instance, the analysis picked up on how corporate expansion and concentration, along with high rates of profit, count more in the economy than meeting basic human, social needs. The ideological assumption is that economic growth yields well-being for all and that wealth will "trickle down" to those on the bottom of the economic ladder. The differences in attitude and values permeate every issue in everyday life.

In "The World Around Us," the analyses uncovered economic structures and, entangled amongst them, other fundamental ideological patterns. For example:

- "Energy and the Environment" – The way we use the Earth's energy resources alters the environment on a global scale. Drastic climate change is one of the "externalities," an unintended but very real consequence of the ideological notion that the environment can be treated as an endless source of economic expansion.
- "Technology from Past to Future" – Progress in the form of rapid technological change is almost an end in itself. Those who stand in the way are branded as Luddites. These are, again, the assumptions of a certain ideology.
- "Globalization and Development" – Progress and development are presumed to go hand in hand with the spread across the world of an industrial model fashioned in Europe and North America. Indeed, it is often assumed that there is no alternative to this form of development. That is because many of us have a deep-seated belief in a form of progress that we associate with the ways in which our own societies have evolved. Given the environmental costs, this model has been labelled *mis-development*, a term that surely has as much legitimacy as the label *underdeveloped*, which is so often applied to poor countries.

Ideological assumptions do not just reflect personal preferences or private points of view. They are social, in the sense that they are socially generated and widely shared and therefore serve to support the dominant structures of a society. The maintenance of an existing social order depends on the majority of people within it subscribing to the main tenets of the dominant ideology.

Who advocates these ideas? Why does an often unjust economic system enjoy people's support? What shapes attitudes and values?

Liberal Capitalism

The prevailing, or dominant, ideology in Canada – what we will call liberal capitalism – is so taken for granted that many people unconsciously accept it as the norm, rather than one specific ideological option. For many Canadians it is indistinguishable from "common sense," and its features are often taken for granted.

Liberal capitalism has evolved over several hundred years. It is *capitalist* because it organizes the economy on the basis of the private accumulation of capital. It is *liberal* because it enhances individual liberty and initiative. It emphasizes the maintenance of justice by the state, although the notion of *social* justice is very much contested terrain.

Most Canadians cherish freedom and equality, perhaps ahead of other values. They believe that everyone should be "free" and should enjoy "equal opportunity." Up to this point, those who uphold liberal capitalism and those who criticize it are on the same wavelength.

According to the dominant ideology in Canada, however, the effective meaning of "freedom and equality" is the right of entrepreneurs to invest their money however, whenever, and wherever they choose. In practice this belief favours those who already enjoy wealth and power. They can make wide-ranging decisions about how their capital is used, and they usually argue that government should not interfere with the free market, even when those decisions have unintended but harmful consequences – to the environment, to workers, to society at large.

George Orwell's famous – and apparently self-contradictory – line from *Animal Farm*, "All animals are equal, but some are more equal than others," highlights the practical contradiction within the ideology of liberal capitalism. Although Orwell was satirizing the dominant ideology of the Soviet Union, his wry comment can just as easily be applied to Canada.

Originally, those who controlled capital demanded unhampered freedom. Anything that interfered with this uncontrolled freedom – for example, laws against child labour and regulations setting minimum wages – was resisted as unnatural and contrary to common sense. The "robber barons" of the nineteenth century were a notable example of this: at that time their unregulated activities were an accepted part of capitalist society. In 1894, fifty years before Orwell wrote *Animal Farm*, the French writer Anatole France satirized liberal ideology in his book *The Red Lilies,* making the famous remark: "The law, in all its majestic equality, forbids the rich and the poor alike, to sleep under bridges, to beg in the streets, and to steal bread."

> The gap between the capitalist illusion and its reality is now so great that the practitioners and indeed the civil authorities have difficulty making economic decisions in a sensible manner. Their problem begins with the democracy = capitalism equation. Running democracy and capitalism together as a single idea is a wonderful Marxian joke. That is to say, in the tradition of the Marx Brothers. Neither history nor philosophy link free markets and free men. They have nothing more to do with each other than the accidents of time and place allow. In fact, free enterprise worked far better in its purer state, when it operated beneath friendly, authoritarian government structures. Unquestioned political authority suits the embracing of financial risk. Authoritarian governments can ally themselves to money without fear of conflict of interest. They can do things faster. Compromise less. Democracy, on the other hand, is subject to ongoing political and social compromise. It tends to want to curb activities of all sorts, business-related or not, in order to protect the maximum number of people.
>
> — John Ralston Saul,
> *Voltaire's Bastards: The Dictatorship of Reason in the West,* 1992.

Free competition in the business world is another basic tenet of liberal capitalism. But (as the examples in chapter four show) more and more economic power tends to concentrate in ever fewer hands. In the past twenty years vigorous lobbying by large business has promoted free trade and deregulation, to the extent that critics now refer regularly to a return to the untrammelled freedom of the bad old days by calling it "neo-liberalism" (see chapter nine).

Liberal capitalism has evolved and adapted. Political agitation for social justice has led to changes that promote more equal (but often still unjust) relations between those who sell their labour and those who have the capital to buy it. Trade unions, once seen as an obstacle to the freedom of business, were legalized and won improvements for their members. Government outlawed child labour and brought in the minimum wage. With the growth of the welfare state, pensions, social welfare programs, medicare, and (un)employment insurance arrived in Canada. Such programs, taken together, are called the "social wage." It is a wage that fluctuates according to the tenor of the political times, and the rise of neo-liberalism in the 1980s reduced it significantly.

The media disseminate the ideology of liberal capitalism in both subtle and obvious ways. For example, the news does offer sympathetic features on people who are poor and unemployed; but it rarely questions the priorities of corporations whose exclusive preoccupation with growth and profitability can result in downsizing (and therefore unemployment), dangerous working conditions, or environmental damage.

People are not just passive consumers of news, entertainment, and advertising. The letters to the editor page of any newspaper attests to that. Many people can and do look critically at media information. Members of a striking union are often the first to see how the coverage and the language selected tend to favour their employer over their union. People can tell when news or advertising presents a view of things that runs contrary to what they know from their own life

experiences. And not everyone comprehends media messages in the same way.

Within the dominant media there are many journalists who attempt to swim against the mainstream ideology. Although they have little power, and their perspective has to rise above the mass of intense, familiar news and the advertising torrent, they do try to do investigative reporting, let people who are usually excluded speak for themselves, and make connections that are fresh and out of the ordinary. Outside the mainstream, alternative media dig more deeply into social issues. Community newspapers, critical film and video productions, Aboriginal broadcasting, small and medium-sized magazines, and book publishers together form a vibrant sector. They face the problem of reaching out to the same mass audiences enjoyed by major television networks, newspapers, and magazines.

A call to a local Indigo bookstore revealed that there was no record in their system of the Canadian feminist magazine *Herizons*.[28] This despite the claim of the publication's website that the latest issue ("Turbo Chicks: Talkin' 'bout My Generation") was then on the newsstands – an issue challenging the image of young women as apathetic, apolitical dupes of an anti-feminist backlash. The magazine section at Indigo, with its slogan "The World Needs More Canadian," featured dozens of U.S. fashion magazines packed with ads. Cogeco, a leading cable-TV provider, offered "Even more freedom to choose" from packages that included New Rock Edge TV, Sex TV, X-Treme Sports, and dozens of others. But channel-hoppers will only rarely find a documentary with an explicit point of view.

The Internet has made it cheaper and easier for citizens with an explicit point of view to create their own media by publishing electronically what was once expensive to print or produce.

Distribution costs are also much lower for social movements and citizen networks that want to communicate with anyone who has the resources to connect electronically. Although the Internet has become more commercialized and is subject to total surveillance by security forces (see chapter nine), it still represents a free space in which both movements and marketers seek to get their messages out.

The analysis in *Getting Started* often conflicts with the viewpoint of the dominant ideology, which, for example, might favour the end of social programs previously available to all while uncritically lauding the latest hand-held computer-in-a-cellphone. The dominant ideology does not question Canada's need to become competitive in the new global marketplace, while *Getting Started* wonders about who wins and who loses in this global race.

Social analysis gets at ideological assumptions not so much by talking about ideology as by asking further questions and pushing beyond what is conventional wisdom or what seems, on the surface, to be simple common sense. For example, the values of a just, sustainable, participatory society promise to serve the interests of workers, consumers, and other citizens, but these ideals are often pitted against the conventional wisdom of business and government decision-makers.

The structures that buttress society and the values of private enterprise and private profit, corporate growth, and progress are constantly assumed and positively enforced. The ideology itself is hardly ever questioned. The idea of ordering the Canadian economy according to any norms other than liberal capitalism would seem puzzling to many citizens, especially those in control of the command posts of the economy.

Welcome to "People and Perspectives"

Elements of Canada's dominant ideology are lodged within our heads. This book, in its efforts to analyze, interpret, and judge Canadian reality, tries to shed light on our ideological blind spots. What might have been taken for common sense before now deserves to be questioned and – possibly – changed.

The next part of the book, "People and Perspectives," deals with social issues (though not exclusively social, any more than the previous chapters were exclusively economic). It analyzes the experience of three groups of people: the aged, Aboriginal peoples, and women. In different ways these three groups are kept out on the edge of society. The reality of their lives clashes with the dominant ideology of Canadian society. They are often presented in an unfavourable light or incomprehensible fashion. But at the same time they are struggling for freedom and equality.

In a sense the groups in the next three chapters face the same basic issues and economic issues that have already been analyzed. But how do they look from their point of view? If the media usually give a distorted picture of their needs, rights, and demands – or leaves their real concerns out

---

The World Wide Web is too expensive for millions of people in developing countries, partly because of the cost of computers that are the standard entry point to the Web: in January 2001 the cheapest Pentium III computer was $700 – hardly affordable for low-income community access points. Further, the text-based interface of the Internet puts it out of reach for illiterate people.

To overcome these barriers, academics at the Indian Institute of Science and engineers at the Bangalore-based design company Encore Software designed a handheld Internet appliance for less than $200. Based on the Linux open source operating system, the first version of the Simputer will provide Internet and email access in local languages, with touch-screen functions and microbanking applications. Future versions promise speech recognition and text-to-speech software for illiterate users. The intellectual property rights have been transferred for free to the non-profit Simputer Trust, which is licensing the technology to manufacturers at a nominal fee.

— United Nations Development Programme, *Human Development Report 2001.*

altogether on a consistent basis — is it possible to break through the stereotypes and hear from them?

The next three chapters together hold up a mirror to Canadian society: this is how Canada looks to people whose voices are all too often shunted to the side in this land.

Questions

❑ What role do the media play in creating taste? What are other mechanisms for communicating the dominant ideology? How do they work? Who controls them? Identify some sources of alternative, questioning viewpoints.

❑ The media usually defend their selection of events and editing of stories by claiming that they are giving consumers what they want. Do the media in fact give us what we want? Does the news industry have any responsibility to society beyond catering to its tastes? Should the news industry be allowed to consider itself "a private enterprise owing nothing to the public"?

❑ Ideology is sometimes described as a set of ideas that are commonsensical, a way of looking at the world. How would you describe your own ideology? Where did it come from? In what ways, if any, does it differ from the ideology that prevails in Canadian society?

❑ To what extent do you find out about the news of the days on the Internet? How do you choose which sites to visit? Do you consider them more or less reliable than television, radio, newspapers, and magazines? Are some controlled by companies that also own other communications media?

❑ Images, brands, slogans, and logos appear wherever we turn — pop-ups on the Internet, ads on rented DVDs, embedded in the ice at hockey games, on clothing of all sorts. Does this torrent influence how we see the world? If so, how?

❑ Look for quotations. Who did the reporter talk to — government officials, recognized experts, "usually reliable sources," or anony-mous "informants"? If quotes come from a prepared press release, does the paper usually say so? What are the interests and motives of the people quoted? Do their opinions represent conventional wisdom?

❑ Review the story. Do you believe that you understand the conflict? Are some participants in the event absent from the story? Have credible witnesses been neglected or presented in a dim light? Comparing two or more reports, does the situation seem to have been confused by a particular news outlet, and might there be a reason? Are there clues about where to look for more reliable information?

❑ Evaluate your sources of information on one of the issues in this book. Do you rely on the major networks, newspapers, and news-magazines? Are you familiar with alternative sources, such as church, labour, or special-interest publications? Compare an alternative source with a major news outlet, with an eye on the selection of stories, the depth of coverage, and the viewpoint of the journalist.

❑ Evaluate the target audience for a TV program by watching its commercials. Note the kind of commercials (beer for football games? detergents for soap operas?). Do the commercials match (or contradict) the content of the programs? What are the values involved?

Resources

• Kay Armatage, Kass Banning, Brenda Longfellow, and Janine Marchessault. *Gendering the Nation: Canadian Women's Cinema.* Toronto: University of Toronto Press, 1999. A definitive collection of essays that address the impact and influence of a century of filmmaking by women in Canada — a refreshing and empowering perspective on women in the media.

• John Berger. *Ways of Seeing.* Harmondsworth, Middx.: Penguin Books, 1972. Based on a BBC television series, *Ways of Seeing* is a classic that raises questions about words and images in art and advertising.

• Michael Clow. *False Pretenses: Canadian Newspapers and Nuclear Power*. Halifax: Fernwood Publishing, 1993. The Canadian nuclear industry has argued that the media have treated them unfairly. Clow's study, which looks at nuclear coverage in four dailies in Ontario and New Brunswick, finds that the promoters rather than the opponents of nuclear energy have dominated the news.

• Todd Gitlin. *Media Unlimited: How the Torrent of Images and Sounds Overwhelms Our Lives*. New York: Metropolitan Books, 2001. The relentless saturation of daily life with media images does not herald a "new information age," argues U.S. media critic Gitlin. Rather, it threatens to erode democracy by substituting everything from personality cuts and irony for commitments to public life.

• Robert W. McChesney, Ellen Meiksins Wood, and John Bellamy Foster, eds. *Capitalism and the Information Age: The Political Economy of the Global Communication Revolution*. New York: Monthly Review Press, 1998. A collection of essays that examine how new communications technologies have reshaped the labour force and changed the nature of communication itself.

• M. Nourbese Philip. *Frontiers: Essays and Writings on Racism and Culture*. Stratford, Ont.: Mercury Press, 1992. A collection that critically explores – from the point of view of people of colour living in Canada – our political and economic systems and the various "isms" woven into them.

• Herbert I. Schiller. *Culture, Inc.: The Corporate Takeover of Public Expression*. New York: Oxford University Press, 1991. Schiller examines the effects of a half-century of corporate growth on American culture.

• *Manufacturing Consent: Noam Chomsky and the Media*. Canada, 1992. Directed by Mark Achbar and Peter Wintonick. NFB. Video. Two parts, 167 min. Explores the political life and ideas of U.S. radical philosopher Noam Chomsky, who believes that the media play a pivotal role, not just in shaping how we view our world but also in the political decision-making process. Also available in a six-video classroom version.

• *Adbusters* is a not-for-profit magazine based in British Columbia and devoted to reporting the truth behind many of the world's corporate giants and the devastation and social injustice that comes at the hands of their colossal profits. *Adbusters* describes itself as a "global network of artists, activists, writers, pranksters, students, educators and entrepreneurs who want to advance the new social activist movement of the information age. Our aim is to topple existing power structures and forge a major shift in the way we will live in the 21st century." See also their website <www.adbusters.org>.

Websites:

The expansion of alternative and critical sources of news and media analysis has accompanied the growth of the Internet. Websites and links abound. The Media Channel is a global internet community with over a thousand affiliates focused on media issues. They range from the Institute for Public Accuracy to Newslink Africa. Organizations like the Canadian Journalists for Free Expression scrutinize the Canadian media scene. For other alternative news and viewpoints, see the websites for Rabble.ca, which combines activism and journalism, and Straight Goods – "Canada's Independent On-Line Source of News You Can Use."

Chapter Eleven
Aging – Out of Sight

"I must be getting old."

It's an offhand remark that any of us might mutter, perhaps when we become breathless after running up a flight of stairs. Or perhaps after we've forgotten someone's name, or when we haven't been able to do something we used to be able to do. It's an offhand remark that speaks volumes about our feelings towards aging.

To a certain degree aging should mean that things get better. We are all continually growing and changing, and as we gain in experience we also potentially gain in wisdom and skill. We can put things in a larger perspective. Some of the older generation find themselves gradually endowed not only with a new sense of freedom but also with new energy and vitality.

It is, indeed, an accomplishment to arrive at a state of oldness. There can be a lust for life that younger people only dream of. Older people "have journeyed through life. They have survived, many to find peace – even serenity – most to find a welcome self-acceptance."[1]

It can be an enriched period, this time that the French refer to as the "Third Age." For a few

– especially those able to buy a house early on in their lives and pay off the mortgage – advanced age can even mean economic freedom, a greater ability to travel, to do things that had been put off for years. With the growing demographic shift involving the aging of the population, newspapers have been extolling the employment benefits – reliability, experience, skills – of hiring seniors.[2]

Aging affects everyone. Except for the unfortunate few who die young, we will all be old someday, and more people than ever before are living longer. Just *how* we grow old is determined largely by two factors: society's assumptions about what it means to be old; and our prosperity in the younger years.

But more often in our society, growing old has a bleak side. In Canada the idea of aging seldom suggests an improvement in a person's general situation. On the contrary, old people are frequently viewed as frail, forgetful, confused, infirm – perhaps even dangerous to themselves. Above all, old people are seen as people in need of help.

The analysis in this chapter touches on several ideas about old people that are common in Canada:

- *Separate* – Old age is a distinct period separate from the earlier years of life. Old people are a special group whose unique problems separate them from the rest of society.

> Men often gain great honour as they grow old, but there is a double standard in the chronicle of aging. For a man, the signs of great age, the wrinkles, the lines, the heavy paunch suggest character, fortitude. They indicate a maturity and celebrate his engagement with life. For a woman they signal obsolescence. We are all aware that in Western society old women should hide themselves, ashamed that we no longer fit the mold of perfection that our society demands.
>
> — Shelagh Wilkinson,
> "Old Woman, 'Bearer of Keys to Unknown Doorways,'"
> *Canadian Woman Studies/les cahiers de la femme*,
> Winter 1992.

- *Hidden* – The experience and plight of the elderly, far from being taken into account by society, somehow remain "out of sight" and hidden from view.
- *Dependent* – Because they may be in need of some help, the aging lose their right to independence. Old people become dependent on others.
- *Useless* – Old people have no useful purpose and are a drain on society's resources. In a way they're seen as useless, and they often feel pretty useless themselves.

The Golden Years

What is old? An Aboriginal Canadian told the Ontario Advisory Council on Senior Citizens: "At 75 or 80 you can still chop wood; when you can't then you are old."[3]

In earlier times – and still today in certain societies – people performed socially recognized work for as long as they were physically able. Canada's Inuit, like many other traditional peoples, look to their elders as a rich source of wisdom and advice. The Inuit have no word for "senior citizen."

The concept of "who is old" varies from culture to culture, and also according to factors like gender. Until 1965 Air Canada stewardesses faced compulsory retirement at age thirty-two. While few people are forced to retire that early any more, most expect eventually to give up full-time employment and make the move into retirement. Nowadays most Canadians can expect to spend at least one-fifth of their lives in retirement.

Retirement is a relatively recent phenomenon. In industrialized countries in the 1930s between 40 and 70 per cent of all men aged sixty-five and over were working for pay. By 1971 the proportion of aged men doing paid work in Canada had declined markedly to 25 per cent, and by 1998 that number had fallen to 10.3 per cent. In the 1920s and 1930s one elderly woman in five was working for a wage, but by 1998 this had shrunk to less than one in thirty.[4]

While compulsory retirement at age sixty-five has been eliminated in Quebec and challenged under the Charter of Rights and Freedoms in some provinces, it is still routine in some provinces. In the 1990s the Supreme Court reversed its earlier position on the question of whether mandatory retirement constitutes discrimination. In 1982 it had rejected ageist stereotypes on grounds similar to the rejection of racism and sexism. But in 1990 the court returned to those stereotypes. In its judgment regarding the retirement of a University of Guelph professor, the court stated that "there is a general relationship between advancing age and declining ability," which makes age a legitimate basis for discrimination.[5] The mean age of this panel of judges was sixty-five.

While forced retirement is an unfair restriction on people's options, especially for those who love their career, for others retirement also presents opportunities. Retirement can serve as a well-earned rest, but only if it includes economic security. Mandatory retirement can mean forced unemployment for two different sorts of workers: those with higher educations; and low-paid workers or those who have had significant career interruptions. Arguments for the right to continue working have quite different meanings for these different kinds of workers. If low-paid workers could afford to leave their jobs, retirement might be exactly what they need to pursue further education or take up the inherently interesting activity that makes continuing on the job so attractive to more highly educated workers.

Objections to age discrimination, while legitimate, can mask other social problems. The same problems came up, for instance, in objections to child labour laws based on the argument that children in poor countries need to be able to work to support themselves and their families. Such problems are symptomatic of the view that each individual alone has to earn her or his basic economic security, rather than that security being a right — something that we as a society should work to ensure for all members of our community, especially those who are most vulnerable.

Retirement can also be "forced" by other factors, such as pressing family responsibilities. In Canada more women than men retire early. While women decide to retire for a variety of reasons, they are much more likely than men to retire because of the ill health of a spouse or other family member. Indeed, one study showed that family responsibilities ranked third as the most common reason for women to retire, while it barely ranked at all for men.[6] In those cases, women who have to leave the paid workforce often lose their economic security. They are hardly retiring for a "rest," or because they are unwilling or unable to keep up with the demands of the workplace.

How people react to retirement depends in many ways on their previous work. Those who spent their working lives in jobs that were boring, frustrating, dirty, or dangerous are more likely to embrace retirement eagerly. Many workers don't want to wait until sixty-five to retire. By 1994 only 60 per cent of men aged fifty-five to sixty-four remained in the labour force, and the average age of retirement had reached as low as sixty-two.[7] With the slogan "thirty and out," some unions have won contract clauses permitting employees to take their pensions after thirty years' service, no matter what their age. But since only a minority of workers are unionized, few enjoy this option.

People who found their work challenging, enjoyable, and satisfying are not likely to be satisfied with sudden joblessness. In a society in which individual status and personal dignity are so intimately bound up with a job (see chapter five), the sudden termination of work can easily lead people to feel useless and lacking in purpose.

Society has come to define retirement and old age as the end of a certain part of life — the useful part. This is especially true in a period when traditional skills are quickly being replaced with new ones. As both public and private institutions become ever larger and more remote, feelings of obligation between employer and employee evaporate. The labour market is often biased against the older worker, especially in times of high unemployment. When large numbers of employees are threatened with layoffs, older workers are often pressured to take early retirement so that jobs can be kept for younger people. All of a sudden "these old people" are less valuable to society than they were before. This "state of reality" is driven home when retirement suddenly and dramatically drives down a person's income level.

Advertisers favour images of fun-loving groups of smiling, attractive people in their twenties and thirties. This imagery links positive feelings about youth with particular products. Elderly people are only rarely seen in beer or soft drink commercials. "Pepsi – for those who think young" used to be a sales pitch. Vigour, imagination, energy, and purpose are frequently associated with youth. This assumption is not only faulty in itself, but also leads to negative attitudes about old age.

Getting old and being retired acquire a kind of stigma: not really the golden but the declining years in which old people now have to deal with age discrimination and lack of choice in many aspects of their lives, including work and/or retirement.

Unfortunately, for over half of Canada's elderly citizens, the "golden years" are all too often tarnished by poverty and insecurity.

Pensions . . .

In 1907 the federal government introduced a scheme whereby people could purchase an annuity with government assistance. "I doubt extremely the expediency of having recourse to a system of old age pensions," one senator said:

> But I do believe there is great opportunity for the state to avail itself of the machinery at its disposal for the purpose of placing within the grasp of every industrious man in Canada the opportunity, at an easy rate and at a very small cost to the state, of providing a reasonable annuity for his support at an advanced period of life.[8]

The emphasis was on individual thrift, and at that time pensions were a long way off. But today discussions of pension reform still tend to reflect this individualistic perspective.

When the idea of Canadians receiving an old age pension was discussed in the 1920s, some politicians opposed the idea on the principle that it would place a premium on laziness. But as compulsory retirement spread and fewer people remained economically active in their later years, pensions became widely accepted. By 1951 everyone seventy and over was entitled to an old age pension. The qualifying age for pensions was later lowered to sixty-five.

There are now various pension plans to support people when they leave the labour market. These are the safety nets that should protect people from poverty when their active participation in the paid labour force ends.

- The oldest form of income security is individual savings. Workers are expected to squirrel some money away to support themselves when they can no longer work. Government uses a tax incentive to encourage personal savings for retirement through Registered Retirement Savings Plans (RRSPs).
- Job-related or employer-sponsored pension schemes. People who work for government agencies and large firms contribute a portion of their salary to a pension plan. In 1997 four out of every ten Canadians in the paid labour force were participating in occupational pension plans.[9]
- Old Age Security (OAS), the oldest form of government pension. The federal government provides all senior Canadians with a basic pension and pays for it out of general revenues.
- Guaranteed Income Supplement (GIS). The government "tops up" the OAS with a means-tested supplement for those with no other source of income over and above the basic pension. Each province also has a system of payments to supplement the OAS.
- The Canada Pension Plan (CPP) and the Quebec Pension Plan (QPP). Begun in 1966,

the CPP is similar to private plans in that employees contribute through their wages, and the employers also contribute. CPP is a portable fund that workers carry with them as they move from job to job.

This list of programs protecting people against old age poverty seems comprehensive. But RRSPs and private savings exclude those who cannot afford to save for retirement because they need all their income to get by in their earlier years. Except for the OAS/GIS combination — which by itself fails to keep the recipient above the poverty line — all pensions are geared to previous performance in the labour market. Those who were paid higher wages get bigger pensions, while low-income people receive less. People who were frequently unemployed or who had taken time off work for child care or to fulfil other family responsibilities are left out.

Those without a good track record in the labour market are condemned to continuing poverty in their later years. Thus the inequalities characteristic of economic life in Canada are reproduced in old age. Despite all the programs, each person has primary responsibility for his or her own well-being in old age. The guiding principle of an individualistic ethic remains unchanged. The social system scarcely guarantees economic security to retired Canadians.

. . . or Poverty?

The programs established in Canada have worked to a degree. Shortly before the Economic Council of Canada was closed down by the government, its researchers noted, "The dramatic decrease in poverty among the elderly was the result of political decisions taken some 25 years ago, when it was felt that the extent of hardship among this group was no longer tolerable."[10]

The proportion of seniors who live on low incomes fell from 34 per cent in 1980 to 19 per cent in 1997. Still, even with that decrease, almost two-thirds of a million people aged sixty-five or over remain living below the official low-income cut-off line. Many more hover just above that level. In 1998, 37 per cent of aged Canadians

had incomes so low that they were eligible for the Guaranteed Income Supplement.[11] Many of them are in the group that statisticians call the "near poor" — often a worse situation financially than those designated as poor, because the "near poor" do not qualify for the meagre services available to the officially "poor." Some groups of old people are at particular risk of poverty: very old people, women, and unattached individuals.[12]

Aged Canadians cite low income as their number one concern. This was obvious in the storm that broke out on Parliament Hill in 1985, when the federal government announced its plan to de-index pensions. Senior citizens' groups from across the country denounced the proposal as indecent and unjust. With support of large sections of the population, including leading business groups such as the Canadian Chamber of Commerce and the Canadian Organization of Small Business, older Canadians organized and mounted a strenuous lobby. The plan was withdrawn. The reason for the government's blunder was simple, according to the press — it had underestimated "Grey Power."

The government soon went on the attack again with an assault on the universality of Canada's social service programs. Its 1989 budget introduced a tax measure known as the "clawback" of Old Age Security, in which the government would tax back OAS income from people with incomes above a certain level. The cut-off point established in the 1989 budget was $50,000. But the reality was more harsh. The Ecumenical Coalition for Economic Justice analyzed the policy:

The government chose a fifty thousand dollar threshold to create the impression that the clawback would only affect the wealthy. Yet the threshold was partially deindexed and set to rise annually at three percentage points less than the rate of inflation. Accordingly, the fifty thousand dollar threshold would be equal to only forty thousand dollars in real terms after eight years and to just twenty thousand dollars after 30 years.[13]

Retirement planning is only for men; women are the caregivers, and in the eyes of society must continue working at this volunteer labour as long as the need for our services persists.

Once the need is no longer there, life does get brighter for some older women. In the government-built and subsidized senior citizen highrises, women proudly showed me through their apartments, which were decorated with photographs of children, grandchildren, and great-grandchildren. They pointed out their access to running water, heat and other amenities they never knew as younger women. Those who still enjoy good health and are sociable are busy with many activities and have formed supportive circles of friends close by.

— Anne Smart,
"Representing Older Women in Saskatchewan," *Canadian Woman Studies/les cahiers de la femme, 1992.*

Statistics Canada projected that the number of old people with a middle-class standard of living would decline by about one-third. By 2036 there could be more than six times the present number of elderly Canadians living in poverty.

Canada has the resources to properly look after our aging population, even in the case of "relatively modest economic growth" and "even taking into account increased public spending on health care and pensions."[14]

Yet most Canadians anticipate their old age with foreboding, wondering whether they will be living in poverty. The individually oriented pension leaves many people in the lurch. Women are particularly vulnerable. Senior women have the highest incidence of poverty of any age group in Canada. Many older women are poor because there is a presumption both on their part and on the part of governments that women are family members first and workers only second.[15] The situation is worsened by women's second-class status in the paid workforce, where women's wages are only about two-thirds of men's. This condition has a key impact on the value of both public and private pension benefits for women.

Occupational pension benefits in 1997 made up 25 per cent of the incomes of men over sixty-five, but only 14 per cent of the income of women over sixty-five. Since Canada Pension Plan benefits are based on an individual's earning history, the CPP benefits that many women receive do not lift them above the poverty line. In 2002 the average CPP benefit paid to women was $287.01 per month; for men it was $503.51 per month. While the number of women contributing to Registered Retirement Savings Plans has increased markedly in recent years, women are still less likely to make these contributions than are men. Small wonder, then, that almost one out of every four elderly women in Canada lives in poverty, and that for unattached women the figure rises to one in two.[16]

In Canada over half of all women now hold paying jobs, and many raise children at the same time, often alone. While the responsibility to care for other adult family members also falls mainly on women, those who take time away from paid work to care for family forfeit future income security as well as current earnings. As a result, the retirement income of a mother and home-maker usually depends on her husband's income or pension and savings. Without this support, or if the spouse dies without leaving any survivor's benefits, she is condemned to poverty, dependent on the inadequate OAS/GIS combination.

A single woman who has worked all her life to earn a living is often in a precarious state when she grows older. Anne Smart, a former member of the Saskatchewan legislature, tells a story she heard while campaigning door to door — a story that combines the basic and economic issues of housing, unemployment, and new technology with the social issues of aging and gender:

At one door I was ushered into a one-room apartment by a woman who was just moving in. Her kitchen area was behind a curtain, her bathroom down the hall to be shared with strangers. She spoke to me softly, with tears in her eyes. She had been a business receptionist for nearly 25 years and was still appropriately dressed for the job. She was certain that her sudden lay-off was the result of her employer considering her too old to be retrained to deal with the new computer technology being introduced in the office. She was still a long way from sixty-five, her pension would be very small, she had not had any luck finding another job. This was the cheapest place she could find in a hurry. How was she going to manage?[17]

Seniors who belong to visible minority groups are also very vulnerable. A person of Caribbean origin told the Ontario Advisory Council on Senior Citizens that many Blacks spend a good portion of their lives working in low-paying service jobs because of prejudice: "Sadly, they won't be able to afford those services for themselves once they retire."[18]

New immigrants can face an even worse situation. It can take ten to twenty years for a recent immigrant to reach an income level equal to the Canadian average.[19] For immigrants, hard work does not translate into equal pension benefits. Residence requirements introduced in 1977 mean that anyone who has lived in Canada for less than ten years gets no government pension benefits. Other immigrants may get less than full benefits depending on how late in their adult life they came to Canada.[20]

Elderly Aboriginal people living in remote communities continue to be plagued by difficult situations and poor health, with pensions that are far from adequate for food. Their houses are not insulated and they worry about being able to continue to cut firewood to keep warm. They live in fear of getting seriously ill and being shipped off to a distant hospital to spend their last days among strangers.[21] Changes in attitudes towards older people have also proven painful. "When I was growing up elders were always respected for their knowledge and experience," says Margaret Labillois, elder and former Micmac chief. "They were our teachers, our books, our education, our babysitters, our story tellers, and our special helpers — in short, a way of life. . . .

Today elders are no longer elders but just old people."[22]

In general, older Canadians who live out their lives in poverty must struggle to find housing that is not cramped, dirty, and draughty. The press occasionally features stories of pensioners forced to subsist on pet food. Towards the end of the month, when the pension runs out, there is often nothing left for the barest necessities.

People caught in the daily throes of material poverty have to cut out many of the small things in life — newspapers, trips downtown, a new item of clothing — that other people take for granted. But reading a newspaper and getting around town are important because they can provide a sense of participating in the day to day life of society. When old people are deprived of these "little things," they are denied the opportunity to participate. They feel excluded, no longer a part of the busy life they once knew, and separate from what is happening around them.

The "Demographic Bulge"

The idea of *separation* of the elderly from the rest of society is reinforced when pension experts focus on conflicts between generations that, we are told, suddenly arise when one generation comes to depend on another. But generations have always depended on each other — and in any case, the whole notion of dependency is overblown.

While the popular resistance to the pension clawback was spearheaded by senior citizens, it garnered widespread support across other sectors of the population. More recent attacks on the pension system structure the "problem" of universality as one that pits a burgeoning elderly population — the "demographic bulge" — against an overstressed younger generation. A move to privatize public pensions is necessary, we are told, to prevent a pending crisis in the system. The threat is said to come from the increasing size of the population drawing pensions in proportion to the numbers of working-age people required to put money into the fund.

Pension experts who have studied the effects

of pension privatization efforts, for example in the United Kingdom and Chile, identify talk of "demographic time bombs" as misleading scare tactics.[23] For one thing, "dependency," the statistical category that represents older people simply as needy, is itself oversimplistic. It ignores how retired people do pay various kinds of taxes and user fees, in addition to the various ways in which they contribute to the life of the community.

For another thing it fails to take other demographic shifts into account, and especially decreasing "youth dependency." Statisticians calculate elderly dependency by dividing the number of people over age sixty-five by the number of people aged twenty to sixty-four. They determine youth dependency by dividing the number of people under nineteen by those between twenty and sixty-four. While elderly dependency rates increased from .09 in 1921 to .19 in 1991, with a projected increase to .42 in 2036, the youth dependency rates decreased, from .84 in 1921 to .46 in 1991, with a projected decrease to .40 in 2036.[24] Combining these figures generates a net decrease in overall dependency.

A closer look at intergenerational support patterns also reveals that they strongly favour younger people. One Canadian study found: "Up to age seventy older people give more support to their children than they receive. And they continue to give to their children throughout their lives."[25]

"Homes for the Aged"

Some people live in their own homes until they die. Others stay with relatives who provide whatever assistance is required. Still others live out their years in places established to care for the elderly. But in recent years the pattern of family life has been changing. Family members are more likely to live in different parts of the country than ever before. Many daughters and daughters-in-law were once in a position to care for aging relatives because they worked at home as housewives. (Many of them also earned money by taking in boarders or doing sewing and laundry.) Now many more women work outside of the home as well. As family size has declined, so too has the ability of families to assist their elderly members.

In the 1990s most people over the age of seventy-five stayed in their own homes, which is where they preferred to be. Although government policies began to reflect and support this trend, it remains to be seen whether there is sufficient political will to back these policies with adequate resources.

While most seniors still live with family members, a significant and growing number live alone. By 1996, 29 per cent of seniors lived alone, a figure that has grown steadily from 20 per cent in 1971. In Quebec the number of older people living alone more than tripled between 1956 and 1976 (from 5.5 per cent to 19.1 per cent). In Canada, between 1961 and 1991 the proportion of senior women living alone more than doubled.[26] In part these changes are due to shifting family structures and social expectations; in part they are due to the combination of widowhood and higher average age among senior women in comparison with senior men; and in part to the greater independence that even a small pension, housing subsidies, and community-based health-care supports make possible. Older women make up the largest group in subsidized housing and the greatest proportion of subsidized home-care consumers.[27]

With "social housing" or "subsidized housing," tenants' rent is geared to their income, with people paying higher rents when their incomes are higher. The demand for this kind of affordable and well-maintained housing far exceeds the supply. People can spend years on social housing waiting lists.[28] Because of the drop-off in construction of social housing units in recent years — a decrease in Canada of 65 per cent between 1989 and 1998 — this situation has become more acute for younger seniors who have only recently come to need that kind of subsidy. (See also chapter three.)

Over the past several decades the percentage

of old people living in institutions such as hospitals and special-care homes has gradually decreased, from 10.2 per cent in 1971 to 7.3 per cent in 1996. The rate of institutionalization increases slightly according to age and gender; and it also varies more significantly from one part of the country to another, ranging from a low of 5 per cent in British Columbia to a high of 10 per cent in Quebec.[29]

In the early days of medicare public money supported institutional care, giving institutionalization a running start that developed a momentum of its own. People were forced to opt for institutions because only those costs were insured. A whole industry grew up to maintain, expand, and profit from "homes for the aged." As a newspaper report in the early 1980s put it, "Private enterprise has been making inroads into the healthcare field in recent years — particularly in the delivery of geriatric services — as governments have found themselves strapped for both capital and operating funds."[30]

This business has gone transnational, with firms like Extendicare Inc. ready to maximize the "opportunities for growth" presented, for example, by the Ontario "market." To companies like Extendicare, Ontario looks like a good place to control costs (that is, to minimize labour costs) and a good place to gain access to public funds. Canada as a whole presents a less regulated environment than, say, Texas or Florida — states that Extendicare withdrew from in order to avoid further "exposure to litigation."[31]

In some long-term care facilities — the new term for nursing homes or "homes for the aged" — the care is startlingly inadequate — although, with few regulations and inspections in place, the quality of care is difficult to assess. Keeping people in institutions, even if they are called homes, is expensive. With better community-care facilities, more old people could remain in their own homes and, indeed, get out more. Those living at home may also feel less separated from society. If they have a choice, most seniors, like the young and middle-aged, will choose an autonomous life where they make their own decisions. Many

elderly are shut in through no choice of their own, and even the label "shut-in" evokes the pejorative image of a prison.

Support for home care continues to be limited, despite increased public discussions about the value of community support for older people and people with disabilities. This translates into an uneven quality of service for people who need care, and exploitive working conditions for people with jobs in this underfunded sector. In late 2002 the Romanow Commission recognized the problem when it made recommendations for at least some improvements (see chapter two). Investors have recognized the profit-generating potential of home-care services as more and more health-care and social support services are downloaded from provincial to municipal governments and from there out into the private market. As long as this field remains under-regulated, the quality of care as defined by consumers and front-line caregivers is likely to take a back seat to economic performance indicators as defined by private investors.

"Community care" can also be a misleading expression. While staying at home may be the best option for older people, so far the system of supports and services necessary to assist that lifestyle for many old people is lacking. The job tends to be done by women who already carry the load of two jobs.[32]

Community care ought to be provided by a caring community, one that recognizes the value of all its members, and the value of having a home and being able to participate in the life of the community. A home, more than just a place to live, is a personal space, a place to belong. At home people are more likely to feel they have some control over what they do. These are intangibles that all of us – old and young – cherish.

An Aging World

"Population aging is a universal force that has the power to shape the future as much as globalization." So states the United Nations in the Madrid International Plan of Action on Aging, a plan that was accepted by 156 nations at the United Nations Second World Assembly on Aging that took place in Spain in April 2002. As a member of the Canadian delegation, I had the privilege of learning first-hand about the huge challenges – and opportunities – that aging poses around the world and comparing them to our experience in Canada.

Aging isn't a "side" issue internationally. It's a central concern that must be in the mainstream of global development agendas. And while the specifics differ depending on what part of the world you're from, delegates from all regions at this Second Assembly agreed on several common goals: ensure dignity, security and equality for all older persons (especially for women, who face more discrimination); enhance solidarity among generations; support families; create opportunities for productive activity for all ages and fight poverty. . . .

As a signatory to the Plan, Canada is accountable to Canadians and to the international community to achieve the goal of a society for all ages. The Second World Assembly on Aging is over. It's time for action.

— Patricia Raymaker,
chairperson, National Advisory Council on Aging, 2002.

The End of Separatism

Even if we are not in our own later years, most of us have accompanied parents or grandparents through old age – or will have to do so in the future. We cannot help but wonder what will become of us when we become old ourselves. Perhaps the most important discovery is that we all share the problems of the old, not simply because we will one day be old ourselves, but because the problems of the old are closely linked with other social difficulties.

The level of material comfort in old age is largely a function of class and sex. If you are a middle-class man who had a steady job with a pension plan during your working life, your retirement is likely to be materially secure. But if you are a working-class woman who spent part of your life working at home looking after family and part of your life in paid work, you will likely be one of the many senior Canadians who depends on an inadequate government pension.

If you were poor in your earlier years, chances are you will be poor in your old age. If you fail to save enough, the state will dole out some limited support, but this small stipend condemns you to poverty. In Canada, it seems, a comfortable and secure old age is a privilege to be earned, not a right that is guaranteed. According to this do-it-yourself attitude towards retirement, each person is responsible for his or her own income, through private savings or a private pension plan. As seniors try to supplement pension funds, the increased number of retirees could lead to a growth in part-time employment. Among those seniors who did work for pay after sixty-five, in 1998, 41 per cent worked part-time.[33]

How people live in retirement is a function of how their worth was measured by a pay cheque, not necessarily of what they contributed to society over the course of their lives.

Society has come to treat aging as something that is *done* to people who happen to be in the later years of life. But contrary to popular belief, older people are actually quite independent. "For the most part," concludes a Statistics Canada report, "Canadian seniors look after themselves."[34] In general they devote about as much time to household chores as do younger people, with women continuing to spend more time on this kind of work. This does not mean that seniors do not get social support. In 1996, 84 per cent of all people aged sixty-five and over got some sort of help with household work and personal chores as well as emotional support. Mostly this help comes from family and friends rather than from paid caregivers. This kind of help is not the mark of a relationship of dependence, but rather of interdependence. Seniors also devote a lot of their time, energy, and expertise in providing support to others.[35]

With institutionalization the ability of older people to take care of themselves and to contribute to the community declines, just as it declined with the rise of compulsory retirement and the reduced capacity to earn an income. Institutionalization imposes a heavy financial burden on everyone, and the load will become more onerous as the demographic bulge grows older. The practical issues of pensions and enabling old people to be autonomous citizens cannot be tackled simply by providing more community care and adjusting pensions upward.

The tendency to treat the greying of society as some kind of huge problem is a socially imposed and self-fulfilling verdict in Canada. The attitudes of looking at old people as a group apart, as using retirement as a form of waste disposal, are institutionally supported.

Poverty and isolation can lead to abuse, especially in the case of widowed women who become dependent on caregivers. Little attention has been paid to documenting the incidence of elder abuse. One study found that about 4 per cent of older adults living in private homes experienced abuse or neglect, usually at the hands of a family member.[36] Poor conditions in unlicensed nursing homes can also create a breeding ground for abuse.

Abuse is linked to social vulnerability, isolation, poverty, and the low social value accorded to certain kinds of people. Although older men report higher rates of abuse than younger men do, the term elder abuse can mask the relation between gender and vulnerability to abuse in old age. Older women are more vulnerable to abuse than older men because of "the relative powerlessness of women throughout life."[37] This vulnerability is reproduced in old age and aggravated by the vulnerability associated with aging and social attitudes towards aging.

While the old in Canada face hardship and uncertainty, we do not hear or see much of them, because they tend to be hidden away. Elder abuse, for instance, has been an almost taboo topic. Old people also separate themselves mentally and spiritually, because they get the sense that society considers them useless and unproductive. This separatism makes no sense for old people and ignores the skills and accumulated experience they have to offer in helping to solve the many problems society faces.

Still, despite the very real problems of poverty, isolation, and abuse, surveys have shown that most old Canadians living at home — and about two-thirds of those aged seventy-five and over — feel good about themselves, their health, and their prospects.[38] Although disability rates are higher among older people, disability is not an all-pervasive phenomenon among the elderly. In 1996-97, one in four people aged sixty-five or over had a long-term disability or handicap.[39] Still, as Mark Novak and Lori Campbell put it: "Chronic conditions do not necessarily translate into functional disability. That is, while over three quarters of elderly persons have at least one chronic condition, only about half experience some functional disability. Even fewer, about one fifth, require assistance with basic activities."[40] Indeed, a great many seniors provide help to friends and family and more generally to the community. In 1997, 58 per cent of seniors participated in what Statistics Canada calls "informal volunteer activities," babysitting, helping with shopping and transportation, providing care and support to the sick, helping with the gardening, and so on. The rate of participation in formal volunteer activities does decline somewhat with age, although those seniors who do perform these services on average devote more of their time to it than do younger volunteers.[41]

This kind of involvement means that we have to cast off the prevailing ideas of useless and dependent, and our attitudes to aging have to be redefined so that old people are not hidden but seen, not impoverished but living with dignity, not separate but playing a useful, independent, and participatory role in society.

Power and New Approaches

Older people themselves are doing what they can to play a full role in Canadian society. Half of all seniors, for instance, report involvement in a political organization. Many have focused specifically on issues affecting them as seniors – as witnessed by the protests over the de-indexing of pensions. This kind of activism has a long history in Canada. The Old Age Pensioners Organization, one of the first seniors advocacy groups in the country, was set up in British Columbia in 1932 by people who wanted to protest the rigid use of a means test for pensioners. In recent years senior advocacy has grown in Canada.[42]

Active seniors emphasize their abilities and power as a group, working not only on their own behalf but also as Canadians concerned with the future that faces all of us. This movement includes groups like the Older Women's Network, founded in Ontario, the Fédération de l'Âge d'Or du Québec, and the vibrant "Raging Grannies," a protest group originating in Victoria, B.C. with branches all across the coun-

try, specializing in street theatre and satirical song. These groups give older people a voice, not only on issues of aging but also on everything from disarmament and peace to the environment.

The aged are nevertheless not a homogeneous group. Their needs vary greatly depending on their gender and ethnic background, their economic situation, their health, and their living situation. An older man is more likely to be married; an older woman is more likely to be widowed. The social support networks of the elderly differ from those of the general population.[43]

Aged immigrants recently settled in Canada have special problems. A Vietnamese senior told the Ontario Advisory Council on Senior Citizens that in Canada the older Vietnamese "see themselves as being stripped of power because they have little or no income and do not speak the language," whereas in Vietnam they had more economic power and were more independent.[44]

Despite the growth of the seniors movement, power is unequally shared by those who work with old people. Old people become easy targets for physical abuse because they are powerless. One reason for this lack of power is that they are marginalized by society. For all old people, any new approaches to aging need to emphasize this issue of power – making sure that old people have the power to provide for themselves, to use their skills to help each other, to be active subjects in their own lives rather than passive objects of institutional policy.

Different approaches are needed. Here are some suggestions.

■ Rather than encouraging everyone to retire at an arbitrary age like sixty-five, take a more flexible approach. Then those who want to retire could do so, and others who want to could stay on the job for as long as they are capable of working.

- Explore options to phase in retirement with reduced hours of work. Then people can gradually become accustomed to new routines and explore new options.

- Restructure the pension system so that it recognizes rather than penalizes women for the contributions made in fulfilling family responsibilities and doing unpaid work.

- Structure the pension system in ways that avoid reproducing the poverty experienced earlier in life. For instance, the replacement rate of CPP/QPP pensions could be increased for low-income workers, and pensions could be indexed to wages rather than prices.

- Many family members could and would provide more assistance to their elderly members if subsidies were available for effective family care rather than just for institutions. Support must be structured, however, so that the responsibility does not fall inequitably on women already carrying the load of other jobs.

- Meals-on-wheels is a service that enables seniors with mobility limitations to have regular, hot food of good quality in their own homes. Given the poverty of many old people, this meal is frequently the only source of decent sustenance each day, a break from diets of tea and toast. These often underfunded and understaffed services need more public support.

- Day hospitals and visiting health-care workers can meet many of the medical needs of older people at much less than the cost of chronic care institutions.

- Vehicles designed for wheelchairs can bring transportation to the homes of those who have trouble getting out. With adequate transit, old people could live at home and still be able to participate in the life of the community and have access to many services they need.

- Multi-service community centres can meet a variety of old people's needs: food, health care, companionship, recreation, and legal aid.

- Government commitment to barrier-free designs in buildings and services could lead the

way in preventing as well as removing many of the barriers that get in the way of seniors' equal participation in society as well as that of younger people with disabilities.

- Increased media representation of real rather than stereotypical seniors would help to overcome some of the stigma associated with aging, and bring some of the reality of this part of all our lives to light.

"Change, not charity" is what many Canadians are demanding: programs to provide them with whatever support they need to care for themselves. To stop separating old people from society and to reintegrate them means to change society itself.

Alternatives do exist. Putting an end to the problems of the elderly requires, in the most basic terms, ending the equation of old age with poverty. It also requires discarding the conception of old age itself as a problem. Old people need access to facilities and services that enable them to participate actively in every dimension of life. But they also need greater autonomy and greater recognition of their continuing capacity to contribute to society.

Given the way that Canada is organized, the social and economic forces at play have worked on old people in the same way that they have worked on the rest of us. But they have done so for longer, with more extreme — and final — consequences. Is it any wonder that older people want the enforced separation and dependency to end?

We pensioners constitute a reservoir of experience and of seasoned capacity for coping with personal and social problems. We have a widespread experience of our country's political processes, and the numbers now to carry political weight. Above all, we have time – most citizens now can look forward to spending at least one-fifth of their productive lives in relatively good health with about 2,000 hours a year of time at their own disposal. The potential for the good of society and for a personally fulfilling citizen role is enormous.

— G.C. Gifford,
Canada's Fighting Seniors, 1990.

Questions

❏ If you have not retired, what do you imagine yourself doing when you do retire? How would you like to describe who you are then?

❏ If you are not yet retired, do you think you will be able to afford to retire when you are ready to? What sorts of changes are necessary in Canada to make sure that people will be able to choose retirement without fear of poverty?

❏ In Canada various provisions are made for people who retire from lifelong paid employment. Fewer provisions are made for people who were under-waged, underemployed, or did not participate in the wage economy at all. How can we recognize the contributions that have been made by members of this segment of society throughout their lifetime – for example, as homemakers and caregivers?

❏ Do we live in a youth culture? At what age do we believe that men and women reach their "peak"? When do they make their most valuable contributions to society or reach their highest levels of personal achievements? Do you think of men or women of a certain age as being "past it"? What does this tell us about the standards against which we measure human worth? Do these standards need changing? What would it take to change them?

❏ Should retirement be compulsory? Should older workers be required to "make way" for younger people? Do people have a right to work regardless of age?

❏ Do we live in a society that is segregated by generations? How much contact do you have with people who are a generation or two older or younger than you? Is this contact restricted mostly to family members? How much access do you have to the insights, perspectives, and experiences of members of different generations? How much opportunity do you have to share your experience with members of other generations? If you have good intergenerational contact, explain why this is valuable. What makes this contact possible for you? If you don't have such good intergenerational contact, do you feel this as a lack? How might this be remedied?

❏ Dream a little! If you are not yet a senior citizen, imagine what your needs might be as you age. Imagine the kinds of opportunities you would want for self-development, for contributing to your community, for simply enjoying your life. What would it take, from you personally, and from the society around you, for these dreams to become a reality? If you are already a senior citizen, do you experience gaps between your dreams and reality? What would it take to narrow these gaps? What has enabled you to realize your dreams as you age?

❏ How is aging represented in the mass media? In movies and on television, at what age do men and women disappear from the ranks of those enjoying or pursuing active love lives? How often are older men and women represented as dependants, as interfering, or as a burden on the younger generation? In proportion to other age groups, how often are older people represented at all? In a group, brainstorm a list of characters or types of older people you have seen represented in the mass media. Can you relate to these images? How would you like to be seen as you age?

Resources

• Jeanette A. Auger and Diane Tedford-Litle. *From the Inside Out: Competing Ideas of Growing Old*. Halifax: Fernwood Publishing, 2002. Written from the perspectives of older persons, in deliberate contrast to those of gerontological professionals. Includes voices from various communities, including Black Nova Scotians and Mi'kmaq.

• Canada, National Advisory Council on Aging. *Seniors in Canada: A Report Card*. Ottawa, 2001. This study evaluates the status of Canadian seniors in relation to health, the health-care system, economic well-being, living conditions, and participation in society.

• Margaret Laurence. *The Stone Angel*. Toronto: McClelland and Stewart, 1964. A literary masterpiece that explores the complex reactions – and brief rebellion – of ninety-year-old Hagar Shipley, who is being pushed into a retirement home. The story, told from Hagar's viewpoint, unfolds as a recollection of her life.

• Colin Lindsay. *A Portrait of Seniors in Canada*. 3rd ed. Ottawa: Statistics Canada, 1999. A comprehensive report on the demographic characteristics, living arrangements, family situation, health, education, work patterns, and related activities, income, and expenditures of Canada's sixty-five and over population.

• Rohinton Mistry. *Family Matters*. Toronto: McClelland and Stewart, 2002. A modern *King Lear*, set in Bombay by a Canadian author, this novel tells the story of Nariman Vakeel, an elderly widower living at home with his two middle-aged unmarried stepchildren, who plot to move him out into the cramped flat of their younger step-sister and her family.

• Marika Morris et al. *The Changing Nature of Home Care and Its Impact on Women's Vulnerability to Poverty*. Ottawa: Status of Women Canada, 1999, cat. no.SW21-42/1999E. In light of cutbacks and other policy changes and women's position as the majority of home-care recipients and paid and unpaid caregivers, this national research report provides an essential gender-based analysis.

• Phil Mullan. *The Imaginary Time Bomb: Why an Aging Population Is Not a Social Problem*. New York: I.B. Tauris & Co, 2001. While the World Bank warns of an aging crisis and the pension industry talks of a "demographic time bomb," analysts like Mullan argue that the "crisis" is overblown, that it is a device to justify the privatization of public pension systems.

• Mark Novak and Lori Campbell. *Aging Society: A Canadian Perspective*. 4th ed. Toronto: Nelson, 2001. One of the most highly used and comprehensive textbooks on aging in Canada. It covers health, economic, cultural, social, and policy issues.

• Monica Townson. *Pensions under Attack: What's Behind the Push to Privatize Public Pensions*. Ottawa: Canadian Centre for Policy Alternatives, 2001. An analysis of the politics of pension privatization specifically in Canada.

• Monica Townson. *Reducing Poverty among Older Women: The Potential of Retirement Incomes Policy*. Canada Status of Women Policy Research. Ottawa: Canada Communications Group, 2000. Also available on-line at <www.swc-cfc.gc.ca/pube.html>.

• *The Company of Strangers*. Canada, 1990. Directed by Cynthia Scott. NFB. Video, DVD, and 16mm. 101 min. A group of elderly women, stranded miles from nowhere when their bus breaks down, take refuge in an abandoned farmhouse. They improvise beds and forage for food and gradually get to know each other, "turning the crisis into a magical time of humour and friendship."

• *Ojigkwanong: Encounter with an Algonquin Sage*. Canada, 2000. Directed by Lucie Ouimet. NFB. Video. 26 min.. French with English subtitles. The story of highly respected Algonquin elder Ojigkwanong (William Commanda), born on the Maniwaki reserve in 1913. Interviews and archival footage tell the story of his early life and personal struggles, and of how he embarked on a mission to promote reconciliation and healing between peoples.

• *Time on Earth*. Canada, 1997. Directed by Patricia Fogliato and David Mortin. NFB. Video. 51 min. This film follows three seniors as they each travel the highways of North America in their motorhomes, seeking community, companionship, and new vistas.

• *You Won't Need Running Shoes Darling*. Canada, 1996. Directed by Dorothy Todd Hénault. NFB. Video. 54 min. A renowned Canadian documentary filmmaker captures the life of her aging parents during a critical two-year period of declining health, and finds that their passion for living carries them through difficult times.

• *When Shirley Met Florence*. Canada, 1994. Directed by Ronit Bezalel. NFB. Video. 27 min. This film explores the lifelong friendship of two women – one lesbian one heterosexual – and the differences in their lives and the music and care they share.

Websites:

Various government and non-profit advocacy organizations are devoted to issues of particular concern for older Canadians, and many of them maintain websites. Among these, look for Health Canada's Aging and Seniors site, which includes a valuable link to the Canadian Seniors Policies and Programs Database <www.sppd.ga.ca>.

Among the advocacy groups, look for the Canadian Association of Retired Persons at <www.fifty-plus.net/carp> and The Older Women's Network web page. The Seniors Can internet program is a guide for retirees and older adults to Manitoban, Canadian, and international information and services. Visit its website at <www.crm.mb.ca>.

Several Raging Grannies groups have mounted websites. The Woodstock, Ont., chapter has posted a Raging Grannies starter kit on their website at <www.ocl.net/projects/grannies> (hosted by the Oxford County Library).

Chapter Twelve
A Home and Native Land

Canada's ten million square kilometres make it the world's second biggest country. How do we relate to all this land? For realtors it is real estate, something to be parcelled up and sold on the market. Investors in mining and logging operations see land as a repository of natural resources. For farmers too, land is the source of their livelihood and of the country's vital food supply. For cottagers and golfers it is a recreational opportunity.

But the land is more than just something people use. Indigenous peoples recognize land as an essential part of the web of relations within which human beings live. It nurtures and sustains human and non-human life. It is home – not just in the way that an address is home, but in the way that family is home.

It was the defence of land that led to the 1990 confrontation between the Quebec police, the Canadian army, and the Mohawk (*Kanienkehaka*) of Kanesataké. The nearby town of Oka was planning to take over a piece of land to expand a golf course. But the land contained a Mohawk cemetery in the forest known as "The Pines." The showdown with the Quebec Police led to an exchange of gunfire and the death of officer

Marcel Lemay. Four days later the army was brought in. It surrounded the area with tanks and bulldozers. The People of the Pines were besieged for seventy-eight days.

The confrontation at Oka was a watershed event in recent history. According to some observers, it was a wake-up call that prompted the federal government to address larger issues. The prime minister promised a Royal Commission on Aboriginal People. He promised to speed up the rate of land claims, improve conditions on reserves, and include Aboriginal peoples in constitutional negotiations. Some of these initiatives were more successful than others. The constitutional process failed, but the Royal Commission went on to complete a three-thousand-page report in 1996.

The issues that sparked the events at Kanesataké also defy simple solution. The federal government purchased the disputed land, with plans to turn it over to the Mohawks, but many remain sceptical of the response. Some ten years after the conflict Ellen Gabriel, a key Mohawk spokesperson, concluded:

> The issue of the land that we were protecting is still in question. The government keeps saying, "We have negotiations underway." They have the band council that they're negotiating with. And the traditional people, the longhouse people whose government predates European arrival on this continent, is still not recognized and is still outlawed.[1]

As concerned observers, including the United Nations, have noted, something that has not changed is the tendency to respond with enormous, often deadly, force when Aboriginal people assert their rights to land. This pattern of response has been seen again and again: at the standoff at Camp Ipperwash, Ontario, where Anthony Dudley George was fatally shot by provincial police in 1995; that same year's siege of members of the Shuswap nation at Gustafsen Lake, British Columbia, in "the largest Canadian police or military operation on land since the Korean War," and the government's approach since 2000 to the fisheries conflict at Burnt Church, New Brunswick, labelled "gunboat diplomacy" by Christian Peacemaker Teams.[2]

Aboriginal Peoples in Canada: Identity and Diversity

Who are the people whose lives are at the centre of these issues? They are called Native and Aboriginal, names that can encourage solidarity, but obscure diversity. They may also misleadingly suggest that the basis of identity is race. This is a view that the Royal Commission on Aboriginal Peoples rejected:

> We believe strongly that membership in Aboriginal nations should not be defined by race. Aboriginal nations are political communities, often comprising people of mixed background and heritage. Their bonds are those of culture and identity, not blood. Their unity comes from their shared history and their strong sense of themselves as peoples.[3]

Their diversity reflects specific relationships with enormously diverse climactic conditions and physical geographies. This diversity is also expressed linguistically. Today there are more than fifty distinct linguistic groupings among First Nations, as well as several dialects within the Inuit language Inuktitut. Many Métis people speak Michif, a language that evolved out of their mixed linguistic heritage, and many speak a variety of First Nations languages such as Cree, Ojibwa, and Chipewayan.[4]

Yet within all this diversity some shared identity remains. One sense of identity occurs at the level of nations or peoples. The Mi'kmaq, Innu, and Anishnabe, for example, are defined as Aboriginal nations because each group has a shared sense of national identity and makes up the main population in a certain territory.[5] While there are about a thousand reserve and settlement communities in Canada, the members of those communities belong to between sixty and eighty Aboriginal nations.

Aboriginal elders point to broader spiritual grounds of identity. Shuswap leader George Manuel explains that just as European cultures show wide variations, Aboriginal cultures display similar differences. But, he says, "It seems to me that all of our structures and values have developed out of a spiritual relationship with the land on which we have lived."[6]

History also provides a basis of identity. Since contact and colonization by Europeans, a common thread running through the history of Aboriginal peoples is displacement from or confinement to a shrinking land base. For Aboriginal people, access to the land that once provided both material and spiritual nourishment has long been threatened on both an individual and community level. Traditional lands have been encroached upon, expropriated, and "developed." Meanwhile, well over half of Canada's Aboriginal population has migrated into Canadian cities, largely in response to the economic and social difficulties that have become associated with life on many reserves. By 1996, about three of every ten Aboriginal people lived on rural reserves, and another three in ten lived in metropolitan areas. One-quarter lived in other urban areas, and one-fifth in rural areas other than reserves.[7]

What's in a Name?

According to the 2001 census, almost one million people – 976,310 – identify with at least one Aboriginal group (North American Indian, Métis, or Inuit). That number amounts to 3.3 per cent of Canada's total population. An even larger number, over 1.3 million, reported Aboriginal ancestry. Amongst those who identified with one of the three Aboriginal groups, 608,850 identified as North American Indian, 292,310 as Métis, and 45,070 as Inuit.[8]

The federal government further subcategorizes the North American Indian population of Canada into Status and Non-Status Indians. The question of who is entitled to be registered as a Status Indian, and what this entitlement means, is determined by the Indian Act, which has been continually changed since 1876. In general, the Act determines a person's relationship to an Indian Band, a political unit itself defined by the Indian Act and the federal Department of Indian Affairs and Northern Development. This relationship in turn determines the possibility of reserve residence and access to treaty rights, tax exemptions, and special federal programs. There are 612 bands, 2,633 reserves, and 558,175 registered Indians in Canada.[9]

While this approach to defining identity is resisted by many of those it categorizes, nonetheless the government has created further subcategories of "legal Indians." Some are categorized according to whether or not they have "taken treaty" – that is, whether or not their ancestors signed a treaty with the federal government. This category excludes, for example, Indians in British Columbia (with the exception of Vancouver Island, and very recently the Nisga'a people), the Yukon, Quebec, and the Atlantic Provinces who did not sign any treaties. Other groups, like the Iroquois of Brantford and Tyendinaga, who emigrated from the United States, are also considered non-treaty Registered Indians.[10] Pursuing even finer distinctions, the government also subdivides Status Indians into reserve or non-reserve, according to whether or not the state provided their ancestors with reserve lands.

Non-Status Indians may be North American Indians who lost status for a variety of reasons: for example, in exchange (prior to 1960) for the right to vote, or due to being a child of someone who had lost status. Others may have missed out on status because they lived in remote areas or were absent from their communities during registration. At different times the government has applied various, often arbitrary criteria. At one point even having a university degree meant loss of status.[11]

Sometimes Aboriginal people of mixed heritage call themselves Métis, indicating a relation to historical communities, such as those formed by the descendants of First Nations and French settlers near Manitoba's Red River or, in the East, by the Labrador Métis. Some persons of mixed ancestry simply identify themselves as Native people.

The Inuit, the majority population in the Canadian Arctic, have never fallen under the Indian Act. They have no reserves and had no treaties until the 1975 James Bay and Northern Quebec Agreement. Most of the Inuit people of Canada live in Nunavut, the newest territory in Canada, established in 1999.[12]

Aboriginal communities are home, as well, to other distinct perspectives: those of women, elders, youth, rural communities, Northerners, and urban Aboriginals. Still, despite all of these differences, Aboriginal people in Canada have important goals in common: control over their own land and resources, self-government, healing from the devastating effects of colonization, and the preservation and promotion of their distinct cultures.

Land and the Culture of Colonization

Long before Europeans first arrived on this continent, its indigenous peoples occupied specific, recognized territories. Some practised a "sedentary" way of life, farming, fishing, and mining in the same vicinity year round. Others migrated, following the movements of herds, or harvesting wild plants. But even migratory peoples followed definite paths, which generated a clear sense of their "home" on the land.

Before the European arrival, this land was criss-crossed with trade routes. For example, to sell the copper they mined, the Anishnabe developed extensive trade relations throughout the eastern part of the continent. Artefacts from as far away as Florida and Ohio found in three-thousand-year-old Mi'kmaq burial mounds attest to the historical and geographical extent of indigenous trade relations.[13] Prior to contact with Europeans, First Nations peoples were also well practised in the development of nation-to-nation

alliances and sophisticated political structures. The Six Nations Federation, also known as the Iroquois confederacy, was a model that the U.S. statesman and thinker Benjamin Franklin recommended for unifying the English colonists.[14] European newcomers quickly recognized the value of indigenous political achievements, agricultural techniques, methods of transport appropriate to the land, and other technology for survival on that land, even though seldom crediting the original inventors.

The European intrusion came in waves and had varying effects. Aboriginal peoples close to areas of European settlement became partners with the newcomers. Some peoples who once depended on the co-operative activity of hunting switched to the more competitive work of trade – supplying furs and other goods and foodstuffs. Aboriginal people formed political and military alliances, fighting alongside Europeans in wars and making social, economic, and cultural investments in trapping and guiding, and in schools and churches. Just as the early traders and settlers took advantage of indigenous technology, from canoes and corn to constitutions, so too did Aboriginal people recognize the advantages to be gained from some of the goods and know-how brought by the newcomers.

The need for adaptation became even more pressing with the increasing pace and determination of the newcomers to colonize the land that they were claiming to have discovered for themselves. As contact increased, and particularly as Europeans began to settle, epidemics of previously unknown illnesses, such as smallpox and influenza, decimated Indian and Inuit communities – sometimes as a result of deliberate policy.[15]

Indigenous social and economic structures also underwent rapid changes as the various groups adapted to the opportunities and challenges provided by the new contact. But the formation of trade relations and alliances for sharing land and resources is by no means the same as colonization. The distinction between these processes reflects the difference between the destiny of the Americas as it was perceived by its colonizers and as it was imagined by its indigenous inhabitants.

European settlers constantly pushed back the frontier, often betraying, bribing, and coercing Aboriginal peoples into signing treaties and ceding their land. Some indigenous nations made treaties, which they saw not as alienating the lands but as peace treaties granting the Europeans the right to share the land with them.[16] These treaties came to hold enormous importance for later generations, providing tangible evidence of their status and rights as nations and of their special relationship with the Crown.

In the nineteenth and twentieth centuries, as the colonial focus shifted from acquiring lands to "dealing" with the people left on it, the newcomers paid increasing attention to projects of containment and assimilation; and changing economic conditions made the Aboriginal peoples particularly vulnerable to these practices. When the fur trade declined with the depletion of game and a new emphasis on industrial production, many First Nations people became outcasts, relegated to reserve lands in what had formerly been their own home. Reserves became the very model of "internal colonialism" – a colonial approach applied to people within a country rather than in a distant land. South Africa's apartheid regime drew on Canada's reserve system as a model for its restriction of Blacks to the "homelands." South Africa emulated, for example, the "pass" law created in Canada in 1885, which prohibited Indians from leaving their reserves without written permission from the Indian agent.

With the exception of Northern Quebec and the territories, official policy left very little land reserved for use by Aboriginal people. The Aboriginal lands south of the 60th parallel make up less than one-half of one per cent of the Canadian land mass. Moreover, since their original allocation those lands have experienced a steady shrinkage. In addition, because many Aboriginal peoples never did sign any treaties, the precise legal status of much of the land in Canada remains unclear.

Some of the colonizers believed that the problem of land ownership would disappear along with the original inhabitants, and at first, as the European population increased its pressure on the original peoples and their land, the indigenous population did diminish. One colonial politician, Sir Francis Bond Head of Upper Canada, saw the Indians as a "doomed race" who were "melting like snow before the sun." He wanted to consign all Indians in Ontario to Manitoulin Island, where, he speculated, they would eventually die out.[17] That did not happen. As the poet Chrystos declares, Aboriginal peoples are "Not Vanishing."[18]

Since the 1950s the population of Aboriginal people has been increasing at a faster rate than that of the Canadian population as a whole. The Aboriginal population is younger as well: over ten years younger on average than the general population. Children fourteen and under account for about one-third of all Aboriginal people, while only 19 per cent of Canada's total population are that young.[19]

Aboriginal resistance to European attempts to remove them from their lands – indeed, to remove them altogether one way or another – has a long history. But the late 1960s marked the beginning of a new period of increasing activism. In the years since then, enormous energy has also been poured into individual and community healing as well as economic and cultural renewal. Under conditions of colonization, recovery and survival become acts of resistance.

Conditions of Aboriginal Life

In 1993, television and newspaper reports in Canada and abroad were full of images of children and teens sniffing gasoline and solvents in Davis Inlet, Labrador, and other isolated communities. Aboriginal leaders spoke of a "suicide epidemic," which was hitting youth in a

Standard of Living Indicators	Best-off First Nations Communities	Worst-off Non-Aboriginal Regions
% with less than Grade 9*	12	20
% in paid employment	58	57
number of persons per room	0.7	0.6
average annual income	$ 18,200	$ 18,900

*As percentage of population aged 20-64

Source: Based on a table in Robin Armstrong, "Mapping the Conditions of First Nations Communities," *Canadian Social Trends,* Winter 1999 (using data from 1996 Canadian Census).

particularly hard way. In 2000, television crews and reporters returned to Davis Inlet and nearby Sheshatshiu to find the same scene of human devastation. How was such a tragedy possible in a country that the United Nations has, since 1999, been calling the best place to live in the world?

Aboriginal peoples in general have the lowest levels of education, income, employment, and health in Canada, but there are considerable differences from one community to another. Some communities face much worse conditions than others. Yet conditions in the poorest non-Aboriginal communities are still better than those in the best-off First Nations communities.[20]

The conditions are made worse when they are combined with a sense of powerlessness. They also stand in dramatic contrast to the Canadian society in general. In Walkerton, Ontario, illness and death should have been avoided when the water supply became contaminated. But once the tainted water scandal became public, the government responded with free bottled water, an overhaul of the water delivery system, and a public inquiry.[21] "Walkerton" has become a byword for threats to our drinking water. Meanwhile, in Northern Saskatchewan, the Yellowquill First Nation continues to live with a boil-water order that has been in place for more than five years. Its reservoir is filled with run-off from nearby farms.[22]

Suicides, like those at Davis Inlet, have become a dramatic symbol of Aboriginal Canada's despair. Generalizations tell us that the rate of Aboriginal suicides is six to seven times the national average. But equally dramatic is the great variation in suicide rates across communities.[23] For instance, some communities among British Columbia's nearly two hundred Aboriginal groups have suicide rates that are eight hundred times the national average, while in other communities suicide is virtually unknown. In one five-year study, over half the province's bands experienced no youth suicides. The differences in the occurrence of suicide seem to be related to factors that both Aboriginal and non-Aboriginal Canadians can and are doing something about. Communities that have actively attempted to preserve and revive their own cultures have far lower suicide rates. The psychologists who investigated the issue found that the single most important "protective factor" was a community's efforts towards establishing self-government.[24]

That kind of research is valuable because it goes beyond documenting just how bad things are. It seeks to explain how communities can successfully insulate their members against an increased risk of suicide. This is a good example of social analysis shaped by the desire for social change.

Stereotypes of Aboriginal Lives

Social and economic conditions are not the only factors threatening the well-being of Aboriginal peoples. A more subtle but at least as damaging threat exists in the racist stereotypes that so often portray them.

Aboriginal men are sometimes portrayed as wild savages, sometimes as strong, silent, mystic types. In general, Aboriginal people are represented according to their perceived value for those who construct the stereotypes. This creates what Anishnabe writer Drew Hayden Taylor identifies as the "good Indian" and "bad Indian" roles: on the one hand, the Lone Ranger's faithful sidekick, Tonto, and on the other hand the "borderline psychotic, often drunk, out-of-control Indian."[25]

Such stereotypes are used in the war of words and images fought out when Aboriginal people occupy ancestral lands, as they have done on at least two well-publicized occasions since Oka. At Gustafsen Lake, B.C., and Stoney Point, Ontario (Ipperwash), the stereotypes ranged from the gun-toting militant (savage) and the peace-loving negotiator (noble savage). In the Gustafsen stand-off the media portrayed the occupiers variously as cultists, radicals with no support from First Nations, and outside agitators with no link to local communities.[26]

Stereotyped images of Aboriginal women also distort the historical record. The virtue of "Indian princesses" like the legendary Pocahontas are tied to their tendency to save white men from ferocious Indian men, or their talent and inclination to help white men penetrate deep into the natural and cultural wilderness of the "New World."

Indian women are also portrayed as "squaws" available to be used and discarded by anyone who has the inclination. Such images are dangerous. Consider the public response, or lack of it, to the violation and murder of Aboriginal women. Infamous murderer Paul Bernardo is a household name, associated with his accomplice Karla Homolka as well as their victims Leslie Mahaffy and Kristen French. But few Canadians are aware of John Martin Crawford, let alone his victims. Crawford was convicted of the murder of four

Aboriginal women – Mary Jane Serloin, Shelley Napope, Eva Taysup, and Calinda Waterhen – and suspected in the death or disappearance of several others.[27]

When we encounter representations of Aboriginal people we should consider the possible distortions those representations contain and the agendas they may be serving. Overcoming distortions means paying attention to the actual conditions of Aboriginal peoples' lives and in particular what they say about their own experiences, in their own voices.

Colonialism: Land, Hearts, and Spirit

In 1981 a United Nations meeting of indigenous people from around the world analyzed the scandal of Aboriginal living conditions. The explanation had much to do with foreign occupation of the land, the imposition of colonial rule, and a separation from the land that, "even when replaced by money payments – is a concrete form of ethnocide and genocide."[28]

In Canada, the key to the colonizing process was the gradual but relentless destruction of indigenous peoples' relationship with the land. One band after another was removed from its ancestral territory and usually confined to reserves "for their own good."

When Canadians think of the expulsion of the First Nations from their lands, we tend to think of a distant past, but in the early 1940s the federal government moved a thriving Mi'kmaq community at Malagwatch, Cape Breton, to the isolated reserve at Eskasoni, N.S., where there was not enough land for a growing population and limited opportunities for farming. The same period saw federal expropriation of the Stoney Point people's land, to construct Canadian Forces Base Ipperwash – with promises to clean up and return the land when the military no longer had a use for it. Today toxic waste and other military debris remain; the question of legitimate ownership is also undecided.[29]

In the following decade, the Cold Lake nation in Northern Alberta and the Canoe Lake

Cree of Northern Saskatchewan lost 11,655 square kilometres of land when the federal government created the Primrose Lake Air Weapons Range. In 1953, seventeen Inuit families were moved from Northern Quebec to the high Arctic as part of a larger government policy. They were used "as human flagpoles" to assert Canadian sovereignty in the Arctic.[30] In 1963, in another socially devastating move, the Grassy Narrows Ojibwa community north of Kenora was uprooted from its ancestral lands on the English-Wabigoon River and moved to a new reserve.

In 1967 Newfoundland convinced the Mushuau Innu to abandon their traditional home on mainland Labrador, where they had been hunters of caribou for about six millennia. Resettled on the Davis Inlet, they were expected to establish a fishery. Things soon fell apart as the province reneged on promises of fresh water and sewage systems. The Innu still go out on the land to set up hunting camps in the spring and fall. This way of life is threatened by the federal and provincial governments' aggressive promotion of massive development schemes (the proposed nickel mine at Voisey's Bay; the $10-billion Lower Churchill hydroelectric project; the construction of a trans-Labrador highway; the use of Innu airspace for low-level, military flying practice).

In 1970 the Chibougamau Cree, part of the Ouje-Bougoumou Cree, were ordered to move. Their village was bulldozed when a mining company needed sand at Doré Lake. Most of the community left for their winter trapping areas, building shacks beside logging roads. Quebec labelled them "squatters on provincial Crown lands." The mining industry had kept the Chibougamau Cree on the move for sixty years.[31]

Displacement of Aboriginal communities is typically justified in the name of development and progress. But this development has not been of nearly as much benefit to indigenous peoples and other Canadians as it has been to corporations such as Imperial Oil, Amoco, and Canadian Pacific. Improvements in the economic health of company shareholders left Aboriginal communities with little but dangerous side effects: envi-

ronmental degradation and social devastation. This injustice is compounded by the role played by the Department of Indian Affairs and Northern Development. The affairs of developers often conflict with "Indian Affairs," and the Department often favours the industrial interests.

The story of the Lubicon Cree is a case in point. The Lubicon Cree's struggle with the government over land began in 1899, when a government team set off into Alberta to get the Indians to sign treaties and so make way for settlers and mineral exploration. The Europeans, with inadequate maps of the region, failed to locate the Lubicon.[32] A reserve promised in 1940 did not materialize, and without it the Lubicon had to contend with the onslaught of massive resource development on the land they had been using for centuries. The land conflict intensified in the 1980s during an oil boom, and hit new heights in the 1990s when a Japanese company, Daishowa, expressed its interest in the area's valuable timber resources.

In 1990, following a six-year investigation, the United Nations found Canada in violation of Lubicon rights under Article 27 of the International Covenant on Civil and Political Rights. These violations were funded by a $9.5 million federal subsidy for the construction of what was advertised as the largest hardwood pulp mill in Canada. Alberta's $65.2-million support for rail and road access eased outside access to the Lubicon land. The minister who oversaw the federal subsidy also held the Indian Affairs portfolio.

A National Crime

Colonialism usually has cultural as well as political and economic dimensions. In this case the European newcomers and their non-Aboriginal descendants promoted feelings of intellectual, cultural, and religious inferiority among the indigenous population. Governments and churches were concerned about "civilizing" and Christianizing the Aboriginal peoples. Indeed, many saw these two efforts as being closely linked. The Canadian government eventually admitted:

Attitudes of racial and cultural superiority led to a suppression of Aboriginal culture and values . . . suppressing their languages and cultures and outlawing spiritual practices. . . . We acknowledge that the result of these actions was the erosion of the political, economic and social systems of Aboriginal people and nations.[33]

Aboriginal people experienced the process of cultural change in complex, and not necessarily passive, ways. Some saw the act of taking up European tools, language, and culture as necessary to success in this new world. For some, the change meant hiding their Aboriginal languages from their children because they saw no practical advantage in the "old ways." Some saw lines of continuity between the values of traditional and newcomer cultures. Lubicon Cree leader Bernard Ominayak, reflecting on his Quaker education, said that Bible lessons reinforced his parents' teachings about right and wrong, and the value of respecting his elders. Ominayak became a successful student and went on to study at the government school sixty miles away. But this success came at a price, and by Grade 10 he was too homesick to continue. Boarding school in another language and culture had "unsettled his sense of himself."[34]

For many Aboriginal children the pain associated with schooling went way beyond homesickness and restlessness. At the residential schools, produced by a partnership between church and state, students were made to feel ashamed of their culture and heritage. They could be beaten simply for speaking their own languages. Their clothing was replaced by uniforms, which, like their nutrition, their accommodations, and indeed their education, were generally substandard. "Overworked, overtired, and underfed," children in these conditions were particularly vulnerable to illness and disease, and in particular the killer tuberculosis.[35] Still, despite the physical and sexual abuse within their walls, the schools were held up as a "circle of civilized conditions" that provided children with the "care of a mother."[36]

A Message from the Anglican Primate to the National Native Convocation

My Brothers and Sisters:

Together here with you I have listened as you have told your stories of the residential schools.

I have heard the voices that have spoken of pain and hurt experienced in the schools, and of the scars which endure to this day.

I have felt shame and humiliation as I have heard of suffering inflicted by my people, and as I think of the part our church played in that suffering.

I am deeply conscious of the sacredness of the stories that you have told, and I hold in the highest honour those who have told them.

I have heard with admiration the stories of people and communities who have worked at healing, and I am aware of how much more healing is needed.

I also know that I am in need of healing, and my own people are in need of healing, and our church is in need of healing. Without that healing, we will continue the same attitudes that have done such damage in the past.

I know that healing takes a long time, both for people and for communities. . . .

I am sorry, more than I can say, that we were part of a system which took you and your children from home and family.

I am sorry, more than I can say, that we tried to remake you in our image, taking from you your language and the signs of your identity.

I am sorry, more than I can say, that in our schools so many were abused physically, sexually, culturally and emotionally.

On behalf of the Anglican Church of Canada, I offer our apology.

— Anglican Primate Michael Peers, Minaki, Ont., 1993.

Residential schools were phased out in the 1960s and 1970s, but their legacy lives on, transmitted to a new generation whose parents' experiences in residential schools deprived them of positive child-rearing models. By the turn of the twenty-first century, church and state had begun to apologize for the injustices and their continuing aftershocks.

In 1998 Ottawa's minister of Indian Affairs and Northern Development publicly expressed the Canadian government's remorse for its role in the abuse of Aboriginal peoples and proclaimed its commitment to a continuing process of reconciliation.[37] The minister also announced a dedication of $350 million to support community-based healing programs.

The apology seemed to serve as a catalyst for victims' lawsuits. Between 1996 and 2001, the federal government paid out some $27 million in settlements; by then, outstanding claims represented a potential payout of more than a billion dollars. Meanwhile, churches were forced to pay millions in damages. Money is a significant part of a reconciliation process that also involves establishing the facts of what happened as part of the historical record.

Some Canadians have reacted against large cash settlements for Aboriginal victims of abuse in the same way that they resent money paid to First Nations for land-claim settlements. According to this analysis, the injustices and abuses were tragic but they are in the past: Aboriginal people should just get over it and get on with their lives without any special help. But coming to terms with history is not such an easy thing. It is a difficult process, and one that faces everyone in Canada. Aboriginal journalist Kenneth Williams recommends setting aside another fund "to teach Canadians, preferably while they're still in school, about the legacy of residential schools. Sadly, most don't know about them or just have a vague idea. If Canadians knew just what their government did on their behalf, many of them would change their tune about so-called special privileges."[38]

In 2000 the Assembly of First Nations called for a South African-style "truth-and-reconciliation commission," which is an approach to justice and healing that many churches support.[39] (South Africa's truth commission helped to start a process

aimed at healing the gross injustices of apartheid.) A broader healing process in Canada could promote understanding and minimize resentment among Canadians.

Despite the devastation of the residential school system, Aboriginal people see education as an important tool for recovery and self-reliance. After residential schools were phased out, Aboriginal people began to take back responsibility for the education of their children. The number of band-controlled schools increased from fifty-three in 1976 to more than three hundred in the early 1990s. Although Aboriginal education still lags behind levels for the rest of the Canadian population, Aboriginal children are now staying in schools longer. The proportion of on-reserve students completing high school rose dramatically, from 3 per cent to 75 per cent over the thirty-three-year period ending in 1996. The number of First Nations students attending post-secondary schools more than doubled between 1985 and 1995, with the proportion of students going to college and university gradually approaching the level in the Canadian population as a whole.[40]

The Status of Aboriginal Women

Colonialism has undermined Aboriginal culture in ways that have been particularly hard on women, whose well-being has been especially threatened by the harsh and increasing stresses of an uprooted society. The European idea of civilization features a sharp separation of public life from the "private" home and family. Along with a deeply entrenched European habit of excluding women from participation in public decision-making, this tendency has eroded the traditional roles that Aboriginal women play in their communities.[41]

A profit-centred economic system has also degraded the status of Aboriginal women. Capitalism supplanted a different set of values that made the sustaining of community the main priority of economic activity. This shift has had a corrosive effect on the conditions for performing vital work that has traditionally been women's special, though not sole, responsibility. Aboriginal women have been especially subject to cycles of violence – whereas one in ten non-Aboriginal Canadian women is the victim of domestic violence, six in ten Aboriginal women experience violence at one time or another.[42]

Still, Aboriginal women have struggled to adapt to these changed conditions and to do what needs to be done to keep home and community together, in body and spirit.[43] One of the focal points of Aboriginal women's political activism has been the sexist and exclusionary effects of the Indian Act, which imposed a patriarchal system that excluded women from voting in band elections. Only men could grant band membership. According to one Aboriginal woman leader, the patriarchal system became so ingrained that "patriarchy" became viewed as a "traditional trait" of Aboriginal societies: "In other words, even the memory of our matriarchal forms of descent were forgotten or unacknowledged."[44]

Aboriginal women successfully pushed for an amendment to Section 35 of the Constitution Act of 1982, guaranteeing Aboriginal and treaty rights equally to men and women. Similarly, their efforts led to the elimination of sections of the Indian Act that discriminated against women. Some band councils, however, have used the new powers that resulted in changes to the Act to continue discriminatory practices. According to Cora Voyageur, "Indian leaders – that is, Indian men – must loosen their grasp on the power given to them by the government."[45]

Aboriginal women have also pointed out how white feminists should also loosen their grip on the analysis of women's oppression. They note the flaws in any feminist analysis that assumes universal "sisterhood" or the idea that sexism is the same sort of thing for all women. Ignoring the historically specific experiences of non-European women not only makes for faulty analysis, but also gets in the way of the kind of social change that Aboriginal people see as being necessary. Aboriginal women want justice and healing not

Sexism, racism, and the total dismissal of Native women's experiences have little to do with who does dishes and who minds babies. These oppressions result from the accumulations of hurt sustained by our people over a long period of time. Our communities are reduced to a substandard definition of normal, which leads to a sensibility of defeat, which in turn calls the victim to the table of lateral violence and ultimately changes the beliefs and corrodes the system from within. On this table of lateral violence sit the violence of men and women against children and the violence of men toward women. The "healing movement" of the 1980s and '90s, spearheaded by women, is the struggle to clear the table of violence.

What we have not been able to do is remove the table of hurtful oppression and besiegement which spawned the lateral violence.

— Lee Maracle, Preface, I Am a Woman, 2nd ed., 1996.

just for women, but also for the communities in which they play such a vital role.

The efforts and achievements of Aboriginal women have been impressive. Aboriginal women take the lead in education and skills upgrading. More women than men, for example, have returned to high school or studied for equivalency upgrading. Among those with post-secondary education, nearly three times as many Aboriginal women as men have completed schooling in management or administration. Women have been crucial in community efforts at healing, survival, and development.

Development and Self-Determination

"Development" means different things to different people. From the perspective of a corporation operating on traditional Aboriginal land, development is the process of generating profits through the extraction of natural resources and the transformation of those resources into saleable commodities. From the perspective of a community or even a business that sees itself as an organic part of a community, development means something else. It is the process of creating meaningful work, sustainable wealth, and the economic base for self-governance. From the perspective of the community, healthy economic development is connected to self-determination.

Many Aboriginal people have decided that cultural assimilation is an unacceptable price to pay for industrial megaprojects. To shape the future of their societies they want a development that is the product of conscious choices. Their struggle is contributing to changing our understanding of what the word "progress" means in Canada.

Aboriginal people may lead the way in recognizing the threat posed by new trends in international economic development. Indigenous people and their allies were among the participants in the 2001 People's Summit meetings in Quebec City. This conference preceded the meetings of officials drafting the Free Trade of the Americas Agreement. The "Americana Indigenismo" group called for alliances between indigenous and non-indigenous peoples, alliances dedicated to the inherent rights of all people and peoples to safe and sufficient food, shelter, and health care. The group also defined the threat posed by the model of globalization envisioned by the framers of the FTAA:

> The plundering of the great buffalo herds which sustained some of us over millennia, or the wanton destruction of fish stocks off the east coast of North America, or the rush to clear cut the rain forests in Amazonia or British Columbia all stand as testaments and illustrations of the ongoing war against the indigenous ecology of the Americas. This assault on the integrity of the hemisphere's Aboriginal ecologies entails also an ongoing assault on our capacity to renew our own aboriginal economies, cultures and religious freedoms. Rather than putting a halt to this ecocidal destruction, the FTAA would

reward and further concentrate the ill-gotten commercial power of those who have derived huge, monetary fortunes from such short-sighted impoverishment of the real natural wealth of the Americas.[46]

Treaties and Land Claims

For development to take a healthy form for indigenous peoples, it must be built on a recognition of their rights to be here. These rights have a long legal as well as cultural history, and treaties are a cornerstone of that history. Early treaty-making in this country rested on a constitutional foundation known as the Royal Proclamation of 1763. It was proclaimed in response to the news that a confederacy of Indian peoples would resist the British colonization of Canada in the absence of proper recognition of the collectively held title of First Nations peoples to their ancestral lands.[47] It has since been the basis for all treaty-making. The negotiations surrounding the new territory of Nunavut are part of this same history, as is the agreement between Canada, British Columbia, and the Nisga'a that was finally passed into legislation in 1999.

The political achievements of contemporary treaty-making in Canada are the products of long, hard negotiations. It took twenty years to create Nunavut. The Nisga'a agreement marks the end of a process initiated by Nisga'a elders in 1887, when they journeyed by canoe to Victoria to press for recognition of their rights to the Nass Valley.

There is a firm tradition of relationship-building in Canada through the establishment of treaties. Many Aboriginal leaders place their hopes for the future of their people – as well as the integrity of Canadians – in this tradition. The final report of the Royal Commission on Aboriginal Peoples (RCAP) proposed the establishment of a new treaty process that would lead the way to reconciliation between Aboriginal and non-Aboriginal people. "An agreed treaty process," the report states, "can be the mechanism for implementing virtually all the recommendations in our report — indeed, it may be the only legitimate way to do so."[48]

Self-Government and Autonomous Development

The focus on treaties is a focus on relationships between nations. Another key element in the process of development is self-determination, the capacity and right of a people to govern themselves. Aboriginal people say "the ultimate source of their right to be self-governing is the Creator," who "placed each nation on its own land and gave the people the responsibility of caring for the land — and one another — until the end of time."[49] The RCAP report lists three other legal sources of this right: international law, which recognizes the right of peoples to self-determination; the condition that the colonial powers had no rights of conquest, because there was no conquest, nor was North America *terra nullius*, that is, empty and free for the taking; and, finally, recognition of Aboriginal peoples' right of self-governance within the Canadian Constitution.

Proclaimed in 1982, the Canadian Constitution guarantees Aboriginal and treaty rights, although it does not define them. In the years since 1982 the recurring episodes of constitutional review — unsuccessful in various ways — have also failed to adequately include Aboriginal people. According to the Royal Commission:

> Aboriginal self-government is not and can never be a "gift" from an "enlightened" Canada. The right is inherent in Aboriginal people and their nationhood and was exercised for centuries before the arrival of European explorers and settlers. It is a right they never surrendered and now want to exercise once more.[50]

Land and control over natural resources are crucial but so too is the need to think about self-government in a way that encompasses the needs

of a growing urban Aboriginal population. Organizations without a land base have been established in urban areas. Hundreds of friendship centres, scattered across the country, are often part of larger co-ordinating structures. The Vancouver Aboriginal Council is a voluntary association of "service provider" organizations serving the Aboriginal community in Vancouver. The United Native Nations and the Aboriginal Peoples Council speak for the nearly one hundred thousand Aboriginal people in British Columbia who do not live on reserves. Efforts are underway to co-ordinate the work of such organizations and from there to build models of self-government that reflect the needs and strengths of all Aboriginal peoples, wherever they make their home in this country.

Canadian society has much to borrow from Aboriginal conceptions of nature, the land, and development. The land and all it contains — air, water and soil, plants and animals — are sacred gifts received in trust for future generations. Although resources are essential to survival, for the most part Aboriginal peoples resist reducing their relationship to a mere economic relationship — an approach that in the end may prove to be a more sustainable way of life.

There is much to learn, too, from Aboriginal experiences of colonialism. The newcomers undervalued Aboriginal cultures. But the indigenous peoples resisted colonization and struggled to preserve their own values by using a wide variety of strategies. Aboriginal cultures not only survived but also grew stronger. One Aboriginal writer describes never going to a pow-wow during her childhood, while now there are pow-wows from early spring to late autumn all over North America.[51]

In the past, Canadians may have known the names of a few Aboriginal heroes, like Tecumseh or Big Bear. In recent years we have heard about the tragic stories of Helen Betty Osborne, Donald Marshall, Jr., and the children of Davis Inlet. But other names have also become familiar — leaders and activists like Ethel Blondin, Ellen Gabriel, and Ovide Mercredi. Artists, writers, and actors such as Tomson Highway, Susan Aglukark, Daphne Odjig, and Tom Jackson. *Atanarjuat*, the first feature-length fiction film in Canada that was written, produced, directed, and acted by Inuit, won six Genie awards and international acclaim.

The difficulties confronting Aboriginal peoples have deep roots. The issues are complex, from the central questions of culture through distressing social conditions to initiatives for self-government. The Aboriginal peoples of Canada do not necessarily agree on directions to take, and there is no one certain path into the future. There is, though, strength and wisdom in diversity — a diversity of peoples as opposed to the divisions of attempted conquest. The approach to "development" that we take in Canada will influence the future — not just for Aboriginal peoples but also for all the other people who make this land their home.

Questions

❑   Where do you live? Find out which First Nations or Aboriginal peoples have made their home in the region where you live. Are there outstanding land claims in this area? Are old treaties in place? Are new ones being made? Find out as much as you can about the history of these issues in your region. Does the issue look different from various Aboriginal or non-Aboriginal perspectives?

❑   What languages are spoken by the Aboriginal people who live where you live? Are any of these languages taught locally? While indigenous languages are often taught by band schools, they are also sometimes taught through Native Friendship Centres, and even in some community colleges or public schools. Are there any such programs where you live?

❑   Read any good books lately? You can choose from among many engaging, entertaining, and powerfully written books by Aboriginal authors. Look for books by Lee Maracle, Thomas King, Beth Brant, Tomson Highway,

or Richard Wagamese, for example. There are many more names that could be added to the list. Ask your local librarian for suggestions, do an Internet search, look for recommendations in Aboriginal media sources, ask your friends. Read some of these books. Even better, if you belong to a book club, suggest one or two to read together. Perhaps even form a book club dedicated to reading the work of Aboriginal authors.

❑   Many individual Aboriginal people and whole communities suffered deep trauma through the processes of colonization that occurred in Canada. The effects of that trauma are still felt today. Find out what you can about the history of colonization and its consequences. Reflecting on what you learn, what do you think is needed now to support processes of healing and reconciliation? What responsibilities do Aboriginal and non-Aboriginal people have in these processes? What roles can we play?

❑   How are Aboriginal people and the issues affecting them represented in the mass media? Are they represented very often? Look for patterns in the language and images used and types of stories that are repeated. Look at Aboriginal media sources. Do they present different perspectives on the same issues? Do they talk about issues that mainstream mass media fail to cover at all? Compare and share your findings.

❑   What does self-government and self-determination mean to you? Why is self-determination important to an individual? Why is self-government important to a people? What is needed if self-government is to be possible? What sorts of rights, resources, and powers does it depend on?

❑   Canadians have spent many years debating separatism, and these debates often come to mind when questions about the meaning of self-government are raised. But new approaches may be possible. The Royal Commission on Aboriginal Peoples, amongst others, has generated several different models addressing the needs of various different kinds of Aboriginal communities in Canada. Try to learn more about these proposals (in volume 2 of the RCAP report, for example). Discuss how these models might work. What possibilities do they promise for the future? What changes would they require in the lives of Canadians? Do some creative thinking of your own. How else might the goals of community self-determination be met?

❏ "Jobs, jobs, jobs!" "Attract new investments!" "International competitiveness is the key to survival!" We've all heard these slogans. Government leaders all over the world are telling their citizens that economic growth must be the number one priority. Should Aboriginal people adopt the same attitude in order to flourish? What other goals and values should also enter into decision-making about Aboriginal community development? Are any of these alternatives priorities that should be shared by non-Aboriginal communities as well?

❏ In many traditional First Nations, women played especially important political roles; for example, in the education and selection of chiefs. Long-term community welfare was typically given pride of place amongst Aboriginal peoples; for example, in the guideline that consideration should be given to the impact of a decision on seven generations. And relationships of respect for the land and other parts of the natural environment meant living in that environment in a different way than simply "exploiting" its "resources." How might traditional principles like these play a part in sustainable development for contemporary Aboriginal and non-Aboriginal communities? Are these principles viable in the modern world? How could they be put into action?

Resources

• Kim Anderson. *A Recognition of Being: Reconstructing Native Womanhood.* Toronto: Second Story Press, 2000. An exploration of how stereotypes of Native women have been constructed and, in interviews with forty contemporary Native women, how they are reclaiming powerful and positive images of themselves.

• Canada, Royal Commission on Aboriginal Peoples (RCAP). *For Seven Generations: Report of the Royal Commission on Aboriginal Peoples.* 5 vols. Ottawa, 1996. This massive report contains the most comprehensive collection of information about Aboriginal peoples in Canada, including hundred of research reports on Aboriginal issues, guides for developing Aboriginal awareness curricula for high schools and adults, and thousands of pages of testimony from over two thousand people. It is available in print and on CD-ROM. Highlights from the Report are also available online through the Indian and Northern Affairs Canada website.

• Olive Patricia Dickason. *Canada's First Nations: A History of Founding Peoples from Earliest Times.* 3rd ed. Toronto: McClelland & Stewart, 2001. A survey of the societies and structures of the fifty-five indigenous nations that Europeans encountered on their arrival, and the effects of that contact.

• Louise Bernice Halfe. *Blue Marrow.* Toronto: McClelland & Stewart, 1998. A mixture of prose, poetry, and journal writing that brings voices of the past to new life.

• Lee Maracle. *Sojourner's Truth and Other Stories.* Vancouver: Press Gang Publishers, 1990. A collection of beautifully written, poignant, and spirited short stories focusing on experiences of individual Aboriginal people living through the often dire conditions facing so many. See also *Sojourners and Sundogs: First Nations Fiction* (1999), a book that combines *Sojourner's Truth and Other Stories* with *Sundogs: A Novel* (1992), which tells the story of a Native family profoundly affected by the Oka crisis.

• Christine Miller and Patricia Chuchryk, eds. *Women of the First Nations: Power, Wisdom, and Strength*. Winnipeg: University of Manitoba Press, 1997. An anthology of diverse perspectives – scholarly, personal, activist, academic, Aboriginal and non-Aboriginal – on political, cultural, economic, environmental, and other issues facing Aboriginal women in Canada.

• John S. Milloy. *A National Crime: The Canadian Government and the Residential School System, 1879 to 1986*. Winnipeg: University of Manitoba Press, 1999. Begun as research for the Royal Commission on Aboriginal Peoples, this work documents the ideology behind the system and the experience of the thousands of Aboriginal children forced to endure it.

• Patricia Monture-Angus. *Journeying Forward: Dreaming First Nations' Independence*. Halifax: Fernwood Publishing, 1999. A former law professor examines the "challenges" that the Canadian legal system presents in the face of indigenous independence struggles, and exposes a racist legal history that this system must confront.

• Daniel N. Paul. *We Were Not the Savages: A Mi'kmaq Perspective on the Collision between European and Native American Civilizations*. 21st-century edition. Halifax: Fernwood Publishing, 2000. This book presents the tortured history of contact between one of the East Coast indigenous peoples and the Europeans, from the earliest encounters prior to 1492 right up to the present.

• Hundreds of Aboriginal newspapers (national, provincial, and local) are available in print and on-line. Look for such titles as *Windspeaker*, *Raven's Eye*, *Saskatchewan Sage*, *Innu News*, *GenXMagazine*, *The Drum*, *Fourth World Journal*, *Mi'kmaq News*, *Eastern Door*, *Anishnabek News*, *First Perspective*, *Métis News*, *Redwire*, and many more. Ask about them at your local library or Native Friendship Centre. On-line versions as well as subscription information are also available though the Aboriginal media websites listed below.

• *The Gift*. Canada, 1998. Directed by Gary Farmer. NFB. Video. 49 min. Through interviews, dance, and song, this film explores the spiritual, economic, and political significance of corn for the indigenous peoples of the Americas, from the history of its cultivation to current conflicts over genetic manipulation, intellectual property, and free-trade deals.

• *Kahnesetake: 270 Years of Defiance*. Canada, 1993. Directed by Alanis Obomsawin. NFB. Video. 120 min. Documentary about the People of the Pines and their determination to protect their land during the 1990 Oka crisis.

• *Keepers of the Fire*. Canada, 1994. Directed by Christine Welsh. NFB. Video. 55 min. Mohawk, Haida, Maliseet, and Ojibwe women tell their stories of passionate struggle for their culture and dignity.

• *Redskins, Tricksters and Puppy Stew*. Canada, 2000. Directed by Drew Hayden Taylor. NFB. Video. 55 min. Exploring issues like Native identity, politics, and racism, this comedic "road trip" draws on the revealing and healing powers of Aboriginal humour.

• *Whose Land Is This?* Canada, 1997. Directed by Richard Hersley and Renae Morriseau. Mongrel Media. Video. 44 min. Against the historical background, spiritual perspectives, and contemporary politics of land claims in British Columbia, this film addresses the question of what exactly constitutes land ownership.

Websites:

There are many Aboriginal websites available, with more coming on-line every day. To start, try the websites of the Aboriginal Multi-Media Society (AMMS) and the Turtle Island Network, which has up-to-the-minute news from a variety of sources and links on just about every Aboriginal subject you can think of.

Chapter Thirteen
A Woman's Place

Some Canadians believe that a woman's proper place is at home, raising children and doing domestic work, while her husband – the head of the household – goes out to win the daily bread. They believe that the words "housewife" and "homemaker" describe exactly what women are and should do. Although these beliefs about women's work are common and strongly held, the actual work that women do is only weakly valued. In our society women are economically and politically penalized for doing what is expected of them.

Beliefs about women's place are not merely personal, private opinions. Rather, they are assumptions widely accepted as normal and built into nearly all of society's major institutions. In fact, in Canada the pattern of husband away on the job and wife at home emerged less than a century ago. Maybe it is really not so "normal" after all.

Their Proper Place
Nineteenth-century Canada was a largely rural society, with an economy based on agriculture. At that time the family unit was the centre of

production. In rural areas men, women, and children all contributed to the family's survival, helping the land yield its bounty. Women maintained the household, made the clothing, grew the garden, milked the cows, and did dozens of other tasks. They bore and nursed the infants, but the children grew up living and working beside their parents.

A poem that appeared in the *Farmer's Advocate and Home Journal* in 1910 sums up the facts of life for most married women in nineteenth-century and early twentieth-century Canada:

> She rose before daylight made crimson the
> east
> For duties that never diminished.
> And never the sun when it sank in the west
> Looked down upon work that was finished.
>
> She cooked an unending procession of meals,
> Preserving and canning and baking.
> She swept and she dusted,
> She washed and she scrubbed,
> With never a rest from it taking.
>
> A family of children she brought in the
> world.
> Raised them and trained them and taught
> them.
> She made all the clothes and patched, mended
> and darned
> 'Til miracles seemed to have wrought them.
>
> She watched by the bedside of sickness and
> pain
> Her hand cooled the raging fever.
> Carpentered, plastered, upholstered and
> scraped
> And worked just as hard as a beaver.
>
> And yet as a lady-of-leisure, it seems,
> The government looks on her station
> For now, by the rules of the census report
> It enters her – No Occupation.[1]

With ironic humour this poem celebrates women's pivotal role in production and indispensable role in reproduction. Without their labour

the farm could not have functioned. Yet at the time when the poem was written, women could neither own a farm nor vote. Economically and legally, socially and politically, they were second-class citizens. Like children, they did not exist as persons in the public sphere.

Although sex discrimination had its expression in laws, its basis was in beliefs about the nature of women, about their capacity and place in society. In the twentieth century many discriminatory laws were taken off the books, but discriminatory patterns remained entrenched in our social institutions, even taking new forms as new ways of organizing labour developed.

As Canada industrialized, women gradually began filling positions of all sorts in the paid economy – in factories, as teachers and nurses, and as workers in the service sectors. Women were recruited from overseas, as well as from among Aboriginal, Black, and other poor communities in Canada, to perform domestic labour for wealthier employers. The participation of married women in industrial production depended greatly on ethnic origin.[2] Meanwhile, the government erected immigration barriers that kept out the wives of railway workers who had emigrated from China.

When the factory began replacing the farm as the main area of production, more men, women, and even children worked for wages in towns and cities, selling their labour to others rather than contributing as before to a family-based enterprise. The women who moved into wage labour at this time were mostly young and single. They would leave the jobs when or if they got married – in fact, many employers forced any woman who got married to quit her job.

By the turn of the century, child-labour laws and other improvements won through early trade union struggles eliminated some of the worst injustices of the factory system. But the pattern of family life had changed. Husbands now spent the day away from home earning money. Wives and other female relatives had almost exclusive responsibility for the tasks that made it possible for a man to work for wages, for children to be raised, and for sick or disabled adults to be cared for.

The public world of work and politics was a man's world, while the domestic sphere was women's. That at least was the official picture, which tended to reflect the world as men experienced it rather than as women did. Many women always found it necessary, or useful, to participate in wage work as well as in unpaid work. As for politics, the myth that what occurs in the private sphere is not political has been debunked by researchers who include gender in their social analysis.

One area of interest for such analysis has been the use of women as a "reserve army of labour." As a category of workers, women have been relatively easily and cheaply transported back and forth across the public-private divide. When Canada entered World War II and men enlisted in the armed forces by the tens of thousands, women took up the slack in the workplace. They filled many of the jobs that the men had been doing on assembly lines and in mills and smelters. Government advertising extolled their role in war production, picturing women marching to the plant in overalls, lunch buckets in hand. Women proved they could do "non-traditional" jobs. But when the men came back from the war, women returned to their "proper place" in the home.

By 1954 only 23.6 per cent of women were in the paid workforce.[3] Government policy and propaganda encouraged this arrangement, and public opinion supported it. This view of a woman's place persisted for decades. In 1988 nearly two-thirds of Canadian women believed that, if at all possible, a mother should not leave for work when there were small children in the home. Yet by 1999, 61 per cent of Canadian women with children under three were participating in the paid labour force.[4]

Social policy since the 1990s has been pushing mothers to work for pay at wage levels that barely sustain them as workers or enable them to pay for child care. Although the demand for women's work in the paid economy fluctuates, the undervaluing of that work remains a constant.

What is also a constant is the social necessity of the work that women have traditionally performed to reproduce a new generation of workers and to care for those participating in, or retired from, the paid economy. This work is undervalued almost to the point of invisibility.

Job Ghettos

Women's participation in the salaried labour force has steadily increased since the 1960s. Indeed, the increase in both the 1960s and 1970s was equal to the total increase in the previous six decades. By the end of the millennium 55 per cent of all women in Canada were working for a wage. Meanwhile, some 67 per cent of men were working at paid employment – which means that women accounted for 46 per cent of the employed workforce.[5]

While women's participation rate increased by 14 percentage points between 1976 and 1999, the rate at which women work part-time has remained stable, making up close to 70 per cent of the part-time labour force. What has changed is the number of mothers in the paid labour force. In 1976, 61 per cent of women under fifty-five with children under sixteen living at home worked for pay; by 1999 the rate was 76 per cent.[6] Most wage-working mothers are members of two-parent rather than single-parent families.

In addition to parental responsibilities, women's participation is influenced by social forces related to identification by race, ethnicity, or culture. Unemployment rates are higher for immigrant than for Canadian-born women, as well as being higher for visible minority and Aboriginal women. One feature of participation in the paid labour force that continues to be shared by women across all groups is their concentration in a relatively small range of lower-paying, traditionally female-dominated occupations. In 1999, 70 per cent of all employed women were working in teaching, nursing, and related health occupations, clerical or other administrative positions, and sales and service occupations. Men's participation in these sectors was at 29 per cent.

Some other sectors have seen improvements for women. In 1999 women made up 49 per cent of business and finance professionals, compared with 41 per cent in 1987. Women now hold more diagnostic and treating positions in medicine and related health professions. Women constituted almost half – 47 per cent – of all doctors and dentists in 1999, up from 44 per cent in 1987. Professionals in social sciences and religion saw an increase from 48 per cent to 58 per cent over the same period. For all managerial positions, the number was 35 per cent, up from 29 per cent, although this shift still tended to be concentrated at lower-level managerial positions. But women remain a minority among those employed in the natural sciences, engineering, and mathematics (20 per cent in 1999), as well as in manufacturing (30 per cent in 1999). In 1999, women made up only 22 per cent of workers in primary industries, and 6 per cent of those in transport, trades, and construction work.

Increases in women's participation in more prestigious and lucrative jobs have not been evenly spread across all groups of women. Immigrant women are more likely than Canadian-born women to be employed as manual workers. In 1995-96, 12 per cent of all immigrant women, and 17 per cent of recent immigrant women, were employed as manual workers, compared with a figure of 6 per cent for Canadian-born women. These same women are less likely to occupy professional positions, especially if they are recent immigrants.[7]

In general, based on their education, some immigrant women appear to be overqualified for the positions they hold. For example, recent immigrant women with a bachelor's degree are six times more likely to be manual workers than are their Canadian-born counterparts. Visible minority women, especially young women, are less likely to be employed in paid work than are non-visible minority women. In part this is due to higher unemployment rates; in part it is due to higher levels of participation in educational pursuits.

Aboriginal women are less well represented in the paid workforce than any other group of women in Canada. In 1996, 41 per cent of Aboriginal women were part of the paid workforce, compared with 53 per cent of non-Aboriginal women. Statisticians recommend caution in interpreting these figures – not to equate paid work with socially valuable labour. This is true for women in general, who are more likely than men to be engaged in non-paid work at home, in the extended family, or in the community. It is especially important that we keep this in mind when we consider the occupations of Aboriginal women who are engaged in fishing, trapping, hunting, sewing, and caring for both the children of family and friends and elderly or ailing people. Still, the impact of racism and colonization should not be discounted. Aboriginal people are overrepresented among those who seek paid employment and cannot find it.

The Wage Gap

It was once the legal and socially expected practice in Canada to pay women half of what men earned for the same work. Those laws have changed, but their legacy continues today in the form of women's concentration in low-paying job sectors and what economists call the wage gap. Although the Canadian gap is no longer as large as 50 per cent, the difference between women's and men's wages remains embarrassingly high. A 2001 study of twenty-nine industrialized countries revealed that Canada had the fifth-largest wage gap when the earnings of full-time male and female workers were compared. Only Spain, Portugal, Japan, and Korea had larger wage gaps.[8]

Comparing the earnings of full-time, full-year workers, women in 1997 earned on average only 73 per cent of what men earned. When adjustments are made for all workers, keeping in mind that women are more likely than men to work part-time or have temporary jobs, the gap increases. In 1997 the average earnings for all women were only 64 per cent of those of all employed men.

On average, women attain higher levels of education than men. Nonetheless, though women with more education tend to earn more than women with less education, at all levels of educational attainment women's earnings are still lower than their male counterparts. This pattern holds true in all occupational fields. But there are also significant differences among women. These differences are most acute for Aboriginal women and women with disabilities. As the National Association of Women in the Law noted in a 1998 presentation to the United Nations, Aboriginal women earn 15 per cent less, women of colour earn 8 per cent less, and women with disabilities earn 17 per cent less than do all employed women.[9]

Given that wages largely determine access to pensions, unemployment insurance, and other social benefits, the wage gap has a great cost to women. The biggest impact is on pensions, which are tied to a person's lifetime earnings (see chapter eleven). The gap also compromises other forms of income support especially geared to women's needs. Recent changes have sharply reduced access to a wide range of maternity benefits that had been introduced for women in the paid labour force in 1971. The Employment Insurance Act of 1997 included changes in eligibility rules – increasing, from three hundred to seven hundred hours, the minimum number of hours a person has to work in the past year to qualify for maternity benefits. These changes are particularly hard on women who already have children and are more likely to be part-time or temporary workers.

The gender-based income gap is even greater than the wage gap. In 1997 women's average income reached only 62 per cent that of men. It should come as no surprise, then, that women constitute a disproportionate part of the Canadian population living under the poverty line. According to 1997 statistics, women are about 20 per cent more likely to live in poverty than men.[10] The biggest group of women in poverty is mothers, in particular single mothers who are young or have small children. In 1995, 83 per cent of single mothers with children under seven and 83 per cent of single mothers under twenty-five lived under Statistics Canada's low-income cut-off (LICO). Some 56 per cent of all single mothers live under the LICO.

Other women with high rates of poverty include those marginalized by racism or age: 49 per cent for unattached women over 65; 43 per cent for Aboriginal women; 37 per cent for visible minority women; and 32 per cent for immigrant women.[11] Women with disabilities face an especially acute risk of poverty. Depending on age, women with disabilities, living in a household rather than an institution, and who had any income at all, had incomes in the mid-1990s that ranged on average between a low of $13,000 and a high of $17,000. At best, disabled women earn only 55 per cent of what men with disabilities in their age range earn.[12]

The biggest predictor of poverty for women with disabilities, as for all other women, is single parenthood. Women with disabilities are five times as likely as men with disabilities to be lone parents and twice as likely as women without disabilities to be lone parents, due to the greater likelihood of women with disabilities to be divorced, separated, or widowed. Cultural attitudes towards women's work affect all women, and for women with disabilities it affects them in a more complex way. Like all women, they assume an uneven share of domestic as well as child-care responsibilities. These factors interact with disability to produce low levels of participation in the paid labour force.[13]

Unequal wages in the paid workforce and motherhood are the two major factors to take into account in understanding poverty as a gender issue. Do women earn less than men because they are confined to the lowest-paying jobs? Or are these jobs badly paid because they are filled by women? And how is the answer to these chicken and egg questions related to the value accorded to caring labour? Women do work, cheaply or freely, to raise the next generation, to support the efforts of the current one, and to tend to the needs of elders. Why is this work so undervalued? These questions take our analysis to the heart of the matter.

Exploring the Wage Gap

One old justification given for paying women less is that female workers are not the real breadwinners – men are. Based on this view, a man's wage is higher because his wage is the "family wage." Women, the argument goes, are financially dependent on men; a woman's place is in the home; she does not really need a salary. If she works, it is supposedly to earn so-called "pin money," a little extra on the side for her personal whims or to help pay for a family holiday. Of course, this argument makes assumptions about just what is a reasonable amount for a single woman to live on. It also rests on mistaken assumptions about the economic realities facing two-parent families, realities that motivate both parents to participate in the paid workforce.

The so-called traditional family in which the father is the only breadwinner is now relatively rare. By 1997 the percentage of families with one parent who stays out of the paid labour force in order to care for children hit a low of 22 per cent, compared with 52 per cent in 1976. While there has been a slight increase in the number of men who have gone against the grain of traditional gender roles as stay-at-home parents (4 per cent in 1997), the biggest change in roles has been in the increases of the labour-market participation of mothers. One income is usually not enough to support a two-parent family.

The percentage of families led by a single parent, most of them women, is also increasing. By the late 1990s almost one out of every five families was a sole-support family headed by a woman.[14] Combine unequal wage rates with the complications of finding adequate child care, and the increasing necessity of having two incomes to support a household, and it should come as no

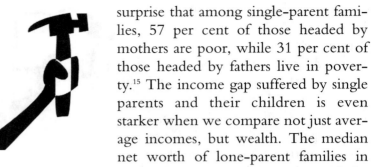

surprise that among single-parent families, 57 per cent of those headed by mothers are poor, while 31 per cent of those headed by fathers live in poverty.[15] The income gap suffered by single parents and their children is even starker when we compare not just average incomes, but wealth. The median net worth of lone-parent families in 1999 was $14,600, a mere 12 per cent of the $119,300 average for all families combined.

Another justification offered for paying women less is what's seen as their unreliable participation in the workforce. But, despite commonly held perceptions, the employee turnover rates of women and men differ only slightly, and women are staying in the paid workforce longer. Still, given the misconception, many employers show a reluctance to hire women for jobs that require lengthy training, and this tendency limits opportunities. Of course, the last weeks of pregnancy and early months of a child's infancy can take a woman temporarily out of the paid workforce. But it is not simply pregnancy and birthing that restrict a woman's access to better paid jobs or a more secure career. Rather, it is a woman's "duties" at home that can affect her eligibility for more prestigious and better paid work. But why should we assume that the care of the family is a woman's rather than a man's duty? And why should we make this activity invisible as work, by thinking of whoever does it as a consumer of paycheques or welfare rather than a provider of a socially necessary and valuable service?

Ironically, another supposed justification for underpaying women in the public sphere is that their domestic labour is not paid either. Cooking, cleaning, raising children, caring for the sick, chauffering – these are vital tasks, often eulogized as such. But domestic labour has long been taken for granted and usually earns nothing at all: "No Occupation" – salary, zero. If that is what women's work is worth, why pay them much more when they go out to work in a day-care centre or long-term care facility, or a call centre or assembly line, for that matter?

Perhaps the economy does not need all members of society to work without interruption. The "in and out" arrangement guarantees greater profits in many sectors. It is to the employers' advantage to have available a "reserve army" of workers, with no choice but to accept lower pay, vulnerable to dismissal when they are no longer needed. And if employers can get away with relying on an unpaid sector of society to do socially necessary work, rather than paying workers enough money to support this activity, why challenge social expectations about the value of the work women do? There is a vested interest in the unequally valued sexual division of labour.

Low-paid jobs and part-time positions are usually not held in high esteem, and unpaid work is even less so. If, despite that, women (or men) who recognize the social and personal value of caring work choose to do it, whether for family, friends, patients, or clients, they should be able to do so. As it stands, those who do this work, whether by choice or the pressure of social conditioning, are punished economically and pushed to the margins of society, where their interests and concerns carry little weight with political decision-makers.

A basic change would mean paying women the same as men who are doing jobs of comparable social worth – equal pay for work of equal value, which is now usually referred to as pay equity. Eliminating gendered job ghettos will also require employment equity and affirmative action programs; access to training and promotions; changes in work design and social environments; accessible maternity and parental leave provisions; and access to affordable, quality child care.

When the unequally valued sexual division of labour is done away with, along with the low-paid job ghettos that it has generated, women and men will be free to choose from among all the jobs that need doing, including homemaking, childrearing, and community-building.

> Critics of affirmative action describe these programs as reverse discrimination. I do not believe in such a phenomenon because to discriminate we must first wield power. Logically, those without power cannot meaningfully discriminate. More important, what action or movement are we aspiring towards in an affirmative action initiative? The norm we sanction is that of the "white male." This does not affirm my experience or reality! It is not likely I will wake up tomorrow and discover I have become a white male! What we need to consider are programs of "equity." Equity is what is just or what should have been all along. This description brings us around full circle, back to paying careful attention to language and the related power of naming.
>
> — Patricia A. Monture,
> "I Know My Name: A First Nations Woman Speaks," in
> *Limited Edition: Voices of Feminism*, ed. Geraldine Finn,
> 1993.

The Double Day

It is often difficult to reconcile family and work. At the beginning and end of each weekday, after leaving their paid jobs, many women shop, provide meals for the family, transport the children to school or child care, wash the clothes, do the dishes, and clean the house. The "double day" is a term applied to these two daily shifts, one typically low paid and the other unpaid. For many a working woman, these unpaid tasks are hers to shoulder alone. In the 1990s more than one-half of all mothers working full-time at a paid job were still solely responsible for all daily household chores.[16]

While men and women put in around the same number of hours of work a day, the split between paid and unpaid work is so uneven as to be almost mirror images. One study, which averaged hours worked per day over a seven-day week, found that while women spent 4.4 hours per day on unpaid work, and 2.8 in paid work, men spent 2.7 hours on unpaid work and 4.5 hours per day in paid work. The uneven split applies even to women who work full-time for pay. They simply work more hours in total.[17]

Many women's unpaid work responsibilities extend beyond child care and housekeeping. Women perform proportionately more unpaid community work than men do, as well as providing the bulk of unpaid care for elderly or disabled relatives. Combining all of these tasks is a challenge facing many more women than men. "Role complexity," or the number of different responsibilities that a person has to cope with, can lead to "time stress." Thus, not surprisingly, 38 per cent of married mothers aged twenty-five to forty-four and employed full-time in 1998 reported that they were time-stressed, in comparison with 26 per cent of their male counterparts.[18] This unequal burden of stress takes its toll on women's careers.

For many women the cost of this time stress is paid in foregone promotions and pay raises, or a shift to part-time or temporary jobs. Spending increased hours in unpaid labour carries other costs for women besides lost income, pension contributions, or the right to employment insurance benefits when they have difficulty returning to the paid labour force. It also often means working in isolation, foregoing training opportunities and job experience that will be recognized by potential employers. It means being exposed to health and safety risks without being able to take sick days, and without access to supplementary health care, disability plans, or workers' compensation. Fulfilling domestic responsibilities costs women in all these ways – while the work itself remains invisible, ironically, precisely because it is unpaid.

The Pitfalls of Caregiving

Many women sacrifice their careers or earning potential because they feel responsible – or they've been left responsible – for looking after others. Given the dearth of affordable alternatives, they have little choice. Consider the shortage of good affordable child care, for example. While the number of licensed day-care spaces available over the last several decades has increased substantially, it still nowhere near meets the need. In 1998 there were just under 470,000

licensed child-care spaces in Canada, almost five times more than in 1980. But the rate of increase has slowed in recent years, and in some provinces it has even reversed. Cuts in public spending in Ontario, for example, hit child care hard. Between 1995 and 1999 the Ontario government reduced spending on regulated child care by about 40 per cent.[19]

A million and a half Canadian children need care while their parents work or attend school.[20] Their needs are being addressed not by a comprehensive strategy but by a patchwork of programs that depend increasingly on private, informal arrangements. A glance at most local newspapers will reveal classified ads placed by women willing to offer child care in their homes. Although this type of unregulated care, when provided by experienced women, may be stimulating and of high quality, it can also sometimes be mere supervision-by-television and even dangerous. But a well-equipped child-care centre staffed by trained workers who receive good wages can easily cost more than a year in private school for a teenager.

Quebec maintains a successful five-dollar-a-day child system in which regulated care is equally available to everyone. Much of the rest of Canada relies on individuals competing in the market as buyers and sellers of the commodity that is "child care." The situation puts a lot of pressure on women. Some try to make a living looking after toddlers in their homes. Many struggle to find suitable care. The solution is not simply to cheer on the women who have managed to find work in more highly paid sectors, because the work of caring will remain. Someone has to do it, and as long as it remains a low-value commodity, not a job that is highly esteemed because it is important for society, it will be left to the society's most vulnerable members.

Immigration policies targeted at poor countries have long been part of Canada's approach to solving such problems – an approach we see even today in Canada's "Live-in Caregiver Program." Under this program women (and a few men) who are unable to enter the country as either family-status or independent immigrants apply for a work permit in the hope that after meeting its requirements they will be eligible to apply for permanent resident status. The program requires that they live with the employer whose name appears on the work permit and that they work as live-in nannies and maids for a period of two years. They live in physical and social isolation with little or no privacy, vulnerable to physical and sexual abuse.[21]

The Live-in Caregiver Program also contributes to the loss of occupational skills by some women in the program. The number of nurses from the Philippines who come to Canada under the LCP is increasing, and university graduates from that country discover that their training is not recognized in Canada despite the shortage of workers in their field. During the mandatory twenty-four months of domestic work in Canada, they cannot work part-time as nurses. All this time away from the profession decreases their chances of ever practising it again. Some professional bodies require that they take refresher courses if they have been away from nursing for five years – a heavy expense for women with already low incomes.[22]

People who need care, whether they are disabled, ill, or elderly, are most often looked after by women who have witnessed a recent shift in their caregiving work from institutional to community settings. This has happened because people are more comfortable at home and because it is less costly to look after them at home. A gender analysis shows that the way this shift has happened has meant that the *social costs* have been borne by the women who provide the care.

Many community-care programs, from housekeeping for the elderly to changing dressing for post-operative patients, have been placed in the hands of commercial operators who submit the lowest bids on government community-care contracts. Once the preserve of not-for-profit charities like the Victorian Order of Nurses, whose workers were often unionized, these services tend now to be provided on the quicker, leaner time schedules that are most efficient from a cost-accounting perspective. In metropolitan areas, home-support workers are mainly low-income women, increasingly drawn from immigrant populations.[23]

Private contractors rely both on untrained workers and, at the same low rates of pay, on trained workers who have lost their positions in hospitals because of cutbacks. While many women who work as caregivers are expected to function with little or no specific training, others find their professional skills underused and underpaid. Meanwhile, the commercial home-care sector depends on the holistic knowledge that women have acquired over generations about the nature of caring work – about, for instance, how important it is to pass the time talking with someone who is ill or lonely.

If we follow Canadian physicist Ursula Franklin's advice and look at how work is organized as a technological decision (see chapter eight), then we can see that commercial home-care labour is "prescriptive" because it is organized from above and broken down into small bits of work, whereas a "holistic" approach puts the one who does the work in control.[24]

Yet more and more the way these jobs are organized requires working faster, in ways that contradict what many women know about the holistic nature of care. When fewer women are hired to look after more people for purposes of cost reduction, the social and psychological elements of caring work, like simple listening, get neglected. "Care plans" typically do not make allowance for the intangibles of real care, treating them as an unproductive waste of time even though they have been shown to improve things for people in need.[25]

The costs of the restructuring of care are borne by its recipients as well as its front-line providers. Just as the vast majority of home-care providers are women, so too are the majority (67 per cent) of subsidized home-care recipients.[26]

Women are more likely to rely on subsidized home care than men are. Women tend to live longer than men, and they are less likely to have a spouse who will provide this unpaid service, or sufficient income to pay for private home-care services. This situation, again, reveals how women are particularly vulnerable to public policy moves that reflect the low social value accorded to "care."

Family

Women's experience is distorted by myths about the nature of work in the private sphere – and also by the myth that home and family are a haven and refuge from the world of work. Not only is the home a workplace for most women, but for many it is also a site of violence and vulnerability.

The pressures on family life are illustrated by rising divorce and separation rates. Between 1972 and 1997 the divorce rate for Canadians rose by 75 per cent.[27] When families do stay together, they often do so at a cost. While both men and women experience violence at the hands of a spouse (about 8 per cent for women and 7 per cent for men), women tend to be more severely abused than men.[28] Female victims were almost two and a half times more likely to report having been beaten. Women are more likely than men to be victims of repeated incidents of spousal violence, and more likely to suffer physical injury. Women are also five times more likely to have required medical attention as a result of the violent incident. In many cases, the violence or threat of violence is so severe that the victims (38 per cent of women and 8 per cent of men) fear for their lives.

Often these fears become reality. Women are more likely to be murdered by someone they know than by a stranger. In 1998, eight out of ten female murder victims were killed by someone they knew – most likely a family member, particularly a spouse. Indeed, three out of the ten women murdered in 1998 were killed by a spouse, while only 3 per cent of the men murdered that year were killed by a spouse.[29] The more socially marginalized a woman is, the more vulnerable she becomes to physical violence. If a woman has a disability, or is an Aboriginal woman or woman of colour, the chances of her being subjected to violence increase dramatically; at the same time the chances of her violation being taken seriously decrease proportionately.

Despite its seriousness, less than half of the incidents (37 per cent) of spousal violence against women are reported to police.[30] Such incidents were kept almost completely hidden in the privacy of the home until the women's movement forced them out into the open. Now there are shelters for women whose intimate partners attack them. Nearly one hundred thousand women were admitted to 448 shelters for abused women across Canada in 1999-2000.[31] In these places a battered woman can get counselling and help in finding a job, and gain the support of other women who have also suffered violence. Still, more shelters for battered women are needed, while the existing ones are vulnerable to government cutbacks. The shelters are operating at maximum capacity, and many have long waiting lists.[32]

Although, for many, home can be a site of violence and abuse, for women who belong to communities whose members are the targets of racist discrimination and violence the situation is more complicated. Family and community can be a place of shared understanding and support, especially for coping with experiences of hostility and discrimination. Yet when things go wrong within a family, members of marginalized communities face additional barriers in getting culturally sensitive support, or in simply being taken seriously within a judicial system that they can experience as systematically discriminatory. Women may also be held back by fear of betraying the community to a society that is all too ready to have its prejudices confirmed, poised to respond with an attack on the family or community rather than provide appropriate support for its more vulnerable members.[33]

> Eliminating violence against women requires fundamental changes in many areas, not only the criminal law system, but also in social security policies, housing, equal pay and the eradication of racism, for example. Social and economic inequality places women in situations where they are more vulnerable to abuse, be it sexual harassment in the workplace, violence in the home or sexual abuse in private and public institutions.
>
> — Canadian Women's March Committee, World March of Women, "It's Time for Change: Demands to the Federal Government to End Poverty and Violence Against Women," September 2000.

Images

Violence in interpersonal relationships is not something that women experience only at home. It occurs also as sexual harassment in contexts that should be categorized as professional rather than personal. Supported by images everywhere of women as sex objects, some popular ways of thinking about sex and gender influence have a subtle but powerful impact on perceptions of women's participation in the world of waged work. Some people see the presence of women as automatically bringing with it a personal or even sexual element. Some see women's presence as a kind of *intrusion* into the (male) public sphere. Acting on this kind of assumption, some men treat female workers as if they were inviting sexual attention simply by being in the workplace. This kind of harassment, whether it takes the form of unwanted comments of a sexual nature or goes as far as forced sexual contact, is aimed at taking sexual advantage of workers on the basis of workplace power differences.

Between 40 and 70 per cent of Canadian women and around 5 per cent of men report that they have experienced sexual harassment, usually from supervisors.[34] Sometimes the harassment of women in the workplace is aimed at forcing them out altogether. This hostile response can take many forms, some subtle, resulting in an uncom-fortable working environment or what has been called a "chilly climate." In more serious cases it can take forms that jeopardize the health and safety of women workers.

Some two decades after having been hired as part of a Corrections Canada project to bring female guards into men's prisons in the early 1980s, former participants in the program went public about the harassment they had faced, ranging from pornography strewn around the security office to having their cars vandalized. One former guard reported being told that she would be put into a cell to deal with any trouble with an inmate and that her male co-workers would not help. Another remembered, "I actually found cells left open from the previous shift."[35]

In extreme cases, resentment against women's presence in a man's world has turned into deadly attacks. The best-known and most shocking case in Canada happened on December 6, 1989, at the École Polytechnique in Montreal. A twenty-five-year-old man, Marc Lepine, walked into an engineering faculty classroom armed with a semi-automatic rifle. After ordering the male students out of the room, he yelled out to the women students left in the room, "You're all a bunch of feminists, and I hate feminists." He opened fire on them, killing fourteen young women. In a three-page suicide note, Lepine blamed feminists for ruining his life.

Lepine was a mentally unbalanced young man, but as women's experience and the statistics both show, his spasm of hatred was not an isolated act of madness. It fits within a broader context that narrowly defines women's place in society and punishes them for stepping out of it.

Violence, abuse, and harassment experienced by women at home, at work, and in the streets are related to the images that circulate in our culture. Women and men and children are exposed every day to images in advertising, art, and pop culture that equate women with their sexuality and define that sexuality in ways that make domination sexy. In these images, attractiveness in women is tied to characteristics like helplessness or passivity, a focus on stimulating male desire, and a tendency to use sex as a way of manipulating men.

Since women are represented as always "wanting it," tying images of female sexuality to commercial products turns out to be a very successful marketing strategy, encouraging the male consumer to feel desirable and powerful. This marketing strategy doesn't only sell cars and beer. It also sells an image of women that has been coming off the cultural production line for centuries. The very success of selling the image not only contributes to women's vulnerability to violence but also makes that vulnerability socially invisible. If a woman always "wants it," how could she ever really mean "no" when she says "no"? It is hard enough for a woman, already disadvantaged by the social and economic devaluation of her work, to ensure that what she says is taken seriously. It is even harder in a culture that puts words in her mouth, words that invite sexual and other forms of exploitation.

Power: Patriarchy, Class, and Racism

Patriarchy is a word that describes social structures that justify and support male dominance over women. Historians understand patriarchy as a very specific form of male domination, namely domination by fathers or father figures, like monarchs or bishops. Many men as well as women have revolted against such domination. Participants in the American and French revolutions argued against the paternal domination of some men over others. Their ideal was one of equality among brothers, as professed in slogans like, "Equality, liberty and fraternity."

Unfortunately, "fraternity" was meant quite literally by its male champions to encompass only male members of society, and not even all men at that. In the laws of the new republics they created, all women were excluded, as were men and women of colour, Aboriginal peoples, and others regarded as not quite fit to be included in the brotherhood of man. Early liberal egalitarians somehow saw no contradiction between this and their argument for the equal dignity of men.

Social analysts have dubbed the thinking and institutions that supported these exclusions as the sexual and racial contracts.[36] This analysis sheds new light on the "social contract" – the assumed agreement between citizens to govern themselves in ways that maximize their liberty and equality. The idea of the sexual contract explains a new phase of patriarchy, called "fraternal patriarchy," to indicate the power over women held by (some) men as fraternal equals rather than as father figures. This can be seen in the legal rights that men have had over women, as husbands rather than fathers. Until very recently a husband had a right to physically "discipline" his wife – that is, to beat her. Marital rape was not recognized as a crime in Canada until 1983, on the assumption that upon marriage a woman gave consent to any and all sexual relations that her husband might initiate, regardless of her feelings about it at any particular time, even after separation from him.

In the centuries that have passed since patriarchal power passed from fathers to sons, the status of personhood has been extended more broadly. Slavery was abolished; Aboriginal peoples are engaged in land-claim negotiations; sex and race have been eliminated as grounds for legal discrimination; and in recent years there has been an unprecedented amount of reform in the area of sexual assault and family law. Given these changes, some people say that feminists who protest against patriarchy are the ones who are behind the times. Not only do we see little evidence of men controlling women as fathers might control children, but most of the laws that gave some men privilege over others on the basis of their race and sex have also been eliminated, they say. Equality is enshrined in our Constitution; it is a watchword in our society. The law has become sex and colour-blind.

Closer analysis suggests that the privilege of sex and race, as well as what Aboriginal peoples regard as the perspective of settlers, has become such an integral part of the institutions, practices, and assumptions that structure our society that there is no longer any need to protect them by law. The information we have about who lives in poverty and at risk of violence is not consistent with a culture that genuinely supports equality.

Labour force statistics and public policy on child care and home care reflect a persistent male model of citizenship. Legal barriers to women's participation in "non-traditional" kinds of work have been removed, but traditional woman's work still has to be done.

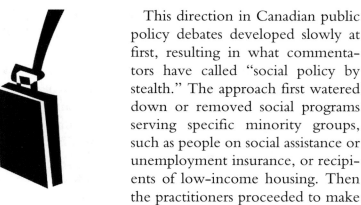

The male model of citizenship assumes a separation of private from public, family from market. It is reflected in the way we talk, for example, about the "rights" of wage-earners who act independently in the labour market. This talk contrasts with the "needs" of people (most often women) who work but do not get paid. To have their needs met, these consumers are dependent on (usually male) wage-earners or the government, either as wives or as welfare recipients. This way of picturing social participation means that the benefits of the social contract are restricted to the mostly male entitled members of society who "contribute" to the economy, as opposed to the mostly female "charity" and excluded cases who are "non-contributory" and marginal to the social contract.[37]

This picture depends on equating productive activity with waged activity, not with social usefulness. Thus a woman who prepares nutritious meals for her children, elderly relatives, or even as a volunteer at a local soup kitchen is defined as being engaged in unproductive activity, as a consumer of the resources brought home by productive labourers, while a woman who takes orders at a fast-food outlet is defined as being engaged in productive activity. These kinds of value-laden definitions figure in an increasingly popular public policy that emphasizes moving people off the welfare rolls and into "productive activity" while withdrawing public funding for social programs upon which "unproductive" members of society were said to have become "dependent."

This direction in Canadian public policy debates developed slowly at first, resulting in what commentators have called "social policy by stealth." The approach first watered down or removed social programs serving specific minority groups, such as people on social assistance or unemployment insurance, or recipients of low-income housing. Then the practitioners proceeded to make fundamental changes to the major social programs, such as pensions, health care, and education.[38]

Social citizenship rights determine access to the social goods available through the government – everything from education, roads, clean water, and health care to employment insurance, pensions, and so on. Political citizenship rights have to do with our capacity to participate in democratic government. This element includes not just the right to vote, but also the opportunity to participate in political movements aimed at influencing the kind of rights and access to social goods that members of society receive. A male model of citizenship harms both of those sets of rights.

Critics sometimes say that the efforts to represent the interests of women as a group are the work of a "special interest," of a group with special needs, and therefore illegitimate – as opposed to reflecting the rights of individuals, taxpaying citizens, or participants in the productive economy. Without ever referring to men, this language reflects the assumptions of the male model of citizenship. In the name of neutrality and of not giving in to the special claims of one group on the basis of gender, the stance systematically ignores and devalues women's experiences of a society that remains structured along gender lines.

The Women's Movement

Women have a long history of organizing for change, for improvement in their status, and improvements more generally in the communities in which they play a vital role. The past hundred years have been marked by important steps along the road known as women's liberation. The women's movement has won significant advances – the right to vote, the right to equal access to education, recognition in human rights legislation, reform in sexual assault law, and prohibitions against sexual harassment. Equality rights have even been enshrined in the Canadian Charter of Rights and Freedoms.

Since the 1960s a renewed feminist movement has struggled to put women's issues on the political agenda. In the process participants in the movement discovered the need to more intensely focus their analysis of gender and social justice and at the same time to make connections that broaden their analysis. The first lesson resulted from demands made by women whose experiences were not being adequately considered, even though the movement professed to represent all women. Just as a male model of citizenship functions to exclude women while making that exclusion invisible, some women's experiences were privileged as the norm. In the 1960s feminists like Betty Friedan who complained about the social isolation of middle-class suburban housewives were assuming a middle-class lifestyle as the norm. But that lifestyle was unlikely to be shared by Aboriginal women and women of colour. Similarly, the discussion of inequalities in sexual relationships proceeded as if all such relationships were heterosexual.

Over the past thirty years Black women, Aboriginal women, Métis women, lesbians, disabled women, and immigrant and visible minority women have analyzed the ways in which Canadian society has oppressed and discriminated against them, organizing to assert their rights.[39] But women organizing within their communities is not a new phenomenon. Women have long played a central cultural role among indigenous peoples, a role that is vitally important today as Aboriginal communities struggle for survival and renewal. Amongst newcomers, too, women played key roles. As early as 1659 the Sisters of the Hospitaliers of St. Joseph were managing the first medical mission in New France, and later, in

the early eighteenth century, Marie-Marguerite D'Youville and her followers, attending to the housing needs of the poor, established the Grey Nuns. Since the early eighteenth century, Black women have played a key role in benevolent societies, especially in Nova Scotia and Southern Ontario. Their work, begun by aiding those escaping slavery, continued to help Black people overcome and to thrive despite the economic and social legacy of slavery and racism.

Organizing to get women's interests on the political agenda has also meant making links between the ways in which women are oppressed as women and oppression based on racism and economic class. Women have long been active in the union movement in Canada – for example in the earliest days of the garment industry.[40] More recently, union activists have made explicit links between women's issues and the issues facing workers. Unions have begun to take a leading role in organizing for pay equity, child care, and parental leave, as well as in including anti-harassment policies and anti-discrimination clauses in contracts. They have been especially involved in unionizing female-dominated workplaces.

Some of the victories of the women's movement have been subjected to counterattack. Through the 1980s and 1990s a whole range of government bodies dedicated to women's issues were cut, and funding to women's organizations was radically reduced and then eliminated. Progress made in the field of employment equity was undermined in the 1990s by provincial government repeals and federal government refusals to pay up. Although both the provincial and federal government actions were eventually found to be unconstitutional, governments continue to invest public money in continuing legal appeals rather than in equality. Meanwhile, government sources of funding for groups that lobby for gender justice continue to be choked off.

Although no legal barriers to women's participation in electoral politics remain, and Canada has even had a female prime minister, most women continue to be shut out of the country's political institutions. In the federal election of

2000, only 62 out of the available 301 seats in the House of Commons were held by women. Women's representation in executive positions in the federal civil service was only slightly better, 27 per cent in 1999.[41]

For organizers in the women's movement, an increasingly important goal in the face of economic globalization is establishing solidarity across various lines. The prevailing trends in globalization reflect a vision of the "free" market that increases women's risk of poverty and violence. The creation of broader free markets, tax and government cuts, privatization of health care and public institutions, deregulation of work, and the removal of environmental protections are most threatening to the poorest among us, and all over the world – as in Canada – that means women.

Social analysts are drawing further connections between two mindsets: one that makes women's work and its exploitation invisible and another that encourages plundering the Earth for its resources. These mindsets enable many people to ignore, on the one hand, the essential life-support activity performed by the "undeveloped" natural environment and, on the other, the significance of the work done by women in fulfilling their "natural" role.[42] When progress is premised on economic development that transforms ecological and cultural systems into machines for productive activity, with no regard for how they sustain themselves and indeed sustain the life of the planet, then the basis of all activity and all life is undermined.

These analyses, and others like them, are invigorating a new generation of activists in the women's movement – activists like those who, with serious intent, playfully dub themselves "eco-grrrls."[43] Members of this media-savvy generation engage in "culture jamming": playing with images and producing spoof ads, for example – not just telling but showing how sexism functions in the media. Trading tactics and tips on the Internet, these activists think globally and act locally, in groups like the Radical Cheerleaders, a loose affiliation of protestors

> ## My Definition of Feminism
>
> In the dictionary, it might say something about the movement towards political, social and economic equality between men and women. The gang of girls I work with just finished a zine on feminism, and they added things to the definition including beauty, power of choice, power to stand up for yourself. I think that the main thing for me is that feminism has always boiled down to choice. For everyone to have a chance to make choices, lots of things have to be addressed, and feminism has always been about making choices.
>
> — Emmy Pantin,
> "The Personal Is Political," in *Turbo Chicks: Talking Young Feminisms*, ed. Allyson Mitchell, Lisa Bryn Rundle, and Lara Karaian, 2001.

who bring their message to streets all across Canada.

The women's movement has become invigorated by bringing diverse analyses out of the margins as well as by coalitions with unions and other groups working in solidarity nationally and internationally. It has been revitalized too by the energy of radical elders like the Raging Grannies (see chapter eleven), who also play with stereotypes and protest (with serious intent) in song and street theatre.

Towards Equality and Well-Being for All

The same society that wants a woman at home gives her two jobs, pays her low wages, and limits her choices. The same society that eulogizes the family and puts the ideal woman on a pedestal treats her as a disposable consumer good and a target of violence.

The law used to deny equality explicitly to women. In Canada, women first won the right to vote in 1916, in Manitoba. Only in 1929 were women recognized officially by the courts as "persons." And it was not until 1940 that women in Quebec could cast a ballot. In 1981 Canadian women succeeded in pressuring the federal government to include in the Charter of Rights of the country's new Constitution a section guaranteeing women equal rights under the law. This victory, after an intense political fight, was a step forward for half the population, but it was only one step in a long journey. Women continue to struggle for autonomy, dignity, and a decent standard of living.

Only when patriarchy is abandoned – along with the other forces of oppression that are intertwined with it – will all people achieve liberation from oppressive and exploitive structures and ideologies. The issues that the women's movement has addressed – from rape and unequal pay to universal suffrage and child care, and the relationships between sexism, racism, and the social structures that keep people in poverty – all have their roots in the way society is organized. Each advance towards greater dignity and equality has been won with great effort, and each contributes to a society in which justice will prevail.

Questions

❑ Housework, and caring for children and often for adult relatives when they are sick or need special care, are jobs that fall disproportionately to women. This work often interferes with paid work or is simply added on top of it, leaving women stressed and economically more vulnerable. What can be done about this? Can these responsibilities be shared more fairly? How can the value of this work be properly recognized and rewarded? Is this just a private matter to be worked out among family members? Are there ways we can address this issue collectively in Canada?

❑ The women (and some men) who provide child care or home-care services, or perform domestic labour for pay, are among the worst-paid workers in Canada, often working in insecure, unsafe, or unstable working conditions. What does this tell us about social values in Canada? How do we account for the gap between this bottom line and what most of us say about the importance of home and family? What would it take to close this gap?

❑ What does equal pay for work of equal value

mean? How should we measure and compare the value of different kinds of activities? Should we leave it to the marketplace to decide, accepting that what we do is only worth what others are willing to pay for it? Are there alternatives?

❑ Why are there so few women in political office compared to men? What would it take to have a government made up of at least as many women as men?

❑ Too many women live in dangerously violent relationships. The causes of violence can be complex, and women often feel that leaving is not a viable option. What is needed to prevent domestic violence? What would enable a woman in an abusive relationship to make a better life for herself and her children? Are there ways of supporting reconciliation and healing that don't risk health and safety? What if the violence won't stop? What does it take to make leaving a viable option? What is necessary to recover from an abusive past?

❑ It takes a lot of energy and hard work to maintain a home and care for children on a low income. Should a low-income single parent be forced to work for low pay, or enrol in a work for welfare program? Will such programs help her better her situation? Could it harm her, her children, and society more generally in the long run? Who else benefits from these programs?

❑ For some the goal of equality between the sexes means that there should be no rules preventing women from doing anything men can do – women should be able to compete with men in education, the job market, and politics. Few such rules now exist in Canada. When all such rules have been eliminated, will that mean we have achieved equality?

❑ Does concern for the dignity of women mean addressing inequalities between women – for example, those created by racism or economic class differences – as well as inequalities between women and men? How might stressing the right of women to compete equally with men reinforce social and economic structures that threaten the sense of self-respect and economic security of a great many women and men?

❑ Sexism is not the only source of inequality for women. Many women also experience the effects of racism. One way of understanding how this works is to identify sexism and racism as separate social forces, with some people experiencing the effects of only one form of discrimination while others are hurt by more than one. Another possibility is that sexism and racism combine to form unique forms of discrimination. This possibility makes it especially important to listen to what Aboriginal women and women of colour have to say. What is necessary for these voices to be heard more often? Are there ways of listening more attentively? How can we share responsibility for learning about others' perspectives in a way that fairly shares the educational burden?

❑ Consider other possible combinations of discrimination, including, for example, discrimination related to disability, economic class, or sexual preference. How can we find out more about how women experience these combinations? Can we build networks of solidarity across these differences? How might that benefit all of us with an interest in equality?

Resources

• Maria Almey et al. *Women in Canada 2000: A Gender-Based Statistical Report*. Ottawa: Statistics Canada, 2000. An analysis of the situation of women in Canada, exploring demographic and cultural characteristics, living arrangements, income, labour force activity, health, and criminal and victimization rates.

• Shelagh Day and Gwen Brodsky. *Women and the Equality Deficit: The Impact of Restructuring Canada's Social Programs*. Ottawa: Status of Women Canada, 1998. A study that shows not only how restructuring social programs hurt women but also how this violates international human rights treaties and the Canadian Charter of

Rights. An on-line version is available at <www.swc-cfc.gc.ca/direct>.

• Karen Hadley. *"And We Still Ain't Satisfied": Gender Inequality in Canada, A Status Report for 2001*. Toronto: National Action Committee on the Status of Women and the Centre for Social Justice Foundation, 2001. A review of current economic inequalities between the sexes in Canada; it includes analyses of the causes and the promise for improvement offered by unionization and other strategies. Available on-line at <www.socialjustice.org/pubs/pdfs/womequal.pdf>.

• Sophie Harding. *Our Voices, Our Revolutions: Di/verse Voices of Black Women, First Nations Women, and Women of Colour in Canada*. Toronto: Inanna, 2000. Life-writing, poetry, and short auto-fiction are amongst the genres represented in this collection.

• Katherine M.J. McKenna and June Larkin, eds. *Violence against Women: New Canadian Perspectives*. Toronto: Inanna, 2002. A comprehensive collection of articles documenting thirty years of activism against violence against women, with analyses of the incidence, prevalence, and consequences of this violence as well as its relation to social issues like poverty, racism, and rural isolation.

• Amin Nuzhat, Kathryn McPherson, Andrea Medovarski, Angela Miles, and Goli Rezai-Rashti. *Canadian Woman Studies: An Introductory Reader*. Toronto: Inanna, 1999. A broad-ranging introduction to women's issues through a collection of articles previously published in the *Canadian Woman Studies* journal, addressing race, class, sexuality and gender, violence, media stereotyping, work and economy, health, spirituality, and creative writing.

• Tanya Schecter. *Race, Class, Women and the State: The Case of Domestic Labour*. Montreal: Black Rose, 1998. An exploration of the interplay of race and gender in Canadian immigration policy designed to satisfy the demand for a cheap domestic labour force, analyzing the exploitive social and political effects of this policy.

• Veronica Strong-Boag, Mona Gleason, and Adele Perry, eds. *Rethinking Canada: The Promise of Women's History*. 4th ed. Toronto: Oxford University Press, 2002. Essays by Canadian historians on everything from the sainting of Kateri Tekawitha, lesbians in *Chatelaine* magazine, and the impact of the fishery collapse on East Coast women to the effects of globalization on international women's politics.

• Vappu Tyyskä. *Women, Citizenship and Canadian Child Care Policy in the 1990s*. Toronto: Childcare Resource and Research Unit, Centre for Urban and Community Studies, 2001. Policy analysis showing how developments in child-care policy in the 1990s reinforce and reflect a male model of citizenship that constructs barriers in the way of women's full social and political participation in Canadian society. Available on-line at <www.childcarecanada.org/resources>.

• Leah F. Vosko. *Temporary Work: The Gendered Rise of a Precarious Employment Relationship*. Toronto: University of Toronto Press, 2000. A history and analysis of how social norms and relations reflect and shape employment practices along gendered lines. The book includes an especially valuable examination of the relationship between the temporary help industry and workfare programs.

• *An Untidy Package*. Canada, 1997. Directed by Debbie McGee. NFB. Video. 48 min. The 1992 cod moratorium threw 35,000 Newfoundlanders out of work. About one-third of them were women. Their struggles to cope are represented through the experiences of the five women featured in this film.

• *Violence Can Happen to You*. Canada, 1998. Produced by Louise Ford. NFB. Video. 15 min. American sign language with English voiceover and captions. Through discussion and re-enactment, eight deaf/hearing impaired actors portray real stories of violence against women with disabilities.

• *When Strangers Re-Unite*. Canada, 1999. Directed by Marie Boti and Florchita Bautista. NFB. Video. 52 min. Thousands of women every year enter Canada as domestic servants, many from the Philippines. When their families can finally join them the transition is often difficult. This film tells of the challenges they face and the support offered by organizations within the Filipino-Canadian community working for the rights and welfare of migrant workers.

• *Why Women Run*. Canada, 1999. Directed by Meredith Ralston. NFB. Video, 46 min. Using the 1997 election contest between Alexa McDonough and Mary Clancy as a touchstone, this video highlights the accomplishments of women in politics and examines the particular challenges many women face when they participate in the political process.

• There are all sorts of journals and magazines on women's issues in Canada. Look for titles like *Atlantis, Herizons,* and *Canadian Woman Studies* in your local library, or find subscription information on the net.

Websites:

More and more electronic journals by and about women are being produced every day, many especially reflecting the perspectives of younger women. The on-line journal *Expository Magazine* provides a great list of websites linked to other women's e-journals and lists of e-journal websites.

Other key websites where you can find out more about women's issues and activism, with links to publications, associated organizations, and action guides, include those maintained by the Status of Women Canada, World March of Women, and the National Action Committee on the Status of Women.

Chapter Fourteen

We Have Just Begun

"Let's have another cup of coffee."

The example of a cup of coffee, which launched the questioning in *Getting Started* thirteen chapters ago, rounds it out in this chapter with the description of a unique trading company. It is the story of one continuing attempt at a solution. But many, many solutions are needed to all the problems unearthed by social analysis. This book, while not spelling out the solutions, suggests that an inevitable corollary to social analysis is the search for positive action.

That search has to be directed by certain priorities, from addressing the needs of the poor and the marginalized to recognizing the necessity of participation. The search, as we will see, carries social analysis into the realm of the political. It moves that realm closer to everyday life and some of life's obstacles and opportunities.

The Bridgehead Story

A Taste for Justice – that's the name of a Bridgehead Oxfam cookbook published in 1991.[1] The recipes combine ingredients made available to the North American market by a company whose motto is "People before Profit." Along with such items as coffee from Nicaragua, Tanzania, and the Dominican Republic, tea from Sri Lanka, cashew nuts from Honduras, and cocoa from Costa Rica, Bridgehead Trading also offers its customers a stake in international social justice, steadfastly sticking to its objective of bridging the gap between struggling Third World food producers and concerned Canadian consumers.

Begun in Toronto in 1981 by a small group of dedicated people, Bridgehead Trading was taken over by Oxfam-Canada in 1985. Coffee, which was the mainstay of the business, was at first sold through a network of committed volunteers. Over the years the company grew and diversified, dealing eventually in fifty countries and working with over two hundred suppliers. Through its catalogue operation, begun in 1987, and retail stores opened in the 1990s in Toronto, Ottawa, and Vancouver, Bridgehead, at its peak, grossed in the neighbourhood of $6.5 million a year, selling crafts, clothing, food, and furniture as well as coffee.[2] Over the years the complexities and risks of international trade toughened the resolve and educated the Bridgehead staff and volunteers in the realities of everyday economics. One measure of its success is its survival and continued commitment to its principles in a marketplace controlled by transnational corporations.

Bridgehead was a pioneer in what would soon grow into a global movement of alternative trade organizations. It preceded the International Federation for Alternative Trade (IFAT), which was established in 1989 and by 2003 had grown to represent 160 members in fifty countries. Its members include producer associations in Latin America, Africa, and Asia, as well as fair trade groups North and South.[3]

Bridgehead's goal of keeping costs low in order to return as much as possible to Third World producers has been buffeted by the realities of international trade. Although ongoing expenses could be met by sales, Bridgehead discovered that there is more to retailing than merely setting prices high enough to cover costs. Working capital can be a constant problem. In the 1980s, for example, Bridgehead placed a standing order with Nicaragua's National Union of Small Farms and Ranches (UNAG) for container lots of high-quality coffee beans. But each container of coffee tied up $100,000 for three or four months between shipments from the Nicaraguan port and arrival on the distributors' shelves in Canada. Without shareholder investments or its own capital and retained earnings, Bridgehead found itself having to borrow working capital and faced with interest charges that can mount quickly.

In order to survive, Bridgehead has had to evolve through a number of big changes in financing and ownership. In 1998 the company was bought by Shared Interest, a British lending co-op that specializes in financing in the fair trade sector. This was followed by another phase of "restructuring" in 2000, involving the closure of Bridgehead's retail stores and a move to "return the company to its fairly traded coffee and tea roots." This meant a narrower focus on retail and wholesale coffee, tea, and chocolate along with a modest line of giftware, sold on-line as well as through a print catalogue.

In April 2000 the company was sold once again, this time to two members of Bridgehead's management team. They went on to open their first coffeehouse in Ottawa later that year, followed by a second Ottawa coffeehouse in December 2001, with hopes of eventually opening a network of Bridgehead coffeehouses across the country.

Throughout all these changes, the company has remained committed to dealing fairly with its suppliers, and to the education of its customers. It also supports community groups, schools, churches, and others interested in participating in the kinds of action that follow from social analysis — for example, through the advice (and discounted products) it offers to groups engaged in fundraising projects. Bridgehead emphasizes, "You are making a difference by your participation!"

Bridgehead has also made an important difference through its part in the larger fair trade movement — which comprises organizations committed to an economic relationship that sustains producers rather than just the profits of buyers. Doing that means paying more than double the market price to growers. It also encourages growing methods that support communities and the natural environments they live in. Fair trade coffee is grown on small family-run farms and co- ops, and typically in the shade of a forest canopy. Producers are also paid a premium if the crop can be certified as organic. In 1999, 28 per cent of all Fair Trade Certified coffee was organic.

Changes like these are significant in such an enormous industry. Coffee is second only to oil as the world's most actively traded commodity, and in the United States over 70 per cent of this business is owned by only three transnational corporations: General Foods, Proctor and Gamble, and Nestlé. Coffee is also the third most-sprayed crop after cotton and tobacco. More than 70 per cent of the world's coffee is doused with synthetic chemicals, like malathion and DDT, that are illegal in Canada.

Coffee cultivation used to be much less environmentally destructive than other cash crops like bananas and sugar, due to its need for shade. The development of new high-yield varieties has put pressure on producers to turn to large-scale mono-cropping, which leads to soil erosion and land exhaustion as well as reliance on fertilizers and chemical pesticides. These changes in growing practices hurt both the land and the people who live on it. The support provided by fair trade companies for more ecologically and socially sustainable growing practices provides farmers with one of the few viable alternatives available to them.[4]

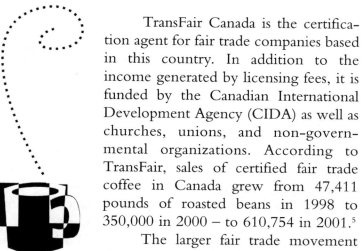

TransFair Canada is the certification agent for fair trade companies based in this country. In addition to the income generated by licensing fees, it is funded by the Canadian International Development Agency (CIDA) as well as churches, unions, and non-governmental organizations. According to TransFair, sales of certified fair trade coffee in Canada grew from 47,411 pounds of roasted beans in 1998 to 350,000 in 2000 — to 610,754 in 2001.[5]

The larger fair trade movement aims to create and sustain equitable partnerships between Western marketers and low-income artisans and farmers throughout the world, producing all sorts of agricultural and hand-crafted goods. This movement, also known as the alternative trade movement, began with the efforts of faith-based non-profit groups, through the sale of handcrafts, to support the economic recovery of people struggling to make a living in postwar Europe. In the 1970s and 1980s this movement shifted its focus to developing trade relationships that would ensure at least a living wage and otherwise help improve the circumstances of their Third World trade partners.

According to the 2002 *Report on Trends in the Fair Trade Industry*, "The fair trade movement is poised to grow dramatically in the next few years."[6] The success of the movement as a whole enables trading companies to better fulfil their commitment to bringing greater stability to what, especially in the case of coffee, is an extremely volatile market. The success of the movement means, among other things, that when companies like Bridgehead have to restructure, there is someone there to maintain trade relationships that might otherwise be in danger. It was a great relief to Tracey Clark of Bridgehead to be able to report, "Ten Thousand Villages, a fair trade organization operated by the Mennonite Central Committee in both Canada and the United States, purchases from virtually all of the handicraft producers who supplied Bridgehead, so the work will continue."[7]

Bridgehead is an example of social analysis leading to action. Its founders and owners, through their work in development education, have been working to raise Canadian awareness of the inequality and injustice of a complex economic system dominated by Western banks and governments and by transnational corporations that dominate production, processing, marketing, technology, and Third World commodity prices. According to this analysis, Canadians should not be condemned to serve as accomplices in the economic exploitation and political oppression of poor agricultural workers in the Third World. Bridgehead, and other organizations like it, represent one way, other than boycotts of certain products, to act in solidarity with these workers.

As the Canadian Conference of Catholic Bishops once put it: "It is not enough to see injustice, disorder, and violence at home and abroad and to worry about the future. These conditions will not improve on their own. We, the people, have the responsibility to change them."[8]

"After years of analyzing global poverty, you have to do something, take a stab at it yourself," said Peter Davies, one of Bridgehead's founders. "We didn't start out as another charity – but as a way of bringing producers and consumers together in new and fairer relationships."

Bridgehead Trading is based, then, on a sharp

> Northern consumers can, and should, rely on fair-trade labeling in supermarkets. But . . . a label is, of itself, quite worthless. It may be imbued with all the mystique of a "brand" – the costs of which account for a sizable chunk of the price you pay – but for fair-traders it has another job to do, identifying people you are better able to trust because you know who they are. Where conventional trade hides behind a veil of commercial secrecy, fair trade makes a virtue of telling you more. You may not be able to change the world as much as you would like by shopping with your eyes open – but keeping them closed makes absolutely certain that it stays the same.
>
> — David Ransom,
> *The No-Nonsense Guide to Fair Trade*, 2001.

critique of unjust marketing structures, national no less than global. It counters the excesses of the profit motive by recycling earnings. Its alternative trading approach challenges the dominant structures of ownership, marketing, distribution, and retail sales. It expresses solidarity and eschews the unfair competition of giant transnational corporations versus tiny Third World producers. Compared with the dimensions of the problem it has been attempting to address, Bridgehead is at once a modest and successful venture.

The Bridgehead example not only provides valuable lessons but also leads to further special analysis. Bridgehead's successes and difficulties raise questions about the food industry in Canada. If alternative trading can be successful, what are the obstacles to establishing thousands of bridge-building companies? If alternative trading makes sense for Third World producers, could Canadian farm products be marketed in a similar way?

The Game

In some ways we are encouraged to think of the struggle for social and economic survival in Canada as one great game. According to the Canadian sense of fair play, everyone has a good chance to win and no one should triumph at the expense of others. The final goal of the game is power – which in essence means some kind of control over the rules of the game. Unfortunately, relatively few people ever achieve that goal.

Commercials on TV serve up the Canadian game in its slickest form. Secure and youthful families, made happy by the products they consume, relax on warm summer afternoons. There is always clean air, good food, and abundant energy.

But for people who do social analysis, the TV commercials raise questions. Where are the blizzards, the polluted rivers, the Aboriginal peoples, the bag ladies, the unemployed? What about the housing crisis, the older Canadians shunted off to the side, the upheaval caused by rapidly changing technologies?

According to conventional wisdom, there must be something wrong with people who ask such questions.

- They are a downer, pessimists who will always go on about the glass being half-empty.
- They have proved unable to compete in Canada as it is. They're just poor losers.
- They resent the success of others. As moralizers and chronic complainers, they enjoy criticizing. They like to take all the fun out of the game.
- They exaggerate the plight of the poor and disadvantaged, who, after all, are relatively few in an otherwise prosperous and egalitarian country.
- They overlook the countless benefits of life in Canada and don't know how good they have it. They are simply ungrateful.
- They have an anarchistic or subversive streak in them. They seem to be addicted to change for its own sake.

But there is a different explanation for why people ask such critical questions. Social analysis, which begins with the ordinary problems of everyday life, soon makes it clear that commercial advertisements portray a false Canada. In the real Canada, the environment is imperilled, machines threaten to displace workers, many people live out on the edge, and corporate rather than human values often seem to prevail.

The game is rigged, social analysis tells us, and the deck is stacked. The stated rules and principles are one thing, but how they work is quite another. Talk of "a just society" and "equal opportunity" and "free competition" masks unfair advantages possessed by a relatively few "winners," whose access to these advantages is predetermined by accidents of birth: class, sex, and ethnic origin. Some people have a head start. Many others — like women, the aged, Aboriginal people, people with disabilities, people of colour, or in general the poor and unemployed who can't find decent work or housing — never get into the official game at all.

Getting Started analyzes Canadian society from the viewpoint of those who have been cheated or unfairly penalized. The analysis speaks up for those who remain on the sidelines with no public role to play. It makes visible the essential labour of those who are permitted only to work behind the scenes (with little or no financial or other credit).

But is it enough to point out, over and over again, that the game is rigged? Do social analysis and the concerns it nourishes translate into anything besides talk and more analysis?

"What Can We Do?"

Spontaneously bursting into action may satisfy one or two people for a little while, but it rarely proves effective. Action requires careful planning. Just as analysis is best developed in the give and take of discussion, so too is action best decided upon in co-operation with other people. The decisions to be made are many: pursuing a question further, getting into deeper research, joining a group, contacting others, taking collective action.

The question of action seems to come "at the end." Yet social analysis is oriented towards action right from the start. Social analysis, as defined in *Getting Started*, means *raising questions about society and seeking answers*. It helps to *develop a critical awareness* of the world — that is, of how and against whom the deck is stacked, how the rules are bent or broken, and for whose benefit. By uncovering concrete, particular instances of foul play that people can do something about, social analysis also helps to *lead towards social justice*.

"We Can't Afford to Change"

Social analysis seems to cry out for answers, but easy answers, ideal models of society, or perfect social organizations waiting to be copied do not exist. Thorny problems abound. Bridgehead Trading, ultimately a success story, is no easy answer. A package of recipes for change or one overarching scheme of reforms won't be found in *Getting Started*.

If there are no answers, then what is the point, many will ask themselves, of getting involved in social analysis and change? (See the "Social Paralysis Quiz" at the end of chapter one.) Here are several reasons why Canadians feel reluctant to get involved.

■ Some people are comfortable and don't want to be disturbed – even though their comfort starkly contrasts with the pain of many others. Some are merely cynical and believe that *"plus ça change..."*

■ Others feel sorry for the victims of injustice. They hope the poor, whether in Canada or the Third World, will get a better shake. But these sentiments are short-circuited by other values – for example, faith in "the marketplace" or in "freedom of opportunity."

■ Some believe that there are no class barriers in Canada – just as there are supposed to be no racial or sexual barriers – and some people also believe the poor can "make it" if they only put in the effort.

■ Some Canadians who do admit to the existence of social injustices are blocked by the fear that any potential solution will prove as expensive and messy as the original problem.

■ Many Canadians long for peace and security, but are convinced that they can do nothing to change the injustices that inevitably lead to poverty, violence, and war. Their longing remains abstract and sentimental.

■ Personal comfort and security, vague longings for peace, empty sympathy for the unfortunate, fear of future complications – these attitudes leave many Canadians feeling paralyzed and powerless. The dominant ideology either denies that the problems are real or claims that they can be solved by tinkering. This only reinforces the sense of paralysis. Proposed solutions are easily dismissed as idealistic, partial, and unfeasible. Thus the status quo is – apparently – justified.

But not addressing the issues proves very costly. For the status-quo argument overlooks the tremendous human, economic, and social costs of accepting the current patterns of social and economic relationships. Each chapter of this book demonstrates that the current situation is an all-too-messy and unfair one. The system not only fails to work, but also cannot work for significant numbers of Canadians:

■ women, old people, people with disabilities, Aboriginal peoples, people of colour
■ the unemployed and the underemployed
■ workers threatened by the revolution in new technology
■ several million people in search of affordable housing
■ all of us who are losing the right to a safe and healthy environment.

The decision to maintain things as they are contains its own acute contradictions and holds out little promise for the future. The burden of proof should be on those who would claim that change will be too costly and painful. Anyone who begins to do social analysis will quickly be forced to ask, "How can we afford not to change?"

Beyond Paralysis

The stories about community health centres (chapter two), citizens using new technologies as tools for global organizing (chapter nine), Aboriginal peoples struggling for self-government (chapter twelve), and Bridgehead challenging world trade patterns (earlier in this chapter) – these are all good examples of solutions in progress.

In each case, people saw that something was wrong, or found an injustice. They figured out what was going on, developed a strategy, and began to build an alternative. Other examples can be found in the Resources at the end of nearly every chapter, where we have listed further information and groups to contact.

Envisaging alternatives and shaping solutions involve people's beliefs and values. How do social analysts sort out the various voices, the conflicting interests, and the competing needs, rights, and demands? A simple principled commitment provides the guiding thread. In the words of David Hollenbach, a Catholic social philosopher: "The needs of the poor take priority over the wants of the rich. The freedom of the dominated takes priority over the liberty of the powerful. The participation of marginalized groups takes priority over the preservation of an order which excludes them."[9]

These three points make challenging criteria for orienting social analysis and grounding the solutions that emerge. Many people in Canada would affirm them wholeheartedly, at least in theory. But can they be put into practice? Yes, if the problem is concrete and if it carries with it the possibility of concrete solutions.

First, the needs of the poor and the exclusion of the marginalized need to be clearly considered. To come to an appreciation of these needs, this exclusion *in the concrete*, is a task of social analysis. By providing the necessary tools for understanding the real problems in particular cases (instead of producing merely vague feelings about social injustice in general), social analysis can help people to honour these priorities in practice.

Second, people need to envisage concrete, viable solutions – solid alternatives to the problems analyzed. People need to imagine change. Most chapters of *Getting Started* contain examples of people working together – often with the help of others from outside their group or class – and solving their own problems. Stories of change taking place, the failures no less than the successes, need to be exchanged among people doing social analysis.

The moral of all the stories: The way things are is not how they have to be.

Participation

In recent years we've heard a lot about how Canadians have become thoroughly disillusioned with the political process. Opinion polls and the media alike indicate that we have developed a deep distrust of politicians and their promises.

On a national scale this mood expressed itself repeatedly in the final decade of the last millennium. It was reflected in the failure of the Meech Lake constitutional process and the "no" vote in the 1992 referendum on the Charlottetown Accord. So too was it expressed in the 1993 federal election, when Canadians elected a large number of MPs from what were then two new upstart parties (Reform and the Bloc Québécois) and humiliated two old parties, the Progressive Conservatives and the NDP.

Things went from bad to worse in the federal election of 2000, which had the lowest voter turnout in seventy-five years. Observers noted that nearly 40 per cent of the eligible voters were "no longer bothering to cast their ballots" and that many Canadians were feeling "cut off by remote governments and powerless to change the system."[10] The trend in voter apathy, particularly among the young and poor, had become so worrying that the Law Commission of Canada embarked on its own study of the problem. In 2002 the Commission reported: "There are signs that the debate about electoral reform is gaining momentum. It is important for all Canadians to be engaged meaningfully in this debate. After all, discussing such an important component of Canadian political life is itself a way to maintain a healthy democracy." The Commission suggested that a system of proportional representation might encourage "higher voter turnout, better

Canada's current voting system and federal government structure effectively violate the fundamental democratic principles of one-person, one-vote, representation by population, and free and fair elections. . . . Many changes are needed to have a voting system and government that respects the rights of voters to have their votes count equally, and to have representative, elected and honest government. . . . Among the undemocratic aspects of the current voting system and federal government structure are as follows: one political party usually forms a majority government after winning support from only a minority of voters; the Senate is appointed, not elected; and political parties and governments can make fraudulent and misleading statements with no accountability.

— Democracy Watch, "Democracy Watch Launches Voter Rights Campaign, Calling for Representative, Elected and Honest Government," Nov. 27, 2001.

representation of women and minority groups, and more open government."[11]

While voting is obviously important, between election and referendum campaigns the impact of our participation in public decision-making seems no more effective than the "vote" about what will be on the supermarket shelf (see chapter four). Unless they are party activists, few Canadians participate in the electoral process in any significant way. Maybe it is normal for people who feel powerless to also feel apathetic about party politics. Some would argue that there is more participation in a Stanley Cup playoff game.

Referendum campaigns like those we've had nationwide over the constitution, or in Quebec over sovereignty, allow everyone to focus on and debate a single issue. Referenda, however, are rare. Some critics advocate holding referenda more regularly, on a variety of issues. But such votes have their pitfalls. They can reduce complex issues to a simple yes/no response – and they "empower" those who pose the question.

Election campaigns tend to avoid in-depth discussions of social policies, concentrating instead on political strategy and reducing issues to twenty-second sound bites for TV news or two-sentence quotes for newspapers. Indeed, one of the perils that democracy faces is that citizens have often been reduced to the role of spectators, fascinated by the unfolding drama – whose "handler" or pollster is more effective? What tactic is candidate A following to discredit candidate B? Or we become cynical about politics as a game of manipulation by backstage managers. Either way, political life – in which people engage with important issues – is eroded.

What falls into the realm of the political? At first sight, politics refers to elections, town councils, and legislatures. Between elections Canadians tend to leave not only party politics but also social issues in the hands of parliamentarians and city councillors. That is a pity. Federal, provincial, and local representatives can be made responsive to pressure from their constituents and enlisted to help resolve certain issues. Public administrators can also be identified, informed, and pressured to help solve social difficulties. These methods are effective to a degree. But some Canadians have concluded that more intervention, more activity, is necessary to grab the attention of political leaders.

Canadians are becoming more upset at the lack of responsiveness of elected leaders to the views of the populace. For many this disregard was vividly symbolized by the concrete and chain-link fence erected by the government around the heart of Quebec City at the Summit of the Americas in 2001. Defended by six thousand heavily armoured police officers, the wall was meant to protect representatives of powerful nations and business leaders from the voices of dissent in the streets.[12]

There were plenty of voices to be heard – 30,000 according to police estimates, over 60,000 according to media and protest organizers – from all over Canada, the Americas, and other parts of the world, places that were feeling the impact of free-trade policies on which they had not been consulted. Even more were there in spirit if not in body. According to one poll, one in five adult Canadians – that's 4.4 million people – would have been part of the Quebec City protests if they had been able to afford the travel and time.[13]

The social action at Quebec City did not take place only on the streets. It also occurred in the hundreds of formal and informal meetings that took place there at the People's Summit, where, in contrast to the official summit, the emphasis was on participation. Participants educated themselves on the issues, shared their knowledge, and exposed themselves to the experience and analyses of people from many other walks of life. They asked critical questions, explored answers, and produced statements meant to share the perspectives achieved through this process and to inspire the kind of continuing reflection and action that is the hallmark of social analysis. The protest actions were also characterized by creativity, from multilingual banners and signs to the person with a ukelele singing "Don't Fence Me In." Some participants danced alone and in groups. Others performed street theatre in costumes (like the cow outfits worn by a group calling itself "Mad Cows Against Globalization").[14]

Creativity and humour are effective vaccines against rigid and dogmatic thinking, and a tonic for the openness and critical questioning essential for social analysis. It becomes even more necessary when critical questioning and organized expressions of dissent are regarded as threats rather than the lifeblood of democracy. Amnesty International condemned the police response in Quebec as an excessive use of force – it included tear gas, water cannons, rubber bullets, and electric shock devices even though there was no threat to police or private property.[15] One participant later wrote:

> In a democracy isn't it the role of citizens to take a vigilant interest in public affairs? When people see their rights stunted and diminished (indeed privatized) isn't it their democratic duty to rally and defend them? It felt like what the conference organizers really wanted was not active citizens at all. What they wanted felt more like consumers of "good news" who would sit in front of their TV sets and nod enthusiastically at all the limos, photo ops and final communiqués.[16]

Hostility towards criticism intensified in Canada and the United States after the attacks on the World Trade towers and the Pentagon on September 11, 2001. After that tragic day, following the U.S. lead, the Canadian government added hastily enacted anti-terrorist legislation to its "national security" arsenal. Spending on security and intelligence was increased, and sophisticated surveillance technology became used in increasingly intrusive ways.

These methods of fighting a "war against terrorism" pose a serious threat to democratic participation in Canada. When criticisms of a given economic and social order are confused with attacks on democracy, the "war against terrorism" has a chilling effect on the peaceful expression of discontent, and on action aimed at redressing injustice. Social analysis is crucial here too.

When government officials tell us that everything from agricultural subsidies to Canadian control of its own borders may "undermine the war on terrorism," it is time to ask critical questions.[17] Fortunately, concerned Canadians are doing this. Individual citizens as well as diverse religious, legal, social, and community groups have gathered to consider these issues and publicly express their concerns. In November 2001, for example, the Canadian Association of University Teachers (CAUT) unanimously voted to urge the government to withdraw its proposed anti-terrorism act and "initiate a process of public consultation during which time a genuine discussion could occur over the measures necessary to safeguard the rights and freedoms of Canadians." While the government was less than responsive, CAUT remained committed:

> The ascendance of "national security" as a state priority is particularly tragic because the real security of Canadians can best be measured by the strength of the civil liberties and human rights that its residents enjoy. In this regard, academic staff – a profession that depends on the unfettered examination of ideas no matter how popular or unpopular and relies for its continued vitality and relevance upon freedom of speech, freedom of thought and the free flow of information – have a special role to play in defending these fundamental values. At the same time, they have much to lose as these rights are diminished by the "war on terrorism."[18]

Social analysis is both a condition for, and a form

of participation. Without social literacy (see chapter six), people cannot take an intelligent – much less an active and creative – part in the issues unfolding around them. At the same time the very activity of social analysis, especially in a group, helps to "lift the fog" and overcome ideological confusion (see chapter ten). It can lead directly into effective action.

Through social analysis, citizens can overcome their sense of intimidation – or cynicism – in the face of bureaucracy and conventional politics. The experience of social analysis can gradually involve people more and more in the decisions that have an impact on their own lives. At the same time, to do social analysis in Canada is to realize how truly complex and ambiguous is the Canadian game. It is not a simple conflict of good guys versus bad. No one is conspiring to gain complete power over the rules.

The only just – the only democratic – approach to these complexities is found in the sometimes boring, often rewarding process of participation. In this way, the notion of democracy expands beyond the ballot box, and the notion of politics stretches to include daily life.

Participation, not a new theme, runs throughout all of *Getting Started*.

- "Issues in the Everyday" – Confronting basic health, housing, food distribution, and workplace problems, people gather information, develop their own expertise, and set up alternative organizations. A food co-op, a tenants' group, a neighbourhood task force to set up a health centre, a group of workers seeking unionization – the participants may solve the immediate problem and at the same time win some control over fundamental aspects of their lives. They also lay the groundwork for understanding and acting on the economic structures that frame their lives. A just, participatory, and sustainable society requires whole new ways of organizing production, work, distribution, and consumption. Beginning to provide the needed creativity are all sorts of union initiatives, new small businesses, workers' and consumers' co-ops, government projects, and self-help groups – or, in other words, people participating in what we might call economic democracy.

- "The World Around Us" – When we take a look around, we see that "the environment" is not some wilderness or nature preserve. It is where we live; it is the world we are a part of. Its survival and ours depend on an increased awareness of the impact of our actions on the world around us, especially when we act on government or corporate policies and programs that don't include environmental damage in their cost-benefit analyses. Technological change and developments in global economics are often presented as if they are forces of nature, as powerful and inevitable as the weather. Powerful they certainly are, but like global climate change they result from human actions – actions that are as open to questioning and redirection as any other conditions.

- "People and Perspectives" – When we look at basic and economic issues from the specific viewpoints of excluded groups of people, it helps us to see things in a different light. Each group – old people, Aboriginal peoples, and women – has contributed to society in important but typically unrecognized ways, and the value of those contributions will not be recognized or their full potential realized unless those groups – and others like them – gain a new level of self-determination. Third World peoples struggling to improve their own lot in life not only win our concrete support for that struggle, but can also inspire us to face our own problems.

Participation grows and increases in interrelated steps: basic control and economic democracy, local action, global awareness, and political self-determination. At no stage does participation provide ready-made solutions; but it does provide the means of approaching solutions. Participation is not a platform or a stopgap measure, nor is it just a means or a temporary tactic. Participation is a goal that makes many other goals possible. It is one very important fruit of social analysis.

At the same time, participation is a first step and often a very small one. The crime, as a philosopher once said, is to do nothing because we fear we can do only a little. But small changes are important in themselves. Moreover, they can generate a so-called critical mass, a movement that eventually turns a seemingly impossible change into an inevitable one. Each of these local, partial solutions helps to improve the workings of society. At the same time, few of these solutions will endure or fulfil their total promise without large-scale reforms of structures in this country and internationally.

People come together to analyze a problem. They overcome social paralysis and discover a power of their own. They run into blocks, difficulties, and obstacles. As they confront them, they generate more power. They move beyond the ballot box. They press for significant change, demanding adequate public notice and more opportunity for input when major decisions are made. Social analysis guides this progression through basic, economic, and social issues. Participation nourishes the connections among people across the country who are doing social analysis, working on concrete issues locally and regionally, contributing in novel ways.

What can happen in Canada if people link up, raise questions together, and participate in a collective analysis and a search for collective solutions? We have truly just begun.

> Just as structures of domination support one another, so do our efforts at justice. The sum of the changes that we seek eludes us as a total system because those working for change have less power than the complex and entrenched institutions of hierarchical power that dominate our world. But lured on by the ground already attained and by the ground of that ground that empowers us, we remember the words of Mishnah Avot 2:16: "It is not incumbent upon us to finish the task, but neither are we free to desist from it altogether."
>
> — Judith Plaskow,
> *Standing Again at Sinai,* 1990.

Resources

We hope that users of *Getting Started* who want to reflect further on social analysis or compare the approach taken here with other approaches will find the following list useful.

- Rick Arnold, Bev Burke, Carl James, D'Arcy Martin, and Barb Thomas. *Educating for a Change.* Toronto: Between the Lines and Doris Marshall Institute for Education and Action, 1991. Decades of experience in social education provide both introductory theory and practical tools for applying the principles of democratic practice to daily work.
- Ken Battle and Sherri Torjman. *Social Policy That Works: An Agenda.* Ottawa: Caledon Institute of Social Policy, 2002. Informed by a social justice perspective, this report outlines the key areas of social policy that demand analysis and action in Canada today, with recommendations for effective alternatives.
- Bev Burke, Jojo Geronimo, D'Arcy Martin, Barb Thomas, and Carol Wall. *Education for Changing Unions.* A follow-up to *Educating for a Change*, this book is a storehouse of ideas, practical exercises, and debate aimed at building action and understanding within a union context.
- Tony Clarke and Sarah Dopp. *Challenging McWorld.* Ottawa: Canadian Centre for Policy Alternatives, 2001. This workbook is designed to help concerned youth develop skills for confronting globalization in their daily lives, with tools developed in workshops conferences and teach-ins with young people and their allies.
- Tara Goldstein and David Selby. *Weaving Connections: Educating for Peace, Social and Environmental Justice.* Toronto: Sumach Press, 2000. Committed to the view that education is crucial to building social progress, this collection of articles describes educational models based on the principles of tolerance, equity, and justice. With its focus on ideas and practice developed over the past three decades by teachers, students, parents, and activists, it is a call to action by progressive educators.

• The Harmony Institute, Victoria, B.C. <www.harmonyfdn.ca> has issued "workshop manuals," including *Community Action Workshop Manual* (2001) and a companion volume, *Climate Change: A Profile for Community Action*, as well as others on biodiversity, water, and Northern climate issues.

• Brian K. Murphy. *Transforming Ourselves/Transforming the World: An Open Conspiracy for Social Change*. Halifax: Fernwood Publishing, 1999. The author explores the social and personal dilemmas that hold people back from social engagement and how these obstacles can be overcome. A book for community workers, social activists, adult educators, and everyone else who wants to overcome pessimism and play a part in changing things for the better.

• Darryl Novak and Linda Vieregge. *Action for Change: A Guide to Activism with Public Interest Research Groups*. WPIRG, University of Waterloo, 2000. This handbook for starting and running public interest research groups is available through any of the twenty-one PIRG groups across Canada. PIRGS are non-profit organizations funded and directed by university students; they conduct research education and action on social and environmental justice issues. Links to local chapters can be found at <www.opirg.org>. The handbook is also available on-line.

• The Otesha Project, Kanata, Ont., is just one example of a group taking action "to change the world." The word "Otesha" means "reason to dream" in Swahili, and the organization was created as a means of spreading this message. "We are a growing organization of young people dedicated to helping our generation of youth become aware, hopeful and empowered global citizens" <www.otesha.ca>.

• Maureen Wilson and Elizabeth Whitmore. *Seeds of Fire: Social Development in the Era of Globalization*. Halifax: Fernwood Publishing, 2000. All over the world, in popular movements, ordinary citizens are working to rebuild their lives and communities in the wake of economic globalization. The authors explore "globalization from below," social change led by people at the local level. They explain how this change can be supported by "accompaniment," a model of solidarity practised internationally through global grassroots alliances.

• *Democracy à la Maude*. Canada, 1998. Directed by Patricia Kearns. NFB. Video. 61 min. A portrait of Maude Barlow, Canadian activist and leader of the Council of Canadians, this country's largest citizen's rights group. "How dare we give this up without a fight?" she asks, "It will probably take the rest of our lives to turn this around. But then, what else have we got to do?"

• *Journey to Justice*. Canada, 2000. Directed by Roger McTair. NFB. Video. 47 min. This documentary pays tribute to five Canadians who led a historic struggle against racism in this country: Viola Desmond, Fred Christie, Hugh Burnette, Bromley Armstrong, Donald Willard Moore, and Stanley G. Grizzle. Between the 1930s and 1950s each of these people took their case against racism to court, helping to secure justice for all Canadians.

Websites:

Bridgehead Trading and TransFair Canada both have websites. To learn more about fair trade, visit the website of the Fair Trade Federation. Included among its links is the *2002 Report on Fair Trade Trends in the U.S. and Canada* (Washington D.C.: Co-Op America Business Network, April 2002).

One of the most valuable electronic gateways to information and organizations involved in social justice analysis and action is located at the Canadian Social Research Links website, with links to hundreds of sites, including the Canadian Centre for Policy Alternatives, Caledon Institute of Social Policy, Centre for Social Justice, Inter Pares, and many more.

Notes

Chapter One

Welcome to Social Analysis

1. "Coffee Cartel Shuts up Shop," BBC News, Oct. 19, 2001, <news.bbc.co.uk/hi/english/business> (July 12, 2002).

2. Liz Armstrong and Adrienne Scott, *Whitewash: Exposing Health and Environmental Dangers of Women's Sanitary Products and Disposable Diapers – What You Can Do About It* (Toronto: HarperPerennial, 1992), p.9.

3. "Oxfam Paper on EU Common Agricultural Policy (CAP) Reform," Canadian Sugar Institute, Toronto, August 2000 <www.sugar.ca> (Dec. 17, 2002).

4. Canadian Conference of Catholic Bishops, *Ethical Choices and Political Challenges*, Ottawa, 1983, p.2.

5. Canadian Council of Churches, "*Just* Trade, not Just Trade: Towards a more Neighbourly Economy," Quebec Summit Statement, April 9, 2001 <www.ccc-cce.ca/ english/jp/ quebecsummitstatement> (July 12, 2002).

Chapter Two

In Sickness and in Health

1. Canadian Institutes of Health Research (CIHR), Institute of Gender and Health, Institute News, "Institute of Gender and Health Recommendations Relevant to Romanow Commission Report, IGH Citations," Ottawa, 2002 <www.cihr-irsc.gc.ca>, p.155 (Jan. 22, 2003). See also Esyllt Jones and Anna Ste Croix Rothney, "Women's Health and Social Inequality," paper, Canadian Centre for Policy Alternatives (CCPA), Ottawa, November 2001.

2. National Forum on Health, *Canada Health Action: Building on the Legacy*, Final Report, vol. 1, Ottawa, 1997, p.15.

3. See, for instance, Manitoba Centre for Health Policy, "The Health and Health Care Use of Registered First Nations People Living in Manitoba: A Population-Based Study" (short title: "Health and Health Care: Manitoba's First Nations"), University of Manitoba, Winnipeg, March 2002.

4. National Forum on Health, *Canada Health Action*, p.9.

5. David Suzuki, "Expanding the Health Care Debate," *Canadian Medical Association Journal*, vol. 166 (June 25, 2002), pp.1678-79.

6. Canadian Public Health Association Board of Directors, "Health Impacts of Social and Economic Conditions: Implications for Public Policy," discussion paper, Ottawa, March 1997, p.14.

7. "Comparing the Canadian and U.S. Health Care Systems," *The CCPA Monitor*, May 2002, p.26.

8. Michael Rachlis and Carol Kushner, *Second Opinion: What's Wrong with Canada's Health-Care System* (Toronto: Collins, 1989), p.174.

9. "Antismokers Cheered by 'Fantastic Numbers,'" *The Globe and Mail*, Jan. 22, 2002, p.A7.

10. Jean Swanson, *Poor-Bashing: The Politics of Exclusion* (Toronto: Between the Lines, 2001), p.80.

11. Nancy Milo, Promoting Health through Public Policy (Ottawa: Canadian Public Health Association, 1986), p.75, quoted in the Premier's Council on Health Strategy, "Nurturing Health: A Framework on the Determinants of Health," Toronto, March 1991, p.3.

12. Amy Zierler, "Socio-Economic Status and Health Care Services," summary of a report by Cam Mustard et al., "Socioeconomic Gradients in Mortality and the Use of Health Care Services at Different Stages in the Life Course," Manitoba Centre for Health Policy, University of Manitoba, Winnipeg, September 1995.

13. Richard Swift, "Health Hazard: We Don't Have to Live on the Critical List," *The New Internationalist*, January/February 2001, p.10.

14. Richard Schabas, "Public Health: What Is to Be Done?" *Canadian Medical Association Journal*, vol. 186 (May 14, 2002), p.1282.

15. Wendy Mitchinson, "The Medical Treatment of Women," in *Changing Patterns: Women in Canada*, 2nd ed., ed. Sandra Burt, Lorraine Code, and Lindsay Dorney (Toronto: McClelland & Stewart, 1993), p.394.

16. Premier's Council on Health Strategy, "Nurturing Health," p.3.

17. Alvin Finkel and Margaret Conrad, with Veronica Strong-Boag, *History of the Canadian Peoples*, vol. 2, *1867 to the Present* (Toronto: Copp Clark Pitman, 1993), pp.440-41.

18. E.M. Hall, Canada's National-Provincial Health Program for the 1980's, Ottawa, 1980, p.2.

19. M.A. Baltzan, "Deductible Insurance Could Rationalize Medicare," *Canadian Medical Association Journal*, vol.126 (1982), p.550.

20. Ivan Illich, *Limits to Medicine – Medical Nemesis: The Expropriation of Health* (Harmondsworth, Mddx.: Pelican Books, 1977), p.11.

21. Canadian Institute for Health Information, "Health Care in Canada, 2002," report, Ottawa, May 29, 2002.

22. Manitoba Centre for Health Policy, "Socio-Economic Status and Health Care Services."

23. Premier's Council on Health Strategy, "Nurturing Health," p.3.

24. Michael Rachlis, Robert G. Evans, Patrick Lewis, and Morris L. Barer, "Revitalizing Medicare: Shared Problems, Public Solutions," paper, Tommy Douglas Research Institute, January 2001, p.6; Monique Bégin, "Legislative Reforms Needed to Strengthen, Expand Medicare," *The CCPA Monitor*, May 2002, p.18.

25. Martin Mittelstaedt, "Harris Gives Job Loss New Spin, Hospitals Likened to Hula-Hoop Fad," *The Globe and Mail*, June 3, 1997.

26. Canadian Institute for Health Information, "Health Care in Canada, 2002."

27. Ibid., p.27.

28. Canada, *Building on Values: The Final Report of the Commission on the Future of Health Care in Canada* (Romanow Report), Ottawa, Nov. 28, 2002.

29. Kevin Taft and Gillian Steward, *Clear Answers: The Economics and Politics of For-Profit Medicine* (Edmonton: Duval House Publishing, University of Alberta Press, and Parkland Institute, 2000), p.97.

30. Rachlis et al., "Revitalizing Medicare," p.6.

31. Thomas Walkom, "Behind the Push for Private Clinics," *The Toronto Star*, June 25, 2002.

32. Ibid.

33. Canada, *Building on Values*. See also "Romanow's $15-Billion Cure," *The Globe and Mail*, Nov. 29, 2002, p.A1; and the various responses to the report in that issue. The Romanow report followed closely on the heels of the report of the Senate Standing Committee on Social Affairs, Science and Technology, chaired by Senator Michael J.L. Kirby, issued in October 2002.

34. Dr. Michael Rachlis, "Building Relationships: Developing an Organized Approach to Facilitating the Management of Chronic Illness in British Columbia," paper, Victoria, B.C., April 2002.

35. Canadian Policy Research Networks, "Citizens' Dialogue on Health Care Yields Fascinating Results," a paper prepared for the Commission on the Future of Health Care (Romanow Commission), June 26, 2002.

36. Canada, *Building on Values*, p.116. See also "Non-health Spending 'Getting Squeezed Out,'" *The Globe and Mail*, Nov. 29, 2002, p.A10; and "Romanow Recommendations a Boost for CHCs in Ontario," press release, Association of Ontario Health Centres, Toronto, Nov. 29, 2002.

37. Canadian Auto Workers, "Let's Unite to Keep It So: CAW Summary of Roy Romanow's Report," press release, Nov. 29, 2002, p.4 <www.ca.caw/campaigns&issues>.

38. Terrence Sullivan and Patricia Baranek, *First Do No Harm: Making Sense of Canadian Health Reform* (Toronto: Malcolm Lester, 2002), p.23; Pat Armstrong et al., *Take Care: Warning Signals for Canada's Health System* (Toronto: Garamond Press, 1994).

39. National Forum on Health, *Canada Health Action: Building on the Legacy*, synthesis reports and issues papers, Ottawa, 1997, p.19.

40. Canadian Institute for Health Information, "Health Care in Canada," 2002; Joel Lexchin, "A National Pharmacare Plan: Combining Efficiency and Equity," paper, Canadian Centre for Policy Alternatives, Ottawa, March 2001.

41. Lexchin, "National Pharmacare Plan"; see also "Pharmacare Is Both Needed and Affordable," *The CPPA Monitor*, May 2001, p.7.

42. Prithi Yelaja, "More Die in For-Profit Hospitals, Study Says," *The Toronto Star*, May 28, 2002; the study was published in the May 28, 2002, issue of *Canadian Medical Association Journal*.

43. Rachlis et al., "Revitalizing Medicare."

44. These examples are described in detail in Rachlis et al., "Revitalizing Medicare."

45. Rachlis et al., "Revitalizing Medicare." p.v.

46. Canada, Building on Values, p.116, and appendices; "Romanow's Forecast for 'Primary Health Care' Means Community Health Centres for Ontario," op-ed article, Association of Ontario Health Centres, Toronto, Nov. 29, 2002. <www.aohc.org>.

Chapter Three

No Place Like Home

1. National Housing and Homelessness Network (NHHN), *State of the Crisis, 2001: A Report on Housing and Homelessness in Canada*, Toronto, Nov. 26, 2001, p.5.

2. J. David Hulchanski, "Housing and a Sustainable Social Fabric," review draft, housing paper, Canadian Policy Research Networks (CPRN), December 2002, p.8.

3. Jeanne M. Wolfe, "Canadian Housing Policy in the Nineties," *Housing Studies*, vol.13, no.1 (1998), pp.121-33.

4. Hulchanski, "Housing and a Sustainable Social Fabric," p.10.

5. *Today*, Jan. 30, 1980.

6. John Ota, "2. Lead a Sheltered Life," in "7 Habits of Highly Effective Nations," *This Magazine*, January/February 2001, p.22.

7. Doug Faulkner, interviewed by Frances Bula, "No Place Like Home," *Ideas*, CBC Radio, Oct. 25, 26, 1999.

8. Dan Devaney, "Duct Tape and Cardboard: Governments Downgrade Social Housing Commitments While Improving Tax-Shelters for the Rich," *Briarpatch*, April 2001, p.14.

9. Barbara Loevinger Rahder, "Women Plan Toronto: Incorporating Gender Issues in Urban Planning," *Planners Network Online*, no.130 (July/August 1998).

10. Hulchanski, "Housing and a Sustainable Social Fabric," p.8. See also J. David Hulchanski, "A Tale of Two Canadas: Homeowners Getting Richer, Renters Getting Poorer, 1984 and 1999," *Research Bulletin*, no.2, Centre for Urban and Community Studies, University of Toronto; Hulchanski, "The Evolution of Property Rights and Housing Tenure in Post-War Canada: Implications for Housing Policy," *Urban Law and Policy*, vol.9, no. 2 (1988), pp.135-56; and Hulchanski, interviewed by Bula, "No Place Like Home."

11. NHHN, *State of the Crisis*.

12. Federation of Canadian Municipalities, *National Affordable Housing Strategy*, Ottawa, Oct. 11, 2000, p.4. See <www.fcm.ca/english/national/strategy2-e.pdf>.

13. *Golden Report*, with emphasis added, quoted by Jack Layton, *Homelessness: The Making and Unmaking of a Crisis* (Toronto: Penguin Canada and McGill Institute, 2000), p.29.

14. *The Toronto Star*, Sept. 5, 1992.

15. Elaine Carey, "High-Rise Ghettos: In Toronto, Visible Minorities Are Pushed into 'Pockets of Poverty,'"

The Toronto Star, at Ontario Network for Human Rights website <www.geocities.com/CapitolHill/6174/housingghettos> (July 12, 2002).

16. Margaret Philp, "Poor? Coloured? Then It's No Vacancy: Housing Discrimination Rampant, Says Poverty Report, Despite Fact That Visible Minorities Are Poised to Become City's Majority," *The Globe and Mail*, July 18, 2000.

17. Carey, "High Rise Ghettos." See also Grace-Edward Galabuzi, "Canada's Creeping Economic Apartheid: The Economic Segregation and Social Marginalization of Racialized Groups," CSJ Foundation for Research and Education, Toronto, May 2001, p.76: "Research shows that the quality of a neighbourhood significantly affects the life chances of its residents."

18. Quoted in Carey, "High Rise Ghettos."

19. Canada, *Report of the Royal Commission on Aboriginal Peoples*, cited in Layton, *Homelessness*, p.126.

20. Devaney, "Duct Tape and Cardboard"; Layton, *Homelessness*, p.51.

21. NHHN, *State of the Crisis*. The figures were 1.4 million in 1987 and 2.4 million in 1999.

22. Hulchanski, interviewed by Bula, "No Place Like Home."

23. Bula, "No Place Like Home."

24. Toronto, Mayor's Homelessness Action Task Force, 1999, p.19, cited in Hulchanski, "Housing and a Sustainable Social Fabric." See also Ken Dion, "Immigrants' Perceptions of Housing Discrimination in Toronto: The Housing New Canadians Project," *The Journal of Social Issues*, vol.53, no.3 (2001), pp.523-39; and Sylvia Novac, Joe Darden, David Hulchanski, and Anne-Marie Seguin, *Housing Discrimination in Canada: The State of Knowledge* (Ottawa: Canada Mortgage and Housing Corporation, February 2002), both also cited in Hulchanski.

25. Quoted in Layton, *Homelessness*, p.68.

26. J. David Hulchanski, "The Human Right to Adequate Housing in Canada," report submitted to the United Nations Committee of Economic, Social and Cultural Rights, Geneva, by the Rupert Coalition Community Residential Services of Toronto, October 1998; Layton, *Homelessness*, pp.54, 103.

27. Dr. Stephen Hwang, "Homelessness and Health," January 2001, quoted in NHHN, *State of the Crisis*.

28. Hulchanski, "Housing and a Sustainable Social Fabric," p.11.

29. "New Export Strategy to Aid Canadian Housing Industry," *Construction Innovation*, vol.1, no. 4 (Spring 1996).

30. See, for instance, "The Current Performance of the Housing Industry in Canada," Canadian Home Builders' Association, Ottawa, December 1999.

31. Federation of Canadian Municipalities, "Building Foundations for the Future: Considerations in the Design of a Capital Grant Program to Support Affordable Housing," January 16, 2001; Federation of Canadian Municipalities, *National Affordable Housing Strategy*.

32. See, for instance, Jeanne M. Wolfe, "Canadian Housing Policy in the Nineties," *Housing Studies*, vol.13, no.1 (1998), pp.121-33.

33. Federation of Canadian Municipalities, *National Affordable Housing Strategy*.

34. Devaney, "Duct Tape and Cardboard," p.15.

35. See, for instance, Richard Harris, "Is Canadian Housing Policy More Benign Than That of the US?" *Housing Studies*, vol.13, no.5 (1998).

36. Catherine Dunphy, "City Limits: Barriers to the Disabled – Barriers Falling One Ramp at a Time," *The Toronto Star*, Sept. 17, 2000.

37. Elizabeth Plater-Zyberk, interviewed by Bula, "No Place Like Home."

38. Velma Michel and Faith Funk, interviewed by Bula, "No Place Like Home."

39. Press release from the Village of Ouje-Bougoumou, Aug. 20, 1997. See <www.nativeweb.org/pages/legal/ouje.html> (July 12, 2002).

40. Figures from the Co-operative Housing Federation of Canada, Ottawa, December 2002.

41. E.A. Flichel, "Housing and the Quality of Life," *Canadian Housing*, vol.8, no.1-2 (Spring/Summer 1991), p.10.

Chapter Four

Lost in the Supermarket

1. Oliver Bertin, "Kraft Launches $5-Billion (U.S.) IPO," *The Globe and Mail*, March 17, 2001; "International Menu Solutions Corp. (MENU)," *The Wall Street Transcript*, Oct. 11, 1999.

2. For more on alternatives to the hidden costs of food globalization, see Helena Norberg-Hodge, Todd Merrifield, and Steven Gorelick, *Bringing the Food Economy Home: The Social, Ecological and Economic Benefits of Local Food* (Dartington, Devon: The International Society for Ecology and Culture, October 2000).

3. Import Control Systems Task Force, Canadian Food Inspection Agency, "Towards a National Import Strategy and Policy," discussion paper," draft, Nov.15, 2000 <www.inspection.gc.ca/english/ppc/psps/imppol/dispae.shtml> (July 12, 2002).

4. M. and R. Friedman, *Free to Choose* (New York: Avon Books, 1981), p.57.

5. *Canadian Grocer*, June 1982.

6. National Anti-Poverty Organization (NAPO), "What Is Poverty?" Ottawa, n.d. See their website <www.napo-onap.ca>. Even Statistics Canada "does not itself consider the LICO to be a poverty line." See Jim Silver, "Appendix: The Debate about Poverty Lines," in "Persistent Poverty and the Push for Community Solutions," in *Power and Resistance: Critical Thinking about Canadian Social Issues*, 3rd ed., ed. Les Samuelson and Wayne Antony (Halifax: Fernwood Publishing, 2003).

7. Canadian Association of Food Banks, "Food Banks Left Alone to Fight the Battle for Food Security," *The CCPA Monitor*, September 2002, p.36 (a position paper prepared for the World Food Summit, Rome); "Food Bank Use Has Doubled," *The CCPA Monitor*, December 2002/January 2003, p.3.

8. Canadian Association of Food Banks, "Food Banks Left Alone," p.36.

9. See, for instance, Paul Martin, quoted in Beth Wilson and Carly Steinman, "Hunger Count 2000: A Surplus of Hunger – Canada's Annual Survey of Emergency Food Programs," Canadian Association of Food Banks, Toronto, October 2000.

10. Wilson and Steinman, "Hunger Count 2000."

11. Sylvia Ann Hewlett, interviewed in Mary O'Connell, "The Trouble with Poverty," *Ideas*, CBC Radio, May 2000.

12. Steve Kerstetter, "Rags and Riches: Wealth Equality in Canada," paper, Canadian Centre for Policy Alternatives, Ottawa, December 2002, pp.9, 10; see also Kerstetter, "Top 50% of Canadians Hold 94.4% of Wealth, Bottom Half 5.6%," *The CCPA Monitor*, vol.9, no.6 (November 2002), pp.1, 7. See also Wayne Ellwood, *The No-Nonsense Guide to Globalization* (Toronto: New Internationalist and Between the Lines, 2001), p.101, for similar figures.

13. Julia Drake, "2000: The Year That Was," *Canadian Grocer*, December 2000.

14. Ken Lubas and Adrienne Simmons, "Looking Ahead," *Canadian Retailer*, May/June 2001.

15. Kathy Showalter, "Wal-Mart to Expand Supercenter Presence," *Business First*, May 11, 2001.

16. *Canadian Grocer*, May 1982.

17. *Canadian Grocer*, May 1993.

18. Quoted in Drake, "2000: The Year That Was."

19. *68th Annual Report of the Grocery Industry*, supplement to *Progressive Grocer*, April 2001.

20. Phil Bereano and Florian Kraus, "Consumers' Resistance to GM Foods Stronger in Europe. Why?" *The CCPA Monitor*, vol.7, no.10 (April 2001).

21. See, for instance, Jennifer Story, "Field of Genes: Some of the World's Worst Polluters are Fixing Dinner," *Canadian Perspectives* (Council of Canadians), Fall 1999, p.8. See also "Europe Adopts the World's Strictest Legislation for GE Labeling," press release, Greenpeace Canada, Toronto, Nov. 28, 2002.

22. OPIRG McMaster, *The Supermarket Tour*, Hamilton, Ont., 2002, p.34.

23. "You Are What You Eat," *The CCPA Monitor*, vol. 8, no. 2 (June 2001), p.24.

24. David Ransom, "Banana Split," and "Bananas – The Facts," *The New Internationalist*, Issue 317 (October 1999), pp.8, 19.

25. United Nations Development Programme, *Human Development Report 1992* (New York: Oxford University Press, 1992), p.1.

26. *The Globe and Mail*, May 24, 1979, p.B2.

27. Richard Barnet and R.E. Muller, *Global Reach: The Power of the Multinational Corporations* (New York: Simon and Schuster, 1974), pp.14-15.

28. Jan Kainer, "Gender, Corporate Restructuring and Concession Bargaining in Ontario's Food Retail Sector," *Relations Industrielles/Industrial Relations*, vol.53, no. 1 (1998).

29. Ibid.

30. Deborah Barndt, *Tangled Routes: Women, Work, and Globalization on the Tomato Trail* (Aurora, Ont.: Garamond Press, 2002), p.126. "By 1995, 85 percent of retail food workers were part-time."

31. Kart Saver press release, quoted in Consumers Against Privacy Invasion and Numbering (CASPIAN), "Shopping Carts to Track Customer Movements," *Food Industry News*, CASPIAN website <www.nocards.org/news/supermarketnews.shtml> (Jan. 27, 2003).

32. These "alternatives" come from OPIRG McMaster, *Supermarket Tour*, pp.26-27.

Chapter Five

The Brave New World of Work

1. Statistics Canada, "Canadian Economic Observer," cat. no.11-010-XPB, July 2002.

2. Statistics Canada, *Labour Force Survey*, cited in Andrew Jackson and David Robinson, "Falling Behind: The State of Working Canada, 2000," Canadian Council for Policy Alternatives (CCPA), Ottawa, 2000, p.56.

3. Andrew Sharpe, "The Nature and Causes of Unemployment in Canada," in *Employment Policy Options*, ed. K. Battle and S. Torjman (Ottawa: Caledon Institute of Social Policy, 1999), p.39.

4. Arthur Donner and Fred Lazar, "Restructuring Canada's Labour Market for the New Millennium," in *Employment Policy Options*, ed. Battle and Torjman, p.116.

5. Statistics Canada, *Labour Force Survey 2000*.

6. Statistics Canada, *Labour Force Survey*, Ottawa, April 2001.

7. Personal observation by Jamie Swift, May 2002; Gordon Laird, *Power: Journeys Across an Energy Nation* (Toronto: Penguin Viking, 2002), pp.278-80.

8. Jackson and Robinson, "Falling Behind," pp.70-71.

9. Statistics Canada, "Canadian Economic Observer," cat. no.11-210-XPB, 2000-2001, p.34.

10. Judith Maxwell, in *Canadian Unemployment*, ed. Surendra Gura (Ottawa: Economic Council of Canada, 1991); Statistics Canada, "Canadian Economic Observer," 2000-2001, p.34.

11. *The Globe and Mail*, Dec. 5, 1992.

12. C. Wright Mills, *The Sociological Imagination* (New York: Evergreen, 1961), pp.8-9.

13. Adam Smith, *The Wealth of Nations 1776* (New York: Random House, 1937), p.355.

14. Economic Council of Canada, *Good Jobs, Bad Jobs: Employment in the Service Economy*, Ottawa, 1990.

15. Jackson and Robinson, "Falling Behind," pp.56-57.

16. Ibid., p.65.

17. Peter Nares, "Self-employment," in *Employment Policy Options*, ed. Battle and Torjman, pp.360-61; see also Jackson and Robinson, "Falling Behind," p.59.

18. Donner and Lazar, "Restructuring Canada's Labour Market," pp.113, 116.

19. Statistics Canada, *Canadian Economic Observer*, cat. no.11-010, February 1993; emphasis added.

20. Jackson and Robinson, "Falling Behind," p.63.

21. *The National Post*, Jan. 22, 1999.

22. Jim Stanford, "Canadian Labour Market Developments in International Context: Flexibility, Regulation and Demand," *Canadian Public Policy*, vol.26, supplement 1 (2000), p.S46.

23. Yves Gingras and Richard Roy, "Is There a Skill Gap in Canada?" *Canadian Public Policy*, vol.26, supplement 1 (2000), pp.S162, 167-68.

24. Organization for European Cooperation and Development (OECD), *Human Capital Investment*, Paris, 1998, cited in Gingras and Roy, "Is There a Skill Gap in Canada?" p.S170.

Chapter Six

Social Analysis Again

1. Statistics Canada, *Reading the Future: A Portrait of Literacy in Canada* (1996). See <www.nald.ca/nls/ials/introduc.htm> (July 12, 2002).

2. Margaret Wente, "The Ridiculous $3-Million MRI Machine Problem," *The Globe and Mail*, Dec. 5, 2002, p.A27.

3. J. Holland and P. Henriot, S.J., *Social Analysis: Linking Faith and Justice*, rev. ed. (Maryknoll, N.Y.: Orbis Books, 1983), p.28.

Chapter Seven

Energy and the Environment

1. Norman Myers, *Gaia: An Atlas of Planetary Management*, rev. ed. (New York: Doubleday, 1993), p.136.

2. Michael T. Klare, *Resource Wars: The New Landscape of Global Conflict* (New York: Henry Holt & Co., 2001), pp.19, 55.

3. United Nations Development Programme (UNDP), *Human Development Report 2001: Making New Technologies Work for Human Development* (New York: Oxford University Press, 2001), Table 18, pp.200-1.

4. D.F. Owen, *What Is Ecology?* (Oxford: Oxford University Press, 1974), p.1.

5. Quoted in Keith Bradsher, *High and Mighty: SUVs –* *The World's Most Dangerous Vehicles and How They Got That Way* (New York: Public Affairs, 2002), p.51.

6. Bradsher, *High and Mighty*, pp.401-2.

7. City of Toronto Staff Report, "By-law Amendment to Regulate Drive-Through Facilities in the City of Toronto," Toronto, 2002, pp.7-8.

8. Quoted in Dinyar Godrej, *The No-Nonsense Guide to Climate Change* (Toronto: New Internationalist and Between the Lines, 2001), p.112.

9. Henry Hengeveld, Environment Canada senior science advisor on climate change, presentation to Energy Policy Committee, Communications, Energy and Paperworkers Union, Ottawa, Aug. 21, 2001.

10. U.S. Department of Energy, data cited in Klare, *Resource Wars*, p.37.

11. Eric Reguly, "Economic Fear-Mongering Protects the Gas Guzzlers," *The Globe and Mail*, March 16, 2002.

12. Bradsher, *High and Mighty*, pp.88-89.

13. Jeremy Leggett, *The Carbon War: Global Warming and the End of the Oil Era* (London: Penguin, 2000), ch.1, passim.

14. John Mason, "U.S. Pressure Forces Removal of Climate Change Chief," *Financial Times* (London), April 21, 2002.

15. Fuel economy data from Bradsher, *High and Mighty*, p.243; per capita CO_2 emissions from UNDP, *Human Development Report 2001*, p.200; Canada adopting U.S. vehicular air pollution standards, Bradsher, *High and Mighty*, p.261.

16. Bradsher, *High and Mighty*, p.xvii.

17. In 1991 the company changed its name to New Brunswick Power Corporation (NB Power).

18. New Brunswick Power Commission, *Annual Reports*, Fredericton, 1983-86.

19. "A New Dawn for Nuclear Power?" and "A Renaissance That May Not Come," *The Economist*, May 19, 2001.

20. Conservation Council of New Brunswick, *Submission to the Board of Commissioners of Public Utilities of New Brunswick*, Fredericton, June 18, 2002.

21. Gordon Laird, *Power: Journeys Across an Energy Nation* (Toronto: Penguin Viking, 2002), pp. 181,185.

22. Data from U.S. Energy Information Administration, Canadian Association of Petroleum Producers, cited in Matt Price and John Bennett, *America's Gas Tank: The High Cost of Canada's Oil and Gas Export Strategy* (Ottawa:

Natural Resources Defence Council and Sierra Club of Canada, 2002), p.2.

23. Stephen Clarkson, *Uncle Sam and Us: Globalization, Neo-conservatism, and the Canadian State* (Toronto: University of Toronto Press, 2002), p.336.

24. Clarkson, *Uncle Sam and Us*, p.341; Martin Mittelstaedt, "Firms Breaking Promises on Emissions, Study Says," *The Globe and Mail*, Oct. 18, 2002.

25. Price and Bennett, *America's Gas Tank*, p.4; Laird, *Power*, pp.206, 208.

26. Communications, Energy and Paperworkers Union of Canada (CEP), "National Energy Policy," Ottawa, 2002, pp.15–16, 49–52.

27. Commissioner of the Environment and Sustainable Development, *Government Support for Energy Investments*, Ottawa, 2000, cited in Price and Bennett, *America's Gas Tank*, p. 6.

28. United Nations Development Programme, *Human Development Report 1998* (New York: UNDP, 1998), pp.29, 50.

29. World Commission on Environment and Development, *Our Common Future* (Oxford: Oxford University Press, 1987), p.43.

Chapter Eight

Technology from Past to Future

1. Statistics Canada, *The Digital Divide in Canada*, cat. no.56F0009FIE, Ottawa, Oct. 1, 2002.

2. Tom Forester, *High Tech Society: The Story of the Information Technology Revolution* (Cambridge, Mass.: MIT Press, 1988), p.17.

3. United Nations Development Programme, *Human Development Report 2001* (New York: Oxford University Press, 2001), Table A2-4, p.60.

4. E.P. Thompson, *The Making of the English Working Class* (Harmondsworth, Middx.: Penguin Books, 1969), ch.14.

5. Eric Hobsbawm, "The Machine-Breakers," in Hobsbawm, *Uncommon People: Resistance, Rebellion and Jazz* (London: Weidenfeld & Nicholson, 1998), pp.12–13.

6. Quoted in *Canadian Interchange*, no.38 (1981).

7. Personal communication with Jim Stanford, Canadian Auto Workers (CAW), Nov. 22, 2002.

8. Quoted in David Robertson and Jeff Wareham, *Changing Technology and Work: Northern Telecom*, CAW Technology Project, Toronto, 1989, p.32.

9. See Shoshona Zuboff, *In the Age of the Smart Machine: The Future of Work and Power* (New York: Basic Books, 1988).

10. Quoted in Robertson and Wareham, *Changing Technology and Work*, p.47.

11. Quoted in Joan Kuyek, *The Phone Book: Working at the Bell* (Toronto: Between the Lines, 1979), p.69.

12. Communication, Energy and Paperworkers Union of Canada (CEP), "Submission to Bell Canada," Ottawa, Sept. 30, 1993; personal communication with Jamie Swift, Gananoque, Ont., April 15, 1993.

13. Quoted in Meyer Siemiatycki, "The Microchip Battleground," *Ideas*, CBC Radio, March/April 1983.

14. Dwayne Winseck, "Netscapes of Power: Convergence, Network Design, Walled Gardens and Other Strategies of Control in the Information Age," in *Surveillance as Social Sorting*, ed. David Lyon (London: Routledge, 2003), p.192.

15. American Management Association, "More Companies Watching Employees, American Management Association Annual Survey Reports," press release, April 18, 2001 <www.amanet.org/press/amanews/ems2001>.

16. Michael Geist, "Computer and E-Mail Workplace Surveillance in Canada: The Shift from Reasonable Expectation of Privacy to Reasonable Surveillance," Canadian Judicial Council, Ottawa, 2002, pp.12–13.

17. David Zweig and Jane Webster, "Where Is the Line between Benign and Invasive? An Examination of Psychological Barriers to the Acceptance of Awareness Monitoring Systems," *Journal of Organizational Behaviour*, vol.23, no.5 (2002).

18. Quoted in "Workplace Monitoring: Can Employers Go Too Far?" *Management and Economics Review* (University of Toronto at Scarborough), vol.1, no.2 (2002). <www.utsc.utoronto.ca/~mgmt/journal>.

19. Lewis Mumford, "The Myth of the Machine: Technics and Human Development," in *The Lewis Mumford Reader*, ed. D. Miller (New York: Pantheon Books, 1986), pp.317-18.

20. David H. Flaherty, "Visions of Privacy: Past, Present, and Future," in *Visions of Privacy: Policy Choices for the Digital Age,* ed. Colin J. Bennett and Rebecca Grant (Toronto: University of Toronto Press, 1999), p.33.

21. David Lyon, "Surveillance in Cyberspace: The Internet, Personal Data, and Social Control," *Queen's*

Quarterly, vol.109, no.3 (Fall 2002), p.352, passim.

22. David Lyon, "Surveillance as Social Sorting: Computer Codes and Mobile Bodies," in *Surveillance as Social Sorting,* ed. Lyon, p.15.

23. "Market Segments – Clusters," PCensus, Tetrad Computer Applications Inc., Vancouver <www.tetrad.com/pcensus/can/py951st>.

24. René Laperrière, "The 'Quebec Model' of Data Protection," in *Visions of Privacy,* ed. Bennett and Grant, p.191.

25. Lyon, "Surveillance as Social Sorting," pp.20-21.

26. Lewis Mumford, *Technics and Civilization* (New York: Harcourt, Brace, 1934), pp.12-18.

27. Janet Abbate, *Inventing the Internet* (Cambridge, Mass.: MIT Press, 2000), pp.2-6.

28. Ursula Franklin, *The Real World of Technology,* rev. ed. (Toronto: Anansi, 1999), ch.1.

Chapter Nine

Globalization and Development

1. William Greider, *One World, Ready or Not: The Manic Logic of Global Capitalism* (New York: Simon & Schuster, 1997), p.341.

2. Noami Klein, *No Logo: Taking Aim at the Brand Bullies* (Toronto: Alfred A. Knopf Canada, 2000).

3. Quoted in Gustavo Esteva, "Development," in *The Development Dictionary,* ed. Wolfgang Sachs (London: Zed Books, 1992), p.6.

4. United Nations Development Programme, *Human Development Report 1999* (New York: Oxford University Press, 1999), pp.36-37.

5. Wayne Ellwood, *The No-Nonsense Guide to Globalization* (Toronto: New Internationalist Publications and Between the Lines, 2001), p.49.

6. Joseph Stiglitz, *Globalization and Its Discontents* (New York: W.W. Norton, 2002), p.30.

7. United Nations Development Programme, *Human Development Report 1997* (New York: Oxford University Press, 1997), ch.3.

8. Stiglitz, *Globalization and Its Discontents,* pp.30-33, 54-55.

9. Bank for International Settlements, "Triennial Central Bank Survey of Foreign Exchange and Derivatives Market Activity – Final Results," Basel, Switzerland, 2001 <www.bis.org/publ/rpfx02>.

10. Stiglitz, *Globalization and Its Discontents,* p.95.

11. James Tobin, interviewed by Jamie Swift, *Ideas,* CBC Radio, November 1995.

12. United Nations Development Programme, *Human Development Report 1999,* pp.33-34.

13. International Labour Organization, Sectoral Activities Program, *The Employment Impact of Mergers and Acquisitions in the Banking and Financial Services Sector,* Geneva, 2001.

14. United Nations Development Programme, *Human Development Report 1999,* p.31.

15. Ellwood, *No-Nonsense Guide to Globalization,* p.92.

16. United Nations Development Programme, *Human Development Report 2001* (New York: Oxford University Press, 2001), Table 18, pp.200-1.

17. Karl Polanyi, *The Great Transformation: The Political and Economic Origins of Our Time* (Boston: Beacon Press, 1957), p.132.

18. Ibid., p.135.

19. Quoted in Canadian Council for International Co-operation, *What We Can DO: A 10-Point Global Action Plan against Poverty,* Ottawa, 1998, p.17.

20. See Stephen Clarkson, *Uncle Sam and Us: Globalization, Neoconservatism and the Canadian State* (Toronto: University of Toronto Press, 2002), pp.349-50.

21. Ibid., pp.243-50.

22. United Nations Development Programme, *Human Development Report 2001,* p.3.

23. Esteva, "Development," p.10.

24. See Benjamin Barber, *Jihad vs. McWorld: How Globalism and Tribalism Are Reshaping the World* (New York: Ballantine Books, 1995).

25. Stiglitz, *Globalization and Its Discontents,* p.153.

26. Amartya Sen, *Development as Freedom* (New York: Alfred A. Knopf, 1999).

Chapter Ten

Media and Ideology

1. Calculated from Canadian Cable Television Association, *Annual Report 2000-2001*, Ottawa, 2001.

2. Statistics Canada, *The Digital Divide in Canada*, cat. no.56F0009FIE, Ottawa, Oct. 1, 2002.

3. Statistics Canada, *Household Internet Use Survey*, 2001, CANSIM, Tables 358-0002 to 358-0006.

4. Quoted in James Winter, "Canada's Media Monopoly: One Perspective Is Enough, Says CanWest," in *Extra!* (Fairness & Accuracy in Reporting), May/June 2002.

5. Gully Cragg, "Canada: CanWest 'Muzzles' Staff: Corporate Censorship," *Index on Censorship*, April 18, 2002 <www.indexonline.org/news>.

6. Ibid.

7. William H. Metcalfe, *The View from Thirty* (Winnipeg: William H. Metcalfe, 1986), pp.136-37.

8. Anthony Winson, *The Intimate Commodity: Food and the Development of the Agro-Industrial Complex in Canada* (Toronto: Garamond Press, 1993), p.167.

9. Ibid., p.170.

10. Linda McQuaig, "Read All about It: The Truth about Free Press" *The Toronto Star*, June 23, 2002.

11. Quoted in *The Financial Post*, July 16, 1983.

12. See Harry Glasbeek, *Wealth by Stealth: Corporate Crime, Corporate Law, and the Perversion of Democracy* (Toronto: Between the Lines, 2002), p.132.

13. Debra Clarke, "Constraints of Television News Production: The Example of Story Geography," in *Critical Studies of Canadian Mass Media*, ed. Marc Grenier (Toronto: Butterworths, 1992), p.114.

14. Quoted in Lawrence Weschler, "The Other Democratic Revolution of 1989," *UTNE Reader*, no.40 (July/August 1990), p.44; reprinted from *The Columbia Journalism Review*, March/April 1990.

15. Michael J.L. Clow, "False Pretenses: Canadian Newspapers and Nuclear Power," in *Critical Studies of Canadian Mass Media*, ed. Grenier, p.165.

16. Henry F. Heald, "Covering Aboriginal Issues: Traditional Reporting Just Won't Do," *Content*, March/April, 1992, p.16.

17. *The Globe and Mail*, Feb. 3, 2003.

18. Clarke, "Constraints of Television News Production," p.120.

19. Weschler, "Other Democratic Revolution of 1989," p.39.

20. Ezekiel Makunike, "Out of Africa! Western Media Stereotypes Shape World's Portrait," *Media&Values*, no.61 (Winter 1993), pp.11-12.

21. Clow, "False Pretenses." The study analyzed coverage in *The Globe and Mail, The Toronto Star,* the *Fredericton Daily Gleaner*, and the Saint John *Telegraph-Journal*. See also Michael Clow and Susan Machum, *Stifling Debate: Canadian Newspapers and Nuclear Power* (Halifax: Fernwood Publishing, 1993).

22. Mediawatch, "Global Media Monitoring Project: Women's Participation in the News," and "Women Strike Out: 1998 Newspaper Survey" <www.mediawatch.ca/research>.

23. Cited in Augie Fleras and John Lock Kunz, *Media and Minorities: Representing Diversity in a Multicultural Canada* (Toronto: Thompson Educational Publishing, 2001), p.30.

24. Krishna Rau, "How the Media Covered the Terrorist Attacks," DiversityWatch, Ryerson University School of Journalism, Toronto, 2001 www.diversitywatch.ryerson.ca/media/archive>.

25. Statistics Canada, 1998 General Social Survey, cited in Kerry Daly, "It Keeps Getting Faster: Changing Patterns of Time in Families," Vanier Institute of the Family, Ottawa, 2000, p.6.

26. Todd Gitlin, *Media Unlimited: How the Torrent of Images and Sounds Overwhelms Our Lives* (New York: Metropolitan Books, 2001), p.116.

27. United Nations Development Programme, *Human Development Report 1998* (New York: Oxford University Press, 1998), p.7.

28. Personal communication with Indigo Books, Kingston, Ont., Dec. 3, 2002.

Chapter Eleven

Aging – Out of Sight

1. Editorial, *Canadian Woman Studies/les cahiers de la femme*, vol.12, no.2 (Winter 1992), p.3.

2. "Short Staffed? Senior Can Help," *The Bulletin: The Baking Association of Canada Newsletter* (July 2001) <www.bakingassoccanada.com> (July 13, 2002); Ann Duffy and Norene Pupo, *Part-Time Paradox: Connecting Gender, Work and Family* (Toronto: McClelland & Stewart, 1992), p.241.

3. Ontario Advisory Council on Senior Citizens, *Aging Together: An Exploration of Attitudes towards Aging in Multicultural Ontario*, Toronto, 1989, p.69.

4. Statistics Canada, *Labour Force Annual Averages*, Table 1, cat. no.71-220, Ottawa, 1993; Colin Lindsay, *A Portrait of Seniors in Canada*, 3rd ed., cat. no.89-519-XPE, Ottawa, 1999.

5. C.T. Gillin and Thomas R. Klassen, "Retire Mandatory Retirement," *Policy Options*, July/ August 2000, pp.60, 61.

6. For more on women retiring because of ill health of a family member, see Anne Martin Matthews and Joseph A. Tindale, "Retirement in Canada," in *Retirement in Industrialized Societies: Social, Psychological and Health Factors*, ed. S. Kyriakos, S. Markides, and Cary L. Cooper (Toronto: John Wiley and Sons, 1987). On the ranking of family responsibilities, see Lindsay, *Portrait of Seniors in Canada*.

7. D. Gower, "Men Retiring Early: How Are They Doing?" *Perspectives*, Winter 1995, pp.30-34; V.W. Marshall, "The Older Worker in Canadian Society: Is There a Future?" in *Rethinking Retirement*, ed. E.M. Gee and G.M. Gutman (Vancouver: Gerontology Research Centre, Simon Fraser University, 1995), pp.31-50.

8. Quoted in Canada, *Report of the Special Committee of the Senate on Aging*, Ottawa, 1966, p.71.

9. Mark Novak and Lori Campbell, *Aging Society: A Canadian Perspective*, 4th ed. (Toronto: Nelson, 2001), p.166.

10. Economic Council of Canada, *The New Face of Poverty: Income Security Needs of Canadian Families*, Ottawa, June 1992, p.13.

11. Lindsay, *Portrait of Seniors in Canada*, p.10; National Council of Welfare, *A Pension Primer*, cat. no.H68-49/1999E, Ottawa, 1999.

12. Novak and Campbell, *Aging Society*, p.158.

13. The Ecumenical Coalition for Economic Justice, *Reweaving Canada's Social Programs: From Shredded Safety Net to Social Solidarity*, Toronto, 1993, p.14.

14. Monica Townson, *Pensions under Attack: What's Behind the Push to Privatize Public Pensions* (Ottawa: Canadian Centre for Policy Alternatives, 2001).

15. Maria Almey et al., *Women in Canada 2000: A Gender-Based Statistical Report*, cat. no.89-503-XPE (Ottawa: Statistics Canada, 2000), p.279; Susan A. McDaniel, "The Changing Canadian Family: Women's Roles and the Impact of Feminism," in *Changing Patterns: Women in Canada*, 2nd ed., ed. Sandra Burt, Lorraine Code, and Lindsay Dorney (Toronto: McClelland &

Stewart, 1993), p.440.

16. Canadian Union of Public Employees (CUPE), "Calculate My Lifetime Wage Loss," Ottawa, April 9, 2000 <cupe.ca/campaigns/womenswages> (July 13, 2002); Almey et al., *Women in Canada 2000*, pp.142, 279.

17. Anne Smart, "Representing Older Women in Saskatchewan," *Canadian Woman Studies/les cahiers de la femme*, vol.12, no.2 (Winter 1992), p.7.

18. Ontario Advisory Council on Senior Citizens, *Aging Together*, p.72.

19. S. Brotman, "The Incidence of Poverty among Seniors in Canada: Exploring the Impact of Gender, Ethnicity and Race," *Canadian Journal on Aging*, vol.17, no.2 (1998), pp.166-85.

20. Novak and Campbell, *Aging Society*, p.164; Monica Townson, "Equity Issues," presentation to National Pension Conference, Canadian Labour Congress, Ottawa, Feb. 4, 2001; overview available at <www.clc-ctc.ca/policy/pensions/penconf> (July 13, 2002).

21. Ontario Advisory Council on Senior Citizens, *Denied Too Long: The Needs and Concerns of Seniors Living in First Nation Communities in Ontario*, Toronto, 1993, pp.48-50; Rudy Platiel, "Elderly Natives Live in Fear of Sickness," *The Globe and Mail*, July 15, 1993, p.A5.

22. Margaret Labillois, "Aboriginal Housing: A Personal Perspective," in National Advisory Council on Aging, *Aboriginal Seniors' Issues*, Ottawa, 2001, quoted in Novak and Campbell, *Aging Society*, p.120.

23. Monica Townson, "Pension Industry Is Warning of 'Demographic Time Bomb,'" *The CCPA Monitor*, vol. 7, no.8 (February 2001); Phil Mullan, *The Imaginary Time Bomb: Why an Aging Population Is Not a Social Problem* (New York: I.B. Tauris & Co., 2001).

24. B. Desjardins, *Population Ageing and the Elderly*, cat. no.91-533E (Ottawa: Minister of Industry, Science and Technology, 1993).

25. Novak and Campbell, *Aging Society*, p.307. See also L.O. Stone, C.J. Rosenthal, and I.A. Connidis, *Parent-Child Exchanges of Supports and Intergenerational Equity*, cat. no.89-557- XPE (Ottawa: Ministry of Industry, 1998).

26. Lindsay, *Portrait of Seniors in Canada*, p.31; Novak and Campbell, *Aging Society*, pp.197, 198.

27. Novak and Campbell, *Aging Society*, p.198; see also Marika Morris et al., "The Changing Nature of Home Care and Its Impact on Women's Vulnerability to Poverty," cat. no.SW21- 42/1999E (Ottawa: Status of Women Canada, November 1999).

28. Jack Layton, *Homelessness: The Making and Unmaking of*

a Crisis (Toronto: Penguin Canada and McGill Institute, 2000), p.51.

29. Lindsay, *Portrait of Seniors in Canada*, pp.36-38.

30. S. Ward, "Private Nursing Homes Find Gold in Caring for the Elderly," *The Financial Post*, April 14, 1984.

31. Canadian Health Care Coalition, "Extendicare Is Not the Right Model for Health Care Reform," *The CCPA Monitor*, May 2002.

32. Martha Keniston Laurence, "Womancare – Health Care: Power and Policy," *Canadian Woman Studies/les cahiers de la femme*, vol.12, no.2 (Winter 1992), p.33.

33. Duffy and Pupo, *Part-Time Paradox*, p.241; Lindsay, *Portrait of Seniors in Canada*, p.89.

34. Lindsay, *Portrait of Seniors in Canada*, p.34.

35. Ibid., pp.35,36.

36. Health Canada, "Abuse and Neglect of Older Adults," cat. no.H72-22/6-1998E., Ottawa, 1998.

37. Novak and Campbell, *Aging Society*, p.264.

38. Lindsay, *Portrait of Seniors in Canada*, p.61.

39. Ibid., pp.61, 62.

40. Novak and Campbell, *Aging Society*, p.77.

41. Lindsay, *Portrait of Seniors in Canada*, pp.90, 91.

42. Lindsay, *Portrait of Seniors in Canada,* 1990, cited in Novak and Campbell, *Aging Society*, p.301; J.G. Snell, *The Citizen's Wage: The State and the Elderly in Canada, 1900-1951* (Toronto: University of Toronto Press, 1996); H.J. Pratt, *Gray Agendas: Interest Groups and Public Pensions in Canada, Britain, and the United States* (Ann Arbor: University of Michigan Press, 1993).

43. See Pierre Gauthier, "Canada's Seniors," *Canadian Social Trends* (Statistics Canada), no.22 (Autumn 1991), pp.16-20.

44. Ontario Advisory Council on Senior Citizens, *Aging Together*, p.17. See also Gauthier, "Canada's Seniors," p.16; and Monica Boyd, "Foreign Born, Female, Old . . . and Poor," *Canadian Woman Studies/les cahiers de la femme*, vol.12, no.4 (Summer 1992).

Chapter Twelve

Our Home and Native Land

1. Quoted in Paul Barnsley, "Oka: 10 Years Later," *Windspeaker*, July 2000.

2. Tony Hall, "Evidence Presented to Address Canada's Request to Extradite Mr. James Pitawanakwat from the United States for His Involvement in the Gustafsen Lake Standoff in British Columbia in 1995," p.15; Christian Peacemaker Teams, "Gunboat Diplomacy: Canada's Abuse of Human Rights at Esgenoôpetitj (Burnt Church, N.B.)," February 2001 <www.prairienet.org/cpt/enreport> (July 14, 2002).

3. Canada, *Highlights from the Report of the Royal Commission on Aboriginal Peoples: People to People, Nation to Nation*, vol.2, *Restructuring the Relationship*, Ottawa, 1996, p.3 <www.ainc-inac.gc.ca/ch/rcap/rpt> (July 14, 2002).

4. Canada, Royal Commission on Aboriginal Peoples, *Report*, vol.1, Ottawa, 1996, ch.2, p.1. See also Mary Jane Nichols, "Canada's Aboriginal Languages," *Canadian Social Trends* (Statistics Canada), cat. no.11-008, Winter 1998.

5. Canada, *Highlights from the Report*, vol. 2, p.3.

6. George Manuel and Michael Posluns, *The Fourth World: An Indian Reality* (Don Mills, Ont.: Collier-Macmillan Canada, 1974), p.7.

7. Statistics Canada, *The Daily*, Jan. 13, 1998, p.4 <www.statcan.ca/Daily/English> (July 14, 2002).

8. Statistics Canada, "Aboriginal Peoples of Canada: A Demographic Profile," *The Daily*, Jan. 21, 2003; see also "The Census," *The Globe and Mail*, Jan. 22, 2003, p.A6.

9. E-mail correspondence, Department of Indian Affairs and Northern Development, Dec. 31, 2000.

10. James S. Frideres, *Aboriginal Peoples in Canada: Contemporary Conflicts*, 5th ed. (Scarborough, Ont.: Prentice Hall Allyn and Bacon Canada, 1998), pp.28, 29.

11. Ibid., p.26.

12. See "Information Gateway to Nunavut" website <www.nunavut.com> (July 14, 2002). For more on Inuit history and culture and current issues, see also the website of the Inuit Tapirisat of Canada <www.tapirisat.ca> (July 14, 2002).

13. Bonita Lawrence, Institute of Women's Studies, Queen's University, Kingston, personal correspondence, June 14, 2001.

14. Bruce E. Johansen, *Debating Democracy: Native American Legacy of Freedom* (Santa Fe, N.M.: Clear Light Publishers, 1998), p.8. For more on the Haudenosaunee

influence on the U.S. Constitution, see also Donald A. Grinde, Jr. and Bruce E. Johansen, *Exemplar of Liberty: Native America and the Founding of American Democracy* (Los Angeles: UCLA American Indian Studies Center, 1991); Donald A. Grinde, Jr., *The Iroquois and the Founding of the American Nation* (San Francisco: Indian Historian Press, 1977); and Bruce Johansen, *Forgotten Founders: How the American Indians Helped Shape Democracy* (Boston: Harvard Common Press, 1982).

15. There is evidence that some of this devastation was the consequence of what Roger Gibbins identifies as biological warfare. British General Jeffrey Amherst "distributed to First Nations people blankets he knew to be infected with smallpox when it was also known that the disease was often fatal to First Nation individuals due to their lack of natural immunity to it." Gibbins, "Historical Overview and Background: Part I," in *First Nations in Canada: Perspectives on Opportunity, Empowerment, and Self-Determination,* ed. J Rick Ponting (Toronto: McGraw-Hill Ryerson, 1997), p.26. See also Olive Patricia Dickason, *Canada's First Nations: A History of Founding Peoples from Earliest Times* (Toronto: McClelland & Stewart, 1992), p.183.

16. Dickason, *Canada's First Nations*, p.353.

17. P.A. Cumming and N.H. Mickenburg, eds., *Native Rights in Canada*, 2nd ed. (Toronto: General Publishing, 1980), pp.113-14.

18. Chrystos, *Not Vanishing* (Vancouver: Press Gang, 1988).

19. Statistics Canada, *The Daily*, Jan. 13, 1998, pp.2, 6, 8.

20. Robin Armstrong, "Mapping the Conditions of First Nations Communities," *Canadian Social Trends*, Winter 1999, cat. no.11-008. See also Jean Leonard Elliott and Augie Fleras, *Unequal Relations: An Introduction to Race and Ethnic Dynamics in Canada* (Scarborough, Ont.: Prentice-Hall Canada, 1992), p.164.

21. In an extraordinary gesture of support, 2,500 Walkerton residents were treated to a day at the Sky Dome to enjoy a Blue Jays baseball game. The trip was sponsored by the Blue Jays and various other corporate sponsors. Roberta Avery, "Water Victims Get a Trip to Dome," *The Toronto Star*, Sept. 22, 2000.

22. Dan Zareski, "A Bad Taste in Your Mouth: Many Areas in Province are Plagued by Bad Drinking Water," *Saskatoon Star Phoenix*, p.A1.

23. Michael J. Chandler and Christopher Lalonde, "Cultural Continuity as a Hedge against Suicide in Canada's First Nations," *Transcultural Psychiatry*, vol.3, no.2 (June 1998), p.2; see <www.turtleisland.org/front/chandler> (July 14, 2002).

24. Ibid.

25. Drew Hayden Taylor, "Whatever Happened to Billy Jack?" *The Globe and Mail*, Oct 4, 1993, p.A1.

26. Miles Morriseau, "Seeing Savages behind Every Bush: How the Media Missed the Full Story behind Gustafsen Lake and Stoney Point," *Aboriginal Voices*, Autumn 1995, p.6, quoted by Hall, "Evidence Presented to Address Canada's Request to Extradite Mr. James Pitawanakwat," p.15.

27. Warren Goulding, *Just Another Indian: A Serial Killer and Canadian Indifference* (Markham, Ont.: Fitzhenry and Whiteside, 2001).

28. "Statement, International Non-Governmental Organization Conference on Indigenous People and the Land," Geneva, September 1981, published in *Ontario Indian*, vol 5, no.3 (March 1982), p.32.

29. Paul Barnsley, "Camp Ipperwash Occupation Approaches Seven-Year Mark," *Windspeaker*, July 2000 <www.ammsa.com/windspeaker> (July 14, 2002).

30. "Natives Crushed by Land Grab, Federal Report Says," *The Globe and Mail*, Aug. 8, 1993, p.A23; Andrew J. Orkin, "Using the Inuit as Human Flagpoles," *The Globe and Mail*, Dec. 4, 1992, p.A23.

31. John Goddard, "In from the Cold," *Canadian Geographic*, vol.114, no.4 (July/August 1994); reprinted in *The Native Imprint: The Contributions of First Peoples to Canada's Character*, vol.2, ed. Olive Patricia Dickason (Athabaska, Alta: Athabaska University Enterprises, 1996), p.295.

32. John Goddard, "Forked Tongues," *Saturday Night*, February 1988.

33. Excerpted from "Apology to the Nuu-chah-nulth Concerning Indian Residential Schools by the Government of Canada," delivered by Shirley Serafini, Deputy Minister of Indian Affairs and Northern Development on behalf of the Government of Canada, Dec. 9, 2000. The full text of the apology is available on-line at the Turtle Island Native News, Spotlight on Residential Schools web page <www.turtleisland.org/news/apology> (July 14, 2002).

34. Goddard, "Forked Tongues."

35. John S. Milloy, *A National Crime: The Canadian Government and the Residential School System, 1879 to 1986* (Winnipeg: University of Manitoba Press, 1999), p.121.

36. Quoted in Milloy, *National Crime*, p.xv.

37. Jane Stewart, Minister of Indian Affairs and Northern Affairs, "Statement of Reconciliation: Learning from the Past," Jan. 7, 1998. This statement was presented as a

preamble to the unveiling of "Gathering Strength: Canada's Aboriginal Action Plan," the federal response to the work of the Royal Commission on Aboriginal Peoples. Full text available at <www.ainc-inac.gc.ca/ gs/rec_e> (July 14, 2002).

38. Kenneth Williams, "Money Is Not the Issue," *Windspeaker*, February 1998.

39. Rick Mofina, "Natives Want 'Truth' Panel to Study Abuse at Residential Schools: South African-Style Panel Would Hear Tragedies from Past," *The Edmonton Journal*, Dec. 26, 2000.

40. Department of Indian Affairs and Northern Development figures cited in Ponting, ed., *First Nations in Canada*, p.98.

41. See Laura F. Klein and Lillian A. Ackerman, eds., *Women and Power in Native North America* (Norman: University of Oklahoma Press, 1995).

42. See, for example, Rosemary Brown, "The Exploitation of the Oil and Gas Frontier: Its Impact on Lubicon Lake Cree Women," in *Women of the First Nations: Power, Wisdom, and Strength*, ed. Christine Miller and Patricia Chuchryk (Winnipeg: The University of Manitoba Press, 1997); and Miller and Chuchryk, eds., *Women of the First Nations*, pp.3, 4.

43. See, for example, Jennifer Blythe and Peggy Martin McGuire, "The Changing Employment of Cree Women in Moosonee and Moose Factory," in *Women of the First Nations*, ed. Miller and Chuchryk. See also Jeanette Armstrong, "Invocation: The Real Power of Aboriginal Women," in *Women of the First Nations*, ed. Miller and Chuchryk.

44. Gail Stacey-Moore, *Herizons*, Winter 1993.

45. Cora J. Voyageur, "Contemporary Indian Women," in *Visions of the Heart: Canadian Aboriginal Issues*, ed. David Alan Long and Olive P. Dickason (Toronto: Harcourt Brace Canada, 1996), pp.93-115; quoted in Ponting, *First Nations in Canada*, ed. Ponting, p.52.

46. Anthony J. Hall, "Americana Indigenismo: Indigenous Peoples, the FTAA and the Fourth World," conference paper, Quebec City, April 19, 2001, p.4. See <radicalpress .com> (Feb. 13, 2003).

47. For a historic background to contemporary treaty-making, see Tom Molloy, with Donald Ward, *The World Is Our Witness: The Historic Journey of the Nisga'a into Canada* (Calgary: Fifth House Publishers, 2000).

48. Canada, *Highlights from the Report*, vol.2, pp.21-25.

49. Ibid., pp.1, 2.

50. Ibid., p.2.

51. Letter from Trish Fox Roman, Toronto, June 29, 1992.

Chapter Thirteen

A Woman's Place . . .

1. Quoted in Lorna Rasmussen et al., *A Harvest Yet to Reap: A History of Prairie Women* (Toronto: Women's Press, 1976), p.84.

2. Dionne Brand, *No Burden to Carry: Narratives of Black Women Working in Ontario, 1920s to 1950s* (Toronto: University of Toronto Press, 1987).

3. Anne Duffy and Norene Pupo, *Part-Time Paradox: Connecting Gender, Work and Family* (Toronto: McClelland and Stewart, 1992), p.18.

4. Maria Almey et al., *Women in Canada 2000: A Gender-Based Statistical Report*, cat. no.89- 503-XPE, Statistics Canada, Ottawa, 2000, p.119. The 1988 survey appeared in *Chatelaine* magazine, cited in Duffy and Pupo, *Part-Time Paradox*, p.34.

5. Almey et al., *Women in Canada 2000*, p.99; Paul Phillips and Erin Phillips, *Women and Work: Inequality in the Canadian Labour Market*, rev ed. (Toronto: James Lorimer & Co., 1993), p.33.

6. Almey et al., *Women in Canada 2000*, pp.19, 123.

7. Ibid., pp.201, 202.

8. Organization for Economic Cooperation and Development (OECD), *Society at a Glance: OECD Social Indicators* (Paris, 2001).

9. Statistics Canada, *Women in Canada*, 3rd ed., cat. no.89-503E, Ottawa, 1995; and National Association of Women and the Law, "Canadian Women and the Social Deficit," November 1998 <www.nawl.ca/geneva> (July 14, 2002).

10. Almey et al., *Women in Canada 2000*.

11. Karen Hadley, *"And We Still Ain't Satisfied": Gender Inequality in Canada, A Status Report for 2001* (Toronto: National Action Committee on the Status of Women and the Centre for Social Justice Foundation).

12. Statistics Canada, *Women in Canada*.

13. Canada, *Living with Disability in Canada: An Economic Portrait*, Ottawa, 1996.

14. Almey et al., *Women in Canada 2000*, p.43.

15. Statistics Canada, *Women in Canada*.

16. Katherine Marshall, "Dual Earnings: Who's Responsible for Housework?" *Canadian Social Trends* (Statistics Canada), no.31 (Winter 1993), p.11.

17. Almey et al., *Women in Canada 2000*, p.111.

18. Ibid.

19. Vappu Tyyskä, "Women, Citizenship and Canadian Child Care Policy in the 1990s," Occasional paper no.13, Childcare Resource and Research Unit, Centre for Urban and Community Studies, University of Toronto, March 2001, p.14. Full text available at <www.childcarecanada .org/resources/CRRUpubs/pdf>.

20. Ibid.

21. Louise Langevin and Marie-Claire Belleau, "Trafficking in Women in Canada: A Critical Analysis of the Legal Framework Governing Immigrant Live-In Caregivers and Mail-Order Brides," Status of Women Canada, Ottawa, February 2002, p.37.

22. Langevin and Belleau, "Trafficking in Women," pp.37, 38.

23. Jane Aronson and Sheila Neysmith, "The Retreat of the State and Long-Term Care Provision: Implications for Frail Elderly People, Unpaid Family Carers and Paid Home Care Workers," *Studies in Political Economy*, no.53 (Summer 1997), cited in Marika Morris et al., "The Changing Nature of Home Care and Its Impact on Women's Vulnerability to Poverty," cat. no.SW21-42/1999E, Status of Women Canada, November 1999.

24. Ursula Franklin, *The Real World of Technology*, rev. ed. (Toronto: Anansi, 1999).

25. Morris et al., "Changing Nature of Home Care."

26. Kathryn Wilkins and Evelyn Park, "Home Care in Canada," *Health Reports* (Statistics Canada), vol.10, no.1 (1998).

27. Almey et al., *Women in Canada 2000*.

28. Ibid., p.166.

29. Ibid., p.170.

30. Ibid., p.168.

31. D. Locke and R. Code, "Canada's Shelters for Abused Women, 1999-2000," *Juristat* (Statistics Canada), vol.21, no.1 (2001).

32. See Locke and Code, "Canada's Shelters for Abused Women"; and National Action Committee on the Status of Women (NAC), *Review of the Situation of Women in Canada, 1993*, Toronto, July 1993, pp.36-37.

33. See, for instance, Canadian Women's March Committee, "It's Time for Change: Demands to the Federal Government to End Poverty and Violence Against Women," September 2000. Full text available at <www.canada.marchofwomen> (July 14, 2002).

34. *Herizons*, vol.15, no.3 (Winter 2002), p.22.

35. Ibid., p.23.

36. Carol Pateman, *The Sexual Contract* (Stanford, Cal.: Stanford University Press, 1988); Charles Mills, *The Racial Contract* (Ithaca, N.Y.: Cornell University Press, 1997).

37. Tyyskä, "Women, Citizenship and Canadian Child Care Policy," p.7.

38. Ibid., p.8.

39. Status of Women Canada, "In Praise of Canadian Women Volunteers," Ottawa, October 2001 <www .swc-cfc.gc.ca/whm/whm2001/booklet-e> (July 14, 2002). Some of the most important analysis and activism have come from women's groups organized around specific and multiple forms of oppression. In Canada this includes the Congress of Black Women of Canada (founded in 1973); the Native Women's Association of Canada (1974); the Réseau national d'action éducation femmes (1983); the Dis-Abled Women Network Canada (1985); the National Organization of Immigrant and Visible Minority Women of Canada (1986), and the Métis National Council of Women (1992).

40. See, for instance, Mercedes Steedman, *Angels of the Workplace: Women and the Construction of Gender Relations in the Canadian Clothing Industry, 1890-1940* (Toronto: Oxford University Press, 1997).

41. Communication Canada, "From Facts on Canada – Women in Canada," cat. no.PF3-2/24- 2001, Ottawa, 2001 <www.infocan.gc.ca/facts/women> (July 14, 2002).

42. See Marilyn Waring, *If Women Counted: A New Feminist Economics* (San Francisco: Harper & Row, 1988); Maria Mies and Vandana Shiva, eds., *Ecofeminism* (Halifax: Fernwood Publishing, 1993); and Carolyn Merchant, *The Death of Nature: Women, Ecology and the Scientific Revolution* (New York: Harper and Row, 1980).

43. Kimberly Fry and Cheryl Lousley, "Girls Just Want to Have Fun – with Politics," *Alternatives Journal*, vol.27, no.2 (Spring 2001). For an array of interpretations of feminism from young women, see Allyson Mitchell, Lisa Bryn Rundle, and Lara Karaian, *Turbo Chicks: Talking Young Feminisms* (Toronto: Sumach Press, 2001).

Chapter Fourteen

We Have Just Begun

1. Oxfam Bridgehead, *A Taste For Justice* (Toronto: Second Story Press, 1991).

2. "Where to Find a Fairer Cup of Tea," *Citizens Statement of Citizens Bank*, November 2000, Bridgehead Trading website <www.bridgehead.ca> (July 14, 2002).

3. International Federation for Alternative Trade (IFAT) website <www.ifat.org> (Jan. 24, 2003).

4. Fair Trade Coffee Project, "Fair Trade Coffee," Ontario Public Interest Research Group (OPIRG), University of Toronto <www.campuslife.utoronto.ca/groups/opirg/groups/fair_trade/story> (July 14, 2002).

5. TransFair Canada, "Fair Trade Certified Coffee at a Glance," Oct. 15, 2001 <www.transfair.ca/tfc/glance> (July 14, 2002); e-mail from Heather Weinrich, TransFair Canada, Jan. 27, 2003.

6. Fair Trade Federation, *2002 Report on Fair Trade Trends in the U.S. and Canada* (Washington D.C.: Co-op America Business Network, April, 2002) <www.fairtradefederation.org> (July 14, 2002).

7. "Where to Find a Fairer Cup of Tea," *Citizens Statement*, November 2000; see Bridgehead Trading website.

8. Canadian Conference of Catholic Bishops, *From Words to Action*, Ottawa, 1979, para. 1.

9. David Hollenbach, S.J., *Claims in Conflict: Retrieving and Renewing the Catholic Human Rights Tradition* (New York: Paulist Press, 1979), p.204.

10. Rosemary Speirs, "Chair's Update," Equal Voice website, April 28, 2002 <www.equalvoice.ca/news_update> (July 14, 2002).

11. Law Commission of Canada, "Renewing Democracy: Debating Electoral Reform in Canada," discussion paper, Ottawa, November 2002.

12. Brendan Myers, "A Protester's Story of What Really Happened at Quebec City," *The CCPA Monitor*, June 2001.

13. "Over 4 Million Canadians Would Have Participated in the Quebec Protests If They Could Have," *The CCPA Monitor*, July/August 2001.

14. Heather Menzies, "What Really Happened at the Quebec Summit," *Herizons*, Summer 2001; Richard Swift, "The Enclosed Summit," and John Jordan and Jennifer Whitney, "Resistance Is the Secret of Joy," *The New Internationalist*, September 2001; Brendan Myers, "A Protester's Story of What Really Happened at Quebec City," *The CCPA Monitor*, June 2001.

15. "Amnesty International Says Police Used Excessive Force in Quebec City," *The CCPA Monitor*, July/August 2001.

16. Richard Swift, *The No-Nonsense Guide to Democracy* (Toronto: New Internationalist Publications and Between the Lines, 2002), pp.11-12.

17. "Manley Says U.S. Farm Subsidies Undermine War on Terrorism," CBC News on-line, June 14, 2002 <cbc.ca/stories/2002/06/14/manley> (July 14, 2002); Rocco Galati, "Canada's Globalization, Militarization and Police State Agenda," Sarah Blackstock, "Will the Forces Be with You?" and Lorne Brown, "War, Political Repression and Resistance," *Briarpatch*, February 2002.

18. Canadian Association of University Teachers (CAUT), "Civil Liberties, Human Rights and Canada's New National Security Legislation," Ottawa, December 2001; see the CAUT website <www.caut.ca>.

Index